2013

the best campsites
in Italy
Croatia & Slovenia

alan rogers publishing
expert in camping for 45 years

Compiled by: Alan Rogers Guides Ltd

Designed by: Vine Design Ltd

Additional photography: T Lambelin, www.lambelin.com
Maps created by Customised Mapping (01769 540044)
contain background data provided by GisDATA Ltd

Maps are © Alan Rogers Guides and GisDATA Ltd 2013

© Alan Rogers Guides Ltd 2013

Published by: Alan Rogers Guides Ltd,
Spelmonden Old Oast, Goudhurst, Kent TN17 1HE
www.alanrogers.com Tel: 01580 214000

British Library Cataloguing-in-Publication Data:
A catalogue record for this book is available
from the British Library.

ISBN 978-1-909057-19-7

Printed in Great Britain by Stephens & George Print Group

Contents

Alan Rogers - in search of 'the best'

Alan Rogers Guides were first published over 40 years ago. Since Alan Rogers published the first campsite guide that bore his name, the range has expanded and now covers 27 countries in six separate guides. No fewer than 20 of the campsites selected by Alan for the first guide are still featured in our 2013 editions.

This guide contains impartially written reports on over 300 campsites in Italy, including many of the very finest, each being individually inspected and selected. We are including reports on almost 80 of the very best sites in Croatia and Slovenia, destination countries which have seen a substantial surge in interest in recent years. We aim to provide you with a selection of the best, rather than information on all – in short, a more selective, qualitative approach. New, improved maps and indexes are also included, designed to help you find the choice of campsite that's right for you.

Finally, for 2013 we have launched the new Alan Rogers Travel Card. Free to readers, it offers exclusive online extras, money saving deals and offers on many campsites. Find out more on page 10.

We hope you enjoy some happy and safe travels – and some pleasurable 'armchair touring' in the meantime!

" ...the campsites included in this book have been chosen entirely on merit, and no payment of any sort is made by them for their inclusion."

Alan Rogers, 1968

How do we find the best?

The criteria we use when inspecting and selecting campsites are numerous, but the most important by far is the question of good quality. People want different things from their choice of site so we try to include a range of campsite 'styles' to cater for a wide variety of preferences: from those seeking a small peaceful campsite in the heart of the countryside, to visitors looking for an 'all singing, all dancing' site in a popular seaside resort. Those with more specific interests, such as sporting facilities, cultural events or historical attractions, are also catered for.

The size of the site, whether it's part of a chain or privately owned, makes no difference in terms of it being required to meet our exacting standards in respect of its quality and it being 'fit for purpose'. In other words, irrespective of the size of the site, or the number of facilities it offers, we consider and evaluate the welcome, the pitches, the sanitary facilities, the cleanliness, the general maintenance and even the location.

Expert opinions

We rely on our dedicated team of Site Assessors, all of whom are experienced campers, caravanners or motorcaravanners, to visit and recommend campsites. Each year they travel some 100,000 miles around Europe inspecting new campsites for the guide and re-inspecting the existing ones. Our thanks are due to them for their enthusiastic efforts, their diligence and integrity.

We also appreciate the feedback we receive from many of our readers and we always make a point of following up complaints, suggestions or recommendations for possible new campsites. Of course we get a few grumbles too – but it really is a few, and those we do receive usually relate to overcrowding or to poor maintenance during the peak school holiday period. Please bear in mind that, although we are interested to hear about any complaints, we have no contractual relationship with the campsites featured in our guides and are therefore not in a position to intervene in any dispute between a reader and a campsite.

Independent and honest

Whilst the content and scope of the Alan Rogers guides have expanded considerably since the early editions, our selection of campsites still employs exactly the same philosophy and criteria as defined by Alan Rogers in 1968.

'telling it how it is'

Firstly, and most importantly, our selection is based entirely on our own rigorous and independent inspection and selection process. Campsites cannot buy their way into our guides – indeed the extensive Site Report which is written by us, not by the site owner, is provided free of charge so we are free to say what we think and to provide an honest, 'warts and all' description. This is written in plain English and without the use of confusing icons or symbols.

Looking for the best

Highly respected by site owners and readers alike, there is no better guide when it comes to forming an independent view of a campsite's quality. When you need to be confident in your choice of campsite, you need the Alan Rogers Guide.

- Sites only included on merit
- Sites cannot pay to be included
- Independently inspected, rigorously assessed
- Impartial reviews
- Over 40 years of expertise

Written in plain English, our guides are exceptionally easy to use, but a few words of explanation regarding the layout and content may be helpful. This guide is divided firstly by country, subsequently (in the case of Italy) by region. For a particular area the town index at the back provides more direct access.

Index town
Site name
Postal address (including region) T: telephone number. E: email address
alanrogers.com web address (including Alan Rogers reference number)

A description of the site in which we try to give an idea of its general features – its size, its situation, its strengths and its weaknesses. This section should provide a picture of the site itself with reference to the facilities that are provided and if they impact on its appearance or character. We include details on pitch numbers, electricity (with amperage), hardstandings etc. in this section as pitch design, planning and terracing affects the site's overall appearance. Similarly we include reference to pitches used for caravan holiday homes, chalets, and the like. Importantly at the end of this column we indicate if there are any restrictions, e.g. no tents, no children, naturist sites.

Facilities	Directions
Lists more specific information on the site's facilities and amenities and, where available, the dates when these facilities are open (if not for the whole season). Off site: here we give distances to various local amenities, for example, local shops, the nearest beach, plus our featured activities (bicycle hire, fishing, horse riding, boat launching). Where we have space we list suggestions for activities and local tourist attractions. **Open:** Site opening dates.	Separated from the main text in order that they may be read and assimilated more easily by a navigator en-route. Bear in mind that road improvement schemes can result in road numbers being altered. GPS: references are provided in decimal format. All latitudes are North. Longitudes are East unless preceeded by a minus sign e.g. 48.71695 is North, 0.31254 is East and -0.31254 is West. **Charges 2013** (or a general guide)

Maps, campsite listings and indexes

For this 2013 guide we have changed the way in which we list our campsites and also the way in which we help you locate the sites within each region.

We now include a map immediately after our Introduction to that region. These maps show the towns near which one (or more) of our featured campsites is located.

Within each regional section of the guide, we list these towns and the site(s) in that vicinity in alphabetical order.

You will certainly need more detailed maps for navigation, for example the Michelin atlas. We provide GPS coordinates for each site to assist you. Our three indexes will also help you to find a site by region and site name or by the town where the site is situated.

Understanding the entries

Facilities

Toilet blocks

Unless we comment otherwise, toilet blocks will be equipped with WCs, washbasins with hot and cold water and hot showers with dividers or curtains, and will have all necessary shelves, hooks, plugs and mirrors. We also assume that there will be an identified chemical toilet disposal point, and that the campsite will provide water and waste water drainage points and bin areas. If not the case, we comment. We do mention certain features that some readers find important: washbasins in cubicles, facilities for babies, facilities for those with disabilities and motorcaravan service points. Readers with disabilities are advised to contact the site of their choice to ensure that facilities are appropriate to their needs.

Shop

Basic or fully supplied, and opening dates.

Bars, restaurants, takeaway facilities and entertainment

We try hard to supply opening and closing dates (if other than the campsite opening dates) and to identify if there are discos or other entertainment.

Children's play areas

Fenced and with safety surface (e.g. sand, bark or pea-gravel).

Swimming pools

If particularly special, we cover in detail in our main campsite description but reference is always included under our Facilities listings. We will also indicate the existence of water slides, sunbathing areas and other features. Opening dates, charges and levels of supervision are provided where we have been notified. There is a regulation whereby Bermuda shorts may not be worn in swimming pools (for health and hygiene reasons). It is worth ensuring that you do take 'proper' swimming trunks with you.

Leisure facilities

For example, playing fields, bicycle hire, organised activities and entertainment.

Dogs

If dogs are not accepted or restrictions apply, we state it here. Check the quick reference list at the back of the guide.

Off site

This briefly covers leisure facilities, tourist attractions, restaurants etc. nearby.

Charges

These are the latest provided to us by the sites. In those cases where 2013 prices have not been provided to us by the sites, we try to give a general guide.

Reservations

Necessary for high season (roughly mid-July to mid-August) in popular holiday areas (i.e. beach resorts). You can reserve many sites via our own Alan Rogers Travel Service or through other tour operators. Or be wholly independent and contact the campsite(s) of your choice direct, using the phone or e-mail numbers shown in the site reports, but please bear in mind that many sites are closed all winter.

Telephone Numbers

Italy: All numbers assume that you are phoning from within Italy. To phone Italy from outside that country, prefix the number shown with the relevant International Code: 00 39. Do NOT drop the first 0 of the area code.

Croatia and Slovenia: The numbers given assume you are actually IN the country concerned. If you are phoning from the UK remember that a first '0' is usually disregarded and replaced by the appropriate country code: Croatia 00 385, Slovenia 00 386.

Opening dates

These are advised to us during the early autumn of the previous year – sites can, and sometimes do, alter these dates before the start of the following season, often for good reasons. If you intend to visit shortly after a published opening date, or shortly before the closing date, it is wise to check that it will actually be open at the time required. Similarly some sites operate a restricted service during the low season, only opening some of their facilities (e.g. swimming pools) during the main season; where we know about this, and have the relevant dates, we indicate it – again if you are at all doubtful it is wise to check.

Sometimes, campsite amenities may be dependent on there being enough customers on site to justify their opening and, for this reason, actual opening dates may vary from those indicated.

Some campsite owners are very relaxed when it comes to opening and closing dates. They may not be fully ready by their stated opening dates – grass and hedges may not all be cut or perhaps only limited sanitary facilities open. At the end of the season they also tend to close down some facilities and generally wind down prior to the closing date. Bear this in mind if you are travelling early or late in the season – it is worth phoning ahead.

The Camping Cheque low season touring system goes some way to addressing this in that many participating campsites will have all key facilities open and running by the opening date and these will remain fully operational until the closing date.

Taking a tent?

In recent years, sales of tents have increased dramatically. With very few exceptions, the campsites listed in this guide have pitches suitable for tents, caravans and motorcaravans. Tents, of course, come in a dazzling range of shapes and sizes. Modern family tents with separate sleeping pods are increasingly popular and these invariably require large pitches with electrical connections. Smaller lightweight tents, ideal for cyclists and hikers, are also visible on many sites and naturally require correspondingly smaller pitches. Many (but not all) sites have special tent areas with prices adjusted accordingly. If in any doubt, we recommend contacting the site of your choice beforehand.

Our Accommodation section

226

Over recent years, more and more campsites have added high quality mobile home and chalet accommodation. In response to feedback from many of our readers, and to reflect this evolution in campsites, we have now decided to include a separate section on mobile homes and chalets.

If a site offers this accommodation, it is indicated above the site report with a page reference where full details are given. We have chosen a number of sites offering some of the best accommodation available and have included full details of one or two accommodation types at these sites. Please note however that many other campsites listed in this guide may also have a selection of accommodation for rent.

You're on your way!

Whether you're an 'old hand' in terms of camping and caravanning or are contemplating your first trip, a regular reader of our Guides or a new 'convert', we wish you well in your travels and hope we have been able to help in some way.

We are, of course, also out and about ourselves, visiting sites, talking to owners and readers, and generally checking on standards and new developments.

We wish all our readers thoroughly enjoyable Camping and Caravanning in 2013 – favoured by good weather of course! The Alan Rogers Team

Trentino-Alto Adige
page 62

Friuli-Venezia Giulia
page 73

Lake Garda
page 46

SLOVENIA
page 187

CROATIA
page 198

Veneto
page 79

Lombardy
page 41

Piedmont &
Valle d'Aosta
page 21

Emilia-Romagna
page 99

Ligúria
page 33

Marche
page 138

Tuscany
page 109

Umbria
page 131

Abruzzo & Molise
page 151

Lazio
page 144

Campania
page 157

Puglia & Basilicata
page 161

Sardinia
page 178

Calabria
page 166

Sicily
page 171

FREE

The Alan Rogers
Travel Card

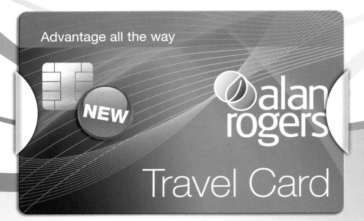

Across the Alan Rogers guides you'll find a network of thousands of quality inspected and selected campsites. We also work with numerous organisations, including ferry operators and tourist attractions, all of whom can bring you benefits and save you money.

Our brand **NEW** Travel Card binds all this together, along with exclusive extra content in our cardholders' area at **alanrogers.com/travelcard**

Advantage all the way

Carry the Alan Rogers Travel Card on your travels and save money all the way.
Enjoy exclusive offers on many partner sites - as well as hotels, apartments and campsite
accommodation. We've even teamed up with Camping Cheque, the low season discount
scheme, so you can load your card with Cheques before you travel. So register today -
hundreds of campsites already have special offers just for you.

Holiday **discounts**, **free** kids' meals, **free** cycle hire, **discounted** meals, **free** sports
activities, **free** gifts on arrival, **free** wine with meals, **free** wifi, **free** tennis, **free** spa day,
free access to local attractions.

Check out all the offers at **alanrogers.com/travelcard**
and present your card on arrival.

Benefits that add up

- Offers and benefits on many
  Alan Rogers campsites
  across Europe

- Save up to 60% in low season
  on over 600 campsites

- Savings on rented
  accommodation and hotels
  at over 400 locations

- Free cardholders' magazine

- Exclusive cardholders' area on
  our website – exchange opinions
  with other members

- Discounted ferries

- Savings on Alan Rogers guides

- Travel insurance deals

Register today - and start saving

Step 1
Register at www.alanrogers.com/travelcard
(you can now access exclusive content
on the website).

Step 2
You'll receive your activated card, along
with a Welcome email containing useful links
and information.

Step 3
Start using your card to save money or
to redeem benefits during your holiday.

Register now at
alanrogers.com/travelcard

The Alan Rogers Awards

The Alan Rogers Campsite Awards were launched in 2004 and have proved a great success.

Our awards have a broad scope and before committing to our winners, we carefully consider more than 2,000 campsites featured in our guides, taking into account comments from our site assessors, our head office team and, of course, our readers.

Our award winners come from the four corners of Europe, from southern Portugal to Croatia, and this year we are making awards to campsites in 10 different countries.

Needless to say, it's an extremely difficult task to choose our eventual winners, but we believe that we have identified a number of campsites with truly outstanding characteristics. In each case, we have selected an outright winner, along with two highly commended runners-up. Listed below are full details of each of our award categories and our winners for 2012.

Alan Rogers Progress Award 2012

This award reflects the hard work and commitment undertaken by particular site owners to improve and upgrade their site.

Winner	
UK0970	Cofton Country Holidays *England*

Runners-up	
FR86010	Castel Camping Le Petit Trianon *France*
CR6765	Camping Kovacine *Croatia*

Alan Rogers Welcome Award 2012

This award takes account of sites offering a particularly friendly welcome and maintaining a friendly ambience throughout readers' holidays.

Winner	
ES80330	Camping Las Palmeras *Spain*

Runners-up	
FR29180	Camping Les Embruns *France*
IT60280	Camping Vela Blu *Italy*

Our warmest congratulations to all our award winners and our commiserations to all those not having won an award on this occasion.

The Alan Rogers Team

Alan Rogers Active Holiday Award 2012

This award reflects sites in outstanding locations which are ideally suited for active holidays, notably walking or cycling, but which could extend to include such activities as winter sports or watersports.

Winner	
DE3003	Camping Wulfener Hals *Germany*

Runners-up	
IT62030	Caravan Park Sexten *Italy*
AU0065	Camping Seehof *Austria*

Alan Rogers Innovation Award 2012

Our Innovation Award acknowledges campsites with creative and original concepts, possibly with features which are unique, and cannot therefore be found elsewhere. We have identified innovation both in campsite amenities and also in rentable accommodation.

Winner	
NL6470	Camping de Papillon *Netherlands*

Runners-up	
FR85625	Camping Les Moulins *France*
ES92120	Camping Monte Holiday *Spain*

Alan Rogers Small Campsite Award 2012

This award acknowledges excellent small campsites (less than 75 pitches) which offer a friendly welcome and top quality amenities throughout the season to their guests.

Winner	
FR58040	Camping l'Etang de la Fougeraie *France*

Runners-up	
UK0115	Tehidy Holiday Park *England*
CZ4896	Camping Country *Czech Republic*

Alan Rogers Seaside Award 2012

This award is made for sites which we feel are outstandingly suitable for a really excellent seaside holiday.

Winner	
IT60450	Camping Marina di Venezia *Italy*

Runners-up	
FR64060	Camping le Pavillon Royal *France*
PO8202	Turiscampo *Portugal*

Alan Rogers Country Award 2012

This award contrasts with our former award and acknowledges sites which are attractively located in delightful, rural locations.

Winner	
FR74140	Camping Les Dômes de Miage *France*

Runners-up	
UK0710	Hidden Valley Touring Park *England*
NL5823	Camping Waalstrand *Netherlands*

Alan Rogers Family Site Award 2012

Many sites claim to be child friendly but this award acknowledges the sites we feel to be the very best in this respect.

Winner	
IT60200	Camping Union Lido Vacanze *Italy*

Runners-up	
NL6710	Recreatiepark de Achterste Hoef *Netherlands*
ES85400	Camping La Torre del Sol *Spain*

Alan Rogers Readers' Award 2012

We believe our Readers' Award to be the most important. We simply invite our readers (by means of an on-line poll at www.alanrogers.com) to nominate the site they enjoyed most.

The outright winner for 2012 is:

Winner	
FR85150	Camping La Yole *France*

Alan Rogers Special Award 2012

A Special Award is made to campsites which have suffered a very significant setback and have not only returned to their former condition, but can fairly be considered to be even better than before. In 2012 we acknowledge a Spanish campsite which suffered a devastating forest fire and we feel is a worthy recipient of this award.

ES80240	Camping Les Pedres *Spain*

Getting the most from **off peak touring**

£**13.95**/night
single tariff
2 people

There are many reasons to avoid high season, if you can. Queues are shorter, there's less traffic, a calmer atmosphere and prices are cheaper. And it's usually still nice and sunny!

And when you use Camping Cheques you'll find great quality facilities that are actually open and a welcoming conviviality.

Did you know?

Camping Cheques can be used right into mid-July and from late August on many sites. Over 90 campsites in France alone accept Camping Cheques from 20th August.

Save up to 60% with Camping Cheques

Camping Cheque is a fixed price scheme allowing you to go as you please, staying on over 600 campsites across Europe, always paying the same rate and saving you up to 60% on regular pitch fees. One Cheque gives you one night for 2 people + unit on a standard pitch, with electricity. It's as simple as that.

Special offers mean you can stay extra nights free (eg 7 nights for 6 Cheques) or even a month free for a month paid! Especially popular in Spain during the winter, these longer-term offers can effectively halve the nightly rate. See Site Directory for details.

Check out our amazing Ferry Deals!

Why should I use Camping Cheques?

- It's a proven system, recognised by all 600+ participating campsites
  - so no nasty surprises.

- It's flexible, allowing you to travel between campsites, and also countries, on a whim - so no need to pre-book. (It's low season, so campsites are rarely full, though advance bookings can be made).

- Stay as long as you like, where you like - so you travel in complete freedom.

- Camping Cheques are valid 2 years - so no pressure to use them up. (If you have a couple left over after your trip, simply keep them for the following year, or use them up in the UK).

Tell me more... (but keep it brief!)

Camping Cheques was started in 1999 and has since grown in popularity each year (nearly 2 million were used last year). That should speak for itself. There are 'copycat' schemes, but none has the same range of quality campsites that save you up to 60%.

Ask for your **FREE** continental road map, which explains how Camping Cheque works

01580 214002

FREE

downloadable Site Directory
alanrogers.com/directory

campingcheque.co.uk

Been to any good campsites lately?
We have

You'll find them here...

The UK's market leading independent
guides to the best campsites

Also available on iPad **alanrogers.com/digital**

... also here...

101 great campsites, ideal for your specific
hobby, pastime or passion

Also available on iPad alanrogers.com/digital

Want independent campsite reviews at your fingertips?

You'll find them here...

...and even here...

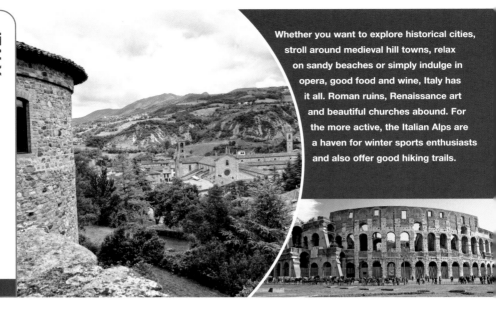

Whether you want to explore historical cities, stroll around medieval hill towns, relax on sandy beaches or simply indulge in opera, good food and wine, Italy has it all. Roman ruins, Renaissance art and beautiful churches abound. For the more active, the Italian Alps are a haven for winter sports enthusiasts and also offer good hiking trails.

Tourist Office

Italian State Tourist Board,
1, Princes Street,
London W1B 2AY

Tel: 020 7408 1254
or 09065 508925 (brochures)
Fax: 020 7399 3567

E-mail: italy@italiantouristboard.co.uk
Internet: www.enit.it

Italy only became a unified state in 1861, hence the regional nature of the country today. With 20 distinct regions, each one has retained its own individualism which is evident in the cuisine and local dialects.

In the north, the vibrant city of Milan is great for shopping and home to the famous opera house, La Scala, as well as Leonardo's Last Supper fresco. It is also a good jumping-off point for the Alps; the Italian Lake District, incorporating Lake Garda, Lake Como and Lake Maggiore; the canals of Venice and the lovely town of Verona. Central Italy probably represents the most commonly perceived image of the country and Tuscany, with its classic rolling countryside and the historical towns of Florence, Siena, San Gimignano and Pisa, is one of the most visited areas. Further south are the historical capital of Rome and the city of Naples. Close to some of Italy's ancient sites such as Pompeii, Naples is within easy distance of Sorrento and the Amalfi coast.

Population
58 million

Capital
Rome (Roma)

Climate
The south enjoys extremely hot summers and mild, dry winters, whilst the mountainous regions of the north are cooler with heavy snowfalls in winter.

Language
Italian. There are several dialect forms and some German is spoken near the Austrian border.

Telephone
The country code is 00 39.

Currency
The Euro (€).

Banks
Mon-Fri 08.30-13.00 and 15.00-16.00.

Shops
Mon-Sat 08.30/09.00-13.00 and 15.30/16.00-19.30/20.00, with some variations in larger cities.

Public Holidays
New Year; Easter Mon; Liberation Day 25 Apr; Labour Day; Assumption 15 Aug; All Saints 1 Nov; Immaculate Conception 8 Dec; Christmas 25, 26 Dec; plus numerous special local feast days.

Fringed by the French and Swiss Alps in the far north of the country, home to several ski resorts, with vine-clad hills in the south, Piedmont and Valle d'Aosta is renowned for its fine wines and local cuisine.

THE REGION IS MADE UP OF THE FOLLOWING PROVINCES: ALESSANDRIA, AOSTA, ASTI, BIELLA, CUNEO, IVREA, NOVARA, VERBANIA AND VERCELLI

In the heart of Piedmont is Turin, home to the most famous holy relic of all time, the Turin Shroud, and the Fiat car company. It also boasts a superb Egyptian Museum, Renaissance cathedral, elegant piazzas plus designer shops and good restaurants. In the east, set in a vast plain of paddy fields along the River Po – which stretches right across northern Italy – is Vercelli, the rice capital of Europe. Further south are the wine producing towns of Alba, renowned for its white truffles and red wines; and Asti, the capital of Italy's sparkling wine industry, where the famous spumante is produced. There are numerous wine museums, vineyards and cantinas in the area, from where you can purchase wine, including those at Barolo, Annuziata and Costigliole d'Asti.

Studded with picturesque castles, the Valle d'Aosta offers great walking and skiing country with its dramatic mountains, beautiful valleys and lush meadows, most notably in the Gran Paradiso National Park. This huge park is also home to over 3,000 ibex, a relative of the deer family, 6,000 chamois, plus golden eagles and rare butterflies.

Places of interest

Aosta: attractive mountain town with Roman architecture and ruins.

Avigliana: small town perched beside two lakes surrounded by mountains, medieval houses.

Biella: renowned for its wool industry.

Domodossola: mountain town of Roman origin, arcaded medieval centre, starting point of a scenic train ride across to Switzerland.

Lake Orta: set among the foothills of the Alps, in the middle of the lake rises the Island of San Guilo, with a basilica.

Saluzzo: medieval town, Gothic church, castle.

Susa: medieval town, 11th-century castle and church.

Cuisine of the region

Bagna cauda: local variation on fondue, vegetables dipped into a sauce of oil, anchovies, garlic, cream and butter.

Fontina: a semi-hard cheese made in the Valle d'Aosta.

Manzo al Barolo: lean beef marinated in red wine and garlic and stewed gently.

Soupe à la cogneintze: soup with rice.

Spumone piemontese: a mousse of mascarpone cheese with rum.

Tora di Nocciole: nut tart including hazelnuts, eggs and butter.

Zabaglione: dessert made with a mixture of egg yolk, sugar and Marsala.

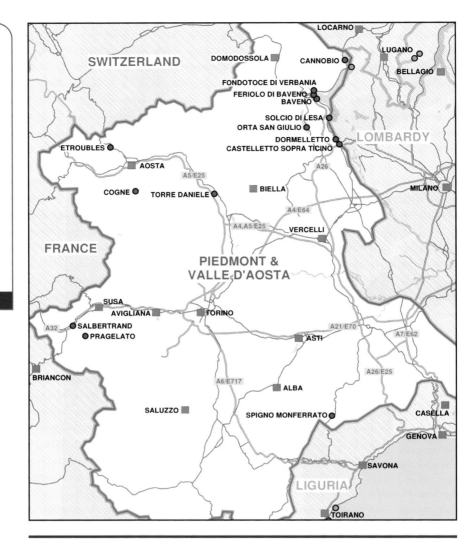

Baveno

Camping Tranquilla

Via Cave-Oltrefiume 2, I-28831 Baveno (Piedmont) T: 032 392 3452. E: info@tranquilla.com

alanrogers.com/IT62470

Tranquilla is a family run site on the western slopes above Baveno, close to Lake Maggiore. The site is in two terraced sections, both with 6A electricity connections. The 55 touring pitches vary in size with trees offering plenty of shade. There is a very pleasant swimming pool with an attractive paddling pool. Reception is housed in an attractive old railway carriage from where the Cagiada family will welcome you. Excellent English is spoken. The site is an ideal base from which to explore this very attractive area.

Facilities

The sanitary block offers the usual facilities including those for disabled visitors. All are kept very clean. British and Turkish style WCs. Laundry. Motorcaravan services. Pizza ordering service. Drinks machine. Swimming pool (10/5-30/9). Aquarium. Play area. Excursions. Free WiFi. Off site: Restaurant 300 m. Fishing and bus service 800 m. Sailing 1.5 km. Golf, bicycle hire and riding 3 km. Shops nearby.

Open: 15 March - 15 October.

Directions

Baveno is 90 km. northwest of Milan on the western shore of Lake Maggiore, and is on the SS33 road between Arona and Verbania. Site is well signed to the west in the northern part of the town.
GPS: 45.91172, 8.49071

Charges guide

Per unit incl. 2 persons
and electricity   € 20.40 - € 29.30
Special discounts for campers with the latest Alan Rogers guide. No credit cards, but travellers cheques and British currency accepted.

For latest campsite news, availability and prices visit
alanrogers.com

Baveno

Camping Parisi

Via Piave 50, I-28831 Baveno (Piedmont) T: 032 392 3156. E: info@campingparisi.it
alanrogers.com/IT62480

Camping Parisi is a quiet, family run site on the beautiful western shore of Lake Maggiore within the town of Baveno. This small and compact site has just 50 touring pitches, all with 6A electricity, which are shaded by mature trees. The site's real strength is the stunning views over the lake. It is possible to paddle and swim from the lake shore which is also good for sunbathing. A lifeguard is present. An early reservation at this site would be necessary if you wish to occupy one of the lakeside pitches (there is an extra charge, but it is well worth it!).

Facilities

Central sanitary facilities are clean with free hot showers and British style WCs but, as yet, no facilities for disabled campers. Washing machine and dryer. No shop (town is 100 m). Coffee machine. Freezer service. Play area. Bar at reception where bookings for local activities are made. Kayaks for hire. WiFi (free). Chalet and mobile home for hire. Off site: Shops nearby. Bus 200 m. Boat launching 1 km. Riding 3 km. Sailing and bicycle hire both 4 km. Golf 10 km. Ferries around the lake every 30 minutes.

Open: 22 March - 30 September.

Directions

Baveno is 90 km. northwest of Milan on the western shore of Lake Maggiore, and on the SS33 between Arona and Verbania. From the A26 take Baveno exit and turn right on main road to site. From Simplon or Gothard the first site sign is in Feriolo. Site is signed to east in town centre. GPS: 45.91245, 8.50555

Charges guide

Per unit incl. 2 persons	
and electricity	€ 23.50 - € 36.50
extra person	€ 5.50 - € 8.00
child (2-12 yrs)	€ 4.00 - € 6.00
dog	free - € 4.00

Low season discounts.

Cannobio

Camping Valle Romantica

Via Valle Cannobina, I-28822 Cannobio (Piedmont) T: 032 371 249.
E: valleromantica@riviera-valleromantica.com **alanrogers.com/IT62400**

This site really lives up to its name! Situated in a wooded mountain valley, it was established about 60 years ago by the present owner's father, who planted some 20,000 plants, trees and shrubs. These are all now well established and maintained to make a delightful garden setting. The 164 numbered pitches for touring units are on flat grass among the trees, which provide good shade. Most have 4/6A electricity, although long cables are necessary in some parts. The site's swimming pool is in a sunny position and there are two areas allowing river access where, except after heavy rain, children can play. The site is used by tour operators (about 24 pitches).

Facilities

Three sanitary blocks provide good facilities with free controllable showers. Washing machines. Gas supplies. Motorcaravan services. Small, well stocked supermarket. Pleasant bar/restaurant with waiter service and takeaway. Pizzeria. Swimming pool (15/5-15/9). Fishing (licence required). Sailing and windsurfing schools. Fridge box hire. WiFi in reception area (charged). Off site: Bicycle hire, boat launching and sailing 1.5 km. Golf and riding 15 km.

Open: 23 March - 15 September.

Directions

Cannobio is 4 km. from the Swiss border on the SS34 Locarno-Verbania road. Follow site signs from SS34 turning west (away from lake) at the southern outskirts of Cannobio and travel 1.5 km. to site. GPS: 46.05758, 8.67737

Charges guide

Per unit incl. 2 persons	
and electricity	€ 30.00 - € 37.00
extra person	€ 7.00 - € 9.50
child (1-11 yrs)	€ 4.00 - € 5.00
dog	€ 4.50 - € 5.00

FREE Alan Rogers Travel Card
Extra benefits and savings - see page 10

Cannobio
Camping Riviera

Via Casali Darbedo 2, I-28822 Cannobio (Piedmont) T: 032 371 360. E: riviera@riviera-valleromantica.com
alanrogers.com/IT62450

With scenic views across the water and the surrounding mountains, this site is directly beside Lake Maggiore. Under the same ownership as Valle Romantica, the site has a well cared for appearance. Over 250 numbered pitches are on flat grass, either side of hard surfaced access roads and divided by trees and shrubs. There are 220 with 5A electricity (long cables may be needed). The site could make a suitable base for exploring the area, although progress on the winding lakeside road may be slow!

Facilities	Directions
Five sanitary blocks are of good quality and two of these include facilities for disabled visitors. Washing machines. Fridge boxes for hire. Gas supplies. Motorcaravan services. Well stocked shop. Bar/restaurants with covered terrace, providing waiter service and takeaway. Fishing (licence required). Boat slipway. WiFi (charged). Off site: The town is only a short distance. Sailing and windsurfing schools nearby. Bicycle hire 500 m. Swiss border 4 km. Golf 11 km. Riding 15 km.	Cannobio is 4 km. from the Swiss border on the SS34 Locarno-Verbania road. It is north of the town, at the lakeside (on the east). Entrance is a few metres north of the bridge over the river. GPS: 46.069, 8.6955

Open: 25 March - 15 October.

Charges guide

Per unit incl. 2 persons and electricity	€ 30.00 - € 43.00
extra person	€ 7.00 - € 9.50
No credit cards.	

Castelletto Sopra Ticino
Camping Italia Lido

Via Cicognola 104, I-28053 Castelletto Sopra Ticino (Piedmont) T: 033 192 3032. E: info@campingitalialido.it
alanrogers.com/IT62430

Arrival here is along the banks of the lake and there is a busy entrance. Reception, the restaurant and all other services are close to the entrance and there is an extremely pleasant beach, unusually with sand, in a quiet area that adjoins the main lake. It is a peaceful spot, apart from the occasional aircraft making for Malpensa airport. The touring pitches are all near reception with a large number of permanent pitches to the rear of the site. Pitches are of varying sizes and informally placed under trees. Most have views of the water with a few really special ones alongside the lake.

Facilities	Directions
The main sanitary block is modern and clean with British and Turkish style toilets with some additional facilities near reception. Showers are very modern and pleasant. Facilities for disabled visitors. Facilities for children. Washing machines and dryer. Bar and good restaurant. Beach on site. Play area. Boat launching. Fishing. Bicycle hire. Tennis. Off site: Town 800 m. Train museum 2 km. Watersports. Boat hire.	Site is on the southern tip of Lake Maggiore. Use A8 from Milan and take exit for Castelletto Sopra Ticino. Follow minor road to the town and site is signed from here. It is at the end of no through road where parking before entering is difficult. GPS: 45.7245, 8.61051

Open: 1 March - 31 October.

Charges guide

Per unit incl. 2 persons and electricity	€ 18.00 - € 25.50
extra person (over 3 yrs)	€ 4.00 - € 5.50
No credit cards.	

Cogne
Camping Lo Stambecco

Valnontey, I-11012 Cogne (Valle d'Aosta) T: 016 574 152. E: infotiscali@campeggiolostambecco.it
alanrogers.com/IT62150

Lo Stambecco is tucked away deep in the Gran Paradiso National Park. After an enthralling mountain drive you will reach this small site with wonderful views of the mountains and glaciers. The grass pitches are informally arranged on slopes and terraces (levelling aids are useful) and all have great views. Electricity is available (3A; long leads useful). Clean crisp air, beautiful views, the rushing clear mountain stream and the delightfully informal atmosphere make this a destination site. You decide whether to hike, bike, raft or simply relax and let it all soak in.

Facilities	Directions
The two toilet blocks are mature but clean. WCs are a mixture of Turkish and British style. Baby baths to borrow. Washing machines. Motorcaravan service point. Bar and lounge. Play area. Barbecues not permitted. Dogs are not accepted. Torches useful. WiFi (charged). Off site: Hotels and restaurants 200 m. Riding 300 m. Bicycle hire 500 m. Gran Paradiso National Park.	Site is south of Aosta. From A5/E25 take Cogne exit south. (From the SS26, take the SR47). A long scenic drive will take you to the Cogne municipality. Follow the signs to Valnontey where site is clearly signed on the left. GPS: 45.58855, 7.34293

Open: 20 May - 20 September.

Charges guide

Per unit incl. 2 persons and electricity	€ 2.00 - € 24.00

For latest campsite news, availability and prices visit
alanrogers.com

Dormelletto

Camping Village Lago Maggiore

Via Leonardo da Vinci 7, I-28040 Dormelletto (Piedmont) T: 032 249 7193. E: info@lagomag.com

alanrogers.com/IT62435

This lively and happy site can be found on the southwestern shores of Lake Maggiore, close to the pretty town of Arona. There are 290 pitches here, of which around 60 are available for touring units. Pitches are all equipped with 6A electrical connections and have reasonable shade. A number of mobile homes, apartments and bungalows are available for rent. The site has direct access to the lake and a sandy beach. On-site amenities include a well stocked shop and a bar/restaurant and there are many opportunities for sports and organised activities.

Facilities

Five toilet blocks in total, of which two are for tourers and a mix of Turkish and British style (a small charge is made for hot water and showers). Private family bathrooms for rent. Motorcaravan services. Bar, restaurant/pizzeria. Shop. Games room. Adventure and play areas. Swimming pools. Beach bar. Children's pool. Sports field. Entertainment and activity programme (high season). Direct access to lake. WiFi. Off site: Supermarket across road from site. Arona 3 km. Watersports. Fishing.

Open: 1 April - 30 September.

Directions

Leave the A26 motorway at the Sesto Calende exit and join the northbound SS33 as far as Dormelletto. The campsite is clearly signed from the village. GPS: 45.73333, 8.57722

Charges guide

Per unit incl. 2 persons and electricity	€ 23.00 - € 41.00
extra person	€ 5.00 - € 9.00

No credit cards.

Etroubles

Camping Tunnel

Via Chevriere 4, I-11014 Etroubles (Valle d'Aosta) T: 016 578 292. E: info@campingtunnel.it

alanrogers.com/IT62160

This is a small, friendly site located near the southern exit of the Gran San Bernado tunnel. The views from the site are really very pleasant with green hills and towering peaks all around. There is a distinct Italian feel about it and the young owners, Silvia and Roberto, are very pleasant and both speak English. The site sits on two sides of a quiet road and steady improvements are being made. There are 95 pitches, with 45 of mixed size for touring units, on both sides of the site. All have 6A electricity with water and drainage nearby. Some have shade and most are on terraces or gentle slopes.

Facilities

One toilet block is beneath the main building and the other is central to the upper part of the site. WCs are mixed British and Turkish styles. Showers are modern in one block, outdoor in the other. Good facilities for disabled visitors. Laundry room. Motorcaravan service point. Bar and restaurant (weekends only in winter). Torches and long leads useful. WiFi area. Off site: Fishing 2 km. Golf 7 km. Riding 16 km. Skiing in season.

Open: All year. Closed for two weeks in May and November (phone to confirm dates).

Directions

From the A5-E25 take Aosta turn and travel north on the E27 towards Col de Gran San Bernado. At Etroubles, the site is signed on left, on a bend, just before the bridge. From the north, ignore first Campeggi sign as you descend the hill. In the village, cross river bridge, turn immediately right. GPS: 45.81840, 7.22891

Charges guide

Per unit incl. 2 persons and electricity	€ 22.00 - € 27.00

Feriolo di Baveno

Camping Holiday

Via 42 Martiri 28, I-28835 Feriolo di Baveno (Piedmont) T: 032 328 164. E: welcome@camping-holiday.info

alanrogers.com/IT62463

Camping Holiday is located on Lake Maggiore's western shores, close to the resort of Baveno and larger town of Stresa. This is a small site with direct access to a sandy beach. There are just 41 touring pitches, all of which are equipped with 6A electricity and satellite TV connections. Premium pitches are available with direct lake access. A number of pitches with shade are suitable for small tents and eight mobile homes are available to rent. Although the site is small, there is a bar/restaurant and a well stocked shop. A cycle track leads from the site to the village of Feriolo, 600 m. away, and beyond to Baveno.

Facilities

The single, clean sanitary block has both British and Turkish style toilets and good showers. Bar. Restaurant and pizzeria with terrace and shop (all season). Direct access to lake and sandy beach. Small play area. Tourist information. Boat launching. Fishing. Internet access and WiFi. Riding and bicycle hire. Off site: Feriolo 600 m. Golf 2 km. Baveno 3 km. Stresa 7 km. Fishing.

Open: 20 April - 22 September.

Directions

Leave the A26 motorway at the Casale exit and join the eastbound S33 as far as Feriolo. Site is clearly signed from the village. GPS: 45.93602, 8.48635

Charges guide

Per unit incl. 2 persons and electricity	€ 18.00 - € 38.00
extra person	€ 5.00 - € 7.50

FREE Alan Rogers Travel Card
Extra benefits and savings - see page 10

Feriolo di Baveno
Camping Orchidea
Via 42 Martiri 20, I-28831 Feriolo di Baveno (Piedmont) T: 032 328 257. E: info@campingorchidea.it
alanrogers.com/IT62465

Camping Orchidea can be found on the western bank of Lake Maggiore, 35 km. south of the Swiss border and 5 km. from Stresa. This site has direct access to the lake, the banks of the River Stronetta and has a sandy beach. Orchidea has a good range of modern amenities, including a shop, bar and restaurant. Watersports are understandably popular here and pedaloes and kayaks can be rented on site. The 234 touring pitches are grassy and generally well shaded, all with 6A electrical connections. Some pitches are available facing the lake (a supplement is charged in peak season). There are apartments and mobile homes for rent. Stresa, nearby, is an important town with 5,000 inhabitants and has a harbour with regular boat trips to the Borromean islands, and also a cable car to the summit of Monte Mottarone, passing the stunning Giardino Botanico Alpinia, world renowned mountain gardens. This site would suit families who prefer a simple and peaceful holiday.

Facilities

Two toilet blocks are kept clean and have hot and cold water throughout. Special facilities for children and provision for disabled visitors. Laundry facilities. Shop. Restaurant. Bar. Takeaway. Direct lake access. Pedalo and kayak hire. Fishing. Playground. Children's club. Mobile homes and caravans for rent. Bicycle hire. WiFi (charged). Off site: Walking and cycle trails. Tennis. Golf 3 km. Stresa 5 km. Riding 15 km. Excursions.

Open: 16 March - 6 October.

Directions

Take the Baveno/Stresa exit from the A26 (autostrada dei Trafori) and head north on the Via Sempione. In Feriolo follow signs to the campsite. GPS: 45.9334, 8.4812

Charges guide

Per unit incl. 2 persons	
and electricity	€ 17.50 - € 41.50
extra person	€ 4.80 - € 8.00
child (2-12 yrs)	€ 3.40 - € 5.80
dog	€ 2.60 - € 5.50

Feriolo di Baveno
Camping Miralago
Via 42 Martiri 24, I-28831 Feriolo di Baveno (Piedmont) T: 032 328 226. E: miralago@miralago-holiday.com
alanrogers.com/IT62464

Miralago is located on the western banks of Lake Maggiore and the bank of the Stronetta river where it runs into the lake, offering many waterfront pitches. It is very close to the little resort of Feriolo which can be accessed via a cycle track. There are 74 neat and easily accessed touring pitches here, all of which have 6A electricity connections. On-site amenities include a restaurant/bar with terrace and a simple play area for children. Miralago is a simple site and would suit those who prefer a quiet and peaceful holiday without all the entertainment and activities of the larger sites.

Facilities

A single sanitary block provides a mix of British and Turkish style toilets and facilities for disabled visitors. Shop. Bar/restaurant (serving pizzas) with terrace (all season). Play area. Tourist information. Direct access to lake and sandy beach. Boat launching ramp. WiFi. Off site: Feriolo and riding 500 m. Golf and bicycle hire 2 km. Baveno 3 km. Stresa 7 km. Walking and cycle routes. Watersports. Fishing.

Open: 1 April - 3 October.

Directions

Leave the A26 motorway at the Casale exit and join the eastbound S33 as far as Feriolo. Site is clearly signed from the village. GPS: 45.93388, 8.48471

Charges guide

Per unit incl. 2 persons	
and electricity	€ 21.50 - € 34.50
extra person	€ 5.00 - € 7.50
child (3-12 yrs)	€ 4.50 - € 6.00

Feriolo di Baveno

Camping Conca d'Oro

Via 42 Martiri 26, I-28835 Feriolo di Baveno (Piedmont) T: 032 328 116. E: info@concadoro.it

alanrogers.com/IT62485

Conca d'Oro is a delightful site with spectacular views across Lake Maggiore to the distant mountains. The first impression is one of spaciousness and colour. There are 21 mobile homes for rent, the rest of the 210 grass plots provide good sized touring pitches. All have 6A electrical connections, some have shade and many have spectacular views especially at night. The land slopes gently down to a fine sandy beach. An attractive terraced restaurant serves a range of regional dishes and there is a pleasant bar and pizzeria plus a well stocked shop. The owners Maurizio and Alessandra are sure to give you a warm welcome. The site is close to the lakeside town of Baveno from where boat trips are available to the three small islands on this part of Lake Maggiore. Fishing and boat launching are possible from the beach at the site, with sailing and other watersports available. There are nature reserves nearby and drives out into the surrounding mountains provide opportunities for walkers, cyclists and climbers.

Facilities

Three toilet blocks provide all necessary facilities kept in immaculate condition, including controllable showers and open style washbasins; some toilets with washbasins. En-suite unit for disabled visitors. Laundry room. Motorcaravan service point. Bar, restaurant, pizzeria and shop (all season). Swimming, fishing and boat launching from beach. Bicycle hire. Dogs must be pre-booked and are not allowed 6/7-17/8. Off site: Shops, bars and restaurants nearby. Riding 700 m. Golf 1 km. Sailing 7 km. Excursions to nearby attractions.

Open: 26 March - 29 September.

Directions

Baveno is 90 km. northwest of Milan on the western shore of Lake Maggiore. Site is off the SS33 road between Baveno and Fondotoce di Verbania, 1 km. south of the junction with the SS34 and is well signed. GPS: 45.93611, 8.48583

Charges 2013

Per unit incl. 2 persons	
and electricity	€ 20.28 - € 43.50
extra person	€ 5.20 - € 8.84
child (6-11 yrs)	€ 3.64 - € 6.76
dog	€ 3.64 - € 5.72

Quiet campingsite, clean and proper, with sanitary blocks and pitches of 100 sqm. Conca d'Oro is situated directly on the lake in a area surrounded by nature. The campsite has a private sandy beach and is child friendly. Market, bar, restaurant, pizzeria, volley, table tennis, canoe and cycling. Special offers in the low season. **www.concadoro.it**

Fondotoce di Verbania

Camping Lido Toce

Via per Feriolo 41, I-28924 Fondotoce di Verbania (Piedmont) T: 032 349 6220. E: info@campinglidotoce.eu

alanrogers.com/IT62455

A relatively dark entrance soon opens up to reveal the type of campsite that some will love – camping as a back to nature experience. The facilities here are of a very high quality and the Perucchini family team, with 50 years experience, are all very keen to make your stay enjoyable. The 80 touring pitches are between 80-140 sq.m, with 6A electricity and larger outfits can access the site easily. There is plenty of shade and greenery, and the beach frontage is attractive with fine views. We met many happy campers here and there is much to do in the local area.

Facilities

Two sanitary blocks with spotless, modern facilities. Good showers. Baby room. Facilities for disabled visitors. Washing machines. Motorcaravan services. Shop. Bar. Restaurant. Takeaway (from April). Play area with climbing frames. Beach frontage onto lake. River alongside (through small wood). WiFi over part of site (charged). Off site: Riding 500 m. Public bus 1 km. Golf 3 km. Bicycle hire 9 km. Excursions to tourist attractions.

Open: Mid March - mid October.

Directions

Leave A26 autostrada at the Casale exit and join the eastbound S33 as far as Feriolo. Site is signed from village and is on the right just before crossing the river bridge. GPS: 45.939232, 8.485774

Charges guide

Per unit incl. 2 persons	
and electricity	€ 15.00 - € 29.90
extra person	€ 4.80 - € 6.50
No credit cards.	

FREE Alan Rogers Travel Card
Extra benefits and savings - see page 10

Fondotoce di Verbania
Camping Continental Lido

Via 42 Martiri 156, I-28924 Fondotoce di Verbania (Piedmont) T: 032 349 6300.
E: info@campingcontinental.com **alanrogers.com/IT62490**

Continental Lido is a large, bustling site situated on the shore of the charming little Lake Mergozzo, about one kilometre from the better known Lake Maggiore. The 413 average size touring pitches are back to back in rows on grass and although a little close together, the rest of the site has a more open feel. All have 6A electricity and there is some shade. There are also 230 mobile homes available to rent. There is an impressive pool complex and a small sandy beach slopes gently into the lake where swimming and watersports can also be enjoyed (no powered craft permitted). A bustling entertainment programme is provided, centred around a very large amphitheatre. Pine-clad mountains and a pretty village directly opposite the beach provide a pleasing, scenic background. An unusual feature here is the nine-hole golf course. There is a busy programme of activities from May to September. Under the same ownership as Isolino Camping Village, this site is managed by the son, Gian Paolo, who speaks good English.

Facilities

Five high standard toilet blocks have free hot water. Facilities for disabled visitors. Washing machines and dryers. Mini-fridges. Well stocked shop and bar/restaurant with terrace and takeaway. Swimming pool complex (28/4-15/9) with slides, rapids and waves, plus free sun loungers and parasols. Snack bars by pool and lake. Large amphitheatre. TV. Tennis. Golf course (9 holes). Playground. Fishing. Windsurfing, pedaloes, canoes, kayaks. Games room. Bicycle hire. Entertainment and activities (mid June-mid Sept). Bus on request to Verbania. Internet access and WiFi. Off site: Riding 1 km. Sailing 5 km.18-hole golf 12 km. Excursions.

Open: 27 March - 15 September.

Directions

Verbania is 100 km. northwest of Milan, on the western shore of Lake Maggiore. Site is off the SS34 road between Fondotoce and Gravellona, 200 m. west of junction with SS33. GPS: 45.94960, 8.48058

Charges guide

Per unit incl. 3 persons and electricity	€ 23.20 - € 45.75
extra person	€ 4.75 - € 8.00
child (6-11 yrs)	€ 3.45 - € 6.60

Fondotoce di Verbania
Camping Village Isolino

Via per Feriolo 25, I-28924 Fondotoce di Verbania (Piedmont) T: 032 349 6080. E: info@isolino.com
alanrogers.com/IT62460

Lake Maggiore is one of the most attractive Italian lakes and Isolino is an impressive site and one of the largest in the region. Most of the 531 touring pitches have shade from a variety of trees. They vary in size, all have 6A electrical connections, 182 are fully serviced and some have lake views. The bar and restaurant terraces overlook the very large, lagoon-style swimming pool with its island sun deck area, water games and a canyon river, and stunning views across the lake to the fir-clad mountains beyond. Often the social life of the campsite is centred around the large bar/terrace which has a small stage inside, sometimes used for musical entertainment. A huge and impressive amphitheatre is where an extensive programme of activities and entertainment takes place throughout the season. The large poolside terrace outside the bar provides an ideal casual eating area for pizzas and ice cream. In the restaurant on the floor above you can enjoy an excellent menu and the magnificent views across the lake. The site is well situated for visiting the many attractions of the region which include the famous gardens on the islands in the lake and at the Villa Taranto, Verbania. The site is owned by the friendly Manoni family who also own Camping Continental Lido at nearby Lake Mergozzo.

Facilities

Six well built toilet blocks have hot water for showers and washbasins but cold for dishwashing and laundry. Good baby room. Laundry facilities. Motorcaravan services. Supermarket, bar and takeaway (all season). Boutique. Gelateria. Swimming pool (27/4-15/9). Entertainment (28/3-6/4, 27/4-15/9). Amphitheatre. Fishing. Watersports. Boat launching. Bicycle hire and guided mountain bike tours. Long beach. Internet access and WiFi. Good English is spoken. Bookings for dogs must be made in high season. Off site: Golf 2 km. Sailing 5 km. Riding 12 km. Swiss mountains and resort of Locarno.

Open: 27 March - 23 September.

Directions

Verbania is 100 km. northwest of Milan on the western shore of Lake Maggiore. From A26 motorway, leave at exit for Stresa/Baveno, turn left towards Fondotoce. Site is well signed off the SS33 north of Baveno and 300 m. south of the junction with the SS34 at Fondotoce. GPS: 45.93835, 8.50008

Charges guide

Per unit incl. 3 persons and electricity	€ 25.50 - € 51.60
extra person	€ 5.65 - € 8.85
child (6-11 yrs)	€ 3.80 - € 7.30
dog	€ 3.80 - € 8.85

For latest campsite news, availability and prices visit
alanrogers.com

Fondotoce di Verbania

Camping la Quiete

Via Turati 72, I-28040 Fondotoce di Verbania (Piedmont) T: 032 349 6013. E: info@campinglaquiete.it

alanrogers.com/IT62495

La Quiete is a small site, attractively located on the shore of Lake Mergozzo, a small lake to the west of the much larger Lake Maggiore. There are 180 pitches here, mostly well shaded and with 6A electrical connections, many of which have fine views across the lake. A number of mobile homes are available for rent. On-site amenities include a shop and bar/restaurant, as well as a sports field and volleyball court. This is excellent mountain biking and walking country and the site owners will be pleased to recommend possible routes.

Facilities

The clean and modern sanitary facilities are well placed along the length of the site. Washing machines. Bar/restaurant. Shop. Sports field. Games room. Play area. Direct access to Lake Mergozzo. Off site: Verbania. Golf and riding 1 km. Bicycle hire 5 km. Lake Maggiore. Watersports. Fishing. Motorboats are not allowed on the lake. Walking and cycle routes.

Open: 1 May - 20 September.

Directions

Leave the A26 motorway at the Casale exit and join the eastbound S34 as far as Fondotoce. Head north here on SP54 and the campsite is clearly signed. GPS: 45.9535, 8.47745

Charges guide

Per unit incl. 2 persons and electricity	€ 20.00 - € 33.00
extra person	€ 5.00 - € 7.50
child (0-12 yrs)	free - € 5.00

No credit cards.

Orta San Giulio

Camping Orta

Via Domodossola 28, I-28016 Orta San Giulio (Piedmont) T: 032 290 267. E: info@campingorta.it

alanrogers.com/IT62420

Lake Orta is a delightful, less visited small lake just west of Lake Maggiore. The site is on a considerable slope, and most of the 90 touring pitches (all with 4A electricity) are on the top grass terrace with spectacular views across the lake to the mountains beyond. There are some superb lakeside pitches across the main road (linked by a pedestrian underpass) although there is some traffic noise here. Amenities include a large games and entertainment room and a traditional Italian bar and restaurant serving good value family meals. Some English is spoken by the Guarnori family, who take pride in maintaining their uncomplicated site to a high standard. Book ahead to enjoy the lakeside pitches. If you are anxious about towing a large caravan to the top terraces, the owner will help out with his tractor!

Facilities

Three modern sanitary blocks are clean and well maintained providing mainly British style toilets, coin operated showers and an excellent unit for disabled visitors. Laundry facilities. Motorcaravan services. Good quality shop. Bar and restaurant with basic menu serving good value Italian family meals. Playground. Large games/TV room. WiFi in reception/bar area. Fishing. Bicycle hire. Boat launching. Lake swimming and watersports. Off site: Riding, golf and sailing within 10 km.

Open: 1 March - 31 December.

Directions

Lake Orta is 85 km. northwest of Milan, just west of Lake Maggiore. Site is on the SR229 between Borgomanero and Omega, 600 m. north of the turn to Orta San Giulio. Parking area for arrivals is on lake side of the road, with reception and main entrance on the opposite side. GPS: 45.80188, 8.42047

Charges guide

Per person	€ 5.50 - € 7.50
child (2-11 yrs)	€ 4.00 - € 5.00
pitch	€ 9.00 - € 18.00
electricity	€ 2.50

No credit cards. Low season discounts.

For latest campsite news, availability and prices visit

alanrogers.com

Pragelato

Gofree Villaggio Touristico Camping

Via Nazionale, I-10060 Pragelato (Piedmont) T: 012 278 045. E: info@villaggiogofree.com

alanrogers.com/IT65050

Gofree, an unusual name for a campsite, is owned by a dynamo in the form of Patrizia Laurent. She will be pleased to welcome you to this site which is open all year and is primarily a modern looking bungalow village. However, the supporting facilities are of a high quality for campers to enjoy. It is one of the very few quality camping sites hereabouts. The 40 pitches (80 sq.m) all have 10A electricity and may be at one end of the site in winter, on what would be the tennis courts in summer season. Tents are placed in a field opposite.

Facilities	Directions
One modern, well appointed, very clean sanitary block. British style WCs. Facilities for disabled visitors. Washing machines. Two special bungalows for disabled campers. Sophisticated bar and excellent restaurant/pizzeria and takeaway. Pleasant play area. Regular bus service at gate. WiFi. Off site: Fishing 100 m. Town and bicycle hire 1 km. Riding 2 km. Golf 3 km. Mountain sports including skiing.	Site is west of Torino and southeast of the Fréjus tunnel exit. From A32 take S24 towards Sestriere. Pass Sestriere and head east for Torino on the R23. Site is 8 km. along this road near the village of Pragelato and well signed. GPS: 45.01667, 6.93333

Open: All year.

Charges guide

Per unit incl. 2 persons and electricity	€ 26.00
person (over 8 yrs)	€ 8.00

Solcio di Lesa

Camping Solcio

Via al Campeggio, I-28040 Solcio di Lesa (Piedmont) T: 032 274 97. E: info@campingsolcio.com

alanrogers.com/IT62440

Camping Solcio is a family run site on the lakeside and has lovely views over the lakes and the surrounding green hills. The 105 neat touring pitches are 60-90 sq.m. with 6A electricity and mostly shaded by trees. A very pleasant restaurant and a bar back onto a large building alongside the site, and there are some views of the lake from the terraces. All manner of watersports are available here and the beach is of coarse sand. The lake is fine for safe swimming. An ambitious entertainment programme is arranged for children in high season, and there is adventure sport for the over tens. This is a pleasant site with modest facilities and it may suit those who do not seek the luxuries of the larger sites. English and Dutch are spoken and the site is very popular with Dutch campers.

Facilities	Directions
One main central toilet block is smart and clean. Toilets here are British style. An older block nearer reception has mixed Turkish and British style toilets. Facilities for disabled visitors. Baby room. Washing machine and dryer. Restaurant and bar with terrace. Basic shop. Full entertainment programme in season. Play areas. Baby club. Bicycle hire. Internet. WiFi (charged). Torches useful. Off site: Public transport 50 m. Town facilities 1 km. ATM 2 km. Riding 5 km. Golf 10 km.	Site is on the west side of Lake Maggiore. From A4 (Milan-Torino) take the A8 to Castelletto Sticino. Then north on SS33 towards Stresa and look for site sign at km. 57 marker at town of Lesa. Take the narrow access road to the site. GPS: 45.81586, 8.54962

Open: 9 March - 20 October.

Charges guide

Per unit incl. 2 persons and electricity	€ 19.90 - € 44.00
extra person	€ 5.50 - € 8.50
child (3-13 yrs)	€ 3.40 - € 6.70
dog	€ 3.70 - € 7.80
Low season discounts.	

FREE Alan Rogers Travel Card
Extra benefits and savings - see page 10

Salbertrand

Camping Gran Bosco

SS 24 del Monginevro km. 75, I-10050 Salbertrand (Piedmont) T: 012 285 4653.
E: info@campinggranbosco.it **alanrogers.com/IT65000**

This is a modern and efficiently run site very near the Fréjus tunnel. The site was chosen to host guests for the winter Olympics of 2006, thus the amenities are very good in an area of notoriously poor campsites. A family site, now being run by the keen younger generation, Gran Bosco has many attractive features, including a smart bar/restaurant with terrace within the clean, new building just inside the entrance, and everything is open all year. The 60 touring pitches are at both ends of the site, all have 6A electricity and are on flat ground with shade.

Facilities

Two modern, well appointed toilet blocks (with piped music) are well placed on the site. Clean WCs are British style, showers are excellent. Superb facilities for disabled visitors. Washing machines. Motorcaravan service point. Shop. Large bar and pleasant restaurant with terraces. Play area and good games room. Entertainment in high season. Children's club. Barbecue area. Torches useful. Off site: Public transport 100 m. Beach and fishing 1 km.

Open: All year.

Directions

Site is east of the Italian exit of the Fréjus tunnel. From A32 Torino-Fréjus autoroute take Oulx East exit. Turn east towards Turin on the SS24 and site is at km. 75 which is 2 km. from the Oulx exit. GPS: 45.06187, 6.866667

Charges guide

Per unit incl. 2 persons and electricity	€ 23.00 - € 24.00
extra person (over 3 yrs)	€ 7.00

Spigno Monferrato

Camping Tenuta Squaneto

Frazione Squaneto, I-15018 Spigno Monferrato (Piedmont) T: 014 491 862. E: info@tenutasquaneto.it
alanrogers.com/IT64045

After years of experience in the camping industry, Barbara and Peter Witschge have built their dream – Tenuta Squaneto, natural camping with brilliant facilities. The 120 sq.m. grassy, level pitches are all fully serviced, with wonderful views and some have their own luxury facilities. The site is in a small valley with trees all around, there is a river to walk along, fish or simply swim and play in. A lovely lake is central to the site and the nearby swimming pool is stunning with a large whirlpool and a children's shallow play pool with wonderful frogs and turtles that spray water. The food in the restaurant is so good that it would be tempting to eat there every night.

Facilities

Single sparkling new sanitary block offers full and luxurious facilities including those for disabled campers. Some pitches have private facilities including cooker, fridge and luxury facilities (€ 6-€ 10 daily). Small shop selling fresh bread. Quality restaurant and bar. Huge swimming pool and paddling pool. Large play area. Beach volleyball. Cooking groups in low season, wine tastings in high season. Lake and river swimming, fishing. Car-free pitch area. Off site: Acqui Terme thermal baths.

Open: 1 April - 12 September.

Directions

From north (Milan) take A7 for Genova then A21 (Torino) and exit for Alessandria South. Take R30 to Acqui Terme. Site is signed at 25 km. on R30 at Spigno Monfferrato. GPS: 44.488978, 8.347126

Charges guide

Per unit incl. 2 persons and electricity	€ 25.00 - € 38.50
extra person (over 2 yrs)	€ 6.00
dog	€ 4.00

Torre Daniele

Camping Mombarone

Settimo Vittone Reg, I-10010 Torre Daniele (Piedmont) T: 012 575 7907. E: info@campingmombarone.it
alanrogers.com/IT62200

This is a small, friendly, all-year site alongside the SS26 road and close to the motorway from the Mont Blanc tunnel, providing a useful stop if entering or leaving Italy via this route. It has 130 pitches, with space for about 60 touring units on the grass area between the permanent units. The site has a small bar and a simple, inexpensive restaurant is 50 m. away. The site is laid out in a valley with attractive plants, shrubs and trees for shade and is surrounded by high mountains and wooded hills, with vines on the eastern slopes. The Peretto family take pride in looking after their guests and English is spoken.

Facilities

The sanitary facilities are adequate and kept clean, with both British and Turkish style toilets and free hot showers. A new, high quality toilet block with facilities for disabled visitors has been opened on the upper level of the site. Washing machine and dryer. Bar (Easter-30/9). Outdoor free-standing pool (1/6-31/8). Free bicycle hire. Fishing. WiFi. Off site: Shops and restaurants nearby. Riding 5 km.

Open: All year.

Directions

From A5 motorway take Quincinetto exit onto SS26 turning right; the site is almost immediately on the left. GPS: 45.5655, 7.8157

Charges guide

Per person	€ 6.00
pitch	€ 4.00 - € 6.00
electricity	€ 2.50
No credit cards.	

For latest campsite news, availability and prices visit

alanrogers.com

Ligúria is a long, thin coastal strip nestling at the foot of olive- and vine-clad mountains. The Italian Riviera boasts an abundance of sandy beaches and charming seaside villages, while inland the mountain resorts offer plenty of walking and a respite from the crowds.

THE REGION HAS FOUR PROVINCES: GENOVA, IMPERIA, LA SPEZIA AND SAVONA

Ligúria divides neatly into two distinct stretches of coastline: to the west is the Riviera di Ponente and to the east is the Riviera Levante. Between the two lies Genoa, Italy's biggest port. It has a fascinating old town with medieval alleyways, and numerous palaces and churches to explore. It was also once the home of Christopher Columbus. The surrounding hills offer a quiet retreat from the city: the picturesque Valle Scrivia has several hiking routes and is easily accessible from the small town of Casella. Stretching across to the French border, the Riviera di Ponente has a number of places of interest: the pretty wine producing town of Dolceacqua; the pleasant resort of San Remo; the charming seafront village of Cervo; and the medieval hilltown of Toirano. There are more coastal resorts along the Riviera Levante including Portofino, the most exclusive harbour and resort town in Italy. With sandy beaches and small coves, this attractive area also offers good walking. Further along is the coastline of the Cinque Terre (Five Lands). The name refers to five tiny villages which appear to cling dramatically to the edge of sheer cliffs: Monterosso al Mare, Vernazza, Corniglia, Manrola and Riomaggiore.

Places of interest

Albenga: small market town.

Camogli: attractive resort.

Cinque Terre: wine growing region, picturesque villages, sandy coves and beaches.

Dolceacqua: medieval stone bridge and ruined castle.

La Spezia: museum with medieval and Renaissance art, ferry trips to Bastia in Corsica.

Lévanto: beachside resort.

Portovénere: village with three islets offshore.

Toirano: caves at the Grotte della Basura and Grotta di Santa Lucia.

Villa Hanbury: impressive botanical gardens.

Cuisine of the region

The best known speciality is *pesto:* made with chopped basil, garlic, pine nuts and grated cheese with olive oil, it was invented by the Genoese to help their long term sailors fight scurvy. Fish and seafood are readily available, often eaten with pasta. Chickpeas grow in abundance, and make *farinata,* a kind of chickpea pancake. Genoa is famous for its *pandolce,* a sweet cake laced with dried fruit, nuts and candied peel.

Burrida di seppie: cuttlefish stew.

Cacciucco: rich stew of mixed fish and seafood cooked with wine, garlic and herbs.

Carpione: fish marinated in vinegar and herbs.

Cima alla Genovese: cold stuffed veal.

Torta pasqualina: spinach and cheese pie.

Trenette al Pesto: noodles with pesto.

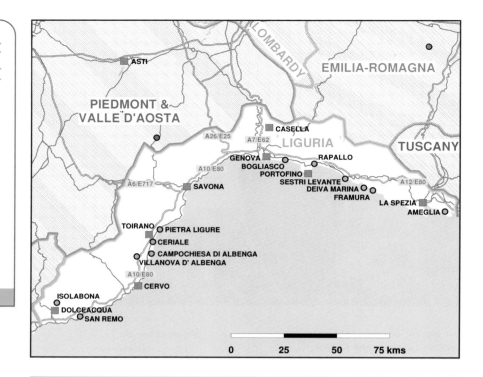

Bogliasco
Camping Genova Est

Via Marconi, localitá Cassa, I-16031 Bogliasco (Ligúria) T: 010 347 2053. E: info@camping-genova-est.it
alanrogers.com/IT64100

This wooded site is set on very steep slopes close to the Genoa motorways and is east of the city. It has very limited facilities, but runs a free bus service to connect with local transport for visiting Genoa. If you are extremely fit a set of steep stairs (125 m. elevation) will take you there in 15 minutes. The approach from the main road twists and climbs steeply with a tight final turn at the site entrance. There are 54 pitches for tents and mobile units with electricity available (3/6A) to the vehicle pitches. A small play area is set on a narrow terrace and children should be supervised. The restaurant/bar with terrace commands fine views over the sea and a pleasant menu, which changes daily, is offered at a good price.

Facilities

Two sanitary blocks provide free hot showers and en-suite cabins (WC, washbasin and shower). Washing machine. Basic motorcaravan services. Shop providing essentials. Bar/restaurant and takeaway (all open Easter-30/9). Towing vehicle available. Gas supplies. Site is unsuitable for disabled visitors. Free WiFi in reception/bar area. Free bus shuttle to local town. Scooters for hire. Off site: Beach 500 m. Fishing and boat launching 1.5 km. Bicycle hire 2 km. Golf and horse riding 20 km.

Open: 23 March - 20 October.

Directions

From autostrada A10 take Nervi exit and turn towards La Spezia on the SS1. In Bogliasco look for a sharp left turn with a large sign for the site. Follow narrow winding road for 2 km. to site. GPS: 44.38453, 9.07308

Charges guide

Per unit incl. 2 persons	
and electricity	€ 25.00 - € 27.60
extra person	€ 5.70 - € 6.60
child (3-10 yrs)	€ 3.90 - € 4.40
dog	€ 2.10

No credit cards. Less 5% for holders of the current Alan Rogers Guide.

For latest campsite news, availability and prices visit
alanrogers.com

Ameglia
Camping River

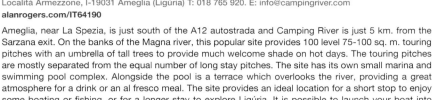

228

Localitá Armezzone, I-19031 Ameglia (Ligúria) T: 018 765 920. E: info@campingriver.com
alanrogers.com/IT64190

Ameglia, near La Spezia, is just south of the A12 autostrada and Camping River is just 5 km. from the Sarzana exit. On the banks of the Magna river, this popular site provides 100 level 75-100 sq. m. touring pitches with an umbrella of tall trees to provide much welcome shade on hot days. The touring pitches are mostly separated from the equal number of long stay pitches. The site has its own small marina and swimming pool complex. Alongside the pool is a terrace which overlooks the river, providing a great atmosphere for a drink or an al fresco meal. The site provides an ideal location for a short stop to enjoy some boating or fishing, or for a longer stay to explore Ligúria. It is possible to launch your boat into the Magra river from the campsite and there are good fishing opportunities further up river. A busy entertainment programme is provided at Camping River from mid June until September. Camping River has something for all the family; we saw fishermen setting off for the afternoon, families playing in the pool, and small children enjoying the large play area while their parents relaxed with a cup of coffee on the terrace. This is a wonderful area to explore with the Cinque Terre nearby, its beautiful coastline and interesting hilltop villages. Liguria is also a well known wine growing area.

Facilities
Two sanitary blocks provide toilets (some Turkish style), washbasins and unisex showers. Facilities for disabled campers. Motorcaravan service point. Restaurant and bar. Shop. Pizzeria. Swimming pool and sun deck. Boat launching. Fishing. Mobile homes and bungalows to rent. Off site: Tennis and riding 200 m. Archery. Sailing. Scuba diving. La Spezia. Le Cinque Terre.

Open: 1 April - 30 September.

Directions
Take Sarzana exit on the A12 (Genoa-Livorno) and follow the signs initially towards Lerici. After 3 km. follow signs to Bocca di Magra and Ameglia where the site is signed off to left. The final access road is narrow and has a tight bend so larger units might experience some difficulty. GPS: 44.07556, 9.96972

Charges guide
Per unit incl. 2 persons and electricity	€ 19.50 - € 53.00
extra person	€ 5.00 - € 11.00

Italia. La Spezia. Ameglia. T : + 39 0187 65920 | F : + 39 0187 65183
E : info@campingriver.com | booking@campingriver.it

Numero Verde Toll-free **800 953 253 Fast Line**

Campochiesa di Albenga
Camping Bella Vista
Reg. Campore 23, I-17031 Campochiesa di Albenga (Ligúria) T: 018 254 0213.
E: campingbellavista@hotmail.com **alanrogers.com/IT64060**

Owned and run by the multilingual, Dutch Kox family, this site has 61 level pitches, separated in places by hedges and trees. The pitches are in rows, loosely ringed by bungalows. Two sizes of pitch are offered: 50 and 80 sq.m. with a sink and tap for every four pitches. Electricity (6A) is available and 17 pitches are fully serviced. Large units will experience manoeuvring difficulties and need to phone ahead for guidance. This is an inexpensive and thus crowded site in high season.

Facilities
The single modern block is clean with British style toilets. Shower water is solar heated, washbasins have cold water only. Single facility for disabled campers although the unit doubles as a baby room with a washing machine and ironing equipment (key at reception). Shop (1/5-15/10). Bar. Takeaway with restrictions (1/5-15/10). Swimming pool and separate paddling pool. Limited entertainment in season. Aviary.

Open: 15 March - 15 November.

Directions
Exit at Borghetto San Spirito onto the SS1 (via Aurelia) towards Ceriale. In Ceriale follow blue signs for Peagna and the campsite. Look for the small signs at regular intervals. GPS: 44.08333, 8.21033

Charges guide
Per person	€ 4.00 - € 8.00
pitch	€ 5.50 - € 13.50
electricity (6A)	€ 2.50

Ceriale

Camping Baciccia

Via Torino 19, I-17023 Ceriale (Ligúria) T: 018 299 0743. E: info@campingbaciccia.it

alanrogers.com/IT64030

This friendly, family run site is a popular holiday destination. Baciccia was the nickname of the present owner's grandfather who grew fruit trees and tomatoes on the site. Tall eucalyptus trees shade the 106 flat pitches which encircle the central facilities block. The pitches are on flat ground and all have electricity. There is always a family member by the gate to greet you, and Vincenzina and Giovanni, along with their daughter and son, Laura and Mauro, work tirelessly to ensure that you enjoy your stay. The pool has a giant elephant slide and there is a vibrant play area for children. The informal restaurant serves delightful seasonal Italian dishes and overlooks a large swimming pool. There is a free shuttle to the site's private beach and the town has the usual seaside attractions.

Facilities

Two clean and modern sanitary blocks near reception have British and Turkish style WCs, and there is hot water throughout. Laundry. Motorcaravan services. Restaurant/bar. Shop. Pizzeria and takeaway. Swimming and paddling pools (1/4-31/10) and private beach. Tennis. Bowls. Excellent play area. Bicycle hire. Wood-burning stove and barbecue. WiFi. Fishing. Diving. Entertainment for children and adults in high season. Excursions. Off site: Department store 150 m. Bus 200 m. Aquapark 500 m. Riding and golf 2 km. Ancient town of Albenga (2,000 years old) 3 km. Parachuting school 10 km.

Open: 20 March - 3 November,
4 December - 10 January.

Directions

From the A10 between Imperia and Savona, take Albenga exit. Follow signs for Ceriale/Savona and Aquapark Caravelle (which is 500 m. from the site) and then site signs. Site is just south of Savona. GPS: 44.08165, 8.21763

Charges guide

Per unit incl. up to 3 persons (over 2 yrs) and electricity	€ 26.50 - € 49.00
extra person	€ 6.50 - € 11.00
dog	€ 2.50 - € 5.00

Discounts for stays in excess of 7 days.
Discount for readers 10% in low season.

Deiva Marina

Camping la Sfinge

Localitá Gea, I-19013 Deiva Marina (Ligúria) T: 018 782 5464. E: info@campinglasfinge.com

alanrogers.com/IT64160

La Sfinge is peacefully located in the famous area of Cinque Terre and stylish Portofino, in a landscape of pine and acacia trees, with excellent panoramic views. The site is particularly suitable for tents as the pitches are located on pleasant terraces with views. There are some permanent residents on the site but they are separated from the touring pitches. A set evening meal is prepared at a good price with barbecues in high season. There is a free private shuttle service to the beach and to the railway station to explore the region. The owners, Tania and Guido, are diligent, keen to please, and speak good English.

Facilities

Modern sanitary facilities including a locked WC for disabled visitors. Washing machines, spin dryers and ironing area. Communal fridge. Small but comprehensive shop. Snack bar producing evening menu. Sports ground and safe play area for children. WiFi. Free mobile phone charging facility. International phone. Animation for children at weekends in July/Aug. 27 tents for hire. Off site: Riding 1 km. Deiva Marina 2 km. Beach, fishing and watersports 3 km. Golf 35 km.

Open: All year.

Directions

From A12/E80 Genova-Livorno motorway take Deiva Marina exit and follow road to Deiva Marina (4 km). Site is on the right as you approach the village. GPS: 44.22625, 9.5502

Charges guide

Per person	€ 6.00 - € 8.00
child (2-12 yrs)	€ 3.00 - € 3.50
pitch	€ 9.00 - € 15.00
car	€ 3.00 - € 3.50
dog	€ 1.00 - € 2.00

Bus service to the beach (June-Sept) included.
Discounts for stays over 5 nights.

For latest campsite news, availability and prices visit

alanrogers.com

Deiva Marina
Villaggio Camping Valdeiva

Localitá Ronco, I-19013 Deiva Marina (Ligúria) T: 018 782 4174. E: camping@valdeiva.it
alanrogers.com/IT64120

A mature and cheerful site, 3 km. from the sea between the famous Cinque Terre and Portofino, Valdeiva is open all year. The 40 touring pitches, with 3A electricity, are in a square at the bottom of the site, some with shade and views, and cars may be required to park in a separate area depending on the pitch and season. There are 100 permanent pitches on the upper reaches of the site. Camping Valdeiva does have a small swimming pool, which is very welcome if you do not wish to take the free bus to the beach. A small busy bar/restaurant offers food at realistic prices. There was late night noise from residents when we stayed in high season. The beach is pleasant and the surrounding village has several bars and restaurants. There are very pleasant walks and treks in the unspoilt woods of Liguria nearby or the most interesting tourist option is a visit to Cinque Terre, five villages, some of which can only be reached by rail, boat or by cliff footpath. Their history is one of fishing but now they also specialise in wines. Unusually, some of the vineyards can only be reached by boat. This is a great site for short stays to visit the Cinque Terre.

Facilities

The toilet block nearest the touring pitches provides cramped facilities. A new block is in the centre of the site. WCs are mainly Turkish. Washing machines and dryers. Shop (15/6-10/9). Bar/restaurant and takeaway (15/6-10/9). Small swimming pool. Play area. Excursions. Free bus to beach. Torches required. Bicycle hire. WiFi. Off site: Beach, fishing and boat launching 3 km. Tours.

Open: All year excl. 10 January - 10 February and 4 November - 4 December.

Directions

Leave A12 at Deiva Marina exit and follow signs to Deiva Marina. Site signs are clear at the first junction and site is on left 3 km. down this road.
GPS: 44.22470, 9.55168

Charges guide

Per unit incl. 2 persons and electricity	€ 20.00 - € 36.00
extra person (over 6 yrs)	€ 6.50

Framura
Camping Framura

Localitá La Spiaggetta, I-19014 Framura (Ligúria) T: 018 781 5030. E: hotelriviera@hotelrivieradeivamarina.it
alanrogers.com/IT64180

Framura is an unusual, small, cliff-side site of 160 pitches including just 12 pitches for touring units. These pitches are at the end of the seasonal units and are on the site of the old railway line, as is the whole steeply terraced site. The pitches themselves are fabulous as they are directly above the crystal clear waters here. Access to the site is through an old railway tunnel and there is absolutely no shade. The supporting amenities are basic but have a certain charm, some being cut into the rock face. The site is unsuitable for children, the infirm and has no facilities for disabled campers.

Facilities

Five very mixed blocks offer clean but basic toilets, mostly Turkish but some British style. Innovation has been used here and one very small shower block is carved into the rock face. Cold water at sinks. Washing machine. Very basic snack bar and takeaway (1/6-15/9). Bar (1/4-30/10). Small shop (15/6-15/9). Canoeing and windsurfing is possible. Fishing. Dogs are not accepted. Off site: Sister hotel with restaurant 400 m. Town 500 m. Boat launching 1 km. Bicycle hire 3 km.

Open: 1 April - 30 October.

Directions

From A12 take exit to Deiva Marina. Proceed to town centre. Take care to find site signs – road to north is impassable for larger units! Cross narrow bridge and negotiate narrow approach road. Check for cyclists in the dark railway tunnel and drive through to site! GPS: 44.21670, 9.56440

Charges guide

Per unit incl. 2 persons and electricity	€ 25.00 - € 36.50
No credit cards.	

FREE Alan Rogers Travel Card
Extra benefits and savings - see page 10

Isolabona

Camping delle Rose

Via Provinciale, Regione Prati Gonter 4, I-18035 Isolabona (Ligúria) T: 0184 208 130.
E: info@campingdellerose.eu **alanrogers.com/IT64015**

Camping delle Rose can be found close to the French border, and a few miles inland from the Italian Riviera. This is a peaceful spot, set deep in the Maritime Alps, and surrounded by unspoilt medieval towns, picturesque churches and bustling markets. This is a friendly, family site where Lorena, Mauro and Lorenzo will guarantee a warm welcome. The site is located on a terraced hillside, surrounded by eucalyptus and mimosa. Pitches are of a good size, and most have electrical connections. A number of mobile homes and apartments are available for rent.

Facilities

Swimming and paddling pools. Bar. Restaurant/pizzeria. Play area. Tourist information. Mobile homes and chalets for rent. Off site: Shops, cafés and restaurants in Pigna and Dolceacqua. San Remo 12 km. Monaco 32 km. Walking and mountain biking. Fishing.

Open: 1 April - 31 October.

Directions

From Ventimiglia, head north on SP54 to Dolceacqua and continue to Isolabona. The site is well signed from here. GPS: 43.894573, 7.646905

Charges guide

Per unit incl. 2 persons
and electricity € 28.50 - € 30.50
extra person € 8.00 - € 9.00
Camping Cheques accepted.

Pietra Ligure

Camping Dei Fiori

Viale Riviera 11, I-17027 Pietra Ligure (Ligúria) T: 019 625 636. E: info@campingdeifiori.it
alanrogers.com/IT64040

This is a small, family owned site with basic facilities, situated around 500 metres from the beach in an old olive yard and offering reasonable prices for your stay. A road runs past the entrance and the restaurant terrace is partly overlooked by an elevated section of this road. There are 232 pitches, which are on the small side, with lots of seasonal pitches for Italian campers, and some bungalows. The 60 flat touring pitches are mainly on the lower terraces of the site, with some shade and 6A electricity. Some of the smallest pitches may be challenging when manoeuvring with large units.

Facilities

Two blocks are old with a mixture of British and Turkish toilets. A new Portacabin-style unit offers better showers and toilets, but the majority are Turkish. Water is solar heated and free throughout. The facilities can be under pressure at peak times. Sinks have cold water only. Facilities are provided, but we do not recommend this site for disabled campers. Motorcaravan service point. Fridges for use by campers. Bar/snack bar. Takeaway (June-Sept). Shop. Swimming pool (May-Sept). Fabric paddling pool. Limited entertainment programme in season. Bicycle hire.

Open: All year.

Directions

From the A10/E80 take Pietra Ligure exit between Finale Ligure and Loano. Site is just southwest of the town of Pietra Ligure and is clearly signed off the beach road onto a minor road heading northwest. GPS: 44.14183, 8.27833

Charges guide

Per unit incl. 3 persons
and electricity € 23.00 - € 41.00
extra person € 5.00 - € 8.00
No credit cards.

Pietra Ligure

Camping Pian dei Boschi

Viale Riviera 114, I-17027 Pietra Ligure (Ligúria) T: 019 625 425. E: info@piandeiboschi.it
alanrogers.com/IT64107

Camping Pian dei Boschi can be found on the Ligurian Riviera, 700 m. from the sea, close to the resort of Pietra Ligure. Pitches are well shaded and most have electrical connections. A number of mobile homes are available for rent, as well as apartments (for 4-6 people). There is a large swimming pool surrounded by a wide sun terrace, with a paddling pool adjacent. The campsite restaurant includes a wood-fired pizza oven, and offers an enticing range of Mediterranean cuisine. Other on-site amenities include a tennis court and sports field.

Facilities

Shop. Bar/restaurant/pizzeria. Takeaway. Swimming pool. Paddling pool. Play area. Tennis. Sports field. Activity and entertainment programme. Tourist information. Mobile homes and apartments for rent. Off site: Nearest beach 700 m. Shops and restaurants in Pietra Ligure. Golf. Watersports.

Open: All year.

Directions

Approaching from France (Menton) on A10 motorway, leave at the exit to Pietra Ligure and head south on Viale Riviera towards the town centre, from where the site is well signed. GPS: 44.14906, 8.26856

Charges guide

Per unit incl. 3 persons
and electricity € 27.00 - € 42.00
extra person (over 2 yrs) € 5.00 - € 8.00
dog € 2.00 - € 3.50

For latest campsite news, availability and prices visit
alanrogers.com

Rapallo
Camping Miraflores

Via Savagna 10, I-16035 Rapallo (Ligúria) T: 018 526 3000. E: camping.miraflores@libero.it

alanrogers.com/IT64110

Camping Miraflores is located on the Ligurian coast, close to the famous resort of Portofino and the Cinque Terre. It is a small, uncomplicated site with a tiny restaurant and bar offering pizzas and a reasonable menu of the day. The 87 pitches are fairly flat and arranged around the lower levels of the site with separate terraced areas for tents (small pitches) and caravans or motorcaravans with electricity (6A Europlug). There are eight mobile homes on higher terraces. A small swimming pool is free to campers (hats required) and showers are now free. Rapallo is an attractive resort in its own right with an interesting old town centre. The A12 motorway is very close, so some road noise should be expected.

Facilities

Single central traditional sanitary block with a small number of toilets (some Turkish style). Showers. Washing machine. Shop. Restaurant/pizzeria and takeaway meals. Basic games room. Playground. Swimming pool (hats compulsory). WiFi (free). Mobile homes for rent. Tours and visits booked by reception. Off site: Golf 500 m. Tennis and riding 1 km. Nearest beach, fishing and boat launching 1.5 km. Rapallo centre 1.5 km.

Open: All year.

Directions

Site is located extremely close to the Rapallo exit from the A12 motorway. From this point, follow signs to Rapallo town and immediately around a roundabout to the left for the site entrance, which is well signed. GPS: 44.35772, 9.20964

Charges guide

Per unit incl. 2 persons
and electricity   € 25.50 - € 29.50
No credit cards.

San Remo
Camping Villaggio dei Fiori

Via Tiro a Volo 3, I-18038 San Remo (Ligúria) T: 018 466 0635. E: info@villaggiodeifiori.it

alanrogers.com/IT64010

Open all year round, this open and spacious site is a member of the Sunêlia group and maintains very high standards. It is ideal for exploring the Italian and French Rivieras or for just relaxing by the enjoyable, filtered seawater pools or on the private beach. Unusually, all of the pitch areas at the site are totally paved, with some extremely large pitches for large units (ask reception to open another gate for entry). Electricity (3/6A) is available (at extra cost) to all 107 pitches; 20 also have water and drainage, and there is an outside sink and cold water for every four pitches. There is ample shade from mature trees and shrubs, which are constantly watered and cared for in summer. The gold pitches and some wonderful tent pitches are along the seafront and have great views. There is a path to a secluded and pleasant beach with sparkling water, overlooked by a large patio area. The rocky surrounds are excellent for snorkelling and fishing, with ladder access to the water. The friendly management speak English.

Facilities

Four clean and modern toilet blocks have British and Turkish style WCs and hot water. Controllable showers. Baby rooms. Facilities for disabled campers. Laundry facilities. Motorcaravan services. Gas. Bar sells essentials. Large restaurant. Pizzeria and takeaway (all year; prepaid card system). Seawater swimming pools (small charge in high season) and heated whirlpool spa (June-Sept). Tennis. Play area. Fishing. Satellite TV. WiFi (charged). Bicycle hire. Dogs are not accepted. Off site: Bus at gate.

Open: All year.

Directions

From SS1 (Ventimiglia-Imperia), site is on right just before San Remo. There is a very sharp right turn into site if approaching from the west. From autostrada A10 take San Remo exit. Site is well signed. GPS: 43.80117, 7.74867

Charges guide

Per unit incl. 4 persons
and electricity   € 35.00 - € 72.00
Some charges must be paid on arrival.

FREE Alan Rogers Travel Card
Extra benefits and savings - see page 10

Sestri Levante

Camping Mare Monti

Via Aurelia km 469, I-16039 Sestri Levante (Ligúria) T: 018 544 348. E: info@campingmaremonti.com

alanrogers.com/IT64130

Mare Monti is a neat and tidy site with 140 pitches. It is set high in the hills with spectacular views overlooking the small town of Sestri Levante. The owner and his staff are relaxed and very friendly. The site has 40 touring pitches with 3A electricity, all set on terraces overlooking the wonderful countryside. The remaining pitches are taken by seasonal units. A small shop and a bar with its terrace overlook a neat swimming pool. Access to the site and within is difficult and the site is therefore only suitable for smaller units and tents. However the rural location, together with good facilities offers a quiet and relaxing retreat away from city life. English is spoken.

Facilities

Two refurbished toilet blocks are modern, bright and spotlessly clean. British style WCs. Hot showers. Washing machine and dryer. Small shop, bar with takeaway (April-Oct). Outdoor swimming pool with separate pool for children (June-Oct). WiFi (free). Minibus to town (July/Aug). Off site: Bars, restaurants, shops and ATM in Sestri Levante 2 km. Fishing 2 km. Bicycle hire 4 km. Riding 5 km. Golf 15 km.

Open: 1 March - 31 October.

Directions

From autostrada A12 take exit for Sestri Levante. Follow road SP1 in an easterly direction to km. 469. Site entrance is on the left set back from road and difficult to see. The road is steep in places and winding. It is not suitable for large units.
GPS: 44.26365, 9.441901

Charges guide

Per unit incl. 2 persons and electricity	€ 25.00 - € 32.00
extra person	€ 6.00

Villanova d'Albenga

Camping C'era una Volta

Localitá Fasceti, I-17038 Villanova d'Albenga (Ligúria) T: 018 258 0461. E: info@villaggioceraunavolta.it

alanrogers.com/IT64050

An attractive campsite, C'era una Volta is about 6 km. back from the sea, situated on a hillside with panoramic views. Pitches are on terraces in different sections of the site. Varying in size, most have shade from the young trees which harbour crickets with their distinctive noise. Some of the upper pitches have good views. Cars are required to park in separate areas at busy times. There are electricity connections, with water and drainage close by. Charges are high in season but the site has an enjoyable atmosphere and is a good choice for families. A private beach is 7 km. and a bus runs to the beach in July and August.

Facilities

The main toilet block is modern and above average with hot water throughout. Four additional smaller blocks are spread around the site. Maintenance can be variable. Shop. Bar and pizzeria (15/5-10/9). Restaurant. Takeaway (evenings only 1/4-30/9). Disco (July/Aug). Swimming pools (15/5-20/9). Small gym. Fitness track. Miniclub. Health centre with Finnish sauna. Hydromassage bath/shower. Turkish bath. Hydrojet massage bed. Tennis. Large adventure playground. Boules. Internet. Satellite TV. Communal barbecue. Off site: Riding 500 m. Golf 2 km. Lake fishing 4 km. Beach, boat launching and sailing 6 km.

Open: 1 April - 30 September.

Directions

Leave A10 at Albenga, turn left and left again at roundabout for the SS453 for Villanova. At T-junction turn left (Garlenda), turn right in 200 m. and follow signs up a long winding narrow road beyond the Stadium. GPS: 44.04433, 8.1137

Charges guide

Per unit incl. up to 3 persons	€ 25.00 - € 49.00
tent pitch	€ 20.00 - € 38.00
extra person	€ 7.00 - € 12.00
child (3-6 yrs)	€ 3.50 - € 6.00

Electricity included. No credit cards.

Advantage all the way

alan rogers Travel Card

Got yours yet?

Extra benefits and savings - see page 10

For latest campsite news, availability and prices visit
alanrogers.com

The region of Lombardy stretches from the Alps on the border with Switzerland, down past the romantic lakes of Como and Maggiore to the broad, flat plain of the River Po.

THE REGION IS MADE UP OF THE PROVINCES: BERGAMO, BRESCIA, COMO, CREMONA, LECCO, LODI, MANTOVA, MILANO, PAVIA, SONDRIO AND VARESE. WE FEATURE LAKE GARDA SEPARATELY.

Lombardy is one of the most developed tourist destinations in Italy, its major draw being the beautiful scenic lakes. Surrounded by abundant vegetation, Lake Como is set in an idyllic landscape of mountains, tall peaks that seem to rise directly from the water's edge. With a number of places to visit along the shores, including the prosperous towns of Como and Lecco, the area is also great for walking and in most places the lake is clean enough for swimming. Lake Maggiore has a Mediterranean atmosphere, with citrus trees and palms lining the shores, and offers a more sedate pace. There are good walks in the surrounding hills. Lying in the centre of the lake, near Stresa, are the Borromean Islands, of which Isola Bella is the most popular. It is home to the 17th-century Palazzo Borromeo and its splendid garden of landscaped terraces, fountains, peacocks and statues. A lesser known lake, Lake Iseo, is the fifth largest in northern Italy. Situated in wine producing country, surrounded by mountains and waterfalls, it is popular for its watersports and boasts the largest lake-island in Italy, Monte Isola. All three lakes are well served by ferries which zig-zag from shore to shore, and are within easy reach of the vibrant city of Milan.

Places of interest

Bellagio: beautiful town by Lake Como, hilly old centre with steep, cobbled streets.

Bergamo: hill-top town, medieval and Renaissance buildings.

Brescia: Roman ruins, 12th-century church.

Certosa di Pavia: magnificent Renaissance Charterhouse.

Cremona: where the violin was developed, home of famous violin maker Stradivarius.

Lodi: charming medieval town of pastel coloured houses with pretty courtyards.

Milan: fashion capital, great for shopping, art museums, home of famous opera house La Scala and Leonardo Da Vinci's *Last Supper* fresco.

Cuisine of the region

Food varies considerably from town to town. Risotto is popular (the short grain rice is grown in the paddy fields of the Ticino Valley) as are green pasta and polenta. Lombardy is one of the largest cheese making regions in the country – Gorgonzola and Mascarpone are produced here.

Biscotti: biscuits flavoured with nuts, vanilla and lemon.

Cotolette alla Milanese: veal escalope.

La Casoêula: pork stew.

Ossobuco: shin of veal.

Panettone: light yeast cake with candied fruit.

Pizzoccheri: buckwheat noodles.

Risotto alla Milanese: rice cooked in meat stock with white wine, onion, saffron and grated parmesan.

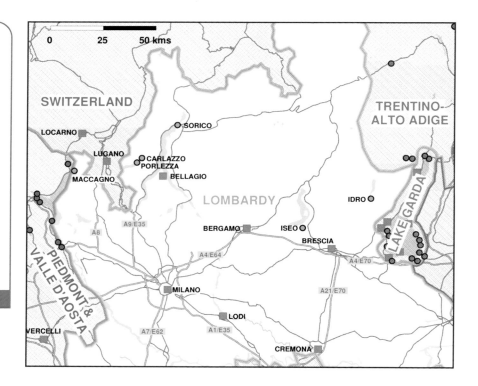

Carlazzo
Camping Ranocchio

Via Al Lago N7, localitá Piano Porlezza, I-22010 Carlazzo (Lombardy) T: 034 470 385.
E: campingranocchio@ngi.it **alanrogers.com/IT62515**

This is a delightful site next to a small lake in a wetland nature reserve, surrounded by tree-clad slopes with views of distant mountain peaks. Such peaceful locations are rare. The very friendly Cremella family are all involved in the running of the site and their welcome is warm and genuine. The 195 touring pitches (all with 3-6A electricity) are on gravel hardstanding or grass. The restaurant, with a bar and terrace, offers a range of Italian dishes and pizzas to eat in or take away. There is a well maintained swimming pool and a paddling pool with safety precautions.

Facilities

Two sanitary blocks provide excellent modern facilities with warm water to some basins; showers are token operated. Good facilities for disabled visitors. Baby rooms. Motorcaravan services. Washing machines. Bar (15/4-30/9). Restaurant/takeaway (15/4-15/9). Pool is charged for (€ 1) but always supervised (15/6-15/9). Gas supplies. Fishing, swimming from small shingle beach (fence and gate, but young children would need watching). WiFi in reception (charged). Off site: Bicycle hire 600 m. Supermarket 800 km. Riding 2 km. Sailing and golf 4 km.

Open: 1 April - 30 September.

Directions

Carlazzo is on the SS340, 6 km. from Porlezza. Ranocchio is clearly signed (turn right) in the centre of the village, and is at the bottom of the lane. The SS340 is very narrow and winding, especially on the Porlezza-Lugano section. The road from Menággio is better. GPS: 46.04078, 9.16828

Charges guide

Per unit incl. 2 persons	
and electricity	€ 21.00 - € 25.00
extra person	€ 5.50 - € 6.50
child (0-6 yrs)	€ 3.00 - € 3.50

No credit cards.
Camping Cheques accepted.

For latest campsite news, availability and prices visit
alanrogers.com

Idro

Azur Camping Rio Vantone

Via Vantone 45, I-25074 Idro (Lombardy) T: 03 65 83 125. E: idro@azur-camping.de

alanrogers.com/IT62580

Lake Idro, one of the smaller of the northern Italian lakes, is tucked away in the mountains to the west of Lake Garda. Rio Vantone is on the southeast shore of the lake with marvellous views across the water to the villages on the opposite bank and surrounding mountains. The ground slopes gently down to the water's edge with many of the 190 touring pitches in level rows divided by hedges, with others between tall trees. All have 6A electricity and there are 46 with water and drainage. The ones by the lake attract a higher charge. The lake is ideal for windsurfing and the surrounding countryside for walking and climbing.

Facilities

The main, heated sanitary block is on the ground floor of a large building and is of excellent quality including cabins. A smaller block is also open in high season. Facilities for disabled visitors. No hot water 22.00-06.00. Washing machines and dryer. Motorcaravan services. Gas supplies. Cooking rings. Shop. Bar. Excellent restaurant (15/5-20/9). Swimming pools. Lake swimming. Windsurf school. Boat and mountain bike hire. Play area. WiFi (charged). Torches useful in some areas. Off site: Shops, bars and restaurants 1.5 km. Riding 8 km.

Open: 1 April - 31 October.

Directions

From A4 autostrada take Brescia Est exit. Go north on SS45bis towards Saló then follow brown signs for Valle Sabia and Lago d'Idro on SS237 via Vobarno, Barghe (bypassed) and Lavenone to Lemprato. Take right turn into narrow road after town sign for Idro. GPS: 45.75418, 10.49821

Charges guide

| Per unit incl. 2 persons and electricity | € 22.00 - € 54.00 |
| extra person | € 6.00 - € 10.00 |

Iseo

Camping Covelo

Via Covelo, 18, I-25049 Iseo (Lombardy) T: 030 9821305. E: info@campingcovelo.it

alanrogers.com/IT62595

Covelo is a modest, family run site in a superb location. It is three hundred metres long, with grassy pitches and mature trees. The average sized, level pitches are in rows parallel with the shores of the lake. As the site is just four pitches deep, all have excellent access to the water plus brilliant views of the mountains across the lake, and the tree-clad escarpment to the rear of the site. The owners take great pride in their site, insisting on high levels of simple family-style enjoyment for their guests.

Facilities

Four sanitary blocks of differing sizes provide pleasant facilities including those for disabled campers. Baby cubicle. Motorcaravan services. Shop. Bar. Restaurant. Play area. Entertainment. TV room. Big screen movies at night. Free bicycles for guests. Fishing. Boat launching. Buoys for boats. WiFi. Off site: Iseo 1 km. Golf 2 km.

Open: 1 April - 31 October.

Directions

From the Milan/Verona A4 Autoroute approach Lake Iseo on the SPX1 from Seriate travelling East, or from any of the many approach roads travelling West from Brescia. At Iseo site is well signed 800 m. south of town on the lakeside. GPS: 45.66667, 10.06694

Charges guide

| Per unit incl. 2 persons and electricity | € 15.00 - € 30.00 |
| extra person | € 5.00 - € 7.00 |

Iseo

Camping del Sole

Via per Rovato 26, I-25049 Iseo (Lombardy) T: 030 980 288. E: info@campingdelsole.it

alanrogers.com/IT62610

Camping del Sole lies on the southern edge of Lake Iseo, just outside the pretty lakeside town of Iseo. The site has 306 pitches, many taken up with chalets and mobile homes. The 180 touring pitches all have 3A electricity and some have fine views of the surrounding mountains and lake. Pitches are generally flat and of a reasonable size, but cars must park in the car park. The site has a wide range of excellent leisure amenities, including a large swimming pool. There is a bar and restaurant with a pizzeria near the pool and an entertainment area, and a second bar by the lake.

Facilities

Sanitary facilities are modern and well maintained, including special facilities for disabled visitors. Washing machines and dryers. Bar, restaurant, pizzeria, snack bar and supermarket (all open all season). Motorcaravan service point. Bicycle hire. Swimming pool with children's pool (21/5-10/9). Canoe and pedal boat hire. Tennis. WiFi. Dog exercise area. Entertainment in high season. Off site: Golf 5 km. Riding 6 km.

Open: 16 April - 25 September.

Directions

From A4 (Milan-Venice) take Rovato exit and at roundabout go north on SPX1 following signs for Lago d'Iseo for 12 km. Site is well signed to left at large roundabout. GPS: 45.65708, 10.03740

Charges guide

| Per unit incl. 2 persons and electricity | € 19.80 - € 42.90 |
| extra person | € 5.90 - € 10.10 |

Camping Cheques accepted.

Iseo

Camping Punta d'Oro

Via Antonioli 51-53, I-25049 Iseo (Lombardy) T: 030 980 084. E: info@camping-puntadoro.com
alanrogers.com/IT62590

Camping Punta d'Oro, at the town of Iseo in the southeast corner of the lake, is a small, delightful campsite. It has been run by the Brescianini-Zatti family for the last 30 years and you will receive a very warm welcome on arrival. The very pretty site slopes gently down to the lake. It has 62 grass pitches (with two static caravans for hire) all with electrical connections, mainly 6A. Trees and shrubs provide some shade and there are lovely views across the lake to the mountains. Lakeside pitches are a little more expensive. There is some occasional noise from the nearby railway.

Facilities

The two small sanitary blocks have been refurbished to a high standard with a mix of British and Turkish style WCs and hot water in washbasins and showers. Suite for disabled visitors. All facilities are kept very clean. Washing machine. Motorcaravan services. Shop. Small bar serving a limited range of snacks. Games room. TV in bar. Lake access for swimming and fishing with two narrow slipways for boat launching. Bicycle hire arranged. Internet and WiFi. Off site: Town within walking distance. Riding 3 km.

Open: 20 March - 26 October.

Directions

Leave A4 Milan-Venice autostrada at Rovato, turn left to roundabout and go north on SPX1 following signs for Lago di Iseo. Punta d'Oro is on northeast side of Iseo. Avoid town centre and turn northeast on SP71 for 1.5 km. before turning back north across the railway and turn right at site sign. GPS: 45.66392, 10.05583

Charges guide

Per person	€ 4.90 - € 7.50
child (1-9 yrs)	€ 3.80 - € 6.10
pitch incl. electricity	€ 9.70 - € 16.40

Maccagno

Parkcamping Maccagno Lagocamp

Via Corsini 3, I-21010 Maccagno (Lombardy) T: 033 256 0203. E: maccagno@lagocamp.com
alanrogers.com/IT62390

Parkcamping Maccagno is an unpretentious site which has immediate access to the shores of Lake Maggiore and a shingle beach. With hills on each side, the views day and night over the lake are spectacular. There is no entertainment or infrastructure, so the site will suit those who just wish to relax on a traditional, older style campsite. The 115 rather cramped pitches vary in size (40-80 sq.m), but are relatively flat and many have shade. They are numbered but demarcation is somewhat informal. The bar and shop have been completely refurbished, with a few snacks added to the menu.

Facilities

One toilet block with old but clean facilities including those for babies (in ladies' toilet) and disabled visitors (key). Laundry facilities. Motorcaravan service point. Newly refurbished bar and shop selling bread and basics. Terrace seating. Basic snacks. Simple play areas and sandpit. WiFi. Off site: Buses 500 m. Golf 20 km.

Open: 18 March - 13 November.

Directions

Site is on the eastern side of Lake Maggiore, a little to the north of the town of Luino. Follow the SS394 towards Maccagno and Locarno. Site is well signed. GPS: 46.038862, 8.734728

Charges guide

Per unit incl. 2 persons and electricity	€ 21.00 - € 36.50
extra person	€ 5.50 - € 8.50

Porlezza

Camping Darna

Via Osteno 50, I-22018 Porlezza (Lombardy) T: 034 461 597. E: informazioni@campingdarna.com
alanrogers.com/IT62505

At the eastern end of Lake Lugano, Camping Darna is in a broad valley with a great view down the lake and mountains on all sides. It is a well run site which becomes lively in high season with plenty of entertainment for young and old; in low season it is much more relaxed. The 304 touring pitches are on flat ground, all with 3A electricity. There are 46 seasonal pitches (not along the lakeside). A pizzeria serves a full range of Italian dishes and has a bar and terrace. There is a good sized swimming pool and paddling pool.

Facilities

Five sanitary blocks, some with controllable showers, are kept very clean. Facilities for disabled visitors. Washing machines and dryers. Motorcaravan service point. Good shop and bakery. Bar/restaurant with takeaway and large terrace. Swimming pool (open to public, € 4 daily to campers) and paddling pool (1/6-30/9). Fishing, swimming and boating. WiFi (charged). Off site: Riding 1 km. Bicycle hire, shops, bars and restaurants 1.5 km. Sailing 3 km. Golf 10 km.

Open: 1 April - 31 October.

Directions

Porlezza is 14 km. east of Lugano on SS340 to Menaggio. Turn right at traffic lights in Porlezza (Via Osteno). Site is 1.5 km. on right. Note: SS340 is narrow and winding, so not for large units. GPS: 46.02514, 9.12603

Charges guide

Per person	€ 5.50 - € 9.00
pitch	€ 12.00 - € 14.50
No credit cards.	

For latest campsite news, availability and prices visit

alanrogers.com

Sorico

Camping la Riva

Via Poncione 3, I-22010 Sorico (Lombardy) T: 034 494 571. E: info@campinglariva.com

alanrogers.com/IT62510

La Riva lies on a waterway at the northern end of Lake Como. It is surrounded by mountains, close to the nature reserve of Pian di Spagna and within walking distance of Sórico, a pretty town with bars, restaurants and shops. The site is beautifully laid out, with 75 level touring pitches on well tended grass, and of a good size. Many have attractive views across the river to the mountains and most have 6A electrical connections. Reception houses a small bar, with limited snack bar and takeaway. Bread and milk to order. The excellent outdoor pool has a sunbathing terrace. Camping la Riva has a happy, friendly atmosphere. This is a small, quiet site which enjoys direct access to the water and is well located for trekking in the surrounding mountains or for mountain biking.

Facilities

The centrally located sanitary building contains modern showers (token), a mixture of Turkish and British style toilets and washbasins (warm water) and is kept very clean. Facilities for disabled visitors. Washing machine. Swimming pool. Bicycle hire. Fishing. Water skiing. Canoe and dinghy hire. WiFi in some areas (free). Off site: Guided walks. Cycling/walking track from site to Sorico. Riding. Golf. Local market.

Open: 1 March - 3 November.

Directions

Sórico is at the northern tip of Lake Como. Approach via the free SS36 dual carriageway from Lecco; just after end of motorway section turn east to Sórico. From Como the SS340 is narrow and winding. Site is on eastern edge of town and well signed. GPS: 46.17067, 9.39268

Charges guide

Per unit incl. 2 persons and electricity	€ 23.00 - € 35.00
extra person	€ 6.00 - € 10.00
dog	€ 4.00

Discounts in low season. No credit cards.

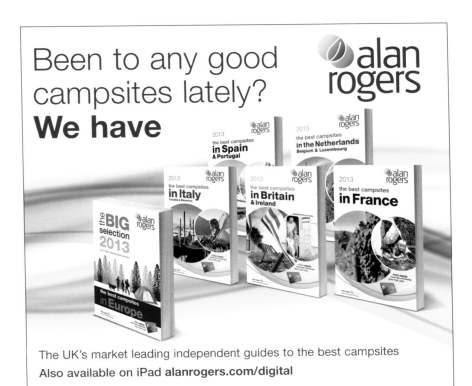

FREE Alan Rogers Travel Card
Extra benefits and savings - see page 10

The largest and cleanest of the Italian lakes, Lake Garda is also the most popular. The low-lying countryside of the southern stretches gives way to the dramatic, craggy mountains of the north, while the western shore is fringed with olive groves, vines and citrus trees.

IN THIS POPULAR TOURIST REGION WE HAVE INCLUDED THE LAKESIDE AREAS OF THE REGIONS OF VENETO, LOMBARDY AND TRENTINO-ALTO ADIGE

The lake's largest town, Desenzano del Garda, lies on the southern shore. Bars and restaurants line the lakefront and a walk to the town's castle affords spectacular views. Nearby, Sirmione is popular with those seeking cures in its sulphurous springs. It has the remains of a Roman spa plus a 13th-century fairytale castle, which is almost entirely surrounded by water. Along the sheltered stretch of the western shore, otherwise known as the Riviera Bresciana, are lush groves and fruit trees; Salò is a good place to stock up on the local produce. Gardone is best known for its exotic botanical garden and Il Vittoriale, the home of the notorious writer Gabriel D'Annunzio, which is filled with curiosities. Up in the mountains behind Gardone is the little alpine village of San Michele, and there are good walks to the springs and waterfalls in the surrounding hills. At the northwest tip of the lake, Riva del Garda is one of the best known resorts and a favourite with windsurfers, as is Torbole, where sailing and mountain biking are popular too. On the eastern shore, Malcesine boasts a 13th-century turreted castle and a funicular which climbs to the summit of Monte Baldo giving panoramic views. Near the lively resort of Garda are white shingle beaches.

Places of interest

Bardolino: home of the light, red Bardolino wine. Festival of the Grape is held between Sept-Oct.

Gargano: olive factory, 13th-century church, good place for sailing.

Peschiera: attractive enclosed harbour and fortress.

Puegnago del Garda: home of Comincioli vineyard that has been producing wine since the 16th century.

Torri del Benaco: considered to be the prettiest lakeside town, with old centre, cobbled streets and a castle.

Cuisine of the region

Fish is popular; there are 40 different species in the lake including carp, trout, eel and pike. Regional dishes include trout filled with oranges and lemons, risotto with tench, and *sisam,* a traditional way of preparing lake minnows. The fruits grown on the western shore are used to make olive oil, citrus syrups and Bardolino, Soave and Valpolicella wines.

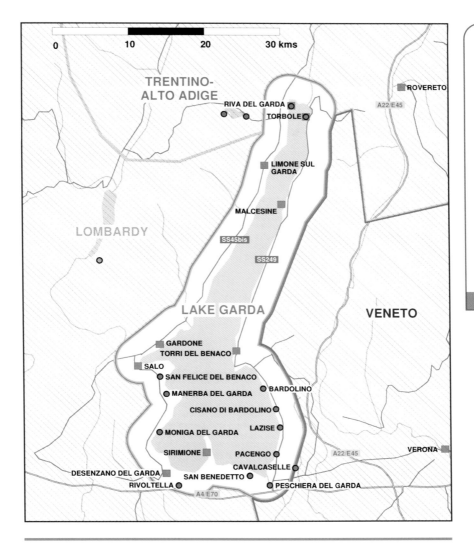

Bardolino
La Rocca Camp

Località San Pietro, I-37011 Bardolino (Lake Garda) T: 045 721 1111. E: info@campinglarocca.com
alanrogers.com/IT63600

This site was one of the first to operate on the lake and the family has a background of wine and olive oil production. La Rocca is in two areas, each side of the busy A249, the upper part being used mostly for bungalows, although some touring pitches are here and these have great lake views. The remaining touring pitches are on the lower part of the site, along with the main facilities. There is access between the two parts via a tunnel. The 445 pitches are mostly on terraces with shade, 6A electricity and access from narrow tarmac roads.

Facilities

Four toilet blocks, two on each side of the site. WCs are mixed British and Turkish style and showers controllable. Facilities for disabled visitors but many steps to pool. Children's facilities and baby baths. Washing machines. Motorcaravan services. Shop and bakery. Restaurant, bar and takeaway. Swimming and paddling pools (lifeguard). Whirlpool. Pool bar. Play area. Entertainment programme in season. Miniclub. Internet point. Bicycle hire. Games room. Watersports. WiFi (charged). Torches useful.

Open: 1 April - 30 September.

Directions

Site is on the east side of Lake Garda, on the lake ring road 249. From the A4 take Pescheria exit and the 249 north for Garda (there are many signs for Gardaland). Site is well signed approaching village of Bardolino. GPS: 45.5645, 10.7129

Charges guide

Per unit incl. 2 persons	
and electricity	€ 19.00 - € 42.00
extra person	€ 5.00 - € 9.50

FREE Alan Rogers Travel Card
Extra benefits and savings - see page 10

Bardolino
Camping Serenella

Localitá Mezzariva 19, I-37011 Bardolino (Lake Garda) T: 045 721 1333. E: serenella@camping-serenella.it
alanrogers.com/IT63590

Situated alongside Lake Garda, Serenella has 300 average size pitches, some with good lake views. Movement around the site may prove difficult for large units (look for the wider roads). The pitches are shaded and have 10A electricity. A long promenade with brilliant views of the mountains and lake runs the length of the campsite. It is dotted with grassy relaxation areas and beach bars where snacks are served and the atmosphere is charming. The pleasant pool complex is near an older style taverna where delicious, sensibly priced food is served. There is some road noise at some of the amenities and the pool. There is an entertainment programme from May to September, with a miniclub for the children. A small market selling a variety of goods and newspapers, and a stall selling fresh fruit and vegetables. Serenella is popular with Italians and international guests. Gardaland is nearby. Professional coaches are available for many watersports and courses may be taken.

Facilities

Five clean, well equipped sanitary blocks include three that are more modern with laundry facilities. British style toilets, free hot water throughout. Facilities for disabled visitors. Infirmary. Washing machines and dryer. Freezer. Bar/restaurant, takeaway and shop (all season). Watersports. Outdoor swimming pool (1/5-18/9). Entertainment and sporting programme for all in high season. Play area. Bicycle hire. Boat launching. Minigolf. Tennis. Satellite TV. Internet and WiFi (charged). Dogs are not accepted. Off site: Beach with fishing and watersports. Town and golf 3 km. Riding 3.5 km. Verona 35 km. Gardaland.

Open: 24 March - 21 October.

Directions

From E70/A4 Milan-Venice autostrada take Pescheria exit and follow signs to Bardolino. Site is on lakeside between Bardolino and Garda, 4 km. south of Garda. GPS: 45.55939, 10.71657

Charges guide

Per unit incl. 2 persons and electricity	€ 18.50 - € 39.00
per person	€ 4.50 - € 10.00
child (0-5 yrs)	free - € 4.40

No credit cards.

Cavalcaselle
Camping Gasparina

Via Gasparina 13, I-37010 Cavalcaselle (Lake Garda) T: 045 755 0775. E: info@gasparina.com
alanrogers.com/IT62660

Gasparina is of average size for this area and of reasonable quality, but a little away from the towns around the lake. It is in a peaceful location and has the feeling of being in the countryside. As the site slopes gently towards the lake, levellers are needed in some parts. There are 363 grass touring pitches in back-to-back rows separated by gravel roads. Many trees and flowers adorn the site, with shade in most parts. The pleasant swimming pools are separated from the restaurant terraces by a neat, well clipped hedge. Just beyond the site fence is a beach and pleasant promenade.

Facilities

Two refurbished and one new toilet block have the usual facilities with warm water in two blocks. Facilities for disabled visitors. Washing machines and dryer. Shop. Bar/restaurant with terrace. Swimming pool. Playground. Tennis courts. Watersports. Entertainment in high season. Dogs and other pets are not accepted. Off site: Bicycle hire 2 km. Riding 3 km.

Open: 1 April - 1 September.

Directions

Leave A4 Milan-Venice motorway at exit for Peschiera, go north on east side of lake on the SS249 towards Lazise for entrance road on your left. GPS: 45.45539, 10.7017

Charges guide

Per unit incl. 2 persons	€ 19.00 - € 34.50
extra person	€ 4.00 - € 8.00
boat trailer	€ 10.00 - € 18.00

Cisano di Bardolino

Campings Cisano & San Vito

Via Peschiera 48, I-37011 Cisano di Bardolino (Lake Garda) T: 045 622 9098. E: cisano@camping-cisano.it
alanrogers.com/IT63570

This is a combination of two sites, each with its own reception. Some of the 700 touring pitches have superb locations along the 1 km. of shaded lakeside contained in Cisano. Some are on sloping ground and most are shaded but the San Vito pitches have no lake views. Both sites have a family orientation and considerable effort has been taken in the landscaping to provide maximum comfort even for the largest units. San Vito is the smaller and more peaceful location, which shares many of the facilities of Cisano. A security fence separates the pitches from the beach, so access involves a short walk. The facilities are constantly upgraded, although visitors with disabilities should select their pitch carefully to ensure an area appropriate to all their needs (there are some slopes in Cisano). On the San Vito site there is a pleasant family style restaurant (some road noise) which also sells takeaway food. San Vito is accessed through a tunnel under the road. Excellent pools and play equipment, along with a children's club and entertainment in high season are all here. The friendly, efficient staff at both sites speak English.

Facilities	Directions
Plentiful, good quality sanitary facilities are provided in both sites (nine blocks at Cisano and two at San Vito). Facilities for disabled visitors. Baby room. Washing machines. Fridge hire. Shop, two bar/restaurants and takeaway (all season). Swimming pool (May-Sept). Whirlpool. Play area. Fishing and sailing. Free windsurfing and canoeing. Archery. Football. Minigolf. Boat launching. WiFi (charged). Car wash. Dogs are not accepted (cats are). Motorcycles not allowed on site (parking provided). Off site: Indoor pool, bicycle hire and tennis 2 km.	Leave A4 autoroute at Pescheria exit and head north towards Garda on lakeside road. Pass Lazise and site is signed (small sign) on left halfway to Bardolina. Site is 12 km. beyond the Gardaland theme park. GPS: 45.52290, 10.72760

Open: 1 April - 8 October.

Charges guide

Per unit incl. 2 persons	
and electricity	€ 18.50 - € 45.00
extra person	€ 4.50 - € 11.00
motorboat	€ 10.00 - € 18.00

Camping Cheques accepted.

NEAR BARDOLINO - LAKE GARDA

CARAVANING BUNGALOWS

CISANO San Vito Camping

Via Peschiera, 48 - C.P. 126 - I - 37010 CISANO DI BARDOLINO (VR)
Tel. +39 045 6229098 - Fax +39 045 6229059
www.camping-cisano.it - cisano@camping-cisano.it

Lazise

Camping Park Delle Rose

Strada San Gaetano 20, I-37017 Lazise (Lake Garda) T: 045 647 1181. E: info@campingparkdellerose.it
alanrogers.com/IT63580

An orderly, well designed site with a feeling of spaciousness, Delle Rose is on the east side of Lake Garda, three kilometres from the attractive waterside village of Peschiera. The 455 pitches are of average size, most with grass and shade and laid out in 30 short, terraced avenues. The ratio of recreational area to pitches is unusually high, particularly for sites at Lake Garda. Unusually, reception is located one third of the way into the site. On approach one sees the attractive restaurant, gardens and comprehensive sporting facilities including the pool complex with its stylish terraced bar and entertainment area close by.

Facilities	Directions
Five clean, modern sanitary blocks have British style toilets, some in cabins with washbasins. Baby rooms. Facilities for disabled visitors. Washing machines. Motorcaravan service point. Fridge hire. Bar/restaurant, takeaway and pool bar. Shops. New swimming pool (mid April-Sept). Tennis. Archery. Minigolf. Play area and miniclub. Fishing (with permit). Beach at site. Watersports.	From A4 Milan-Venice autostrada take exit for Pescheria, west of Verona. Travel north towards Lazise. The campsite is on the southeastern lakeside 2.5 km. north of Pescheria and well signed. GPS: 45.48300, 10.73183

Open: 21 April - 30 September.

Charges guide

Per unit incl. 2 persons	€ 21.00 - € 42.00

Lazise

Camping la Quercia

I-37017 Lazise sul Garda (Lake Garda) T: 045 647 0577. E: laquercia@laquercia.it

alanrogers.com/IT62550

La Quercia is a spacious, popular site on a slight slope leading down to Lake Garda and is decorated by palm trees and elegantly trimmed hedges. Accommodating up to 850 touring units, pitches are mostly in regular double rows between access roads, all with 6A electricity. Most are shaded by mature trees, although those furthest from the lake are more open to the sun. Much of the activity centres around the impressive pool complex with its fantastic slides and the terrace bar, restaurant and pizzeria which overlook the entertainment stage. The daytime activities and evening entertainment are very professional with the young team working hard to involve everyone (some courses require enrolment on a Sunday). La Quercia has a fine sandy beach on the lake, with diving jetties and a roped off section for launching boats or windsurfing (high season). A second restaurant serving traditional Italian food is located closer to the beach. The site is a short distance from the delightful lakeside towns of Lazise and Peschiera, which have a wide choice of restaurants, and is a short drive from Verona, one of Italy's finest cultural centres.

Facilities

Six toilet blocks are perfectly sufficient and are of a very high standard. Laundry. Supermarket. General shop. Bar, restaurant, self-service restaurant and pizzeria. Swimming pools (small charge). Tennis. Aerobics, judo and yoga. Scuba club. Playground with water play. Organised events (sports competitions, games, etc.) and free courses (e.g. swimming, surfboarding). Canoeing. Roller-blading. Archery. Minigolf. Evening entertainment or dancing. Baby sitting service. WiFi (charged). ATM. Free weekly excursion. Dogs accepted (max. 2). Off site: Gardaland, Movieland and Caneva Aqua Park nearby. Bicycle hire 300 m. Golf 10 km. Riding 15 km.

Open: 29 March - 30 September.

Directions

Lazise is on the southeast side of Lake Garda 30 km. west of Verona. From north on A22 (Trento-Verona) take Affi exit then follow signs for Lazise and site. From south on A4 (Brescia-Venice) take Peschiera exit and site is 7 km. towards Lazise and Garda on SS249. GPS: 45.49318, 10.73337

Charges guide

Per unit incl. 2 persons and electricity	€ 21.10 - € 59.00
extra person	€ 5.40 - € 12.85
child (5-7 yrs)	€ 3.15 - € 8.40
dog	€ 4.80 - € 8.00

Lazise

Camping Piani di Clodia

Via Fossalta 42, I-37017 Lazise (Lake Garda) T: 045 759 0456. E: info@pianidiclodia.it

alanrogers.com/IT62530

Piani di Clodia is one of the largest sites on Lake Garda and it has a positive impression of space and cleanliness. It is located on a slope between Lazise and Peschiera in the southeast corner of the lake, with lovely views across the water to Sirmione's peninsula and the mountains beyond. The site slopes down to the water's edge and has 950 pitches, 920 with 6/16A electricity, 290 with electricity, water and drainage, terraced where necessary and back-to-back from hard access roads. There is some shade from mature and young trees. The pool complex is truly wonderful with a range of pools, a pleasant sunbathing area and a bar. A member of Leading Campings group.

Facilities

Seven modern, immaculate sanitary blocks, well spaced around the site. British and Turkish style WCs. All have facilities for disabled visitors and one has a baby room. Washing machines, dryers and laundry service. Motorcaravan service point. Shopping complex with supermarket and general shops. Two bars. Self-service restaurant with takeaway. Pizzeria. Ice cream parlour. Swimming pools (23/3-12/10). Tennis. Gymnastics. Fishing. Boat launching. Bicycle hire. Large playground. Outdoor theatre with entertainment programme. WiFi over part of site (charged). Dog area and shower. Off site: Riding 6 km. Golf 12 km. Theme parks nearby.

Open: 21 March - 13 October.

Directions

Lazise is on southeast side of Lake Garda 30 km. west of Verona. From north on A22 (Trento-Verona) take Affi exit then follow signs for Lazise and site. From south on A4 (Brescia-Venice) take Peschiera exit and site is 6 km. towards Lazise and Garda on SS249. GPS: 45.48272, 10.72932

Charges 2013

Per unit incl. 2 persons and electricity	€ 19.40 - € 58.50
extra person	€ 4.80 - € 12.50
child (1-9 yrs)	€ 3.00 - € 8.20

Your front line seat on Lake Garda!

VR.2012

CAMPING LA QUERCIA, YOUR HOLIDAY FILM

Shady emplacements – Heated toilet bloks for both grown-up's and children – 24 hours Warm water – Restaurant – Pizzeria – Cocktail Bar – Funny Bar on the beach – Swimmingpools with slides – Whirlpool – Full-comfort maxicaravans and bungalows for 4-5 persons with sight on the lake – The widest sand beach on the lake – Theatre – Supermarket – Butcher's shop – Pastry-nd bakers shop – Typical products of the lake – Fresh fruit and vegetables every days – Tobacconist's shop – International newspaper kiosk – Rent a car service – Fax service – Professional nimators – Animation for children and teenagers – Tennis – Canoe – Archery – Surfing – Judo – Football – Fitness gym – Spinning – Horse-riding.

6500 SQUARE METRES OF CLEAN AND SAFE PRIVATE
BEACH, JUST A FEW METRES AWAY FROM ALL THE AMENITIES.

900 SHADY SPOTS
IN BEAUTIFULLY-TENDED GROUNDS.

18 AREAS WITH FACILITIES FOR
SPORTS AND LEISURE ACTIVITIES.

Information and booking:

+ 39.045.6470577

laquercia@laquercia.it
www.laquercia.it

CAMPING ★★★★
LAQUERCIA
... more than a camping!

LAZISE SUL GARDA • VERONA • ITALY

Lazise
Camping du Parc

Via Gardesana, 110, I-37017 Lazise sul Garda (Lake Garda) T: 045 758 0127. E: duparc@camping.it

alanrogers.com/IT62535

Camping du Parc is a very pleasant, family owned site which resembles a Tardis, in that it extends and extends as you progress further through the site. Olive groves are interspersed with the pitch areas which gives an open and green feel. The site is set on a slope which goes down to the lakeside beach of soft sand. The 150 pitches are terraced and all have 5A electricity. Units above 10 m. long will be challenged by some of the corners here. Pitches are separated by trimmed hedges and some have shade, others have fine views of the lake. The restaurant is on the lower level with a terrace to catch the sunsets and the pizzeria also has a patio with sea views. Relax by the beach bar or in the pool whilst the children enjoy the slides and paddling pool. This is a very good site for those who prefer peace and quiet to the noisier atmosphere of the larger sites hereabouts. Buses stop by the gate to take you to Gardaland and other tourist attractions. As a site which caters for families, there is no disco or excessive noise and when we visited there were many happy customers. Entertainment takes place in the lower sports areas and is aimed mainly at children. All facilities are open the whole season. The beach, accessed through a security gate, is safe for swimming and there is a lifeguard.

Facilities

Four modern, heated sanitary blocks have free hot water throughout. Three blocks have facilities for disabled visitors, one for children and babies. Washing machines and dryers. Motorcaravan services. Mini-market. Restaurant with lake views. Pizzeria with terrace and views. Takeaway. Beach bar. Pool bar. Outdoor, heated swimming pool (1/5-31/10). Large paddling pool with slides. Children's entertainment. Baby club. Play area. Tennis. Fitness suite. Multisports court. Fishing. WiFi.

Open: 15 March - 31 October.

Directions

Leave A4 Venice-Milan autostrada by taking the Brennero exit to Lake Garda and then on to Lazise. At the lakeside in town turn left and follow signs for site. GPS: 45.49833, 10.7375

Charges guide

Per unit incl. 2 persons	
and electricity	€ 22.20 - € 45.00
extra person	€ 5.60 - € 10.50
child (2-6 yrs)	€ 1.50 - € 5.80

PARC DUE S.P.A. a socio unico
Via Gardesana, 110 - 37017 LAZISE (VR)
Tel. +39 0457580127 - Fax +39 0456470150

The campsite is located among green trees sloping down toward the lake 500 meters from the village. You can enjoy holidays top quality structures: modern sanitary, accommodations provided with every comforts and piches connected to the water system and to the sewer drain. The beach, heated swimming - pool playground, restaurant, minimarket and bar, together with moniclub, sport and leisure activities contribute to give you a wonderful holiday.

Manerba del Garda
Camping Baia Verde

Via del Edera 19, I-25080 Manerba del Garda (Lake Garda) T: 036 565 1753. E: info@campingbaiaverde.com

alanrogers.com/IT62860

Baia Verde is a smart, luxurious and peaceful campsite located in the southwestern corner of Lake Garda. The 89 touring pitches are in regular rows on flat, open ground where the young trees are giving some shade. The pitches are all fully serviced, and 12 have superb private facilities. The excellent restaurant block and the building housing the other facilities are architect designed and it shows. A great deal of thought and loving care has gone into Baia Verde. We were impressed!

Facilities

Full range of high quality sanitary facilities in an impressive three storey building in the style of an Italian villa. Baby and children's rooms. Superb facilities for disabled visitors. Washing machines and dryers. TV lounge. Rooftop sunbathing area with jacuzzi. Entertainment and activity programme (high season). Bicycle hire. WiFi. Only some breeds of dog accepted. Off site: Beach 400 m. Manerba del Garda 1 km. Golf and riding 2 km. Excursions.

Open: 1 April - 30 September.

Directions

Manerba is on western shore of Lake Garda at the southern end. From A4 Milan-Venice autostrada take Desenzano exit and head north on SS572 towards Salò for 12 km; then turn right following signs to site. GPS: 45.56155, 10.55352

Charges guide

Per unit incl. 2 persons	
and electricity	€ 19.00 - € 46.00
extra person	€ 4.50 - € 10.50

For latest campsite news, availability and prices visit

alanrogers.com

Manerba del Garda
Camping Belvedere
Via Cavalle 5, I-25080 Manerba del Garda (Lake Garda) T: 036 555 1175. E: info@camping-belvedere.it
alanrogers.com/IT62840

Situated along a promontory reaching into Lake Garda, this friendly, traditional campsite has been terraced to give many of the 85 touring pitches wonderful views. They are mostly shaded, on gravel with 6A electricity. There is a long beach and pleasant lakeside pitches; swimming and boat launching is easy. The delightful restaurant and bar with pretty flowers is under shady trees at the water's edge. The facilities are of a high standard, although there are none for disabled visitors, and the site prices are reasonable compared with others in the area. The site has a pleasant, open feel and we enjoyed it here.

Facilities

Five traditional sanitary blocks are well maintained and kept clean. Washing machine. Motorcaravan service point. Shop selling basics. Restaurant, bar and takeaway are all open most of the season. Play area. Tennis. Music and TV in bar. Fishing. WiFi (charged). Torches useful. Mobile homes to rent. Off site: Watersports nearby. Bars and restaurant a short walk away. Golf and bicycle hire 2 km. Riding 4 km. Theme parks.

Open: 4 April - 4 October.

Directions

Manerba is on southwestern shore of Lake Garda. From A4 Milan-Venice autostrada take Desenzano exit and head north on SS572 towards Saló for 11 km. and look for site signs. Turn right off main road, then right again along Via Belvedere. GPS: 45.56207, 10.56315

Charges guide

Per unit incl. 2 persons and electricity	€ 18.00 - € 34.00

Manerba del Garda
Camping la Rocca
Via Cavalle 22, I-25080 Manerba del Garda (Lake Garda) T: 036 555 1738. E: info@laroccacamp.it
alanrogers.com/IT62830

Set high on a peninsula, on the quieter western shore of Lake Garda, la Rocca is a very friendly, family orientated campsite. Eighty attractive touring pitches enjoy shade from the tree canopy and 20 are on open terraces with lake views. It has the choice of two pebble lakeside beaches with a jetty. The beaches can be accessed from the site, and there is a pleasant pool complex. The site has all modern amenities without losing its distinctive Italian ambience with an open feel. Nothing is too much trouble for the management. The owner, Livio, is charming and very engaging with his pleasant, halting English.

Facilities

Two sanitary blocks with smart new units for disabled campers and baby changing areas which are kept in pristine condition at all times. Washing machines. Bar with terrace also offers basic meals. Small shop. Swimming pools. Tennis. Play area. Bicycle loan. Fishing (permit). Boat launching. Music in the evenings. Miniclub (high season). WiFi (charged). Torches required on beach steps and tunnel. Off site: Bars and restaurants a short walk away. Riding 3 km. Golf 5 km. Theme parks.

Open: 1 April - 30 September.

Directions

Manerba is on western shore of Lake Garda at the southern end. From A4 autostrada take Desenzano exit and follow SS572 towards Saló for 11 km. and look for campsite signs. Turn right off main road, then right again along Via Belvedere and it is the second site on Via Cavalle. GPS: 45.56025, 10.56378

Charges guide

Per unit incl. 2 persons and electricity	€ 20.80 - € 39.40
extra person	€ 4.90 - € 9.90

Manerba del Garda
Camping Romantica
Via G Verdi 17, I-25080 Manerba del Garda (Lake Garda) T: 036 654 449. E: info@campingromantica.com
alanrogers.com/IT62820

Camping Romantica is a tranquil site with some lakeside pitches that have beautiful views across the lake to the mountains. The glittering lights across the lake at night are quite romantic and it is a pleasure to sit out and enjoy balmy summer evenings here. The 280 pitches are of 70-80 sq.m, mostly on grass and with tarmac access roads, many having shade. The lake is accessed through a security fence and across a public promenade. It is great here for swimming and watersports and boat launching. A stylish, bistro style restaurant is situated at the front of the site serving good food in a very attractive setting.

Facilities

Seven toilet blocks all clean and pleasant with mixed British and Turkish style WCs and very good, spacious showers. Facilities for disabled visitors. Washing machines. Quality restaurant and bar with large terrace. Large supermarket and bazaar. Play areas. Boat parking and launching. Watersports. WiFi (charged). Torches useful. Off site: Public transport 100 m. in high season. Bicycle hire, ATM 2 km. Riding 4 km. Theme parks.

Open: Easter - 30 September.

Directions

Site is on the western side of Lake Garda near the town of Manerba. From the E70 east of Brescia, take Desenzano exit and turn north for Saló on P572. Then take road to Manerba di Garda and site is well signed. GPS: 45.56639, 10.54972

Charges guide

Per unit incl. 2 persons and electricity	€ 26.00 - € 40.00
extra person	€ 6.00 - € 11.00

FREE Alan Rogers Travel Card
Extra benefits and savings - see page 10

Manerba del Garda
Camping San Biagio

Via Cavalle 19, I-25080 Manerba del Garda (Lake Garda) T: 036 555 1549. E: info@campingsanbiagio.net

alanrogers.com/IT62870

San Biagio is a great site at the tip of an attractive green peninsula surrounded by Lake Garda. Trees, shrubs and flowers have been planted and it has a pleasant, peaceful ambience. Steeply terraced in some parts to maximise views over the water, the 165 pitches are shaded in places, whilst others are in more open lakeside positions. All have 16A electricity. An excellent bar/restaurant is located on the water's edge in a charming old building with views of the small connected island which has a second bar. You can walk there at low tide.

Facilities

The large central toilet block is of a high standard and provides excellent facilities which are kept very clean. Supermarket. Large restaurant and bar. Island bar/snack bar. Play area. Boat launching, moorings for boats. All pitches now have access to satellite TV and WiFi (free). Off site: Bars and restaurants within walking distance. Bicycle hire, tennis, golf and riding 5 km. Sailing 10 km.

Open: 1 April - 30 September.

Directions

Manerba is on southwestern shore of Lake Garda. From A4 (Milan-Venice) take Desenzano exit, head north on SS572 towards Saló for 10 km. and look for campsite signs. Turn right off main road, then right again along Via Belvedere. Site is at the end of Via Cavalle. GPS: 45.56352, 10.56638

Charges guide

Per unit incl. 2 persons, electricity on meter	€ 32.00 - € 56.00
extra person	€ 8.00 - € 12.00

Manerba del Garda
Camping Zocco

Via del Zocco 43, I-25080 Manerba del Garda (Lake Garda) T: 036 555 1605. E: info@campingzocco.it

alanrogers.com/IT62850

Camping Zocco is an excellent, professionally run site in a quiet, scenic location sloping gently down towards the lake where there is a jetty, buoys for your boat and a long pleasant shingle beach with a bar. The Sandrini family, who run this site, give British and Dutch visitors a warm welcome and English is spoken. There are 244 pitches for touring units, all with 6A electricity either on slightly sloping ground or terraced. The position and quality of the facilities make Zocco a most attractive option if you prefer a smaller, quieter site, which improves year on year.

Facilities

Three tiled sanitary blocks are clean and well spaced around the site. Two are very modern with spacious showers and toilets (some Turkish). Facilities for disabled visitors. Washing machines. Motorcaravan services. Good restaurant/pizzeria with terrace and bar. Shop (25/4-20/9). Bar overlooking beach (reduced hours in low season). Pool complex with jacuzzi (free to campers). Fishing. Tennis. Play area. Bocce. Entertainment for children during July/Aug. Bicycle hire arranged. WiFi (first hour free daily).

Open: 20 April - 22 September.

Directions

Manerba is on western shore of Lake Garda at the southern end. From A4 Milan-Venice autostrada take Desenzano exit and head north on SS572 towards Saló for 10 km. Zocco is well signed to right through Manerba. GPS: 45.53967, 10.55595

Charges guide

Per unit incl. 2 persons and electricity	€ 16.00 - € 33.40
extra person	€ 5.50 - € 8.70

Manerba del Garda
Sivino's Resort

Via Gramsci 78, I-25080 Manerba del Garda (Lake Garda) T: 036 555 2767. E: info@sivinos.it

alanrogers.com/IT62900

Sivino's Resort is showing great promise. Its lengthy lakeside position is superb, with many desirable pitches by the beach. The 73 grass touring pitches all have 6A electricity. The pleasant owners' plans include a new bar, followed by a tastefully designed (awaiting permission), restaurant. This is a superb 'get away from it all' location with few extras as yet, but close to all amenities in the nearby villages. There is just one toilet block, a modern reception and a traditional building converted into five apartments.

Facilities

A small, clean, modern sanitary block is located in one corner of the site. The facilities are good although the shower cubicles are quite small. Facilities for disabled visitors. Washing machine. Beach, fishing, boat launching and buoys available on site. WiFi (charged). Dogs accepted by prior arrangement. Off site: Restaurants, bar and supermarket within 1 km. Bicycle hire 2 km. Golf 4 km. Riding 6 km.

Open: 1 April - 30 September.

Directions

Manerba del Garda is on western shore of Lake Garda. From A4 Milan-Venice autostrada take Desenzano exit and head north on SS572 towards Saló for 10 km. Watch for campsite signs. Turn right through Manerba, right again in Via San Sivino and continue for 2 km. along a winding road past other campsites. GPS: 45.5314, 10.5574

Charges guide

Per unit incl. 2 persons and electricity	€ 25.00 - € 46.00

For latest campsite news, availability and prices visit

alanrogers.com

Moniga del Garda
Camping Fontanelle
Via del Magone 13, I-25080 Moniga del Garda (Lake Garda) T: 036 550 2079. E: info@campingfontanelle.it
alanrogers.com/IT62770

Camping Fontanelle, a sister site to Fornella (no. IT62750), is situated near the historic village of Moniga and enjoys excellent views across the lake. The site sits on the southwest slopes of Lake Garda and has 166 touring pitches on slightly sloping and terraced ground. A further 50 pitches are used by tour operators but there is little impingement. All are marked and have 6A electrical connections (36 are fully serviced) and there are some very pleasant lakeside pitches (at extra cost). Some for tents and touring units are very secluded, being distant from the campsite facilities, although small blocks with toilets are close by. This is a peaceful, friendly site. Good English is spoken.

Facilities

The two main toilet blocks and two smaller blocks are modern and clean, with hot water throughout. Facilities for disabled campers are in these blocks. Washing machines and dryers. Motorcaravan services. Large shop with prices to compete with local supermarkets. Pleasant restaurant/bar. Takeaway. Shop. Swimming pools (from 15/5-15/9, supervised). Tennis. Electronic games. Live entertainment in high season. Boat launching. WiFi (charged). Off site: Bicycle hire 1 km. Golf 5 km.

Open: 22 April - 17 September.

Directions

Moniga is on southwestern shore of Lake Garda. From A4 Milan-Venice autostrada take Desenzano exit and head north on SS572 towards Saló for 10 km. watching for campsite signs, turning right then right again in 3 km. GPS: 45.5253, 10.5434

Charges guide

Per unit incl. 2 persons and electricity	€ 25.00 - € 42.00
extra person	€ 6.00 - € 10.00

Pacengo
Camping Lido
Via Peschiera 2, I-37017 Pacengo (Lake Garda) T: 045 759 0611. E: info@campinglido.it
alanrogers.com/IT62540

Camping Lido is one of the largest and amongst the best of the 120 campsites around Lake Garda and is situated at the southeast corner of the lake. There is quite a slope from the entrance down to the lake so many of the 683 grass touring pitches are on terraces which give lovely views across the lake. They are of varying sizes, separated by hedges, all have electrical connections and 57 are fully serviced. This is a most attractive site with tall, neatly trimmed trees standing like sentinels on either side of the broad avenue which runs from the entrance right down to the lake.

Facilities

Seven modern toilet blocks (three heated) have provision for disabled visitors. Three family rooms. Washing machines and dryer. Fridge rental. Supermarket. Bars, restaurant, pizzeria and takeaway. Swimming pool, paddling pool and slides. Superb fitness centre. Playground. Tennis. Bicycle hire. Watersports. Fishing. Activity programme (high season). Shingle beach with landing stage and mooring for boats. Dogs are not accepted in high season (5/7-15/8).

Open: 20 March - 11 October.

Directions

Leave A4 Milan-Venice motorway at exit for Peschiera. Head north on east side of lake on the SS249. Site entrance on left after Gardaland theme park. GPS: 45.46996, 10.72042

Charges guide

Per person	€ 4.70 - € 9.50
child (3-7 yrs)	€ 3.00 - € 5.80
pitch incl. services	€ 9.00 - € 18.00

Pacengo
Eurocamping Pacengo
Via Porto 13, I-37010 Pacengo di Lazise (Lake Garda) T: 045 759 0012. E: info@eurocampingpacengo.it
alanrogers.com/IT63010

Eurocamping is at the southeast corner of Lake Garda, with direct lake access and a pleasant beach. It is a good site for launching boats as there is a little harbour/marina area adjacent. This is the best part of the site, where a pleasant restaurant terrace overlooks the lake and boats. Pacengo includes a large area of mobile homes. Most pitches, although quite small, have very good shade and all have 4A electrical connections. The swimming pool incorporates a jacuzzi and separate children's pool. Although a little untidy, Eurocamping's lower prices may suit some campers.

Facilities

The sanitary blocks, although quite old, are kept fairly clean. Supermarket. Bar, restaurant and pizzeria (closed Tues. in low season). Swimming pools. Second bar at the poolside. Large play area. Tennis. Fishing. Boat launching. Organised entertainment (July/Aug). Off site: Theme parks within 1.5 km. Riding 2 km. Bicycle hire 5 km. Golf 7 km. Sailing 8 km.

Open: 1 April - 24 September.

Directions

From north on A22 (Trento-Verona) autostrada take Affi exit then follow signs for Lazise and site. GPS: 45.46772, 10.71654

Charges guide

Per person	€ 3.70 - € 6.50
child (2-8 yrs)	€ 2.30 - € 3.90
pitch	€ 8.70 - € 14.50
dog	€ 1.00 - € 2.20

FREE Alan Rogers Travel Card
Extra benefits and savings - see page 10

Peschiera del Garda
Camping Bella Italia

Via Bella Italia 2, I-37019 Peschiera del Garda (Lake Garda) T: 045 640 0688. E: info@camping-bellaitalia.it

alanrogers.com/IT62630

Peschiera is a picturesque village on the southern shore of Lake Garda, and Camping Bella Italia is a very attractive, large, well organised and very busy site in the grounds of a former farm, just west of the centre of the village. Half of the 1,100 pitches are occupied by the site's own mobile homes and chalets and by tour operators; there are some 400 touring pitches, most towards the lakeside and reasonably level on grass under trees. All have 16A electricity, water and waste water and are separated by shrubs. There are some fine views across the lake to the mountains beyond. A superb promenade allows direct access to the town. Bella Italia collaborates with Cisano/San Vito (IT63570) and Butterfly (IT62520). The site slopes gently down to the lake with access to the water for watersports and swimming. A feature of the site is the group of pools of varying shapes and sizes with an entertainment area and varied sports provision nearby. A range of supervised activities is organised. Regulations are in place to ensure that the site is peaceful. English and Dutch are spoken by the friendly staff. Although large, this site has not lost its personal touch, and their sixty years of experience has been wisely used.

Facilities

Six modern toilet blocks have British style toilets, washbasins and showers. Baby rooms and facilities for disabled visitors. Washing machines. Motorcaravan services. Infirmary. Shops. Gelateria. Bars. Waiter service restaurant and terrace and two other restaurants (one in the old farm building). Swimming pools (all season). Tennis. Archery. Playgrounds (small). Games room. Watersports. Fishing. Bicycle hire. Organised activities and entertainment. Miniclub. WiFi (charged). ATMs. Dogs are not accepted. Off site: Fishing 1 km. Golf 2.5 km. Riding 3 km. Gardaland, Italy's most popular theme park, is about 2 km. east of Peschiera, with others nearby. Verona 40 minutes.

Open: 24 March - 28 October.

Directions

Peschiera is 32 km. west of Verona. From A4 take exit for Peschiera del Garda and follow SS11 towards Brescia. Site is at the large junction at the western entrance to the village. GPS: 45.44165, 10.67920

Charges guide

Per unit incl. 2 persons	
and electricity	€ 26.30 - € 51.80
extra person	€ 6.40 - € 13.40
child (3-5 yrs)	free - € 5.30

Four charging seasons. No credit/debit cards.

Camping Cheques accepted.

Peschiera del Garda
Camping Butterfly

Lungolago Garibaldi 11, I-37019 Peschiera del Garda (Lake Garda) T: 045 640 11466.
E: info@campingbutterfly.it **alanrogers.com/IT62620**

Camping Butterfly is in the town of Peschiera and has been owned by the same family for 40 years. Giorgio, the younger generation owner, is keen to make your holiday a success. Camping Butterfly is associated with IT62630 Bella Italia. There are 292 flat pitches on grass and sand, with 6A electricity and with some shade from mature trees. Many mobile homes are mixed randomly around the camping area. A pleasant swimming pool with a paddling pool (and lifeguard) is available for cooling off and fun (hats compulsory). The site is keen to welcome children under 12 years of age accompanied by their parents.

Facilities

Three toilet blocks are light and bright. WCs are mainly British style with some Turkish. Facilities for disabled visitors. Washing machines. Shop. Bar and restaurant plus takeaway. Swimming and paddling pools with lifeguard. Play area. Multisport court. Entertainment programme. Miniclub. WiFi (charged). Off site: Public transport and free transport to Gardaland at gate. ATM, beach and sailing 100 m. All town facilities 200 m. Internet 700 m. Golf 1 km.

Open: 10 March - 4 November.

Directions

Site is on south side of Lake Garda in the town of Peschiera. From A4 take Peschiera exit, immediately pick up signs for site as you cross the attractive waterways on the 249. Take care as the signs are not that obvious. GPS: 45.44524, 10.69444

Charges guide

Per unit incl. 2 persons	
and electricity	€ 19.00 - € 46.50
extra person	€ 4.50 - € 12.00
child (3-5 yrs)	free - € 5.00
dog	€ 1.00 - € 5.00

No credit cards.

For latest campsite news, availability and prices visit

alanrogers.com

Peschiera del Garda - Lago di Garda

Reason 13...   Reason 1...   Reason 59...   Reason 56...

Bella Italia welcomes its guests in a relaxing but eventful holiday suitable for everyone from 1 to 100 years old! Families can enjoy a care-free time both resting poolside while children can play in our supervised water-parks or visiting the beautiful surroundings. Too lazy for extensive sport facilities? Delight yourself with the special dishes offered by our famous restaurants.

The evening entertainment starts with our baby dance to continue with shows and musicals. At 23 o'clock vehicle-curfew ensures a quiet sleep for our satisfied campers.

Reason 40...

...63 reasons to visit us!
Discover them all on our website!

camping-bellaitalia.it
info@camping-bellaitalia.it

Peschiera del Garda
Camping del Garda
Via Marzan 6, I-37019 Peschiera del Garda (Lake Garda) T: 045 755 0540.
E: prenotazioni@camping-delgarda.com **alanrogers.com/IT62560**

Camping del Garda is directly on the lake with access through gates which provide security at night. This is one of the largest campsites around Lake Garda and is more of a self contained holiday village with many pitches used by tour operators, although they are generally separate from the touring pitches. The mature trees provide shade for the 659 grass pitches of which 337 are for touring units. Arranged in numbered rows, all have 4A electrical connections and hedges have been cleverly trimmed for maximum attractiveness. Hard roads give access. This is a well kept site with colour added by attractive flower beds.

Facilities
Eleven good quality toilet blocks have the usual facilities with free hot water in sinks, washbasins and showers. Facilities for disabled visitors in two blocks. Washing machines and dryers. Bars, restaurant and takeaway. Supermarket. Swimming pools. Tennis courts and tennis school. Minigolf. Watersports including windsurf school. Fishing. Playground. Organised activities in high season. Bowls. Dogs and motorcycles are not accepted.

Open: 1 April - 30 September.

Directions
Leave the A4 (Milan-Venice) at Peschiera exit and travel through the town towards Garda. After the second town bridge on Via Parcocatullo look for Via Marzan off the complex four road intersection. Site signs are small and difficult to see (site is on Via Marzan). GPS: 45.44797, 10.70125

Charges guide
Per person	€ 5.00 - € 14.00
pitch incl. electricity (4A)	€ 11.00 - € 25.50

Riva del Garda
Camping Brione
Via Brione 32, I-38066 Riva del Garda (Lake Garda) T: 046 452 0885. E: info@campingbrione.com
alanrogers.com/IT62350

Brione is a municipal site situated on the edge of the small town of Riva at the head of Lake Garda. It is about 500 m. from the town centre and lakeside. There are 110 level pitches, 78 with 6A electricity and trees provide some shade. Some also have water and a waste water point. Terraces on the hillside take 21 tents. There are 39 mobile homes to rent, two equipped for disabled visitors. The site is neat and well tended with spectacular views of the mountains from all pitches. Riva is recognised as one of Europe's windsurfing Meccas due to a combination of strong winds with flat water.

Facilities
Two refurbished sanitary blocks, one at either end of the site, have mixed Turkish and British style WCs, washbasins in cabins, and facilities for disabled visitors. New baby/children's room. 8 private en-suite shower rooms for hire. Motorcaravan services. Shop for basics. Bar/breakfast room with buffet breakfast. Good sized swimming pool (15/6-15/9). Minigolf. TV/video. Bicycle hire. Two play areas. WiFi (charged).

Open: 27 March - 15 October.

Directions
Site is on the northeast tip of Lake Garda. From A22 Brenner-Modena motorway, leave at Roverto Sud exit for Lake Garda north, and take SS240 for Nago, Torbole and Riva del Garda. Just before Riva, go through two short tunnels, then immediately turn right at site signs. GPS: 45.88133, 10.86148

Charges guide
Per unit incl. 2 persons and electricity	€ 18.50 - € 30.50

Rivoltella
Camping Village San Francesco
Strada Vicinale San Francesco, I-25015 Rivoltella (Lake Garda) T: 030 911 0245.
E: moreinfo@campingsanfrancesco.com **alanrogers.com/IT62520**

San Francesco is a large, very well organised site situated to the west of the Simione peninsula on the southeast shores of Lake Garda. The 323 touring pitches are generally on flat gravel and sand and enjoy shade from mature trees. There are three choices of pitch of different sizes with 6A electricity; 76 are fully serviced. They are marked by stones but there is no division between them. A wooded beach area of about 400 m. on the lake is used for watersports and there is a jetty for boating. There are delightful lake views from the restaurant and terrace.

Facilities
Spotlessly clean and well equipped sanitary facilities are in two large, modern, centrally located buildings. Excellent facilities for disabled campers. Shop. Restaurant. Bar. Pool bar. Pizzeria. Takeaway and snacks. In a separate area across road: swimming pools (1/5-19/9; disability hoist) and jacuzzi, sports centre and tennis. Playground. Entertainment. Bicycle hire arranged. Torches required in some areas. WiFi (charged). Off site: Riding 5 km.

Open: 1 April - 30 September.

Directions
From autostrada A4, between Brescia and Verona, exit towards Simione and follow signs to Simione and site. GPS: 45.46565, 10.59443

Charges guide
Per unit incl. 2 persons and electricity	€ 25.00 - € 54.00
extra person	€ 6.50 - € 12.50

Camping Cheques accepted.

For latest campsite news, availability and prices visit
alanrogers.com

San Benedetto

San Benedetto Villaggio Turistico

Strada Bergamini 14, I-37019 San Benedetto (Lake Garda) T: 045 755 0544. E: info@campingsanbenedetto.it
alanrogers.com/IT62640

Overlooking Lake Garda and in a position central to local historic attractions and theme parks, San Benedetto is on a slope and has 150 reasonably sized, shaded grass pitches some with lakeside views. The restaurant and bar has a large covered terrace area and there is a comprehensive and reasonably priced menu. Additionally a beach bar serving simple meals is in a pleasant traditional building at one end of the site. A long pathway with reed beds and alternating beach and grass areas for relaxation makes an attractive promenade towards the marina and boat launching area. Two pleasant swimming pools provide a welcome cooling alternative to lake swimming.

Facilities	Directions
Four good toilet blocks provide mainly British toilets but have no facilities for disabled campers. Washing machines and dryers. Motorcaravan service point. Shop. Restaurant and beach snack bar. Two swimming pools. Aerobics. Play areas. Small boat launching. Canoe, motorcycle and bicycle hire. Sub aqua club. Miniclub and entertainment programme all season. Off site: Launderette nearby.	Leave autostrada A4 at Pescheria de Garda exit and take lakeside road to Desenzano. At San Benedetto site is well signed on right. GPS: 45.4482, 10.6697

Open: 15 March - 1 October.

Charges guide

Per person	€ 4.50 - € 8.50
senior (over 60 yrs)	€ 3.50 - € 7.50
pitch incl. electricity	€ 6.00 - € 15.00

San Felice del Benaco

Camping Europa Silvella

Via Silvella 10, I-25010 San Felice del Benaco (Lake Garda) T: 036 565 1095. E: info@europasilvella.it
alanrogers.com/IT62600

This large, traditional, lakeside site is a slightly confusing merger of two different sites with the result that the 345 pitches (about 108 for touring units) appear randomly dispersed around the site. However, those alongside the lake are in small groups and close together; the main bar, restaurant and shop are also located at the lower level. The main area is at the top of a fairly steep hill on slightly sloping or terraced grass and has slightly larger pitches. There is reasonable shade in many parts and all pitches have 4A electricity. An attractive swimming pool complex also has a daytime bar and a restaurant which serves lunch and is the hub of the evening entertainment programme in high season.

Facilities	Directions
Toilet blocks include washbasins in cabins, facilities for disabled visitors and a superb children's room with small showers. Laundry. Shop. Restaurant/pizzeria. Swimming pools (hats required) with bar (11/5-13/9). Tennis, volleyball and five-a-side soccer. Playground. Bowling alley. Entertainment (every night in July/Aug). Disco for children. Tournaments. Fishing and boat launching. First aid room. WiFi (charged). Off site: Golf and bicycle hire 5 km.	From A4 Milan-Venice autostrada take Desenzano exit and head north on SS572 (Saló) for 14 km, turn right towards San Felice and follow brown tourist signs with site name (about 3 km). Enter Manerba del Garda for sat navs. GPS: 45.574474, 10.54857

Open: 23 April - 29 September.

Charges guide

Per unit incl. 2 persons and electricity	€ 19.00 - € 49.00
extra person	€ 6.00 - € 10.50

San Felice del Benaco

Camping Ideal Molino

Via Gardiola 1, I-25010 San Felice del Benaco (Lake Garda) T: 036 562 023. E: info@campingmolino.it
alanrogers.com/IT62650

Molino is a small, garden-like site with much charm and character beside Lake Garda. It is in two main areas divided by the site buildings, and the 85 pitches vary in character, some well shaded on level ground by the lake, some for tents on terraces, and many in rows with pergolas and flowering shrubs. All have electricity, water and drainage. The excellent restaurant has superb lake views and serves traditional Italian food. A friendly family atmosphere is maintained at the site by the daughter of the original owners. Ingeborg is delightful and speaks perfect English.

Facilities	Directions
All three small sanitary blocks have been rebuilt to a very high standard. British style WCs (some en-suite with washbasins) and adjustable hot showers and hot water to all washbasins. Facilities for disabled visitors. Laundry. Motorcaravan services. Shop, restaurant and bar open all season. Bicycle and canoe hire. Fishing. Free organised entertainment in season. Boat launching. Boat excursions. WiFi (charged). Boat and caravan storage.	From A4 (Milan-Venice) take Desenzano exit and head north on SS572 towards Saló for 13 km; turn right towards San Felice. Pass Guardiola sign then follow brown signs bearing site name, turning right and right again. GPS: 45.5785, 10.5542

Open: 23 March - 6 October.

Charges 2013

Per person	€ 6.20 - € 11.50
pitch incl. electricity	€ 46.00

Discount for over 60s in low season.

San Felice del Benaco
Camping Villaggio Weekend

Via Vallone della Selva 2, I-25010 San Felice del Benaco (Lake Garda) T: 036 543 712. E: info@weekend.it
alanrogers.com/IT62800

Created among the olive groves and terraced vineyards of the Château Villa Louisa, which overlooks it, this modern, well equipped site enjoys some superb views over the small bay which forms this part of Lake Garda. On reaching the site you will pass through a most impressive pair of gates. There are 230 pitches, all with electricity, of which about 30 per cent are taken by tour operators and statics. The touring pitches are in several different areas, and many enjoy superb views. Some pitches for larger units are set in the upper terraces on steep slopes, manoeuvring can be challenging and low olive branches may cause problems for long or high units.

Facilities

Three sanitary blocks, one below the restaurant/shop, are modern and well maintained. Mainly British style WCs, a few washbasins in cabins and facilities for disabled visitors in one. Baby room. Laundry. Bar/restaurant (waiter service). Takeaway. Shop. Supervised swimming pool and paddling pool. Entertainment programme all season. TV. Barbecues. All facilities are open throughout the season. Two playgrounds. English spoken. WiFi (charged). Off site: Windsurfing, water skiing and tennis nearby. Fishing 2 km. Golf 6 km. Riding 8 km.

Open: 17 April - 25 September.

Directions

Approach from Saló (easier when towing) and follow site signs. From Milan-Venice autostrada take Desenzano exit towards Saló and Localitá Cisano-San Felice. Watch for narrow right fork after Cunettone roundabout. Pass petrol station on left, then turn right towards San Felice for 1 km. Site is next left. GPS: 45.59318, 10.53088

Charges guide

Per unit incl. 2 persons	
and electricity	€ 17.00 - € 60.50
extra person	€ 4.00 - € 10.50
child (4-12 yrs)	free - € 7.00
dog	€ 1.00 - € 7.50

San Felice del Benaco
Fornella Camping

Via Fornella 1, I-25010 San Felice del Benaco (Lake Garda) T: 036 562 294. E: fornella@fornella.it
alanrogers.com/IT62750

Fornella Camping is one of the few campsites on Lake Garda still surrounded by farmed olive trees and retaining a true country atmosphere. Parts of the crisp, clean site have great lake views, others a backdrop of mountains and attractive countryside. The 180 touring pitches are on flat grass, terraced where necessary and most have good shade, all with 6/10A electricity; 42 have water and waste as well. The staff speak excellent English and Dutch. A superb lagoon pool complex is here, along with a more traditional pool. These are supplemented by a pleasant bar, and a restaurant with terrace overlooking the lakeside. A full entertainment programme runs in high season for both children and adults and there is live music in the evenings.

Facilities

Three very clean, modern toilet blocks, well dispersed around the site, have mainly British type WCs and hot water in washbasins (some in cabins), showers and sinks. Facilities for disabled visitors. Washing machines, dryer and irons. Motorcaravan services. Bar/restaurant. Pizzeria and takeaway. Shop. Supervised swimming pools and paddling pool (15/5-15/9). Tennis. Two playgrounds and entertainment for children in season. Bicycle hire (high season). Beach. Fishing. Small marina, boat launching and repairs. WiFi (charged). Off site: Bicycle hire 4 km. Sailing 5 km. Golf 8 km. Riding 10 km.

Open: 22 April - 25 September.

Directions

San Felice is on western shore of Lake Garda at the southern end. From A4 Milan-Venice autostrada take Desenzano exit and head north on SS572 towards Saló for 13 km; turn right towards San Felice and follow signs. GPS: 45.58497, 10.56582

Charges guide

Per unit incl. 2 persons	
and electricity	€ 24.00 - € 52.60
extra person	€ 6.00 - € 10.30
child (3-7 yrs)	free - € 8.70
dog	free - € 7.00

Charges acc. to season and pitch location. Various low season discounts.

For latest campsite news, availability and prices visit
alanrogers.com

San Felice del Benaco
Villaggio Turistico La Gardiola

Via Gardiola 36, I-25010 San Felice del Benaco (Lake Garda) T: 036 555 9240. E: info@baiaholiday.com
alanrogers.com/IT62700

Located at the end of a narrow lakeside road, this small neat site has just 25 touring pitches, five are fully serviced. The touring pitches are close to the lake with mobile homes on the slope above. The reception, bar, café with a terrace, is modest but attractive, and overlooks the lake. The sanitary amenities are of a high standard and discretely built underground, preventing any intrusion on the beautiful views. We found this a delightful, friendly site with cheerful staff who give you a chance to practise your Italian. The lakeside beach is just five meters from the closest pitches and is brilliant for peaceful picnics in sight of your pitch.

Facilities

The toilet block is just below ground level with a lift system for disabled visitors. The facilities are quite small but are adequate. Hot water is free throughout. Laundry. Small kiosk with terrace for coffee and snacks. Small playground. Fishing. Off site: Restaurants, shops, pizzerias nearby. Golf and riding 1 km.

Open: 24 March - 21 October.

Directions

San Felice is on western shore of Lake Garda at the southern end. From A4 (Milan-Venice) take Desenzano exit and head north on SS572 towards Saló for 13 km; turn right towards San Felice. Site is well signed (La Gardiola) before town. Access is via a long, narrow lane. GPS: 45.57861, 10.55388

Charges guide

Per unit incl. 2 persons, water and electricity	€ 18.00 - € 44.00
extra person	€ 5.40 - € 11.50
child (3-9 yrs)	€ 3.40 - € 8.50
dog	€ 3.50 - € 8.00

Torbole
Camping Al Porto

Via al Cor, 3, I-38069 Torbole sul Garda (Lake Garda) T: 046 450 5891. E: info@campingalporto.it
alanrogers.com/IT62370

This is a small pleasant site built on what was the owner's family farm 50 years ago. It is peaceful, set back from the main road, and a short stroll from the very attractive promenade with its bars and restaurants. The grass pitches are level with mature trees providing shade. Hedges separate the two camping areas, one with 75 touring pitches with 5A electricity. The other area is primarily for tents (no electricity) and has a secure hut for windsurfing equipment. Near the modern reception (with wonderful historic photos on the wall) is a small bar with a terraced area where basic snacks are served. Eight apartments for hire were added in 2012.

Facilities

The clean, modern toilet block has British and Turkish style WCs and hot water throughout. Facilities for disabled campers. Washing machines and dryers. Motorcaravan services. Bar with snacks including light breakfasts (all season). Boat launching. Play area with adventure unit. WiFi throughout (charged). Off site: Mountain biking, hiking, climbing, canoeing, canyoning nearby. Shops and cafés a short walk. Fishing and bicycle hire 100 m. Riding 3 km. Golf 10 km. Swimming, windsurfing and sailing on the lake. Full competitive watersports programme for the season.

Open: 20 March - 3 November.

Directions

Site is on northeast tip of Lake Garda. From A22 (Brenner-Modena), leave at Roverto Sud exit for Lake Garda north, and take SS240 for Nago and Riva del Garda. At roundabout in Torbole, turn right (Riva). Site is signed to left in 200 m. before bridge over river. GPS: 45.87210, 10.87292

Charges 2013

Per unit incl. 2 persons and electricity	€ 24.50 - € 29.00
extra person	€ 7.00 - € 8.50
child (2-12 yrs)	€ 5.00 - € 6.00
dog	€ 2.00 - € 3.00

Discounts in low season. No credit cards.

FREE Alan Rogers Travel Card
Extra benefits and savings - see page 10

Trentino-Alto Adige is a region of mixed Austrian and Italian influences, and much of it has only been part of Italy since 1919. The landscape is dominated by the majestic Dolomites, snow-clad in winter and carpeted with Alpine plants in summer.

THERE ARE TWO PROVINCES IN THE REGION: BOLZANO AND TRENTO

Before 1919, Alto Adige was known as the South Tyrol and formed part of Austria. However, at the end of the First World War, Austria ceded it to the Italians. As a result there are marked cultural differences between the provinces as reflected in the cuisine, architecture and language (both German and Italian are spoken).

The landscape of Trentino-Alto Adige is dramatic and amongst the most beautiful in the country. With only a couple of snow-free months a year, the region is a winter sports haven, and there is also a good network of well established trails, which vary in length from a day's walk to a two week trek or longer. Covering the whole Ortles range and topped by one of Europe's largest glaciers is the Stelvio National Park. One of Italy's major parks, it is popular with skiers, walkers and cyclists; the annual Giro d'Italia, Italy's answer to the Tour de France, passes through here. It also boasts an abundant wildlife, with red deer, elk, chamois, golden eagles and ibex. There are several other parks in the region including the Panevéggio National Park, a predominantly forested area with numerous nature trails and a lake.

Places of interest

Bolzano: 15th-century church, archaeology museum with a 5,300-year-old preserved mummy.

Canazei: mountainside town, good place for exploring the Dolomites.

Cembra: wine producing town.

Merano: attractive spa town.

Ortisei: major centre for wood carving.

Roverto: 15th-century castle converted into a war museum.

Trento: attractive town with 13th/15th-century church, Romanesque cathedral, impressive city square.

Cuisine of the region

The food is a mix of Germanic and Italian influences. Traditional dishes include game and rabbit with polenta, sauerkraut, and sausages with horseradish sauce (*salsa al cren*). Desserts are often based on apples, pears or plums, readily available from the local orchards. The region also produces a variety of wines including the famous Pinot Grigios and Chardonnays.

Apfel strudel: apple pastry.

Canederli: bread dumplings flavoured with smoked ham.

Soffiato alla Trentino: meringue trifle.

Strangolapreti: bread and spinach gnocchi.

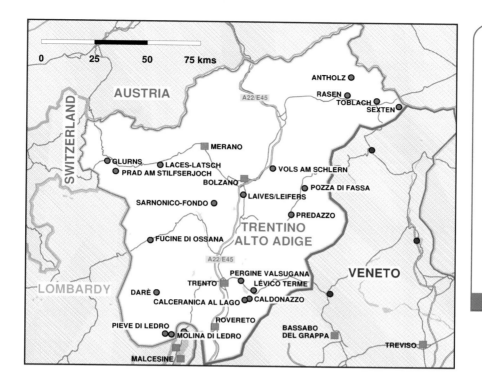

Antholz

Camping Antholz

Antholz Obertal 34, I-39030 Antholz (Trentino - Alto Adige) T: 047 449 2204. E: info@camping-antholz.com
alanrogers.com/IT62010

Camping Antholz is an all-year campsite in the heart of the Dolomites with picturesque meadows, forests and impressive mountain views. The 120 pitches, numbered but only roughly marked out, have at least 4A electricity and 50 have 16A electricity, water and waste water. Just inside the entrance is a traditional building with a welcoming reception and a smart restaurant. High up in the Anterselva valley, there are splendid views of near and distant peaks. This is good skiing country in winter (ski bus, ski school, ski lifts) and nearby is an internationally important Biathlon Centre.

Facilities

The sanitary facilities are of an extremely high standard with underfloor heating, in addition to the normal facilities. Hair salon. Cosmetics room with infra-red sauna. Baby room. Washing machine and dryer. Motorcaravan services. Bar, restaurant and takeaway (all year). Shop for basics. Playground. TV room. Bicycle hire. Limited entertainment programme for children in high season. WiFi (charged). Off site: Skiing and biathlon 1 km. Fishing 3 km. Riding and golf 13 km. Many waymarked tracks for walking and cycling.

Open: All year.

Directions

Antholz/Anterselva is 90 km. northeast of Bolzano. From Bressanone/Brixen exit on A22 (Brenner-Modena), go east on SS49 for 50 km, then turn north (signed Antholz) for 12 km. Pass upper Antholz village and site is on right. GPS: 46.86442, 12.10937

Charges guide

Per unit incl. 2 persons and electricity (4A)	€ 17.00 - € 27.00
incl. full services	€ 20.00 - € 31.00
extra person	€ 6.50 - € 9.00
child (4-16 yrs)	€ 3.00 - € 6.50

Calceranica al Lago
Camping Punta Lago

Via Lungo Lago 42, I-38050 Calceranica al Lago (Trentino - Alto Adige) T: 046 172 3229.

E: info@campingpuntalago.com **alanrogers.com/IT62260**

Camping Punta Lago is in a beautiful setting on Lago di Caldonazzo. This attractive family run campsite, with easy lake access across a small road, has 140 level, shaded pitches on grass. Of a good size, all have 3/6A electricity and 50 are serviced with water and drainage. The campsite first opened 45 years ago and brothers Gino and Mauro continue the friendly family tradition of ensuring you enjoy your holiday. As President of the Consortia Trentino Outdoors, Gino knows all about the range of activities available locally including fishing, lake swimming, windsurfing, sailing and canoeing. There are excellent restaurants within 50 m. of the gate. The site itself has a large terraced snack bar with wonderful views of the lake and the most amazing ice cream (gelato), yoghurt and fruit concoctions.

Facilities

One central sanitary block has superb facilities with hot water throughout. Well designed bathroom and washbasin area. Excellent facilities for disabled visitors and babies. Private units for rent, some with massage baths. Washing machines and dryer. Freezer. Shop. Bar/snack bar. Fishing (with permit). Modern play area. Animation programme (July/Aug). Internet access. WiFi throughout (charged). Cinema. TV. Off site: Bicycle hire, town and ATM 1 km. Watersports. Riding 3 km. Golf 20 km. Train 1 km. to Venice and other cities.

Open: 1 May - 15 September.

Directions

From A22 Bolzano-Trento autostrada take SS47 towards Padova. After 15 km. turn for Lago di Caldonazzo and Calceranica al Lago. Approaching from west by the railway, continue along Via Donegani, turn left at Esso station into Via al Lago and right at lakeside into Via Lungo Lago. Site is on right. From the east follow Calceranica then turn right just before Esso station. GPS: 46.00230, 11.25450

Charges guide

Per unit incl. 2 persons and electricity	€ 16.00 - € 40.00
extra person	€ 5.00 - € 9.00
child (2-12 yrs)	€ 4.00 - € 7.00

Calceranica al Lago
Camping Al Pescatore

Via dei Pescatori 1, I-38050 Calceranica al Lago (Trentino - Alto Adige) T: 046 172 3062.

E: trentino@campingpescatore.it **alanrogers.com/IT62270**

The enchanting small Lake of Calceranica lies just to the east of Trento in the foothills of the Dolomites amidst splendid scenery. Camping Al Pescatore is a very pretty, small, family campsite with a long tradition of camping and where daughter Giulia speaks excellent English. The site has a pool complex, attractive landscaping and a small poolside café with terrace. There are 200 touring pitches, all with electricity connections, on grass under tall trees. A separate area immediately opposite the entrance has one third of these pitches, however all the toilets here are of Turkish style. The lake is very popular and busy at weekends and during the summer season.

Facilities

The two toilet blocks on the main site provide the usual facilities and there is a single unisex block in the overflow section. Facilities for disabled visitors. Baby rooms. Washing machines. Shop, bar and restaurant (June/Aug). Swimming pool with spa, paddling pool and slides. Playground. Organised activities for children and music and dancing for adults in July/Aug.

Open: 20 May - 17 September.

Directions

Leave A22 (Brenner-Modena) motorway at Trento Nord, follow SS47 towards Padova to San Cristoforo and signs to Calceranica and site. Sat nav leads to a no through road. GPS: 46.01000, 11.24100

Charges guide

Per unit incl. 2 persons and electricity	€ 18.00 - € 32.50
extra person	€ 9.00 - € 10.00

For latest campsite news, availability and prices visit

alanrogers.com

Calceranica al Lago

Camping Spiaggia Lago di Caldonazzo

Viale Venezia 12, I-38050 Calceranica al Lago (Trentino - Alto Adige) T: 046 172 3037.
E: info@campingspiaggia.net **alanrogers.com/IT62230**

Camping Spiaggia is a welcoming family run site with private beach access on Lake Caldonazzo. The bar and snack bar is situated on the lakeshore with a beautiful panorama of the lake and surrounding mountains. There are 168 touring pitches (80-100 sq.m), some with shade and all have 6A electricity. On-site activities are limited and there is no swimming pool but swimming is possible in the lake and there are plenty of opportunities nearby for watersports such as kayaking, windsurfing and boating. Other more adventurous sports can also be organised such as rafting, canyoning or hydro speed.

Facilities	Directions
One modern sanitary block with some private cabins for hire. Facilities for disabled visitors. Laundry facilities. Motorcaravan service point. Shop. Bar/restaurant and pizzeria. Direct lake access. Lake swimming. Fishing. Windsurfing. Beach volleyball. Play area. WiFi over site (charged). Tourist information. Mobile homes for rent.	Lake Caldonazzo is east of the A22 autostrada. From Levico Terme, head west on the SP1 road to Caldonazzo and then follow signs to the site. GPS: 46.004343, 11.259763

Open: 16 April - 15 October.

Charges guide

Per unit incl. 2 persons
and electricity € 18.50 - € 36.00

Caldonazzo

Camping Mario Village

Via Lungolago, 4, I-38052 Caldonazzo (Trentino - Alto Adige) T: 046 172 3341.
E: direzione@campingmario.com **alanrogers.com/IT62255**

Camping Mario is a family site, across a small road from Lake Caldonazzo, one of the most attractive small Italian lakes where swimming, fishing and other water-based activities can be enjoyed. The 160 grassy touring pitches (80-150 sq.m) have 6/10A electricity and a further 52 also have water and drainage. Mobile homes are also available for rent. There is a large swimming pool with a new bar/pizzeria/restaurant adjacent and new play areas for children. There is also a well stocked shop. This region is popular for mountain sports, particularly mountain biking, trekking and rafting.

Facilities	Directions
Two well maintained toilet blocks provide all the usual facilities including an area for children and two rooms for disabled visitors (key access). Laundry facilities. Motorcaravan service point. Well stocked shop selling fresh bread. Bar. Restaurant/pizzeria. Large swimming pool with children's pool. New play areas. Miniclub, teenage club and evening entertainment for adults in high season. Bicycle hire. Tourist information. Mobile homes to rent. WiFi throughout (free in low season).	Leave the A22 motorway at Trento Nord and follow SS47 towards Padova. After passing Pergine and Valsugana, follow signs to Calceranica/Caldonazzo. After Caldonazzo railway station turn left and after the level crossing, turn left again towards the lake and site is well signed. GPS: 46.004662, 11.260619

Open: 24 April - 15 September.

Charges 2013

Per unit incl. 2 persons (4 persons
10/7-21/8) and electricity € 19.00 - € 70.00
extra person € 6.00 - € 10.00

Darè

Camping Val Rendena

Via Civico 117, I-38080 Darè (Trentino - Alto Adige) T: 046 580 1669. E: info@campingvalrendena.com
alanrogers.com/IT62135

Set in the National Park of Adamello Brenta, a refuge of the European brown bear, Camping Val Rendena, is an enthusiastically run family site with a very friendly feel. There are 52 level grass touring pitches with some tree shade, all with 6A electricity and spaced between the seasonal pitches. The site's location makes it an ideal base from which to explore this beautiful region, rich in flora and fauna, where wooded hills with many marked paths reach up to 1,800 metres. Beside the site runs the Sarca river, bordered for much of its journey by a cycle way.

Facilities	Directions
Two sanitary units, a small one in the reception block, a larger one at centre of site. Free hot water, controllable showers, some washbasins in cabins. Facilities for disabled visitors. Baby room. Laundry. Motorcaravan service area. Shop selling essential items. Solar heated swimming pool with adjoining children's pool (1/6-30/9). Large playing field. Play area and play room. Bicycle hire. Communal barbecue. Massage and other treatments by appointment. Eight apartments to rent. Off site: Pizza restaurant adjoins site. Thermal baths. Golf. Tennis.	From A22 (E45) Brenner-Verona autostrada take exit for Trento-Centro. Then travel westerly on the SS45b to Sarche, then SS237 to Tione di Trento. North on SS239 (Madonna di Campiglio) for 10 km. to Darè. On entering Darè take slip road to right following signs to site by river. Ignore GPS instructions to enter a small lane to the right before Darè (narrow, height-restricted bridge). GPS: 46.07440, 10.71718

Open: 10 May - 30 September.

Charges guide

Per unit incl. 2 persons
and electricity € 24.60 - € 28.60
extra person € 7.80 - € 8.80

Fucine di Ossana

Camping Cevedale

Via di Sotto Pila 4, I-38026 Fucine di Ossana (Trentino - Alto Adige) T: 046 375 1630.
E: info@campingcevedale.it **alanrogers.com/IT62110**

Nestled under a castle and close to a tiny village, Camping Cevedale has a European atmosphere with very little English spoken, except by Maura, who runs the site. The 197 pitches are grouped in two areas on either side of a fast flowing river (fenced) which can be noisy. The touring pitches, all with electricity (only 2A), are shaded, on grass and slope somewhat; they are in various areas among the well kept seasonal caravans. Some campers come here every holiday and most have built little wooden chalets next to their caravans.

Facilities

Two sanitary blocks with mainly Turkish style toilets are well maintained, modern and spotlessly clean. They include hot water for showers and basins, heating in winter, washing machine and dryer. Small shop. Pleasant bar which serves snacks. Play area with tables and barbecues. Internet access. WiFi throughout (free). Adventure sport courses arranged. Bicycle hire. Dogs are not accepted. Off site: Shops, restaurants and bars in the two nearby villages 1 km. Riding 3 km. Skiing 10 km.

Open: All year.

Directions

From A22 (Brenner-Modena) take San Michele exit north of Trento, then SS43 north for 43 km. to Cles. Turn east on SS42 for 26 km. to Fucine. Go through village and turn south on SP202 (Ossana). Follow signs for site (ignore sat nav!). Entrance is next to the bridge just below castle. GPS: 46.30834, 10.73361

Charges guide

Per unit incl. 2 persons and electricity	€ 25.00 - € 32.00

Camping Cheques accepted.

Glurns

Campingpark Gloria Vallis

Wiesenweg 5, I-39020 Glurns (Trentino - Alto Adige) T: 047 383 5160. E: info@gloriavallis.it
alanrogers.com/IT62130

Gloria Vallis is a style setter. The 92 terraced pitches are well grassed, level and all have 8A electricity, water and drainage. All have lovely mountain views and trees provide some shade. The whole site is most attractive with flowers and landscaping. There is an elegant curved restaurant and bar with a spectacular panorama across the valley with its thousands of apple trees and snow capped mountains beyond. Another more casual eating area is across a grass field alongside a small lake which is stocked with fish. A very modern building houses the excellent sanitary facilities.

Facilities

The excellent sanitary block with underfloor heating is equipped with showers with basin, WC and hairdryer. Excellent en-suite facilities for disabled visitors. Private rooms for hire (from € 15 per day; € 25 final cleaning) with shower, toilet, basin, bidet, hairdryer, safe and music system. Excellent laundry area. Motorcaravan service point. Bar, restaurants and shop (bread can be ordered). Lake for fishing. Picnic and play area. Internet access.

Open: 2 April - 5 November.

Directions

Glurns/Glorenza is 50 km. west of Merano via the SS38 then SS40. Follow signs for the Reschenpass. In Sluderno/Sluderns turn west onto SS41. Site is in 1 km. (signed). Can be approached from north on SS40 from Austria. GPS: 46.67317, 10.57013

Charges guide

Per unit incl. 2 persons and electricity	€ 31.00 - € 37.20
extra person	€ 8.50 - € 11.00

Laces-Latsch

Camping Latsch an der Etsch

Reichstrasse 4, via Nazionale 4, I-39021 Laces-Latsch (Trentino - Alto Adige) T: 047 362 3217.
E: info@camping-latsch.com **alanrogers.com/IT62120**

Gasthof Camping Latsch is 640 m. above sea level between a main road and the river, with splendid views across to the surrounding mountains. About 20 of the 100 touring pitches are on a terrace by reception with the remainder alongside the river. They are in regular rows which are separated by hedges with thin grass on gravel which can look quite dry. All have 6A electricity and 47 also have water and drainage. Trees provide some shade. An underground car park (for 35 cars) protects vehicles from winter snow and summer sun and, if used, gives a reduction in pitch charges. Mountain walkers will be in their element here and several chair lifts give access to higher slopes.

Facilities

The traditional but well maintained sanitary block is on two floors (to serve each section), has all the usual facilities and is heated in cool weather. Excellent private bathrooms for hire. Facilities for disabled visitors. Washing machine and dryer. Motorcaravan service point. Shop, bar and pleasant restaurant. Small heated indoor pool, sauna, solarium and fitness room. Large outdoor pool. Play areas.

Open: 6 December - 10 November.

Directions

Latsch/Laces is 28 km. west of Merano on SS38 Bolzano-Silandro road. Site entrance by the Hotel Vermoi (keep on main road, don't turn off to village). GPS: 46.622592, 10.864921

Charges guide

Per unit incl. 2 persons and electricity	€ 27.60 - € 33.60
extra person	€ 7.20 - € 8.20

For latest campsite news, availability and prices visit

alanrogers.com

Laives/Leifers
Camping-Park Steiner

J. F. Kennedy Strasse 32, I-39055 Laives/Leifers (Trentino - Alto Adige) T: 047 195 0105.
E: info@campingsteiner.com **alanrogers.com/IT62100**

The welcoming Camping Steiner is very central for touring with the whole of the Dolomite region within easy reach. With much on-site activity, one could spend an enjoyable holiday here, especially now the SS12, by which it stands, has a motorway alternative. The 180 individual touring pitches, mostly with good shade and hardstanding, are in rows with easy access and all have 6A electricity. There are also 30 chalets available to rent. There is a family style pizzeria/restaurant, and indoor and outdoor pools. The Steiner Park Hotel provides another restaurant, café and full hotel facilities. This friendly, family run site has a long tradition of providing a happy camping experience in the more traditional style – the owner remembers Alan Rogers who stayed here on many occasions. We met a Danish couple during our visit who were staying for five weeks as it is so easy to get to different parts of the Dolomites and is ideal for walking.

Facilities	Directions
The two sanitary blocks are equipped to a high standard, one having been completely refurbished. They can be heated in cool weather. Shop, bar/pizzeria/restaurant with takeaway (23/3-30/10). Outdoor pool, with paddling pool, and a smaller covered heated pool (all season). Playground. Bicycle hire. Dogs are not accepted in July/Aug. Off site: Fishing 2.5 km. Riding 12 km. Golf and skiing 28 km.	Site is by SS12 on northern edge of Leifers, 8 km. south of Bolzano. From north, at the Bolzano-Süd exit from A22 Brenner-Modena motorway follow Trento signs for 7 km. From south on motorway take Ora exit, then north on SS12 towards Bolzano for 14 km. GPS: 46.25.48, 11.20.37

Open: 24 March - 31 October.

Charges guide

Per unit incl. 2 persons and electricity	€ 28.00 - € 35.00
extra person	€ 7.00 - € 9.00

Southtyrol Dolomites

*** Camping - Park STEINER

SÜDTIROL

Open: 24.03.2012 - 31.10.2012

A well-kept, high quality campsite-park, ideal for families, in South Tyrol/Altoadige, 8 km from Bozen (highway A22, exit Bolzano Sud, direction Trento), on the outskirts of the town of Leifers. Covered and open air swimming pool, mini market, pizzeria, restaurant. Hotel with 50 Rooms. Wooden cabins. Leifers is ideal as a central point for tours in South Tyrol (Dolomites, Merano, Vinschgau region, Gardena valley, Seiseralm mountains and Lake Garda). Bike tours and hiking itineraries. NEW SANITARY FACILITIES. Beach volley with seasand. Playground for kids.

2013 new ringway.
Low saeson children till 9 years free.

WiFi **GPS E 11 20 37 - N 46 25 48**

Kennedystr. 32 · 39055 Leifers/Laives · South Tyrol – Italy
Tel. 0039 0471 950105 · Fax 0039 0471 593141 · info@campingsteiner.com · www.campingsteiner.com

Levico Terme
Camping Due Laghi

Localitá Costa 3, I-38056 Levico Terme (Trentino - Alto Adige) T: 046 170 6290. E: info@campingclub.it
alanrogers.com/IT62250

Due Laghi has a new entrance and reception with very helpful and welcoming staff. This attractive site with flowers and trees is close to the main road but it is quiet, with mountain views and only five minutes walk from Lake Levico, where it has a small private beach. There are over 400 level touring pitches on grass, all with 3/10A electricity. The site has a good pool and excellent facilities for adults and children. A new Camperstop with services, Internet access and restaurant is open all year.

Facilities	Directions
The central toilet block is very large and of good quality with British and Turkish type WCs, some washbasins in cubicles, a baby room and a unit for disabled visitors. Private facilities to rent. Laundry. Motorcaravan services. Shop. Restaurant, pizzeria and café/bar with takeaway. Heated swimming pool (over 300 sq.m) and paddling pool. Animation and music in high season. Playground. Tennis. Bicycle hire. WiFi throughout (charged). Off site: Fishing (for children) 600 m. Boat launching and sailing 1 km. Riding 2 km. Golf 12 km.	Site is just off SS47 Trento-Bassano-Padova road. Take the exit for Caldonazzo/Levico Terme. Site has a new entrance opposite petrol station signed both Due Laghi and Camperstop 47. Look for campsite signs immediately on leaving the main road. GPS: 46.00396, 11.28865

Open: 16 April - 11 September. Campstop all year.

Charges guide

Per unit incl. 2 persons and electricity	€ 19.00 - € 46.00
extra person	€ 4.00 - € 10.00
child (8-16 yrs)	€ 3.00 - € 7.00
Camping Cheques accepted.	

FREE Alan Rogers Travel Card
Extra benefits and savings - see page 10

Levico Terme
Camping Lago di Levico

Localitá Pleina, I-38056 Levico Terme (Trentino - Alto Adige) T: 046 170 6491. E: info@campinglevico.com

alanrogers.com/IT62290

Camping Lago di Levico, by a pretty lakeside in the mountains, is the merger of two popular sites, Camping Levico and Camping Jolly. Brothers Andrea and Geno Antoniolli are making great improvements, already there is an impressive new reception and further developments of the lakeside and swimming areas are planned. The lakeside pitches are quite special. There are 430 mostly grassy and shaded pitches (70-120 sq.m) with 6A electricity, 150 also have water and drainage and 12 have private facilities. Staff are welcoming and fluent in English. The swimming pool complex is popular, as is the summer family entertainment. There is a small supermarket on site and it is a short distance to the local village. The restaurant, bar, pizzeria and takeaway are open all season. The beautiful grass shores of the lake are ideal for sunbathing and the crystal clear water is ideal for enjoying (non-motorised) water activities. This is a site where the natural beauty of an Italian lake can be enjoyed without being overwhelmed by commercial tourism.

Facilities

Four modern sanitary blocks provide hot water for showers, washbasins and washing. Mostly British style toilets. Single locked unit for disabled visitors. Laundry facilities. Freezer. Motorcaravan service point. Good shop. Bar/restaurant and takeaway. Outdoor swimming pool. Play area. Miniclub and entertainment (high season). Fishing. Satellite TV and cartoon cinema. Internet access (free in low season). Kayak hire. Tennis. Torches useful. Bicycle hire. Off site: Boat launching 500 m. Bicycle track 1.5 km. Town with all the usual facilities and ATM 2 km.

Open: 20 March - 15 October.

Directions

From A22 Verona-Bolzano road take turn for Trento on S47 to Levico Terme where campsite is very well signed. GPS: 46.00799, 11.28454

Charges guide

Per unit incl. 2 persons	
and electricity	€ 9.50 - € 38.00
extra person	€ 3.00 - € 14.25
child (3-11 yrs)	free - € 6.50

Molina di Ledro
Camping Al Sole

Via Maffei 127, I-38060 Molina di Ledro (Trentino - Alto Adige) T: 046 450 8496. E: info@campingalsole.it

alanrogers.com/IT62320

Lake Ledro is only 9 km. from Lake Garda, its sparkling waters and breathtaking scenery offering a low key alternative for those who enjoy a natural setting. The drive from Lake Garda is a real pleasure and prepares you for the treat ahead. This site has been owned by the same friendly family for over 40 years and their experience shows in the layout of the site, with its mature trees and the array of facilities provided. Situated on the lake with its own sandy beach, pool and play area, the facilities include an outstanding wellness centre. The site is 70% powered by solar energy.

Facilities

Superb toilet block with well appointed facilities. Private bathrooms with shower, toilet, basin and safe. Excellent facilities for disabled visitors. Baby room. Laundry facilities. Freezer. Motorcaravan services. Well stocked mini-market. Pleasant restaurant/pizzeria with terrace. Bar serving snacks and takeaway. Sun decks and snack bar at the lake. Swimming pool. Play area. Bicycle hire. Boating, windsurfing, fishing and canoeing. Children's club. TV room. WiFi (charged). Torches needed in some areas.

Open: Easter - 2 November, 5 December - 10 January.

Directions

From autostrada A22 exit for Lake Garda North to Riva del Garda. In Riva follow sign for Ledro valley. Site is well signed as you approach Lago di Ledra. GPS: 45.87805, 10.76773

Charges guide

Per unit incl. 2 persons	
and electricity	€ 27.00 - € 48.00
extra person	€ 7.00 - € 10.00
child (2-11 yrs)	€ 5.00 - € 6.50

Pergine Valsugana
Camping San Cristoforo

Via dei Pescatori, I-38057 Pergine Valsugana (Trentino - Alto Adige) T: 046 151 2707. E: info@campingclub.it
alanrogers.com/IT62300

This part of Italy is becoming better known by those wishing to stay by a lake in splendid countryside, but away from the more crowded, better known resorts. Lake Caldonazzo is one of the smaller Italian lakes, but is excellent for watersports. Camping San Cristoforo is a relatively new site on the edge of the small town of the same name and is separated from the lake by a minor road, but with easy access. There are 133 pitches on flat grass with tarmac access roads, and are separated by shady trees. The pitches are of a good size and all have 6A electricity. The site is owned by the friendly Oss family and their aim is to build a happy family atmosphere. Diego, the manager, speaks excellent English.

Facilities

The large, modern sanitary block has some washbasins in cabins and pushbutton showers. Facilities for disabled visitors. Washing machine and dryer. Motorcaravan service point. No shop (but village nearby). Attractive bar/restaurant/takeaway serving reasonably priced food. Swimming pool (20x20 m) with sunbathing area and children's pool. Bicycle hire. Minigolf. Activities (high season). Off site: Fishing and boating 50 m. Village 200 m.

Open: 1 June - 14 September.

Directions

Pergine Valsugana is 10 km. east of Trento. Site is just off the SS47 Trento-Bassano-Padova road, 2 km. south of the town, near village of San Cristoforo. Site is signed from main road or via village. GPS: 46.03855, 11.23698

Charges guide

Per unit incl. 2 persons and electricity	€ 19.00 - € 46.00
extra person	€ 4.00 - € 10.00

Pieve di Ledro
Camping Al Lago

Via Alzer 7/9, I-38060 Pieve di Ledro (Trentino - Alto Adige) T: 046 459 1250. E: mb.penner@libero.it
alanrogers.com/IT62330

This small, family owned campsite has been lovingly rebuilt and refurbished to a very high standard. There are great views over the lakes and the towering mountains surrounding Al Lago. The 105 pitches are of average size, on grass or gravel, with tarmac roads. Some pitches have a slight slope to the lake while others are flat. English and Dutch are spoken at reception and the Penner family is keen that guests enjoy their stay. The small restaurant serves excellent regional food. This site is ideal for watersports, hiking, cycling or for a quiet holiday in a spectacular setting.

Facilities

Two sanitary blocks provide clean facilities with a mixture of Turkish and British toilets. Washing machines and dryers. Basics at the mini-market. New bar/restaurant with balcony. Snacks and takeaway. TV. Limited entertainment in high season. Play area. Bicycle and canoe hire. Boat launching. WiFi (charged). Off site: Riding 6 km. Hiking. Canyoning. Canoeing. Liaison with the local tourist office for various activities.

Open: 6 April - 7 October.

Directions

From Brescia-Verona on the A4 take the S45 or the P572 north to Saló, then the S45 for Riva del Garda. Take the S240 west to Saló and Pieve di Ledro where the site is well signed. Be prepared for narrow winding last section. GPS: 45.8851, 10.7313

Charges guide

Per person	€ 5.50 - € 10.00
child (2-11 yrs)	€ 4.00 - € 6.00
pitch incl. electricity	€ 7.00 - € 12.00

Pozza di Fassa
Camping Vidor-Family & Wellness Resort

Strada de Ruf de Ruacia 15, I-38036 Pozza di Fassa (Trentino - Alto Adige) T: 046 276 0022.
E: info@campingvidor.it **alanrogers.com/IT62090**

This family run site is in a beautiful mountainous setting two kilometres from the town of Pozza. The pitches are of average size with 1-16A electricity, water, hardstanding and drainage. There are some slopes so chocks are advisable. Vidor has excellent facilities including a new reception, camping shop, restaurant and pizzeria (serving local cuisine with special menus for children), and café with terrace and lounge. There is an indoor heated swimming pool (with whirlpool etc) and a superb beauty and wellness centre offering a large variety of treatments and a fitness room.

Facilities

Two excellent hotel standard sanitary blocks provide hot water throughout and good showers. Private bathrooms for hire. Facilities for disabled visitors. Washing machines, drying room and dryer. Bar/restaurant, takeaway and shop. Beauty and wellness centre, heated indoor pool and gym (all season). TV room and cinema. Indoor playrooms and miniclub. WiFi over site. Entertainment programme. Off site: Ski lift 1 km. Town 2 km. Golf 8 km.

Open: All year except November.

Directions

From A22 Trento-Bolzano road take S48 to Pozza di Fassa. In town centre, at roundabout take first exit (Meida and Valle San Nicolo). Site is well signed in 2 km. GPS: 46.41987, 11.70754

Charges guide

Per unit incl. 2 persons and electricity	€ 19.00 - € 41.00
extra person	€ 6.00 - € 11.00
child (2-15 yrs)	€ 4.50 - € 9.00

FREE Alan Rogers Travel Card
Extra benefits and savings - see page 10

Prad am Stilfserjoch
Camping Residence Sägemühle

Dornweg 12, I-39026 Prad am Stilfserjoch (Trentino - Alto Adige) T: 047 361 6078.
E: info@campingsaegemuehle.com **alanrogers.com/IT62070**

This very attractive, well maintained site with beautiful mountain views is alongside a little village. The 160 grass touring pitches are neat and level, some have shade and most have electricity, water and drainage. The high standard indoor pool area is welcoming to cool oneself in the summer and relax in warm water after skiing in winter. The excellent facilities are cleverly placed under the pool area. New for the season is an enlarged reception, well equipped gym and a coffee bar with terrace leading to a very good restaurant. The friendly owners speak some English and Dutch.

Facilities

The main and very modern sanitary facilities are under the pool complex. All WCs are British style and the showers are of high quality. Private cabins for hire. Facilities for disabled visitors. Children's facilities and baby baths. Washing machines. Restaurant and bar. Coffee bar with terrace. Indoor swimming pool with waves, jacuzzi and waterfall. Gym and sauna. Entertainment programme in season. Miniclub. Play areas. WiFi over site (charged). Torches useful. Off site: Town facilities. Bicycle hire 300 m.

Open: All year excl. 8 November - 19 December.

Directions

Site is west of Bolzano. From A38/S40 west of Bolzano, take exit for Pso dello Stelvio/Stilfserjoch (marked S38) and village of Prad am Stilfserjoch. Site is signed from here. GPS: 46.617628, 10.595317

Charges guide

Per unit incl. 2 persons and electricity	€ 27.60 - € 41.10
extra person	€ 8.00 - € 11.00
child (2-15 yrs)	€ 5.50 - € 9.00

Predazzo
Camping Valle Verde

Localitá Ischia 2, Sotto Sassa, I-38037 Predazzo (Trentino - Alto Adige) T: 046 250 2394.
E: info@campingvalleverde.it **alanrogers.com/IT62105**

Beautifully located in the Dolomites, at a height of just over 1,000 meters, Camping Valle Verde is an attractive family run site. There are 125 level pitches with mountain views, set on shallow, grassy terraces with some tree shade; all have 3A electricity. From the site there is plenty of walking in the forests alongside rushing mountain streams enclosed in small rocky canyons, with waterfalls and an abundance of flora and fauna. The site produces its own map of suggested rambling/cycle routes, however a detailed map of the area is an added advantage. The comfortable site restaurant, formally an alpine shelter, with its wood-fired pizza oven and terrace is very welcoming.

Facilities

Modern toilet block with all necessary facilities including those for babies and campers with disabilities. Washing machine/dryer. Motorcaravan services. Restaurant, snack bar, takeaway (mid May-mid Sept). Play area. Sports area. Volleyball. Football. Paddling in adjacent stream. Bicycle hire. WiFi over site (charged). Off site: Indoor pool, tennis, rock climbing, pony trekking, shops, bars and restaurants in Predazzo 2 km. Walking and cycling routes.

Open: 1 May - 30 September.

Directions

Leave A22 Brenner motorway south of Bolzano (Ora). From Ora take SS48 to Calvalese (20 km), then SS232 to Predazzo. Pass Alpine School of Financial Police then first right (Bellamonte and Paneveggio). After minigolf take first right to site. GPS: 46.310565, 11.631764

Charges guide

Per unit incl. 2 persons and electricity	€ 22.80 - € 29.50

Sarnonico-Fondo
Camping Park Baita Dolomiti

Via Cesare Battisti 18, I-38010 Sarnonico-Fondo (Trentino - Alto Adige) T: 046 383 0109. E: campark@tin.it
alanrogers.com/IT61980

Baita Dolomiti is a family campsite located in a splendid mountain region. It was very quiet when we visited in early June, but apparently becomes quite lively in high season, with plenty of organised entertainment for young and old. There is a rustic bar and restaurant providing typical local meals. The 130 grass touring pitches all have 3A electricity and, although they are not large, there is a great sense of space. The Val di Non is a wonderful area for walking and cycling and the more adventurous can explore the canyons on foot or by boat.

Facilities

Two toilet blocks are well equipped and maintained, with a mixture of British and Turkish style WCs, controllable showers, baby room and hot water to all basins and sinks. Facilities for disabled visitors (not conveniently located). Motorcaravan service point. Swimming and paddling pools (July/Aug). Play area. Dogs are not accepted 1/8-15/9. Off site: Tourist train from site to various local villages. Bicycle hire 1 km.

Open: 1 June - 30 September.

Directions

From A22 (Brenner-Modena) take exit for S Michele. Turn right on SS43 (Val di Non), follow signs for Cles, turning northeast after 20 km. on SS43D (Fondo). Continue 14 km. to Sarnonico where site is signed. Avoid route from Bolzano via the Mendel Pass, especially if towing. GPS: 46.41889, 11.14056

Charges guide

Per person	€ 6.80 - € 8.95
pitch incl. electricity	€ 8.50 - € 14.80

Rasen
Camping Residence Corones

Niederrasen 124, I-39030 Rasen (Trentino - Alto Adige) T: 047 449 6490. E: info@corones.com
alanrogers.com/IT61990

Situated in a pine forest clearing at the foot of the pretty Antholz valley in the heart of German-speaking Südtirol, Corones is ideally situated both for winter sports enthusiasts and for walkers, cyclists, mountain bikers and those who prefer to explore the valleys and mountain roads of the Dolomites by car. There are 135 level pitches, all with 16A electricity and many also with water, drainage and satellite TV. The Residence offers luxury apartments and there are authentic Canadian log cabins for hire. The bar/restaurant and small shop are open all season. From the site you can see slopes which in winter become highly rated skiing pistes. A short drive up the broad Antholz/Anterselva valley takes you to an internationally important biathlon centre. An excellent day trip would be to drive up the valley and over the pass into Austria and then back via another pass. Back on site, a small pool and paddling pool could be very welcome. There is a regular programme of free excursions and occasional evening events are organised. Children's entertainment is provided in July and August.

Facilities

The central toilet block is traditional but well maintained and clean. Additional facilities include shower rooms with washbasins, washbasins with all WCs, a delightful children's unit and an excellent facility for disabled visitors. Private shower rooms for hire. Luxurious wellness centre with saunas, solarium, jacuzzis, massage, therapy pools and heat benches. Heated outdoor swimming and paddling pools. Play area. WiFi over site (charged). No charcoal barbecues. Off site: Tennis 800 m. Bicycle hire 1 km.

Open: 6 December - 7 April and 8 May - 27 October.

Directions

From Bressanone/Brixen exit on A22 Brenner-Modena motorway, go east on SS49 for 50 km. then turn north (signed Rasen/Antholz). Turn immediately west at roundabout in Niederrasen/Rasun di Sotto to site on left in 100 m. GPS: 46.7758, 12.0367

Charges guide

Per unit incl. 2 persons,	
electricity on meter	€ 21.50 - € 32.50
extra person	€ 5.50 - € 8.20
child (3-15 yrs)	€ 3.00 - € 7.50

Camping, at home in nature!
SÜDTIROL

VACATION IMMERSED IN NATURE!
- **CAMPSITE** with beautiful pitches
- Alpine style **APARTMENTS**
- Exclusive canadian **CHALETS**

Only 4 km from the Kronplatz - South Tyrols' ski resort N. 1!
Illimited possibilities for biking, mountain biking, walking and more!

Camping-Residence-Chalets
Corones ★★★★

I-39030 Rasun in Valle d'Antersava,
Rasun di sotto 124
Tel. +39 0474 496490,
info@corones.com, www.corones.com

Sexten
Caravan Park Sexten

Saint Josef Strasse 54, I-39030 Sexten (Trentino - Alto Adige) T: 047 471 0444.
E: info@caravanparksexten.it **alanrogers.com/IT62030**

alan rogers
Runner up 2012 Awards

Caravan Park Sexten is 1,520 metres above sea level and has 268 pitches, some very large and all with electricity (16A), TV connections and water and drainage in summer and winter (underground heating stops pipes freezing). Some pitches are in the open to catch the sun, others are tucked in forest clearings by the river. They are mostly gravelled to provide an ideal all year surface. It is the facilities that make this a truly remarkable site; no expense or effort has been spared to create a luxurious environment that matches that of any top class hotel.

Facilities

The three main toilet blocks are remarkable in design, fixtures and fittings. Heated floors. Controllable showers. Hairdryers. Luxurious private facilities to rent. Baby rooms. En-suite facilities for disabled visitors. Laundry and drying room. Motorcaravan services. Shop. Bars and restaurants (entertainment 2-3 nights a week). Indoor pool. Heated outdoor pool (1/6-30/9). Health spa. Play area. Tennis. Bicycle hire. Climbing wall. Fishing. Adventure activity packages. WiFi over site. Off site: Skiing in winter.

Open: All year.

Directions

From Bressanone/Brixen exit on A22 Brenner-Modena motorway follow SS49 east for 60 km. Turn south on SS52 at Innichen/S Candido. Follow signs to Sexten. Site is 5 km. past village (signed). GPS: 46.66727, 12.40221

Charges guide

Per unit incl. 2 persons	€ 22.00 - € 49.00
extra person	€ 8.00 - € 13.00
electricity (per kWh)	€ 0.70

Toblach

Camping Olympia

Camping 1, I-39034 Toblach (Trentino - Alto Adige) T: 047 497 2147. E: info@camping-olympia.com
alanrogers.com/IT62000

In the Dolomite mountains, Camping Olympia continues to maintain its high standards. The 314 pitches are set out in a regular pattern and the tall pine trees, shrubs and hedges make this a very pleasant and attractive site. There are tree-clad hills on either side and craggy mountains beyond. The 238 touring pitches all have 6A electricity and a TV point. There are 21 fully serviced pitches with water, waste water, gas, telephone and satellite TV points. Some accommodation is available for rent, and there are 62 seasonal caravans which are mainly grouped at one end of the site.

Facilities	Directions
The toilet block is of a very high standard. Rooms with WC, washbasin and shower to rent. Baby room. Facilities for disabled visitors. Two small blocks provide WCs and showers. Motorcaravan services. Shop. Bar, restaurant and pizzeria. Pool bar with grill and terrace (10/6-30/9; 20/12-Easter). Heated swimming pool (20/5-15/9). Sauna, solarium, steam bath and whirlpools. Massage and Kneipp treatments. Fishing. Bicycle hire. Play area. WiFi over site. Activities and excursions. Entertainment in high season.	Toblach/Dobbiaco is 100 km. northeast of Bolzano. From A22 (Innsbruck-Bolzano), take Bressanone, Brixen exit and travel east on SS49 for 60 km. Site signed to left just after a short tunnel. From Cortina take SS48 and SS51 northwards then turn west on SS49 for 1.5 km. GPS: 46.734449, 12.194266

Open: All year.

Charges guide

Per unit incl. 2 persons	
and electricity	€ 25.00 - € 34.50
extra person	€ 8.50 - € 11.00

Völs am Schlern

Camping Seiser Alm

Saint Konstantin 16, I-39050 Völs am Schlern (Trentino - Alto Adige) T: 047 170 6459.
E: info@camping-seiseralm.com **alanrogers.com/IT62040**

What an amazing experience awaits you at Seiser Alm! Elisabeth and Erhard Mahlknecht have created a superb site in the magnificent Südtirol region of the Dolomite mountains. Towering peaks provide a wonderful backdrop when you dine in the charming, traditional style restaurant on the upper terrace. Here you will also find the bar, shop and reception. The 150 touring pitches are of a very high standard with 16A electricity supply, 120 fully serviced. Guests were delighted with the site when we visited, many coming to walk or cycle, some just to enjoy the surroundings. There are countless things to see and do here. Enjoy the grand 18-hole golf course alongside the site or join the organised excursions and activities. Local buses and cable cars provide an excellent service for summer visitors and skiers alike (discounts are available). In keeping with the natural setting, the majority of the luxury facilities are set into the hillside. If you wish for quiet, quality camping in a crystal clean environment, then visit this immaculate site.

Facilities	Directions
One luxury underground toilet block in the centre of the site. 16 private units are available. Excellent facilities for disabled visitors. Fairytale facilities for children. Infrared sensors, underfloor heating and gently curved floors to prevent slippery surfaces. Constant fresh air ventilation. Washing machines and drying room. Sauna. Supermarket. Quality restaurant and bar with terrace. Entertainment programme. Miniclub. Children's adventure park and play room. Special rooms for ski equipment. Torches useful. WiFi (charged). Apartments and mobile homes for rent.	From A22-E45 take Bolzano Nord exit. Take road for Prato Isarco/Blumau, then road for Fie/Völs. Road divides suddenly; take left fork as you enter tunnel (Altopiano dello Sciliar/Schlerngebiet) or pay a heavy price in extra kilometres. Climb to Völs am Schlern and site is well signed. GPS: 46.53344, 11.53335

Open: All year excl. 2 November - 20 December.

Charges 2013

Per unit incl. 2 persons	€ 21.10 - € 37.90
extra person	€ 7.00 - € 10.20
electricity (per kWh)	€ 0.60

The flair of the Dolomites all year round!

CAMPING SEISER ALM
I-39050 VÖLS am Schlern, St. Konstantin 16 (BZ)
Tel. 0039 0471 706459 · Fax 0039 0471 707382
info@camping-seiseralm.com · www.camping-seiseralm.com

Friuli-Venézia Giúlia is a beautiful border region nudging Slovenia on the east, Austria and the Carnic Alps to the north with the Adriatic to the south – forming a bridge between the Mediterranean world and central Europe.

THE REGION HAS FOUR PROVINCES: GORIZIA, PORDENONE, TRIESTE AND UDINE

Near the Slovenian border lies the atmospheric city of Trieste, with its long bustling harbour. The prime tourist site is the hill of San Giusto; at the summit is the castle and a walk along the ramparts offers sweeping views over the Gulf of Trieste. Across the bay, Múggia is only a short ferry ride from Trieste, whilst outside the city is an area of limestone uplands, known as the Carso. With an abundance of caves, including the Grotta Gigante, the world's largest accessible cave and second largest natural chamber in the world, the Carso can be easily reached by the tranvia (cable tramway). Sitting on a group of low islands in the middle of the Adriatic lagoon, Grado is attached to the mainland by a long, narrow causeway. A popular seaside resort, it has a long sandy beach and harbour plus a historic centre. A short distance from here is Aquileia, now a small town but once an important city of the Roman Empire and further inland Udine boasts galleries, fine churches, and well preserved historic buildings. Towards the Austrian border in the north, is Carnia. With its lush valleys and flower-filled meadows, which give way to Alpine peaks, it is an area popular with walkers.

Places of interest

Aquileia: Basilica, with mosaic pavement dating from the 4th century.

Cividale del Friuli: market town, medieval walls, archaeology museum.

Forni di Sopra: thickly wooded area, popular for mountain biking, horse riding and hiking.

Gorizia: major shopping town, numerous parks and gardens, castle.

Pordenon: preserved historic centre.

Tarvisio: small mountain resort.

Cuisine of the region

Fish broths, made from squid, octopus, mackerel, sardines and clams, are common. Gnocchi is a Trieste speciality; gnocchi the size of eggs are stuffed with a pitted prune, rolled in breadcrumbs, browned in butter and sprinkled with cinnamon and sugar. Local wines include Tocai, Ribolla Gialla, Merlot and Cabernet Sauvignon.

Brodo di Pesce: fish soup, sometimes flavoured with saffron.

Cialzons: ravioli from Carnia, usually stuffed with spinach and ricotta.

Jota: a soup of sauerkraut and barley.

Spaghetti alle Vongole: spaghetti with fresh clams in a chilli-pepper sauce.

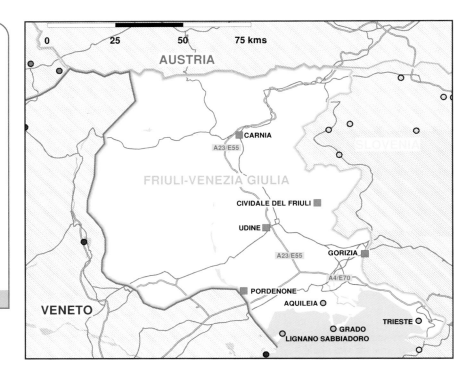

Grado
Camping Residence Punta Spin

Via Monfalcone, I-34073 Grado (Friuli - Venézia Giúlia) T: 043 180 732. E: info@puntaspin.it
alanrogers.com/IT60055

Punta Spin is a large, well maintained site, set between the road and a soft sand beach. The flat pitches vary in size (65-100 sq.m), all with 4/10A electricity, and some are on the beach front (book early for these). A bicycle is an asset here as the sanitary blocks are up to 800 m. distant. The comprehensive amenities are clustered near the entrance and include a wellness centre where you will be pampered, and three pools, one of which is a sophisticated paddling complex. Another is covered and heated. Terraces overlook the pools with the restaurant and pizzeria/bar. A professional team organises all manner of entertainment in high season and an impressive Kids' Club is in full swing all day. The beach offers free loungers and has a lifeguard in high season, as do the pools.

Facilities

Three modern sanitary blocks have free hot water throughout. Mostly British style toilets. Good facilities for disabled campers. Washing machines and dryers. Motorcaravan services. Large supermarket and other shops. Bars and restaurant (April-Sept). Pizzeria. Takeaway. Three swimming pools. Fishing. Minigolf. Disco. Entertainment team in high season. Watersports. Wellness centre. Beach bar. Playground. Tennis. WiFi (charged). Off site: Golf 2 km. Bicycle hire and Grado town 4 km. All manner of sea sports.

Open: 1 April - 30 September.

Directions

Site is 3.5 km. east of Grado on the beach road to Monfalcone. Take 35L road to Grado Pineto and continue to site on same road.
GPS: 45.69467, 13.45255

Charges guide

Per unit incl. 2 persons	
and electricity	€ 17.00 - € 41.00
extra person	€ 5.00 - € 12.00
child (3-16 yrs)	€ 2.50 - € 10.00
dog	€ 3.00 - € 5.00

For latest campsite news, availability and prices visit
alanrogers.com

Aquileia
Camping Aquileia

Via Gemina10, I-33051 Aquileia (Friuli - Venézia Giúlia) T: 043 191 042. E: info@campingaquileia.it
alanrogers.com/IT60020

Situated in former parkland under mature trees providing plenty of welcome shade in summer, Camping Aquileia, with 115 level and grass touring pitches, is a quiet site 10 km. away from the bustling coastal beaches. The pitches, all with 4/6A electricity, are separated from the entrance, swimming pool and play areas by tall hedges, and the more peaceful part of the site with the newer sanitary block is at the rear of the site. The now small town of Aquileia, founded in 181 BC, became one of the most important Roman military and trading posts and is now a UNESCO World Heritage Site. In the basilica, only a short walk from the campsite, along the former harbour, lays one of the world's most magnificent mosaic floors. The campsite is popular with families and for those who seek a quiet base from which to visit the beaches or tour this interesting region. From reception, tours can be organised with the town's tourist office to the region's archaeological sites, and not surprisingly a weekly mosaic course is also on offer.

Facilities

Two sanitary blocks with free hot water, controllable showers and washbasins in cabins. Facilities for disabled visitors. Folding baby changing bench. Laundry facilities. Motorcaravan service point. Restaurant, bar and automat for drinks and ice cream. Large playing field with playground. Swimming and paddling pools. Bicycle hire. Mobile homes and chalets for rent. WiFi (charged). Off site: Supermarket opposite entrance. Riding 12 km. Historic towns of Trieste, Gorizia. Beach resort of Grado.

Open: Easter - 30 September.

Directions

Site is 30 km. west northwest of Trieste. From the A4 (Venice-Trieste) take exit for Palmanova and travel south for 20 km. towards Grado. Just after entering Aquileia turn left at traffic lights, signed Trieste and Goriza and site is 400 m. on the right.
GPS: 45.77585, 13.37084

Charges guide

Per unit incl. 2 persons and electricity	€ 22.00 - € 40.00
extra person	€ 6.00 - € 8.00

CAMPING AQUILEIA

I-33051 Aquileia - Monastero (UDINE)
Tel. 0039/043191042 · Mobile +39 328 3310065
info@campingaquileia.it · www.campingaquileia.it

Welcome to Campsite Aquileia! Just a few steps from the sea, in one of the most important archaeological sites of the Roman period, nearby the marvellous and impressive Basilica complex, in an area rich of excursion possibilities and delicious typical food. 2 swimming pools for adults and children, bar and restaurant of a high level, organized excursions on request, bike rental, workshops for children, wine tasting. How to get here: highway A4 to Tarvisio, exit Palmanova, direction Grado, at the traffic light of Aquileia turn left (400 mt). ***Bungalows and maxicaravans for rent with 2 bedrooms. Open from Mai till September 2012.***

Grado
Camping Tenuta Primero

Via Monfalcone 14, I-34073 Grado (Friuli - Venézia Giúlia) T: 043 189 6900. E: info@tenuta-primero.com
alanrogers.com/IT60065

Tenuta Primero is a large, attractive, well run, family owned site with direct access to its own private beach via a pathway on top of a low bank. Apart from the beach – an ideal place to enjoy the view, sunbathe or take a dip in the Adriatic – the site offers a wealth of facilities and activities catering for all members of the family. The 740 pitches are all level, with 6A electricity, some separating hedges and ample tree shade, and many are reached by branch roads from an attractive palm tree-lined avenue. The site does not accept dogs.

Facilities

Nine well maintained sanitary blocks, 7 with facilities for disabled visitors. Washing machines and dryers. Motorcaravan service point. Swimming pools. Paddling pool. Shop. Bars and restaurants, pizzeria (all April-Sept), takeaway (May-Sept). Beauty salon. Aerobics. Water gymnastics. Football pitch. Tennis courts. Playgrounds. Windsurfing. Marina, sailing, boat launching and boat hire. Bicycle hire. Children's and family entertainment. Live music, disco, dancing. Private beach with sunshades, deck chairs and jetty. Internet corner and WiFi (charged).

Open: 1 April - 3 October.

Directions

Leave A4 autostrada at Palmanova exit and go towards Grado. In Grado, after crossing causeway turn left towards Monfalcone on SP19. Site is on right after 5 km. opposite large golf course.
GPS: 45.7051, 13.4640

Charges guide

Per unit incl. 2 persons and electricity	€ 19.00 - € 49.00
extra person	€ 6.00 - € 12.00
child (0-15 yrs)	free - € 10.00

FREE Alan Rogers Travel Card
Extra benefits and savings - see page 10

Grado
Villaggio Turistico Europa

Via Monfalcone 12, I-34073 Grado (Friuli - Venézia Giúlia) T: 043 180 877. E: info@villaggioeuropa.com

alanrogers.com/IT60050

This large, flat, good quality site is beside the sea and has 500 pitches, with 400 for touring units. They are all neat, clean and marked, most with shade and 6/10A electricity, 300 are fully serviced. The terrain is undulating and sandy in the areas nearer the sea, where cars have to be left in parking places. An impressive, large new aquatic park covers 1,500 sq.m. with two slides (100 m. and 60 m. long) and many other features. With many shallow areas it is very popular with children and there are lifeguards. A new pool bar is an attractive feature. There is direct access to the beach. The water recedes up to 200 m. from the beach, but leaves a natural paddling pool which is enjoyed by children when it is hot. A narrow wooden jetty gives access to deeper water. This is a neat, well managed site which is probably the best in the area.

Facilities

Five excellent, refurbished toilet blocks are well designed and very clean. Free hot water in all facilities, mostly British style WCs and excellent facilities for disabled visitors. Baby showers and baths. Washing machines. Motorcaravan services. Large supermarket, small general shop (all season). Large bar and restaurant with takeaway (all season). Swimming pools (15/5-15/9). Tennis. Fishing. Bicycle hire. Playground. Full entertainment programme in season. Internet access. Dogs are restricted to specific areas and not allowed on the beach. Off site: Golf 500 m. Riding 10 km.

Open: 21 April - 24 September.

Directions

Site is 4 km. east of Grado on road to Monfalcone. Venice-Trieste motorway exit at Reipuglia-Monfalcone, first roundabout take second exit, direction airport and follow Grado signs for 13 km. Site is on the left opposite a golf course.
GPS: 45.69649, 13.45595

Charges 2013

Per unit incl. 2 persons	
and electricity	€ 19.90 - € 46.10
extra person	€ 5.70 - € 10.70
child (3-16 yrs)	€ 3.60 - € 9.70
dog	€ 3.20 - € 6.20

Less 10% for longer stays out of season.

VILLAGGIO TURISTICO
CAMPING EUROPA
I-34073 GRADO (GO)
Tel. 0039 043180877
      0039 043182284
Fax 0039 043182284
www.villaggioeuropa.com
info@villaggioeuropa.com

10% discount in April, May and September for more than 10 days in campsite.
10% discount in bungalows (in the same period) for minimum 14 days.

Grado
Camping Village Belvedere Pineta

I-33051 Grado (Friuli - Venézia Giúlia) T: 043 191 007. E: info@belvederepineta.it

alanrogers.com/IT60070

Belvedere Pineta is situated on the edge of an almost entirely land-locked lagoon, 5 km. from Grado on the northern Adriatic Sea. A minor road runs between the site and the lagoon and a bridge over this connects the site with the beach of fine sand. It is a large site with 900 touring pitches arranged in regular rows with most under shade provided by the many tall pine trees which cover the site. Most are of reasonable size and all have electricity. An area of accommodation to let is to one side of the camping area. In high season a large programme of sport and entertainment for children and adults is organised.

Facilities

Most of the six toilet blocks have been refurbished to a good standard with all the usual facilities including some for children and free hot water in all basins, showers and sinks. Facilities for disabled visitors. Motorcaravan service point. Range of shops. Restaurant, pizzeria and takeaway. Swimming pools. Sports facilities. Play areas. Organised entertainment in high season. Bicycle hire. WiFi (charged). Off site: Riding 10 km. Golf 11 km.

Open: 27 April - 30 September.

Directions

Site is 5 km. north of Grado. Leave A4 Venice-Trieste motorway at Palmanova exit. Go south on SS352 towards Grado. Site is signed after Aquileia on left.
GPS: 45.72867, 13.40109

Charges guide

Per unit incl. 2 persons	
and electricity	€ 19.20 - € 38.50
extra person	€ 4.50 - € 9.00

Camping Cheques accepted.

For latest campsite news, availability and prices visit
alanrogers.com

Lignano Sabbiadoro
Camping Sabbiadoro

Via Sabbiadoro 8, I-33054 Lignano Sabbiadoro (Friuli - Venézia Giúlia) T: 043 171 455.
E: campsab@lignano.it **alanrogers.com/IT60080**

Sabbiadoro is a large, top quality, site that caters very well for children, It is divided into two parts with separate entrances and efficient receptions. It has 1,045 pitches and is ideal for families who like all their amenities to be close by. The level, grassy pitches vary in size, are shaded by attractive trees and have electricity and TV connections. The facilities are all in excellent condition and well thought out, especially the pool complex, and everything here is very modern, safe and clean. The site's private beach (with 24-hour guard) is only 250 m. away and has its own showers, toilets and baby rooms. Open in high season, the smaller and quieter part of the site with an entrance from Viale Central, is only a few metres away from the main site entrance in Via Sabbiadoro. This has four new sanitary blocks, 41 fixed pitches for touring units, an area for tents and a section of mobile homes to rent. Shopping and nightlife can be found in the town of Sabbiadoro itself, more so in Pineta about 1.5 km. away.

Facilities

Well equipped sanitary facilities with free showers includes superb facilities for disabled visitors. Washing machines and dryers. Motorcaravan services. Huge supermarket (all season). Bazaar. Good restaurant (15/5-6/9), snack bar and takeaway (15/5-28/9). Heated outdoor pool complex with separate fun pool area, slides and fountains. Heated indoor children's pool. Swimming courses. TV room. Play areas. Tennis. Fitness centre. Boat launching. Windsurfing school. New children's activity centre (2012) with well organised entertainment (high season) and language school. WiFi. Bicycle hire. Excursions to Venice.

Open: 23 March - 6 October.

Directions

Leave A4 at Latisana exit, west of Trieste. From Latisana follow road to Lignano, then Sabbiadoro. Site is well signed as you approach the town. GPS: 45.68198, 13.12577

Charges 2013

Per unit incl. 2 persons	
and electricity	€ 22.80 - € 41.60
extra person	€ 6.00 - € 11.00
child (3-12 yrs)	€ 3.70 - € 6.20
dog	€ 2.50 - € 2.80

Trieste
Camping Mare Pineta

Sistiana 60 D, Duino-Aurisina, I-34019 Trieste (Friuli - Venézia Giúlia) T: 040 299 264.
E: info@marepineta.com **alanrogers.com/IT60000**

This site is 18 km. northwest of Trieste at the top of an 80 metre cliff from which there are superb views over the Sistiana Bay, Miramare Castle and the Gulf of Trieste. Of the 500 pitches, 340 are reserved for touring units, all with 4/6A electricity and water nearby. They vary in size and location with the most prized being on the cliff top, where there is a 2 km. long pathway, the Rilke Way. Others are in light woodland. Everyone is friendly and good English is spoken. Enjoy a drink and the views at the cliff-top bar.

Facilities

Five toilet blocks have been refurbished (two with solar panels for hot water) and offer some washbasins in cabins. British and Turkish style WCs. Facilities for disabled visitors. Laundry. Motorcaravan services. Shop (all season). Bars. Pizzeria with terrace. Entertainment and disco. Swimming pool (1/5-20/9). Tennis. Fitness studio. New playground. Tennis. Bicycle hire. Fishing. Organised entertainment in season. WiFi (charged). Information point. Dogs permitted in certain areas only and not on the beach. Off site: Beach 1 km. Attractive port of Sistiana. Riding 1.3 km.

Open: 1 April - 16 October.

Directions

From the west on the A4 take Sistiana exit and turn right on S14 towards Sistiana and then Duino. Site is 1 km. on the left past Sistiana. From the east approach on the S14. Site is well signed. GPS: 45.7725, 13.62444

Charges guide

Per unit incl. 2 persons,	
water and electricity	€ 16.00 - € 44.00
extra person	€ 5.40 - € 11.50
child (3-9 yrs)	€ 3.40 - € 8.50

FREE Alan Rogers Travel Card
Extra benefits and savings - see page 10

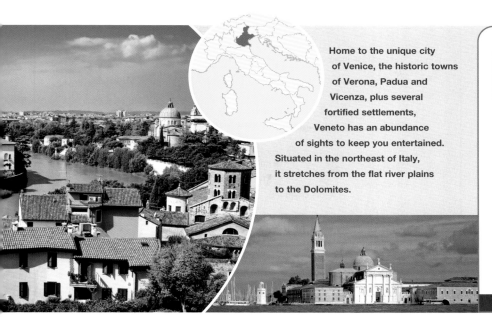

Home to the unique city of Venice, the historic towns of Verona, Padua and Vicenza, plus several fortified settlements, Veneto has an abundance of sights to keep you entertained. Situated in the northeast of Italy, it stretches from the flat river plains to the Dolomites.

THE REGION HAS SEVEN PROVINCES: BELLUNO, PADOVA, ROVIGO, TREVISO, VENEZIA, VERONA AND VICENZA

Built on a series of low mud banks amid the tidal waters of the Adriatic, the main thoroughfare through Venice is the Grand Canal. At nearly four kilometres long, 30 to 70 metres wide, it divides the city in half and palaces, churches and historic monuments line the waterway. The Piazza San Marco is the main focal point of the city, with the Oriental splendour of the Basilica di San Marco, the Palazzo Ducale and the Bridge of Sighs. With another famous bridge and bustling markets, the district of Rialto is one of the liveliest spots, while the lagoon islands offer an escape from the crowds. Murano comprises a cluster of small islands, connected by bridges, and has been the centre of the glass-blowing industry since 1291; Burano is the most colourful with brightly painted houses and a long lace-making tradition, while Torcello boasts a 7th-century cathedral, the oldest building on the lagoon. Outside Venice, the old university town of Padua is rich in art and architecture, and Verona, with its buildings of pink-tinged limestone, is renowned for its Roman ruins including the amphitheatre, which is the third largest in the world. It is also home to Casa di Giulietta, Juliet's house, a restored 13th-century inn with a small marble balcony, immortalised in Shakespeare's Romeo and Juliet.

Places of interest

Bassano del Grappa: well known for its majolica products and Grappa distilleries.

Conegliano: a wine producing region, renowned wine growers' school, grape festival in September, wine routes.

Euganean Hills: hot sulphur springs and mud baths.

Montagnana: fortified settlement with medieval town walls.

Padua: Basilica di Sant'Antonio, one of the most important pilgrimage destinations in Italy.

Treviso: attractive town with medieval, balconied houses overlooking willow-fringed canals.

Vicenza: Roman-Renaissance architecture, home of Europe's oldest surviving indoor theatre, 17th-century stone bridges.

Cuisine of the region

Risottos are popular, especially with seafood, plus pork dishes, polenta and heavy soups of beans, rice and vegetables. The region is also home to Italy's famous dessert *tiramisu*, a rich blend of coffee-soaked sponge cake and mascarpone cheese. Locally produced wines include Soave, Merlot, Cabernet, Pinot Grigio and Chardonnay. Grappa is made from grape husks, juniper berries or plums.

Brodo di Pesce: fish soup.

Bussolai: ring shaped cinnamon flavoured biscuits.

Radicchio alla Griglia: red salad leaves lightly grilled.

Risi e Bisi: soft and liquid risotto with fresh peas and bacon.

Risotto alle Seppie: contains cuttlefish ink.

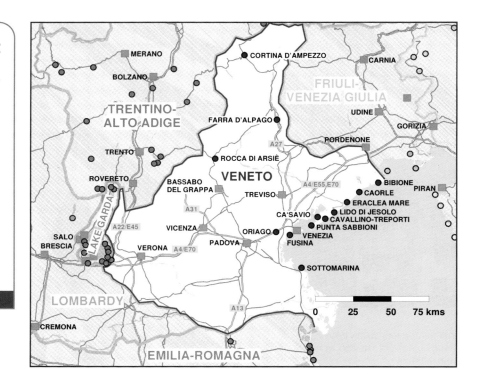

Bibione

Camping Capalonga

Via della Laguna 16, I-30020 Bibione-Pineda (Veneto) T: 043 143 8351. E: capalonga@bibionemare.com

alanrogers.com/IT60100

A quality site right beside the sea, Capalonga is a large site with 787 shaded touring pitches (70-90 sq.m) with 6/10A electricity, 35 fully serviced. The site is pleasantly laid out and permanent pitches are unobtrusive. The new (2010) additional lagoon swimming pool is excellent. Alternatively, the wide, sand beach is very safe. Quality entertainment adds to the enjoyment here and the site has something for everyone. It is roomy and bicycles are a real boon here. The site has a great location between the sea and a large lagoon. Boating (motor or sail) can be undertaken; a landing stage, crane and moorings are available. Security is handled well and all staff are cheerful and attentive. Capalonga is an excellent site, with comprehensive facilities.

Facilities

Nine toilet blocks are of a high standard and frequently cleaned. There are facilities for disabled visitors, and great children's rooms. British and Turkish style toilets, some washbasins in private cabins. Launderette. Dishwashers (€ 1.00). Motorcaravan services. Large supermarket. General shop. Self-service restaurant and separate bar (open all season). Two swimming pools (from 1/5). Boating (170 moorings). Fishing (sea or lagoon). Bicycle hire. Playground. Entertainment programme. Internet access and WiFi. Late arrival parking with electricity. Dogs are not accepted. Off site: Bus by entrance. Riding 2 km. Golf 10 km. Touring and excursions. Boat hire.

Open: 24 April - 23 September.

Directions

Bibione is 80 km. east of Venice, well signed from afar on approach roads. 1 km. before Bibione turn right towards Bibione-Pineda and follow site signs. GPS: 45.63050, 12.99358

Charges guide

Per unit incl. 2 persons	
and electricity	€ 25.80 - € 51.80
extra person	€ 6.90 - € 11.90
child (1-11 yrs acc. to age)	free - € 9.70

For latest campsite news, availability and prices visit
alanrogers.com

Cavallino-Treporti
Camping Miramare

Punta Sabbioni, I-30010 Cavallino-Treporti (Veneto) T: 041 966 150. E: info@camping-miramare.it
alanrogers.com/IT60460

This small, family owned site is well located, being the closest site to the Punta Sabbioni ferry. However, it currently lacks a swimming pool and has no direct access to a beach, so the site provides a free bus service to the ferry and to the local beach. It has an unusually long season compared with other sites in the area. Miramare is ideally located for exploring Venice and its islands, as well as the Lido di Venezia. There are 100 level pitches here, all with 6A electricity. The shop is superb for a small site and the restaurant, 50 m. out of the gate, is renowned for its excellent regional meals. The restaurant has an Internet terminal and WiFi is available over part of the site. Everywhere is kept clean and most pitches have shade from mature trees and are level. Ask about the campsite logo – the Venetian iron – very interesting, and about the local flamingos, which from time to time appear in winter!

Facilities

Two toilet blocks (one heated in low season) with facilities for disabled campers and babies. Motorcaravan service point. Excellent supermarket/shop. Bar, restaurant and pizzas from the oven in the restaurant. Takeaway. Play area. Internet point. Bicycle hire. Dogs are only accepted on 15 specific pitches. Free shuttle bus to Punta Sabbioni square (departure point for trips to Venice and the islands) and to the nearest beach (free sun umbrellas). Barbecues on pitches not permitted. Off site: Boat launching 1.5 km. Beach 1.8 km. Fishing 2 km. Riding 8 km. Golf 15 km.

Open: 23 March - 3 November.

Directions

Leave the A4 autostrada at exit for Venezia Mestre and follow signs to Jesolo and Punta Sabbioni, where the site is clearly signed.
GPS: 45.44035, 12.42110

Charges guide

Per unit incl. 2 persons	
and electricity	€ 22.50 - € 34.00
extra person	€ 5.00 - € 7.80
child (1-10 yrs)	€ 3.30 - € 5.80

Cavallino-Treporti
Camping Dei Fiori

Via Pisani 52, I-30013 Cavallino-Treporti (Veneto) T: 041 966 448. E: fiori@vacanze-natura.it
alanrogers.com/IT60300

Dei Fiori stands out among the other sites in the area. As its name implies, it is ablaze with colourful flowers and shrubs in summer and presents a neat and tidy appearance whilst providing a relatively quiet atmosphere. Of the 310 pitches, the 279 touring pitches are fully serviced with 6/10A electricity, water and drainage. Some pitches are in woodland where space varies according to the trees, which have been left in their natural state. Others are positioned beneath artificial shade, where regular shaped pitches are of reasonable size (55-90 sq.m). Well built bungalows for rent enhance the site and are in no way intrusive, giving a village-like effect. About a quarter of the pitches are taken by static units, all of which are for rent. The site is well maintained by friendly, English speaking management.

Facilities

Three sanitary blocks are of exceptional quality with British style WCs, family rooms, well equipped baby rooms, good facilities for disabled visitors, and laundry facilities. Family rooms (key from reception). Motorcaravan services. Shops. Restaurant. Snack bar. Satellite TV. Swimming pools and whirlpool. Fitness centre, gym, hydro-massage bath (charged in mid and high seasons) and programmes (1/5-30/9). Tennis. Minigolf. Play area. Organised activities, entertainment and excursions. Bicycle hire. WiFi (charged). Dogs are not accepted. Off site: Public transport 200 m. Riding 4 km. Fishing 7 km. Golf 15 km.

Open: 20 April - 30 September.

Directions

Leave A4 Venice-Trieste autostrada either by taking exit for airport or Quarto d'Altino and follow signs for Jesolo and then Punta Sabbioni and site signs just after Ca'Ballarin. GPS: 45.45263, 12.47127

Charges guide

Per unit incl. 2 persons	
and electricity	€ 18.90 - € 42.70
extra person	€ 4.70 - € 10.10
child (2-6 yrs)	free - € 7.80
child (6-12 yrs) or senior (over 65 yrs)	€ 3.90 - € 8.60

Min. stay 3 days in high season (3/7-21/8).

Cavallino-Treporti
Camping Union Lido Vacanze

Via Fausta 258, I-30013 Cavallino-Treporti (Veneto) T: 041 257 5111. E: info@unionlido.com

alanrogers.com/IT60200

This amazing site is very large, offering everything a camper could wish for. It is extremely well organised and it has been said to set the standard that others follow. It lies right beside the sea with direct access to a 1.2 km. long, broad sandy beach which shelves very gradually and provides very safe bathing (there are lifeguards). The site itself is regularly laid out with parallel access roads under a covering of poplars, pine and other trees providing good shade. There are 2,200 pitches for touring units, all with 6/10A electricity and 1,749 also have water and drainage. Because of the size of the site, there is an internal road train and amenities are repeated across the site (cycling is not permitted and cars are parked away from the pitches). You really would not need to leave this site – everything is here, including a sophisticated wellness centre. Overnight parking is provided outside the gate with electricity, toilets and showers for those arriving after 21.00. There are two aqua parks, one with fine sandy beaches (a first in Europe) and both with swimming pools, lagoon pools for children, a heated whirlpool and a slow flowing 160 m. 'river'. A heated pool for hotel and apartment guests is open to others on payment. A huge selection of sports is offered, along with luxury amenities too numerous to list. Entertainment and fitness programmes are organised in season. The golf academy (with a professional) has a driving range, pitching green, putting green and practice bunker, and a diving centre offers lessons and open water diving. Union Lido is above all an orderly and clean site, which is achieved by reasonable regulations to ensure quiet, comfortable camping, and by good management. A member of Leading Campings group.

Facilities

Fourteen well kept, fully equipped toilet blocks which open and close progressively during the season; 11 have facilities for disabled visitors. Launderette. Motorcaravan service points. Gas supplies. Comprehensive shopping areas set around a pleasant piazza (all open till late). Eight restaurants each with a different style plus 11 pleasant and lively bars (all services open all season). Impressive aqua parks (all season). Tennis. Riding. Minigolf. Skating. Bicycle hire. Archery. Two fitness tracks in 4 ha. natural park with play area and supervised play for children. Golf academy. Diving centre and school. Windsurfing school in season. Boat excursions. Recreational events. Church service in English in July/Aug. Hairdressers. Internet cafés. ATM. Dogs are not accepted. WiFi throughout (charged). Off site: Boat launching 3.5 km. Aqualandia (special rates).

Open: 24 April - 29 September (with all services).

Directions

From Venice-Trieste autostrada leave at exit for airport or Quarto d'Altino and follow signs first for Jesolo and then Punta Sabbioni, and site will be seen just after Cavallino on the left.
GPS: 45.467883, 12.530367

Charges 2013

Per unit incl. 2 persons	
and electricity	€ 25.70 - € 50.10
with services	€ 29.20 - € 68.50
extra person	€ 6.60 - € 11.80
child (1-11 yrs acc. to age)	€ 3.70 - € 9.70

Three different seasons: (i) high season 29/6-31/8; (ii) mid-season 18/5-29/6 and 31/8-14/9, and (iii) off-season, outside these dates.

Cavallino-Treporti
Italy Camping Village

Via Fausta 272, I-30013 Cavallino-Treporti (Veneto) T: 041 968 090. E: info@campingitaly.it

alanrogers.com/IT60210

Italy Camping Village, under the same ownership as the better known Union Lido which it adjoins, is suggested for those who prefer a smaller, more compact site. The 180 touring pitches are on either side of sand tracks off hard access roads under a cover of trees. All have 6A electricity connections (Europlug) and 114 are fully serviced. Pitches are between 50-70 sq.m. but access is impossible for large units, particularly in high season when cars are parked everywhere. Fifty-five plots are taken up by units for rental, with 26 being used by tour operators. There is direct access to a gently sloping sandy beach. A heated, swimming pool has a slide and a whirlpool at one end, but for those who want a greater choice of activities, guests can use the facilities at Union Lido for a small additional charge. Strict regulations regarding undue noise here make this a relatively peaceful site and with lower charges than some in the area, this would be a good choice for families with young children. Advance booking is possible.

Facilities

Two good quality, fully equipped sanitary blocks include facilities for disabled visitors. Washing machines. Shop. Restaurant with TV. Bar beside beach. Heated swimming pool (17x7 m. May-Sept). Small playground, miniclub and children's disco. Bicycle hire. WiFi (charged). Only gas and electric barbecues permitted on individual pitches; charcoal only permitted in the designated area. Dogs are not accepted. Off site: Use of facilities at IT60200 Union Lido (extra charge for pool). Sports centre, golf and riding 400 m.

Open: 23 April - 22 September.

Directions

From Venice-Trieste A4 autostrada leave at exit for airport or Quarto d'Altino and follow signs for Jesolo and Punta Sabbioni. Site well signed on left after Cavallino. GPS: 45.46836, 12.53338

Charges 2013

Per unit incl. 2 persons	
and electricity	€ 18.10 - € 38.60
extra person	€ 4.90 - € 9.30
child (1-5 yrs)	free - € 6.70

Three charging seasons.

For latest campsite news, availability and prices visit
alanrogers.com

Cavallino-Treporti
Camping Mediterraneo
Via delle Batterie 38, I-30010 Cavallino-Treporti (Veneto) T: 041 966 721. E: mediterraneo@vacanze-natura.it
alanrogers.com/IT60350

This large site has been considerably improved in recent years and is near Punta Sabbioni from where boats depart for Venice. Mediterraneo is directly on the Adriatic Sea with a 480 metre long beach of fine sand which shelves gently and also two large pools and a whirlpool. Of the 750 touring pitches, 500 have electricity (from 4A), water and drainage. They are partly in boxes with artificial shade, while some are larger without shade; others are in unmarked zones under natural woodland, reserved for tents, are equipped with electric hook-ups. Tour operators use 145 pitches. A well organised and efficient site.

Facilities

Eight modern sanitary blocks are of good quality with British type WCs and free hot water. Laundry facilities. Motorcaravan services. Commercial centre with supermarket and other shops with a restaurant, bars and a pizzeria near the pools. Swimming pool. Playground. Tennis. Bicycle hire. Programme of sports, games, excursions etc. Dancing or shows 3 times weekly in main season. Windsurfing and sailing schools. Dogs are not accepted. Off site: Riding and golf 3 km.

Open: 24 April - 27 September.

Directions

Site is well signed from Jesolo-Punta Sabbioni road near its end after Ca'Ballarin and before Ca'Savio. Follow site signs, not those for Treporti as this village is some way from the site.
GPS: 45.45413, 12.48173

Charges guide

Per unit incl. 2 persons	
and electricity	€ 16.60 - € 49.00
extra person	€ 4.70 - € 11.10
child (2-12 yrs)	€ 0.40 - € 9.50
Four rates.	

Cavallino-Treporti
Camping Silva
Via F Baracca 53, I-30013 Cavallino-Treporti (Veneto) T: 041 968 087. E: info@campingsilva.it
alanrogers.com/IT60310

Silva is a simple site, owned by the same family for many years. It is situated close to the popular beach resort of Cavallino, between the road and the beach (there is some road noise on the pitches near the entrance). It offers direct access to a sandy beach which is its main strength as there is little more beyond the basics of camping here. There are 256 touring pitches (45-60 sq.m) with 6A electricity (long leads needed in places). These are set on grass and sand with a canopy of mature trees providing shade. Some of the trees are positioned quite close together and, combined with vertical metal posts, the site could be difficult for large units.

Facilities

Three older, identically shaped blocks provide basic facilities. A mix of British and Turkish style toilets and hot water throughout. Separate facilities for disabled visitors. Motorcaravan services. Washing machine. Bar, snack bar/pizzeria. Shop. Play area. Direct access to beach. Accommodation to rent. Barbecues are not permitted. Off site: Golf. Riding. Aqualand water park.

Open: 6 May - 19 September.

Directions

Travelling east on the A4 (Milan-Trieste) take exit for Quarto d'Altino. Follow directions for Portegrandi and Jesolo. In Jesolo follow the signs for Cavallino. Site is signed from there. GPS: 45.48150, 12.56467

Charges guide

Per unit incl. 2 persons	
and electricity	€ 17.00 - € 35.00
extra person	€ 4.00 - € 8.00
child (2-6 yrs)	€ 2.00 - € 6.00
dog	€ 1.50 - € 3.00
No credit cards.	

Cavallino-Treporti
Camping Village Europa

Via Fausta 332, I-30013 Cavallino-Treporti (Veneto) T: 041 968 069. E: info@campingeuropa.com

alanrogers.com/IT60410

232

Europa is a large site in a great position with direct access to a fine, sandy, Blue Flag beach with lifeguards. There are 500 touring pitches, 450 of which have 8A electricity, water, drainage and satellite TV connections. There is a separate area for campers with dogs and some smaller pitches are available for those with tents. The site is kept beautifully clean and neat and there is an impressive array of restaurants, bars, shops and leisure amenities. These are cleverly laid out along an avenue and include a jeweller's, a doctor's surgery, Internet services and much more. Leisure facilities are arranged around the site. The touring area is surprisingly peaceful for a site of this size. A professional team provides entertainment and regular themed summer events. Some restaurant tables have pleasant sea views. Venice is easily accessible by bus and then ferry from Punta Sabbioni.

Facilities

Three superb toilet blocks are kept pristine and have hot water throughout. Facilities for disabled visitors. Washing machines. Large supermarket and shopping centre, bars, restaurants, cafés and pizzeria. Takeaway service (30/3-25/9). Excellent pool complex with slide and spa centre (30/3-25/9). Tennis. Games room. Playground. Children's clubs. Entertainment. WiFi (charged). Direct access to the beach. Windsurf and pedalo hire. Mobile homes, chalets and 14 eco apartments for rent.
Off site: Riding and boat launching 1 km. Golf and fishing 4 km. Walking and cycling trails. Excursions to Venice.

Open: 28 March - 30 September.

Directions

From A4 autostrada (approaching from Milan) take Mestre exit and follow signs initially for Venice airport and then Jesolo. From Jesolo, follow signs to Cavallino from where site is well signed.
GPS: 45.47380, 12.54903

Charges guide

Per unit incl. 2 persons and electricity	€ 20.00 - € 50.40
extra person	€ 5.00 - € 10.90
child (2-5 yrs)	€ 3.35 - € 9.90
dog	€ 2.65 - € 5.90

Family feeling in europa!

europa ★★★★
CAMPING VILLAGE

Cavallino-Treporti (Venezia) I-30013
Via Fausta, 332
Tel +39 041 968261-Fax +39 041 5370150
www.campingeuropa.com
info@campingeuropa.com

Cavallino-Treporti
Camping Vela Blu

Via Radaelli 10, I-30013 Cavallino-Treporti (Veneto) T: 041 968 068. E: info@velablu.it

alanrogers.com/IT60280

alan rogers
Runner up 2012 Awards

Thoughtfully landscaped within a natural wooded coastal environment, the tall pines here give shade, while attractive flowers enhance the setting and paved roads give easy access to most pitches. The 241 pitches (137 for tourers) vary in size (55-90 sq.m) and shape, but all have 10/16A electricity and 80 have drainage. A sister site to nos. IT60360 and IT60140, Vela Blu is a smaller family style site and a pleasant alternative to the other massive sites on Cavallino. It is a popular destination for Italian families, booking is essential for high season. A fine sandy beach runs the length of one side of the site.

Facilities

Two modern, well maintained toilet blocks (with attendant) include baby rooms and facilities for disabled visitors. Laundry facilities. Motorcaravan service point. Medical room. Shop. Bar. Gelateria. Restaurant and takeaway. New swimming pool complex. Games room. TV room. Pedaloes. Windsurfing. Fishing. Bicycle hire. No charcoal barbecues. Entertainment. WiFi (charged). Off site: Shops, bars and restaurants. Buses connect with ferry to Venice.

Open: 23 March - 28 September.

Directions

Leave A4 Venice-Trieste motorway at exit for Aeroporto. Follow signs for Jesolo and Punta Sabbioni. Site is signed after village of Cavallino.
GPS: 45.45681, 12.5072

Charges 2013

Per unit incl. 2 persons and all services	€ 18.70 - € 48.60
extra person	€ 4.60 - € 10.30

Camping Cheques accepted.

FREE Alan Rogers Travel Card
Extra benefits and savings - see page 10

Cavallino-Treporti
Camping Villa al Mare

Via del Faro 12, I-30013 Cavallino-Treporti (Veneto) T: 041 968 066. E: info@villaalmare.com

alanrogers.com/IT60290

A small, pleasant family site, Villa al Mare enjoys an unusual location, close to Cavallino's lighthouse and harbour, on the western bank of the River Sile. There is a beach of fine golden sand washed from the Dolomites. There are 100 shaded touring pitches (50-75 sq.m) each with 4/6A electricity, satellite TV connections, water and drainage. There is direct access to the gently shelving beach and during high season a range of activities are organised there. A small pool for children is on a raised area just inside the site and a larger pool is in the centre of the adjoining Résidence Le Dune apartment area.

Facilities

Two traditional style toilet blocks are kept very clean. Facilities for disabled visitors. Washing machines. Bar, restaurant and pizzeria. Shop. Swimming pool (1/5-15/9). Fishing. Playground. Jacuzzi. Children's club. Excursions. Entertainment and activities. Direct access to the beach. Mobile homes and apartments for rent. WiFi over site (charged). Dogs are not accepted. Off site: Aqualandia water park. Bus stop 250 m. Cavallino 2 km. Golf 4 km. Riding 6 km. Ferry terminal for Venice 10 km.

Open: 24 April - 21 October.

Directions

From A4 (from Milan) take Mestre exit and follow signs for Venice airport and then Jesolo. From Jesolo, follow signs to Cavallino. Cross large bridge in Cavallino, take first left turn (Via F Baracca). Continue for 600 m. then left into Via del Faro. Site is at end of road (300 m). GPS: 45.47933, 12.58103

Charges 2013

Per person	€ 5.00 - € 8.90
pitch	€ 8.00 - € 22.00

Cavallino-Treporti
Camping Village Al Boschetto

Via della Batterie 18, Ca'Vio, I-30013 Cavallino-Treporti (Veneto) T: 041 966 145. E: info@alboschetto.it

alanrogers.com/IT60455

Al Boschetto is a good, family owned, beachside site which prides itself on offering a thoughtful service to its customers and has a particular appeal to families. It has an open green and pleasant feel and everything is well maintained. Of 335 pitches, 240 are for touring units and 190 of the flat, variable sized pitches (55-100 sq.m) are fully serviced. The remaining pitches are taken by seasonal units, which do not affect the touring areas. Flowers and trimmed foliage provide a pleasant garden atmosphere. This is a great site for families who do not want the razzamatazz and noise of the bigger sites.

Facilities

Three modern sanitary blocks provide mostly British style toilets and excellent facilities for disabled visitors. Laundry facilities. Motorcaravan services. Supermarket. Bar. Restaurant, pizzeria and takeaway. Entertainment team in high season. Playground. Tennis. Bicycle hire. Beach. ATM. Gymnasium. WiFi (charged). Mobile homes to rent. Dogs are not accepted. Off site: Riding 5 km. Golf 13 km.

Open: 27 April - 15 September.

Directions

Leave A4 Venice-Trieste autostrada either by taking the airport exit or the Quarto d'Altino exit. Follow signs to Jesolo and Punta Sabbioni. Site is well signed from here. GPS: 45.45186, 12.47631

Charges guide

Per unit incl. 2 persons and electricity	€ 19.30 - € 41.90
No credit cards.	

Cavallino-Treporti
Camping Village Cavallino

Via delle Batterie 164, I-30013 Cavallino-Treporti (Veneto) T: 041 966 133. E: info@campingcavallino.com

alanrogers.com/IT60320

This large, well ordered site is run by a friendly, experienced family. It lies beside the sea with direct access to a superb beach of fine sand, which is very safe and has lifeguards. The site is thoughtfully laid out with the 457 large touring pitches shaded by olives and pines. All pitches have 6/10A electricity. There are 264 further pitches which are mainly occupied by mobile homes and chalets available to rent. For visiting Venice, there is a bus to the ferry at Punta Sabbioni which is 20 minutes away. The charming ferry journey takes 40 minutes. and drops you directly at Saint Marco Square.

Facilities

The clean, modern toilet blocks which can be heated, provide a mixture of Turkish and British style WCs with facilities for disabled visitors. Launderette. Motorcaravan services. Supermarket. Restaurant. Takeaway. Pizzeria. Swimming pools and whirlpool (May-Sept). Minigolf. New playground. Bicycle hire. Fishing. Ambitious entertainment programme aimed mostly at younger guests. ATM. WiFi. Dogs are accepted in certain areas. Mobile homes to rent. Off site: Golf 1 km. Riding 2 km. Tours to all attractions.

Open: 24 March - 31 October.

Directions

From Venice-Trieste autostrada leave at exit for airport or Quarto d'Altino. Follow signs, first for Jesolo, then Punta Sabbioni. Site signed just after Cavallino on the left. GPS: 45.45666, 12.50055

Charges 2013

Per unit incl. 2 persons and electricity	€ 20.60 - € 49.90
extra person	€ 6.00 - € 12.90
Min. stay of one week in high season.	

For latest campsite news, availability and prices visit

alanrogers.com

RESERVATION HOTLINE: +39.0421.97.1826
OPEN: 25 APRIL - 29 SEPTEMBER

www.jesolointernational.it / info@jesolointernational.it

Club Camping
★★★★
JESOLO INTERNATIONAL

The best position on the Adriatic: at the shopping-mile of Jesolo, opposite the ferry to Venice, accommodations have an average distance of just 60 mt. from the beach. Unbeatable value for money because of countless services included in the price: Wi-fi, banana boat, loungers and umbrellas on the beach and the pool, free entry to Aqualandia, the best water park in Italy

(as often as you like, 2 Km), free entrance to Adventure Mini Golf, free golfing on the 18 hole course of the Jesolo Golf Club (3 km), diving, pedal boats, canoes, pony riding, heated tubs, tennis, pirate ship, clay shooting, go-kart racing at the race track of Jesolo (4 km), top fitness center, large children's center, animation, all this is for free!

Excellent surveillance system. Exemplary environmental concept. First carbon neutral campsite worldwide.
Camping own luxury mobile homes very well equipped and with top service.
Camping at it's best: new Ultra pitches 170-250 sqm with private bathroom.

ADAC Super-Platz 2012

ADAC CAMPING AWARD
CO 2 Neutral - 2010

AN WB INNO VATION AWARD 2010

KLIMAFREUNDLICHER BETRIE B

camping info AWARD 2012

zoover award 2012
N°1 CAMPING IN ITALY

CARAVANING
BESTER CAMPINGPLATZ EUROPAS 2012

Oriago

Camping della Serenissima

Via Padana 334/a, I-30034 Oriago (Veneto) T: 041 921 850. E: info@campingserenissima.it

alanrogers.com/IT60500

This is a delightful little site of some 155 pitches (all with 16A electricity) where one could stay for a number of days whilst visiting Venice (12 km), Padova (24 km), Lake Garda (135 km) or the Dolomites. There is a good service by bus to Venice and the site is situated on the Riviera del Brenta, at a section with some very large, old villas. A long, narrow and flat site, numbered pitches are on each side of a central road. There is good shade in most parts with many trees, plants and grass. The management is friendly and good English is spoken. The site is used mainly by Dutch and British visitors, with some Germans, and is calm and quiet.

Facilities	Directions
Sanitary facilities are of a good standard and include those for disabled visitors. New additional toilet facilities next to restaurant. Motorcaravan services. Gas supplies. Shop (all season). Bar. Restaurant and takeaway (1/6-31/10). Play area. Fishing. Bicycle hire. Reduced price bus ticket to Venice if staying for 3 days. No organised entertainment but local markets, etc. all well publicised. Off site: Golf and riding 3 km.	Approaching Venice on the A4 take exit for Oriago-Mira then signs for Ravenna, Padova (SS11) to Oriago. On A27 or SS309 take exit for Venezia-Mestre then signs for Ravenna, Padova and Milano. After Padova-Riviera del Brenta follow signs to Oriago. Site is well signed. GPS: 45.451769, 12.183784

Open: Easter - 8 November.

Charges guide

Per unit incl. 2 persons and electricity	€ 28.00 - € 33.00
extra person	€ 7.50 - € 9.00
child (3-12 yrs)	€ 4.50 - € 5.50

Punta Sabbioni

Camping Marina di Venezia

Via Montello 6, I-30013 Punta Sabbioni (Veneto) T: 041 530 2511. E: camping@marinadivenezia.it

alanrogers.com/IT60450

This is a very large site (2,901 pitches) with much the same atmosphere as many other large sites along this appealing stretch of coastline. Marina di Venezia, however, has the advantage of being within walking distance of the ferry to Venice. It will appeal particularly to those who enjoy an extensive range of entertainment and activities, and a lively atmosphere. Individual pitches are marked out on sandy or grassy ground, most separated by trees or hedges. They are of an average size for the region (around 80 sq.m) and all are equipped with electricity and water. The site's excellent sandy beach is one of the widest along this stretch of coast and has five pleasant beach bars. The main pool is Olympic size and there is also a very large children's pool adjacent. The magnificent Aqua Marina Park swimming pool complex is now open and offers amazing amenities (free to all campers), including three heated whirlpools. This is a well run site with committed management and staff.

Facilities	Directions
Nine modern toilet blocks are maintained to a high standard with good hot showers and a reasonable proportion of British style toilets. Good provision for disabled visitors. Washing machines and dryers. Range of shops. Several bars, restaurants and takeaways. Swimming pool complex with slides and flumes. Several play areas. Tennis. Windsurf and catamaran hire. Wide range of organised entertainment. WiFi Internet access in all bars and cafés. Church. Special area and facilities for dog owners.	From A4 motorway, take Jesolo exit. After Jesolo continue towards Punta Sabbioni. Site is clearly signed to the left towards the end of this road, close to the Venice ferries. GPS: 45.43750, 12.43805

Open: 20 April - 30 September.

Charges 2013

Per unit incl. 2 persons and electricity	€ 21.40 - € 47.70
extra person	€ 4.60 - € 10.50
child or senior (2-5 and over 60)	€ 3.80 - € 8.50
dog	€ 1.30 - € 4.20

For latest campsite news, availability and prices visit

alanrogers.com

Rocca di Arsiè
Camping Al Lago
Via Campagna 14, Rocca, I-32030 Arsiè (Veneto) T: 043 958 540. E: info@campingallago.bl.it
alanrogers.com/IT61500

This small, quiet site with its beautiful lakeside setting and surrounded by steep, tree-clad hills, is located at the southern edge of the Dolomites and only 110 km. from Venice and the Adriatic. It is an ideal site to spend some time just relaxing, walking or cycling in this attractive region. The main area slopes gently down to the lake and has plenty of shade; it has 70 touring pitches, all with 3A electricity (long leads may be required) and 30 seasonal caravans. There is also a large open field for both tents and caravans.

Facilities
Central toilet block has controllable showers and a mixture of Turkish and British style toilets. Washbasins (open-style) and sinks (under cover) have only cold water, but there are taps from which to collect hot water. Washing machines and dryer. Motorcaravan service point. Facilities for disabled visitors. Bar (with Sky TV). Restaurant/pizzeria with takeaway. Play area. Games room. WiFi (charged).

Open: 1 April - 30 September.

Directions
Arsiè is 45 km. southwest of Belluno and 65 km. east of Trento on the SS50/SS50bis which links Belluno to the SS47 Padua-Trento road. Site is in Rocca di Arsiè and is signed to the south off the SS47. GPS: 45.96405, 11.75913

Charges guide
Per unit incl. 2 persons and electricity	€ 20.00 - € 26.00

Sottomarina
Camping Miramare
 233

Via Barbarigo 103, I-30015 Sottomarina di Chioggia (Veneto) T: 041 490 610. E: campmir@tin.it
alanrogers.com/IT60560

Camping Miramare is a pleasant, fairly shady site with beach access, a good swimming pool and entertainment programme. The site is divided by a road and reception is on the beach side, along with most of the amenities. The other side is very peaceful with just sports amenities and a sanitary block. The 230 touring pitches are separated from the permanent units. All have 6A electricity and some have water and drainage. The beach is of soft sand and there is a lifeguard. You can hire sunshades and loungers. The restaurant offers traditional food and a plethora of pizzas which can be enjoyed on the terraces. Children have several play areas and there is entertainment all season. The separated swimming pool is excellent, with two diving boards and a lifeguard. The site lies close to the ancient city of Chioggia, famous for its fishing and Venice-like construction. For those wishing to explore the region, there are many other opportunities. An excursion to Venice naturally holds a strong appeal, but other stunning cities are also close at hand, notably Padova, Vicenza, Treviso and, a little further afield, Verona. This is a pleasant, family oriented site which has a distinct Italian feel. English is spoken.

Facilities
Three modern, clean blocks, one of which is in the area of the permanent campers. Push button hot showers and primarily Turkish style toilets. Facilities for disabled guests. Baby room. Laundry rooms. Motorcaravan service point. Bar. Restaurant, pizzeria and takeaway. Shop. Swimming pool. Separate paddling pool (14/5-19/9). Play areas. Multisports court. Bicycle hire. Entertainment and children's activities in high season. WiFi throughout (charged). Mobile homes to rent. No dogs in high season. Off site: Fishing and sailing 1 km. Riding 6 km. Golf 20 km.

Open: 4 April - 23 September.

Directions
Site is off the S309 south of Chioggia. Follow signs to Sottomarina, crossing the Laguna del Lusenzo (look for site signs). Site is off Viale Mediterranneo road to the right (the second of many along this narrow road). GPS: 45.19018, 12.30341

Charges guide
Per unit incl. 2 persons and electricity	€ 20.00 - € 33.90
extra person	€ 4.75 - € 8.20

Sottomarina
Camping Village Oasi

Via A Barbarigo 147, I-30015 Sottomarina di Chioggia (Veneto) T: 041 554 1145. E: info@campingoasi.com

alanrogers.com/IT60540

Camping Oasi is a traditional, friendly, family site where many Italian families return for the summer – you could certainly practise your Italian language skills here. The Tiozzi family will make you feel very welcome. The flat, grass pitches for touring units are in separate areas from the permanent units, some being near the playground and football area. Varying in size (65-80 sq.m) with a choice of shade or sun, all have 6A electricity, 100 have water and drainage. There is a harbour wall walk to the private soft sand beach where a new second bar and restaurant provides drinks, snacks and meals. The touring pitches are near this beach access and some have views of the river leading to the sea.

Facilities

Two good sanitary blocks with mostly British style toilets and free hot showers. There are good facilities for disabled visitors and for children and babies (both some way from the furthest touring pitches). Pleasant swimming pool and paddling pool with flumes (a hoist is available allowing easier access for disabled visitors into the swimming pool). Adventure play area. Multisports pitch. Tennis. Bicycle hire. Riding. Watersports. Fishing. WiFi (charged). Communal barbecue area. Off site: Historical city of Chioggia. ATM 2 km.

Open: 29 March - 29 September.

Directions

Site is off the S309 south of Chioggia. Follow signs to Sottomarina, crossing Laguna del Lusenzo, then look for site signs. Site off this road (Viale Mediterranneo) to the right. Site is at end of this narrow road. GPS: 45.18148, 12.30755

Charges guide

Per unit incl. 2 persons	
and electricity	€ 20.50 - € 35.90
extra person	€ 5.50 - € 8.50
child (1-6 yrs)	€ 2.70 - € 4.50
dog	€ 2.70 - € 3.70

Camping Cheques accepted.

Sottomarina
Villaggio Turistico Isamar

Isolaverde, via Isamar 9, I-30010 Chioggia (Veneto) T: 041 553 5811. E: info@villaggioisamar.com

alanrogers.com/IT60550

This is a very large site with many shops, restaurants and leisure facilities. The camping area, with different pitch sizes, is under pine trees and grouped around the pool complex and covered entertainment centre. The pool complex comprises an Olympic size, saltwater swimming pool, a paddling pool and several new leisure pools. The pitches are arranged on either side of hard access roads and all have 6A electrical connections. There are many other areas containing well constructed chalets and holiday bungalows. The site is right beside the sea, with its own sandy beach. The site has a much higher proportion of Italian holidaymakers than many other sites. It is also popular with Germans and Dutch campers and may become crowded in high season.

Facilities

Four large modern sanitary blocks, are arranged around the main camping area. Fully equipped and of good quality with facilities for children and disabled visitors. Laundry. Motorcaravan services. Gas supplies. Hairdresser. Supermarket and general shopping centre. Large bar/pizzeria and self-service restaurant. Swimming pools. Tennis. Playground. Disco. Games room. Riding. Bicycle hire. Extensive entertainment and fitness programme. Supervised play for children over 4 yrs old. WiFi (charged). Dogs are not accepted. Off site: Fishing and boat launching 500 m.

Open: Second Friday in May - 14 September.

Directions

Turn off the main 309 road towards sea just south of Adige river 10 km. south of Chioggia, and proceed 5 km. to site. GPS: 45.16236, 12.32477

Charges guide

Per unit incl. 2 persons	
and electricity	€ 16.00 - € 47.00
extra person	€ 4.00 - € 11.00
child (2-12 yrs)	free - € 11.00

For latest campsite news, availability and prices visit

alanrogers.com

Once two regions, Emilia-Romagna stretches from the Adriatic coast almost to the shores of the Mediterranean. A prosperous area with historical cities and thriving industry, it is also home to two of Italy's most famous food exports: Parma ham and Parmesan cheese.

EMILIA-ROMAGNA COMPRISES NINE PROVINCES: BOLOGNA, FERRARA, FORLI, MODENA, PARMA, PIACENZA, RAVENNA, REGGIO EMILIA AND RIMINI

One of the richest regions of Italy, Emilia and Romagna only became united in 1947. Its landscape is varied, with the flat fields of the northern plain giving way to the forest-covered Apennine mountains in the south. Carving a route through the heart of the region is the Via Emilia, a Roman military road built in 187 BC that links the garrison town of Piacenza to Rimini on the coast. Most of the major towns lie along this route including Bologna, the region's capital. The historic city boasts a rich cultural heritage with its famous porticos, old university buildings and medieval palaces clustered around bustling town squares. North of Bologna, Ferrara is one of the most important Renaissance centres in Italy, while further inland Modena and Parma are home to some of the region's finest architecture. Parma also boasts one of the country's top opera houses. In the east, Ravenna is renowned for the Byzantine mosaics that decorate its churches and mausoleums, and along the Adriatic coast lie various beaches and the seaside resorts of Cervia, Cesenatico and Rimini. A popular summer destination, Rimini has sandy beaches, a lively nightlife, an abundance of bars and restaurants.

Places of interest

Faenza: home of faïence ceramic-ware.

Ferrara: walled town with impressive medieval castello.

Modena: the home of fast cars: both Ferrari and Maserati have factories on the outskirts.

Montese: wild black cherry festival in July, medieval singing, dancing and classical concerts in August.

Piacenza: historic Roman town, medieval and Renaissance architecture.

Valli di Comacchi: a wetland area, good for birdwatching.

Vignola: best known for its cherries and cherry blossom, spring festival, 15th/16th-century castle.

Cuisine of the region

Bologna is regarded as the gastronomic capital of Italy. Famous regional specialities include parmesan cheese (*parmigiano-reggiano*), egg pasta, Parma ham *prosciutto di Parma*) and balsamic vinegar. Local dishes include *lasagne*, *tortellini* stuffed with ricotta and spinach, *bollito misto* (boiled meats), *zampone* (stuffed pig's trotter). Fish is also popular along the coast of Romagna.

Cannelloni: large pasta tubes stuffed with meat or cheese and spinach, covered in tomato or cheese sauce.

Ciacci: chestnut flour pancakes filled with ricotta cheese and sugar.

Spaghetti al Ragù: pasta with beef and tomato sauce.

Torta di Limone: tart made with lemon and fresh cream.

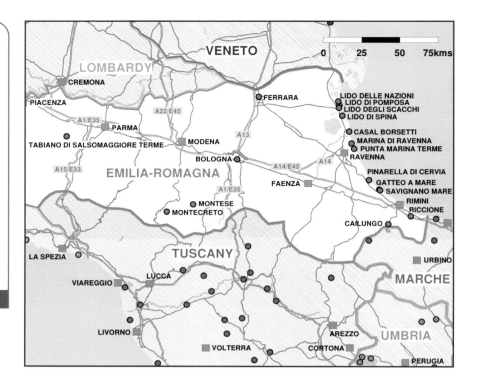

Bologna
Camping Hotel Cittá di Bologna

Via Romita 12-4A, I-40127 Bologna (Emilia-Romagna) T: 051 325 016. E: info@hotelcamping.com

alanrogers.com/IT66020

This spacious site was established in 1993 on the edge of the Trade Fair Centre of this ancient and historic city and is very clean and modern. The 120 pitches are numbered and marked out by trees giving plenty of shade. On level 'grasscrete' hardstandings in two areas, there are 6A electrical connections throughout. We found the toilet block to be exemplary. You will always find space here as there is huge over capacity. Recent improvements include the closure of the poorly used caravan storage area allowing a potential increase to 300 pitches.

Facilities

Modern sanitary blocks include excellent provision for disabled visitors (with British style WCs, free showers and alarms that ring in reception). Washing machines. Motorcaravan services. Smart bar with adjoining terrace where meals are offered (all season), and pizzeria (1/5-15/9). Superb new heated and supervised swimming pool (1/6-15/9). Small play area. Minigolf. Internet access. WiFi over site (charged). Fitness centre. Off site: Bus service to city centre from site. Shops and restaurant 500 m. Bicycle hire 5 km. Fishing 10 km.

Open: 9 January - 20 December.

Directions

Site is well signed from Bologna Fiera exit on the autostrada on the northeast of the city. Look for brown signs. GPS: 44.52366, 11.3741

Charges guide

Per unit incl. 2 persons	
and electricity	€ 24.00 - € 32.00
extra person	€ 5.50 - € 9.00
child (5-9 yrs)	€ 3.50 - € 5.50
dog	€ 2.00

For latest campsite news, availability and prices visit
alanrogers.com

Cailungo

Centro Vacanze San Marino

Strada San Michele 50, Cailungo, I-47893 Repubblica di San Marino (Emília-Romagna) T: 054 990 3964.
E: info@centrovacanzesanmarino.com **alanrogers.com/IT66230**

Centro Vacanze San Marino, at 400 m. above sea level and spreading gently down a hillside, has lovely views across to the Adriatic. This excellent, modern site has a variety of well tended trees offering shade. On level terraces, the main grass pitches are roomy and accessed from tarmac or gravel roads. Separated by hedges, all have electricity (5A). Smaller pitches on lower terraces are for tents. There is a pleasant open feel to this site. Mobile homes and bungalows are available to rent and the site is used by a tour operator (30 pitches).

Facilities	Directions
Four high quality heated toilet blocks, kept very clean have British and Turkish style WCs. Laundry facilities. Motorcaravan services. Gas supplies. Shop (April-Sept). Campers' kitchen. TV room (satellite). Restaurant/pizzeria (all year). Swimming pool (20/5-31/8) with jacuzzi and solarium. Large enclosed play area. Games room with Internet point. Free WiFi over part of site. Tennis. Bicycle hire. Entertainment programme for children (high season).	Leave autostrada A14 at exit Rimini-Sud (or SS16 where signed), follow SS72 west to San Marino. Site is signed from 15 km. GPS: 43.95957, 12.46126

Open: All year.

Charges guide

Per unit incl. 2 persons and electricity	€ 22.00 - € 34.00
extra person	€ 7.00 - € 8.50

Camping Cheques accepted.

Casal Borsetti

Camping Village Adria

Via Spallazzi 30, I-48010 Casal Borsetti (Emília-Romagna) T: 054 444 5217. E: adria@camping.it
alanrogers.com/IT60790

Adria is a modest site at first glance, however one soon realises this is a real gem. Unusually for the Adriatic, the setting is tranquil as there is no road or rail noise. Alongside the pretty beach, the site is surrounded by fields and a nature reserve. The pitches (50-100 sq.m) are level and have 10A electricity. Well shaded in the older area, the trees in the new area are beginning to provide welcome shade. The exciting new pool complex is a fun setting for both day and evening entertainment. This family oriented site really does give value for money. When we visited, children of all ages were having great fun with the entertainment staff. The site is within easy reach of Venice, Verona and other tourist destinations.

Facilities	Directions
Six toilet blocks, four with showers. Facilities for disabled visitors in every block. Very good facilities for children. Washing machines. Three bars including a beach bar, restaurant, separate snack bar and pizzeria with large terrace. Two swimming pools. Excellent entertainment programme in season. Miniclub. Three excellent play areas. Archery. Boules. Multisports courts. Watersports. Bicycle hire. WiFi (charged). Off site: Beach 180 m. ATM 1 km. Riding 3 km. Golf 40 km.	Site is north of Ravenna. From the A13 take the Ferrara road towards the coast at Comacchio and then south on the S309 towards Ravenna. Continue to town of Casal Borsetti and site is well signed. From south, use S309, turning right after crossing new bridge. GPS: 44.55910, 12.27965

Open: 23 April - 15 September.

Charges guide

Per unit incl. 2 persons and electricity	€ 19.60 - € 40.50
extra person	€ 4.60 - € 9.00

Camping Cheques accepted.

Ferrara

Camping Communale Estense

Via Gramicia 76, I-44100 Ferrara (Emília-Romagna) T: 053 275 2396. E: campeggio.estense@libero.it
alanrogers.com/IT60600

Ferrara is an interesting and historic city, well worth a short visit. This pretty municipal campsite on the northern outskirts offers comfortable facilities for all types of units and includes 50 fairly large, grass pitches, with numerous electrical connections. Trees are used to provide shade and to screen the site. Unusual concrete portals are covered in roses, shrubs and other flowers giving a cheerful atmosphere. On-site facilities are limited, with machines for snacks and cold drinks, but there is an excellent trattoria within walking distance (1 km) and a wide choice of other eating places in the city itself.

Facilities	Directions
Two acceptable, adjacent toilet blocks are fully equipped, one heated with British and Turkish style toilets. Separate facilities for disabled visitors. Drinks and snacks machines. Torches required in places. Off site: Restaurant close by. Golf 100 m. Fishing 500 m. Riding 3 km.	Site is signed from the city and is on the northern side of the ring road. GPS: 44.85217, 11.63417

Open: 25 February - 10 January.

Charges guide

Per unit incl. 2 persons and electricity	€ 21.50 - € 24.50
extra person	€ 5.00 - € 6.00

No credit cards.

FREE Alan Rogers Travel Card
Extra benefits and savings - see page 10

Gatteo a Mare
Villaggio Camping Delle Rose

Via Adriatica 29, I-47043 Gatteo a Mare (Emília-Romagna) T: 054 786 213. E: info@villaggiorose.com
alanrogers.com/IT66210

On the Cesanatico coastline of Emília-Romagna, this site is unusually located in a shaded park area just a short distance from the beach. First impressions may be that it is a poor cousin to some of the more highly graded sites in the area, although very shortly after arrival it is clear that this family run site is both efficiently managed and well provisioned for the 300 touring pitches, as well as its permanent and chalet based campers. There is a large swimming pool on site which is very well maintained and a smaller one at the private beach about 450 m. walk away.

Facilities	Directions
Modern facilities are clean and well spaced around this fairly large site. Restaurant, pizzeria and snack bar with takeaway. Supermarket. Swimming pool with pool bar. Paddling pool. Playground. Games room. TV room. Children's club and entertainment (11/6-3/9). Sports field. Off site: Romagna retail centre including supermarkets nearby. Beach 1 km. Mirabillandia water park 5 km.	Take the Cesena exit from the A14 Bologna-Ancona motorway. Head east to join the SS16 and then south to Gatteo a Mare. Site is clearly signed. GPS: 44.16597, 12.43196

Open: 1 May - 26 September.

Charges guide

Per unit incl. 2 persons	€ 23.00 - € 53.00
extra person	€ 6.00 - € 11.50
child (4-10 yrs)	free - € 8.70

Lido degli Scacchi
Kawan Village Florenz

Viale Alpi Centrali 199, I-44020 Lido degli Scacchi (Emília-Romagna) T: 053 338 0193.
E: info@holidayvillageflorenz.com **alanrogers.com/IT60750**

Popular with families for over 40 years, Camping Florenz has many loyal campers who return year after year. This site is among the sand dunes and pine forest along the seafront where there are good sized, shaded and level pitches with views of the water. The gently shelving beach has fine sand and lots of chairs and umbrellas. Away from the beach area there is plenty of shade from the tall pines. The 280 touring pitches are mostly a mixture of sand and grass, of a good size and level, all with electricity (6A). A large restaurant with a terrace overlooks the lively entertainment area.

Facilities	Directions
One excellent, new toilet block. Five mixed, mostly old sanitary blocks with half British, half Turkish style toilets and preset showers, scheduled for upgrade. Some unisex showers at beach. Facilities for disabled visitors. Motorcaravan service point. Supermarket. Restaurant and bar with TV. Large outdoor pool (€ 3). Activities and children's club in season. Play area and games room. Beach for swimming and boat launching. New beach bar and restaurant. Bicycle hire. New sports field. Free WiFi over site. Off site: Town with restaurants and shops 1 km.	Site is at Lido degli Scacchi just off the S309 running between Chioggia and Ravenna. Both Lido degli Scacchi and site are well signed from the S309 (being either Kawan or Florenz). GPS: 44.70111, 12.23806

Open: 4 April - 30 October.

Charges guide

Per person	€ 5.10 - € 10.30
child (3-10 yrs)	free - € 6.50
pitch	€ 11.40 - € 22.50

Camping Cheques accepted.

Lido delle Nazioni
Camping & Thermae Tahiti Centro Vacanze

Viale Libia 133, I-44020 Lido delle Nazioni (Emília-Romagna) T: 053 337 9500. E: info@campingtahiti.com
alanrogers.com/IT60650

Tahiti is an excellent, extremely well run site, thoughtfully laid out less than 1 km. from the sea (a continuous, fun road-train link is provided). Flowers, shrubs, ponds and attractive wooden structures enhance its appearance and, unlike many campsites of this size, it is family owned and run. The 469 pitches are of varying size, back to back from hard roads and defined by trees with shade in most areas. There are 30 pitches with a private unit containing a WC and washbasin. Electricity is available throughout and 100 pitches also have water and drainage.

Facilities	Directions
All toilet blocks are of a very high standard. British and Turkish style WCs. Baby room. Large supermarket. Two restaurants. Bar. Pizzeria. Takeaway. Swimming pools. Fitness and beauty centre. Playgrounds and miniclub. Gym. Tennis. Floodlit sports area. Minigolf. Bicycle hire. Entertainment and excursions (high season). 'Disco-pub'. Internet and WiFi (charged). Torches needed in some areas. No dogs. Off site: Fishing 300 m. Riding 500 m.	Turn off SS309 35 km. north of Ravenna to Lido delle Nazioni (north of Lido di Pomposa) and follow site signs. GPS: 44.73179, 12.22718

Open: 24 April - 23 September.

Charges guide

Per unit incl. 2 persons and electricity	€ 24.80 - € 40.90
extra person	€ 6.80 - € 10.20
child (under 8 yrs)	free - € 7.80

For latest campsite news, availability and prices visit
alanrogers.com

Lido di Pomposa
Camping Vigna sul Mar

Via Capanno Garibaldi 20, I-44020 Lido di Pomposa (Emília-Romagna) T: 053 338 0216.
E: info@vsmcampingvillage.com **alanrogers.com/IT60700**

This quietly situated site, about 8 km. north of Ravenna, has everything required for a happy and active family holiday. Tall, mature trees mark out pitches and give excellent shade in all parts. Some 420 pitches have 6A electricity and satellite TV connections. The private beach is about 100 m. from the centre. The campsite's own beach has a bar with snacks and beach equipment for hire. The site also has an excellent double swimming pool and many sports and recreational facilities, including a small theatre with nightly entertainment of films and dancing.

Facilities
Two of the main toilet blocks have been refurbished to a very high standard and are all kept very clean. Facilities for disabled visitors. Washing machines. Motorcaravan services. Supermarket, greengrocer, ice cream parlour, tobacconist and newsagent. Bar, restaurant, pizzeria and snack bar by pool. Swimming pool (23/5-5/9). Play area. Minigolf. Jogging track. Bicycle hire. Canoe and pedalo hire. Entertainment and excursions (high season). Free WiFi over part of site. Off site: Fishing 4 km. Riding 5 km.

Open: 21 April - 16 September.

Directions
From SS309 Ravenna-Venice road, look for signs for Porto Garibaldi, Lido degli Scacchi and Lido di Pomposa. Follow the coast road northbound, and site is well signed. GPS: 44.72527, 12.23605

Charges guide
Per person	€ 5.40 - € 10.50
pitch	€ 11.50 - € 21.00

Electricity and TV connections included.
Camping Cheques accepted.

Lido di Pomposa
International Camping Tre Moschettieri

Via Capanno Garibaldi 22, I-44020 Lido di Pomposa (Emília-Romagna) T: 053 338 0376.
E: info@tremoschettieri.com **alanrogers.com/IT60760**

Tre Moschettieri (Three Musketeers) is a compact, attractive site alongside the sea at Lido di Pomposa. The gently shelving beach is ideal for swimming and enjoying fun with the family. The site is in a garden setting and has many trees providing excellent shade for the 418 grass pitches (70-80 sq.m; 4A or 8A chargeable electricity). The roads are tarmac to reduce the dust and there are many water points around the site. The friendly management take care that campers are informed of programmed events.

Facilities
Eleven refurbished toilet blocks. Facilities for disabled visitors (check first). Laundry facilities. Restaurant/pizzeria and takeaway with terrace. Bar. Swimming pools on elevated section with a hoist for disabled access (June-Sept). Tennis. Gym. Giant chess. Entertainment in season. Play areas. Miniclub. Windsurfing school. Beach bar. ATM. Disco. Bicycle hire. No dogs on the beach or in the pool area. WiFi over part of site (charged). Off site: Excursions.

Open: 20 April - 16 September.

Directions
Site is east of Ferrara. Take the road to the coast and Comaccio, then the SS309 north to Lido de Pomposa. Site signed. GPS: 44.71666, 12.23333

Charges guide
Per unit incl. 2 persons and electricity	€ 21.00 - € 37.00

Lido di Spina
Spina Camping Village

Via del Campeggio 99, I-44024 Lido di Spina (Emília-Romagna) T: 053 333 0179.
E: info@spinacampingvillage.com **alanrogers.com/IT60780**

This new camping venture in the Adriatic Riviera is a real treat. Upon arrival it is clear that whilst much of the site is devoted to seasonal units and tour operators, every effort is made to meet the needs of touring units. There are lots of choices here – the splendid, private beach or on-site pool, beach sports or games in the superb sports areas. Pitches vary in size, services and setting, from park-like, open areas with rows of trees to heavily shaded pinewoods. The varied types of rental units are also thoughtfully nestled within the site to provide a pleasing mix in an informal layout.

Facilities
The three toilet blocks have been refurbished to a very high standard. Facilities for disabled visitors. Baby rooms. Washing machines. Motorcaravan services. Supermarket. Bakery. Bar with restaurant and terrace. Miniclub. Play areas. Swimming pools (15/5-end August with lifeguard, caps required). Beach bar and pool bar (entertainment in both areas). Watersports. Torches and long electricity leads useful. Communal barbecue area. TV room. WiFi (charged). Off site: Fishing 700 m. Bicycle hire 2 km.

Open: 17 April - 19 September.

Directions
Site is north of Ravenna and east of Ferrara. Take road from Ferrara to the coast at Comacchio, then SS309 south to Lido di Spina. Site is signed from here. GPS: 44.627721, 12.255061

Charges guide
Per unit incl. 2 persons and electricity	€ 15.00 - € 38.00

Camping Cheques accepted.

FREE Alan Rogers Travel Card
Extra benefits and savings - see page 10

Marina di Ravenna
International Camping Piomboni

Viale della Pace, 421, I-48122 Marina di Ravenna (Emilia-Romagna) T: 054 453 0230.
E: info@campingpiomboni.it **alanrogers.com/IT60730**

The pine forest which is home to Piomboni forms part of the Po Delta National Forest, and has been spared the frantic commercial development of other parts of the Adriatic coast. The site, still family owned and run, maintains a totally natural feel with pitches located between the ancient, tall pines and younger, dividing trees. There are 376 pitches, for tiny tents and motorcaravans up to 8 m. Most electrical supply is only 3A, so care is needed when using appliances. Access to the beach is just 100 metres from the site gate and there are large, free public areas.

Facilities

Five toilet blocks, two with hot and cold showers. Baby rooms. Facilities for disabled visitors. Washing machines and dryer. Dog bath. Well stocked shop. Bar, restaurant and takeaway. Dancing and entertainments area. TV room with library. Games and play area with boules pitch. Children's activities programme. Archery. Bicycle hire. Free WiFi. Excursions arranged. Off site: Sandy beach across the road. Restaurants within a short distance. Marina di Ravenna village 2 km. Fishing, sailing and boat launching 2 km. Riding 5 km. Golf 20 km.

Open: 24 April - 16 September.

Directions

Heading north from Ravenna, take the beach road from Punta Marina Terme towards Marina di Ravenna. The site is on the left, but not signed. Coming south from Marina di Ravenna, the site is well signed and is on the right.
GPS: 44.466414, 12.284989

Charges guide

Per unit incl. 2 persons	
and electricity	€ 19.50 - € 36.40
extra person	€ 4.70 - € 8.70
child (2-7 yrs)	€ 3.50 - € 5.60
dog	€ 2.40 - € 4.90
No credit cards.	

Montecreto
Campeggio Parco dei Castagni

Via del Parco 5, I-41025 Montecreto (Emilia-Romagna) T: 053 663 595. E: camping@parcodeicastagni.it
alanrogers.com/IT60980

This lovely little mountain site is well situated on the edge of a small village and is open all year round. It takes its name from the magnificent, centuries old chestnut trees. The owners here have completely cleared a former campsite and started afresh. The sanitary facilities are of top quality, the pool, bar and small restaurant are also very good. The pretty Swiss-style rental chalets and the pitches are on terraced ground and all 15 touring pitches have access to 3A electricity. The amenities here promise to make this site extremely popular with people looking for a quiet site with some dramatic scenery.

Facilities

The new, purpose built toilet block is heated, clean and provides very good facilities. Facilities for disabled visitors. Laundry with washing machines and dryers. Restaurant/bar (all year). Swimming pool (1/6-30/9). Play area. Bicycle hire. Barbecues are not permitted. Off site: Chairlift 50 m. Village with shops and restaurants 300 m. Fishing, golf and riding 6 km.

Open: All year.

Directions

Site is clearly signed from the centre of Montecreto which is near Sestola on the SS324. The site is best approached from Modena as the southern approach, from Pistioa or Lucca via Abetone, involves steep climbs and numerous hairpin bends, but the views are spectacular.
GPS: 44.24667, 10.71194

Charges guide

Per unit incl. 2 persons	
and electricity	€ 24.00 - € 29.00
extra person	€ 7.00 - € 8.00
child (0-12 yrs)	€ 5.00 - € 6.00
dog	€ 2.00

For latest campsite news, availability and prices visit
alanrogers.com

Montese

Camping Eco-chiocciola

Via Testa 80, Fraz. Maserno, I-41055 Montese (Emilia-Romagna) T: 059 980 065. E: info@ecochiocciola.com
alanrogers.com/IT66030

Tucked away in the Apennines in a small village, this interesting little campsite has many surprises. Eco-chiocciola (named after the snail wearing his house on his back) is being developed by the owner Ottavio Mazzanti as a place to enjoy the natural geographic, geological, botanical and zoological features of the area. Comforts such as the swimming pool are designed to offer relaxation when not exploring. The 40 small touring pitches, all with 6A electrical connections, are on level or gently sloping ground with some terraces, many enjoying superb views. This is a peaceful site with a distinctly rustic feel for people who enjoy natural settings. It is best suited to tent campers and small motorcaravans.

Facilities

Two refurbished sanitary blocks have some British style WCs and hot showers (a reader reports they do not always work well in high season). Solar panels have been installed. Facilities for disabled campers. Washing machine. Motorcaravan services. Restaurant. Bar. Large multipurpose room for entertainment. Swimming pool open afternoons and weekend mornings (23/6-3/9). Tennis and volleyball area as well as a tree house. Bicycle hire. Torches necessary. Off site: No shop on the site but the village is 300 m. Local bus stop in village. Riding 3 km. Hotel Belvedere for gastronomic meals. Riding trails, guided tours and mountain biking.

Open: 4 April - 2 December, 19 December - 6 January.

Directions

From the A1 take Modena South exit through Vignola, Montese, Sesta la Fanano, to Maserno di Montese. Site is 200 m. from the village, well signed. GPS: 44.25575, 10.93274

Charges guide

Per unit incl. 2 persons	
and electricity	€ 23.00 - € 39.00
extra person	€ 5.00 - € 8.00
child (2-8 yrs)	€ 4.00 - € 6.00
dog	€ 3.00 - € 5.00

Show this guide and stay for 3 days, pay for 2. Also 7 days for 4 (low season).

Pinarella di Cervia

Camping Adriatico

Via Pinarella 90, I-48015 Pinarella di Cervia (Emilia-Romagna) T: 054 471 537. E: info@campingadriatico.net
alanrogers.com/IT66220

Adriatico, on the Italian Riviera is a busy seaside type of site popular with the Italians. English is spoken and all facilities are clean and well kept. As you would expect, there is occasional noise from the local resort (nearest disco is 200 m), and on the western side you will be serenaded by the voluble frogs in the adjacent allotment. On flat ground, the 210 touring pitches vary in size and are well shaded, but have lots of room to manoeuvre. Some pitches extend over 100 sq.m. The self-service restaurant and bar complex is close to the entrance, as are the supervised pools.

Facilities

Four well kept sanitary blocks, two large two small, have some British style WCs, individual washbasins with cold water and free hot showers. One hot tap in washing areas. Baby rooms. Facilities for disabled campers. Washing machines and a dryer. TV in bar. Small shop. Restaurant/bar, snack bar and takeaway. Swimming pool (15/5-13/9; charged). Bicycle hire. Market. Play area. Excursions and tourist literature. WiFi (charged). Off site: Fishing, boat launching and bicycle hire within 1 km. Riding 3 km. Golf 4 km.

Open: 5 April - 13 September.

Directions

From A14 take Cesena or Ravenna exit and head for Cervia on SS16. Site is south of Cervia, well signed. Drive along the sea front and signs are between the 167/169 markers. GPS: 44.24763, 12.35910

Charges guide

Per unit incl. 2 persons	
and electricity	€ 21.00 - € 34.80
extra person	€ 5.80 - € 9.50
child (2-8 yrs)	€ 3.70 - € 6.30
dog	€ 3.70 - € 6.00

Camping Cheques accepted.

FREE Alan Rogers Travel Card
Extra benefits and savings - see page 10

Punta Marina Terme

Adriano Camping Village

Via dei Campeggi 7, I-48100 Punta Marina Terme (Emília-Romagna) T: 054 443 7230.
E: info@adrianocampingvillage.com **alanrogers.com/IT60620**

Adriano has to be one of the very best campsites in a region renowned for its sightseeing and exploring opportunities. Even so, there is so much to see and do on site that it would be quite believable if visitors remained on site for the whole duration of their holiday. There are 370 touring pitches, some fully serviced, and most shaded by the tall pines. The superb toilet facilities are well maintained and easily accessed, and include wet rooms for disabled visitors. There are swimming pools, a sailing centre, bar, restaurants, shops, minigolf, an amusement arcade, bicycle hire and many sports facilities.

Facilities	Directions
Two first class toilet blocks are fully equipped, one heated with British and Turkish style toilets. Each has facilities for disabled visitors. Drinks and snacks machines. Shop. Bar. Restaurant and takeaway. Swimming pools. Sailing. Sports facilities. Bicycle hire. Amusements. WiFi over part of site (charged). Torches and long EHU leads may be useful. Off site: Close by are the monuments of Ravenna, the Mirabilandia Park and the Po Delta Regional Park. Beach 500 m. Fishing 1 km. Golf and riding 4 km.	Site is well signed from autostrada A14 (toll bridge). GPS: 44.43361, 12.29722

Charges guide

Per unit incl. 2 persons	
and electricity	€ 22.00 - € 50.00
extra person	€ 6.50 - € 12.50
child (4-10 yrs)	free - € 10.50
dog	€ 3.00 - € 7.00

Camping Cheques accepted.

Open: 19 April - 16 September.

Riccione

Camping Alberello

Viale Torino 80, I-47838 Riccione (Emília-Romagna) T: 054 161 5402. E: direzione@alberello.it
alanrogers.com/IT60640

Camping Alberello is a busy holiday site on the Adriatic coast with direct access to the beach via a short underpass below the promenade. The beach is wide with fine sand sloping gently into the sea. The friendly owners of Alberello have designed it with campers in the centre and sports facilities plus entertainment to the rear. The bar, restaurant and reception are at the front. This ensures that campers have the pitches with least road and rail noise. The 100 level, grass pitches are small and well shaded with tarmac access roads and regular water points.

Facilities	Directions
Three traditional toilet blocks are kept very clean. British and Turkish style WCs. Facilities for disabled visitors. Washing machines. Bazaar. Supermarket. Bar, large restaurant with terrace. Pizzeria. TV room. Play area. Limited entertainment programme in season. Miniclub. Watersports. ATM. Free WiFi over site. Dogs are not accepted. Torches useful. Off site: Boat launching 4 km.	Site is southeast of Rimini. From A14 take Riccione exit and follow S16 towards town. Site is well signed and is on the beach road. GPS: 43.98622, 12.68753

Charges guide

Per unit incl. 2 persons	
and electricity	€ 22.30 - € 42.10
extra person	€ 4.65 - € 10.40
child (3-8 yrs)	€ 3.80 - € 8.10

Open: 5 April - 24 September.

Riccione

Camping Riccione

Via Marsala, I-47838 Riccione (Emília-Romagna) T: 054 169 0160. E: info@campingriccione.it
alanrogers.com/IT66200

Situated on the Adriatic coast, 400 metres from the beach, Camping Riccione is a bustling, vibrant campsite with a distinct Italian flavour and would appeal to families with children. The 417 touring pitches are of varying sizes, almost all have shade and 100 are provided with water and drainage. The owner, Luigi Gobbi, and his friendly staff welcome their guests with genuine enthusiasm and many visitors return here year after year. Although there is some road and rail noise, the quality of this site, its services and local attractions make a visit well worthwhile.

Facilities	Directions
Five excellent toilet blocks with mostly British style WCs. Three wet rooms for disabled visitors. Facilities for children and babies. Washing machines. Motorcaravan service point. Supermarket. Two lively bars with TV. Restaurant and pizzeria with terrace. Pool complex. Play areas. Games room. Entertainment in season. Miniclub. Tennis. Five-a-side. Bicycle hire. WiFi over site (first hour free). ATM. Dogs are not accepted in high season. Communal barbecues provided. Off site: Beach 400 m. Fishing 3 km.	Site is in the town of Riccione, south of Rimini. From A14 take road to Riccione and then S16 southeast to Riccione. Site is well signed in the town. GPS: 43.98528, 12.67861

Charges guide

Per unit incl. 2 persons	
and electricity	€ 24.10 - € 62.90
extra person	€ 4.90 - € 10.20
child (3-12 yrs)	€ 4.10 - € 8.10

Open: 5 April - 23 September.

For latest campsite news, availability and prices visit
alanrogers.com

Savignano Mare

Camping Villaggio Rubicone

Via Matrice Destra 1, I-47039 Savignano Mare (Emília-Romagna) T: 054 134 6377.
E: info@campingrubicone.com **alanrogers.com/IT66240**

This is a sophisticated, professionally run site where the friendly owners, Sandra and Paolo Grotto, are keen to fulfil your every need. Rubicone covers over 30 acres of thoughtfully landscaped, level ground by the sea. There is an amazing array of amenities on offer. The 457 touring pitches vary in size (up to 100 sq.m) and are arranged in back-to-back, double rows, most with some shade. In some areas the central pitches are a little tight for manoeuvring larger units. All the pitches are kept very neat with hedges and all have electricity, 160 with water and drainage and 20 with private sanitary facilities.

Facilities	Directions
Modern heated toilet blocks provide showers, washbasins (half in private cabins), mainly British style toilets, baby rooms and two excellent units for disabled visitors. Washing machines. Motorcaravan services. Shop and bars (all season). Restaurant and snack bar (26/5-9/9). Pizzeria. Swimming pools (caps mandatory). Games room with Internet access. Golf (lessons available). Tennis. Solarium. Jacuzzi. Beach with lifeguard. Fishing. Sailing and windsurfing schools. Dogs are not accepted. Bicycle hire. WiFi (charged). Off site: Riding 2 km. Golf 15 km.	Site is 12 km. northwest of Rimini. From Bologna (autostrada A14) take exit for Rimini Nord. Continue on SS16 Adriatica towards Ravenna, then exit for Savignano Mare. Straight on at roundabout to San Mauro Mare. Left immediately after railway. At end of street turn right to site. GPS: 44.16475, 12.441117

Open: 23 May - 16 September.

Charges guide

Per unit incl. 2 persons and electricity	€ 23.20 - € 43.20
extra person	€ 5.30 - € 10.60

No credit cards.

Tabiano di Salsomaggiore Terme

Camping Arizona

Via Tabiano 42/A, I-43039 Tabiano di Salsomaggiore Terme (Emília-Romagna) T: 052 456 5648.
E: info@camping-arizona.it **alanrogers.com/IT60900**

Tabiano and Salsomaggiore Terme are thermal springs dating back to the Roman era and the beneficial waters have given rise to attractive inland resort towns. The focus on water is continued within this family run site by a complex of four large pools, long water slides, a jacuzzi and play area, all set in open landscaped grounds with superb views (open to the public). Camping Arizona is an expanding green site set on steep slopes and is 500 m. from the pretty town of Tabiano. The 300 level pitches with electricity (3A generated on site) vary from 50-90 sq.m. Those on terraces enjoy shade from mature trees, others have no shade. Cars must be parked in the large adjacent car park in shade, under the solar panel array and trolleys are provided. Sporting facilities include the water park area, tennis, volleyball and basketball courts and a five-a-side football pitch on synthetic grass. Younger children will be entertained by the large, supervised play centre and other indoor and outdoor games.

Facilities	Directions
Sanitary facilities in two new blocks provide modern facilities including those for disabled visitors. Laundry facilities. Small well stocked shop. Restaurant/bar with patio. Swimming pools, slides and jacuzzi (18/5-15/9, also open to the public but free for campers). Tennis. Boules. Large play centre. Mountain bike hire. WiFi (charged). Off site: Restaurant outside gate. Riding 2 km. Fishing 4 km. Golf 6 km. Fidenza shopping village 8 km.	From autostrada A1 take exit for Fidenza and follow signs for Tabiano. The site is on left 500 m. after Tabiano town centre. GPS: 44.80621, 10.0098

Open: 1 April - 15 October.

Charges guide

Per unit incl. 2 persons and electricity	€ 20.00 - € 32.00
extra person	€ 6.00 - € 9.00

No credit cards.

Been to any good campsites lately?
We have

You'll find them here...

The UK's market leading independent
guides to the best campsites

Also available on iPad **alanrogers.com/digital**

Tuscany probably represents the most commonly perceived image of Italy, with its classic rolling green countryside, lush vineyards and olive groves with a backdrop of medieval hilltowns and historical cities, where Renaissance art and beautiful churches abound.

TUSCANY COMPRISES THE FOLLOWING PROVINCES: AREZZO, FLORENCE, GROSSETO, LIVORNO, LUCCA, MASSA CARRARA, PISA, PISTOIA, PRATO AND SIENA

One of the most beautiful cities in Italy, much of Florence was rebuilt during the Renaissance, although there are parts which still retain a distinctly medieval feel. The city boasts a wealth of historical and cultural sights, including the Cathedral, the Baptistry, the Campanile, and the church of Santa Croce, to name but a few. It is also home to the Uffizi Gallery, which holds Italy's greatest art collection. Siena is another popular draw. At the heart of the city is the Piazza del Campo, one of the loveliest Italian squares, which plays host to the famous Palio, a bareback horse race which takes place twice a year in summer. Overlooking the piazza is the Gothic town hall of Palazzo Pubblico and bell tower, which is the second highest medieval tower ever built in Italy. Elsewhere in Tuscany, the medieval hilltown of San Gimignano is famed for its thirteen towers, built during the 12th and 13th centuries, which dominate the landscape. Lucca's old town is set inside a ring of Renaissance walls fronted by gardens. Another medieval hill town, Monteriggioni also has beautifully preserved walls, while Volterra is dramatically sited on a high plateau, which offers fine views over the surrounding hills. And Pisa with its famous leaning tower needs no introduction.

Places of interest

Alpi Apuan Nature Park: protected area with hiking trails through wooded valleys.

Arezzo: 13th-century San Francesco church houses famous frescoes by Piero della Francesca.

Bagni di Lucca: spa town.

Cortono: oldest hilltown in Tuscany with maze of old streets and medieval buildings.

Elba: largest island off Tuscan coast with white sandy beaches and woodlands, good for walking.

Fiesole: idyllic hilltop town offering superb views of Florence.

Viareggio: coastal town boasting Art Nouveau architecture.

Vinci: birthplace of Leonardo da Vinci, with a museum celebrating his works.

Cuisine of the region

Soups are very popular, particularly *ribollita* (stew of vegetables, beans and chunks of bread) and the best place to try *cacciucco* (spiced fish and seafood soup) is in Livorno, the town of its birth. Meat is often grilled and kept plain. Local cheeses include *pecorino*, made with sheep's milk, and *marzolino* from the Chianti region, which is also renowned for producing some of the best wines in Italy. Tuscan desserts include *panforte* (a dense cake full of nuts and fruit) and *cantuccini* (hard almond-flavoured biscuits), which are often served together with Vinsato, a traditional dessert wine.

Bistecca alla Fiorentina: rare chargrilled steak.

Pollo alla diavola: marinated chicken, grilled with herbs.

Scottiglia di Cinghiale: wild boar chops.

Torta di Riso: rice cake with fruit.

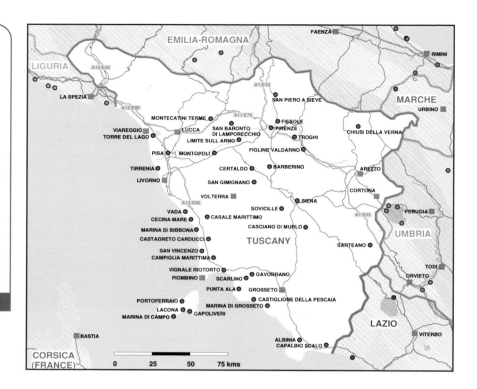

Albinia
Camping International Argentario

Localitá Torre Saline, I-58010 Albinia (Tuscany) T: 056 487 0302. E: info@argentariocampingvillage.com

alanrogers.com/IT66710

Argentario is split into three areas. One is a huge, brick built apartment and bungalow complex; the second is a large, flat, shaded area for motorcaravans and large caravans (4-6A electricity); the third is a separate shaded beach camping area with direct access to the dark sand. The 800 pitches and additional accommodation share facilities, so they can be very busy in high season and involve some walking. The infrastructure is fairly new (2010), and is elegantly designed. There is organised entertainment daily, with something for everyone. Some campers may find the long walks trying, especially as the older style facilities are tired and stressed during peak periods. A traditional restaurant and pizzeria is remote from the touring section and has no views. The beach of dark sand has attractive views across to the mountains. We see this site more for short stays than extended holidays and as unsuitable for disabled visitors.

Facilities

Three mature blocks have mostly Turkish style toilets, a few cramped showers with hot water and cold water at the sinks (showers are very busy at peak periods). Facilities for disabled campers but the sand surface and remoteness of some facilities are unsuitable. Washing machines. Motorcaravan service point. Shop. Restaurant, bar and takeaway. Swimming pools. Tennis. Boat hire. Minigolf. ATM. Free WiFi. Cars are parked in a separate car park in high season. Torches very useful. Dogs are not accepted. Off site: Bar and restaurant on the beach. Boat launching and riding 1 km. Golf 20 km.

Open: 1 April - 30 September.

Directions

Site is south of Grosseto, off the SS1 at the 150 km. mark, signed Porto San Stefano. Ignore the first 'combined' campsite sign and proceed 300 m. to the main entrance. GPS: 42.49623, 11.19413

Charges guide

Per unit incl. 2 persons	
and electricity	€ 24.00 - € 44.00
extra person	€ 8.00 - € 14.20
child (1-6 yrs)	€ 4.00 - € 7.00

For latest campsite news, availability and prices visit

alanrogers.com

Albinia
Camping Marina Chiara
SS Aurelia km. 153, I-58010 Albinia (Tuscany) T: 0564 870304. E: info@marinachiara.it
alanrogers.com/IT66087

Marina Chiara is alongside and twinned with Camping Voltoncino (IT66800) and all facilities are shared. This is a traditional Italian beach site with pitches mainly positioned under a cool canopy of pine trees. There are 133 flat pitches with 3A electricity, of a variety of sizes. They are close to the sea but none have beach views. The bar/restaurant/pizzeria and an attached shop are new (2012) and looked very smart when we visited. They overlook a grassy entertainment area. The combination of amenities at the two sites gives a very large choice of activities and services. The beach is of fine dark sand and covers the length of the two campsites.

Facilities	Directions
Two well positioned sanitary blocks provide some cabins with shower, toilet (mixed styles) and washbasins. Showers are of a very high standard (on payment by token). Cold water only at washbasins, sinks and for laundry. Rooms for children. Facilities for disabled campers. Washing machines. Well stocked shop. Bar and restaurant/pizzeria. Entertainment area. Amenities at the sister site. WiFi over part of site (charged).	Site is south of Grossetto, northeast of Ortobello. From the SS1 (Aurelia) leave at the 153 km. marker towards Albinia. Site is well signed from here and is on a slip road amongst several other sites. GPS: 42.52458, 11.18909

Open: 1 April - 30 September.

Charges guide

Per unit incl. 2 persons and electricity	€ 24.00 - € 37.00
extra person	€ 7.00 - € 11.00

Albinia
Camping Voltoncino
SS1 Aurelia km. 153, I-58010 Albinia (Tuscany) T: 056 487 0158. E: info@voltoncino.it
alanrogers.com/IT66800

Voltoncino has been formally combined with the site next door, Marina Chiara, and now has a long beach of soft, grey sand, and a wide choice of high grade restaurants, sport and entertainment. Voltoncino has 284 flat, shaded pitches, all with 3A electricity, while the area adjacent has 133. The sites are very popular with Italian visitors escaping the heat of Rome. Some motorcaravan pitches are set outside the canopy of pines and there is some traffic noise.

Facilities	Directions
Voltoncino has two modern, clean toilet blocks at each end of the site, with mainly British style WCs, lovely family rooms for children and a bright baby room. Showers are pushbutton (on payment). Facilities for disabled visitors. Washing machines. Motorcaravan services. Shop. Restaurant, pizzeria and bar. Play area. Tennis. Shared entertainment programme. Miniclub (1-8 yrs). Fishing. Barbecues only allowed on communal area. Internet and WiFi (charged). Dogs are not accepted.	Site is south of Grosseto, northeast of Ortobello. From the SS1 (Aurelia) leave at the 153 km. marker towards Albinia. Site is well signed from here. GPS: 42.51666, 11.18333

Open: 1 April - 20 September.

Charges guide

Per unit incl. 2 persons and electricity	€ 19.00 - € 37.00
extra person	€ 7.00 - € 11.00
child (1-8 yrs)	€ 4.00 - € 5.00

Barberino
Camping Semifonte
Via Ugo Foscolo 4, I-50021 Barberino (Tuscany) T: 055 807 5454. E: semifonte@semifonte.it
alanrogers.com/IT66630

Barberino lies in the heart of Tuscany between Florence and Siena. It is an area rich in history and known for that special Italian wine, Chianti. Camping Semifonte is a small, uncomplicated site with fine views over the surrounding, vine smothered hills, but with limited facilities. The 60 shaded pitches, all with 4/6A electricity, are on steep terraces. Some are small and tight for manoeuvring. Each terrace has a tap for water. There is a very small shop selling basics. This site is difficult for disabled campers and infirm visitors. The site facilities are all at the bottom of the site.

Facilities	Directions
Two small sanitary blocks have a mixture of British and Turkish toilets, showers and washbasins. Motorcaravan service point. Shop selling basics, plus local oil and wines. Swimming pools. Supported paddling pool for children with no safety fence – next to small play area. WiFi (charged). Off site: Regular bus route to/from Florence and Siena. Restaurant 500 m. Bicycle hire 500 m. Riding 1 km. Golf 15 km. Trekking.	From Florence-Siena autostrada take Tavarnelle exit to Barberino Val Elsa. Take first left on entering village and site is well signed, 500 m. at end of cul-de-sac. Park outside to check in. GPS: 43.54655, 11.17852

Open: Easter - 10 October.

Charges guide

Per unit incl. 2 persons and electricity	€ 20.00 - € 30.00
extra person	€ 7.50 - € 8.50

FREE Alan Rogers Travel Card
Extra benefits and savings - see page 10

Campiglia Marittima
Blucamp
Via Tuttiventi, 18, I-57021 Campiglia Marittima (Tuscany) T: 056 583 8553. E: info@blucamp.it
alanrogers.com/IT66410

Blucamp is an attractive site in a tranquil setting with fabulous views, near the pretty village of Campiglia Marittima. The islands of Elba and Capraia can be sighted whilst checking in at the reception block. The 88 touring pitches (50-80 sq.m) are terraced, all have 4A electricity (14 are fully serviced) and young trees provide some shade. One area is set aside for tents only and cars are parked off the pitches in numbered bays. This is a very peaceful site with attentive owners and would suit those who prefer not to holiday on the more lively and larger coastal sites.

Facilities

Three toilet blocks have British and Turkish style WCs and free hot showers. Six private sanitary units on pitches for hire. Washing machine. Small friendly restaurant/bar with a pretty terrace is run by a separate family and offers good Tuscan food. Bread and milk available daily. Attractive small swimming pool. Internet point and WiFi. Torches required in some areas. Off site: Bus 200 m. Supermarket 400 m. Riding 2 km. Bicycle hire 5 km. Fishing 8 km.

Open: 18 May - 8 September.

Directions

Site is northeast of Piombino. Take exit for San Vincenzo Sud off the main S1 road (Livorno to Follonica). Follow signs for Campiglia Marittima then camping signs from town. Site is 1 km. from town. GPS: 43.0575, 10.6076

Charges 2013

Per unit incl. 2 persons and electricity	€ 23.65 - € 37.45
extra person	€ 6.65 - € 9.50

Capalbio Scalo
Camping Capalbio
Strada Litoranea del Chiarone, località Graticciaia, I-58010 Chiarone Scalo bei Capálbio (Tuscany)
T: 056 489 0101. E: mauro.ricci@ilcampeggiodicapalbio.it alanrogers.com/IT66810

Camping Capalbio is a simple coastal site with a wide grey sand beach and will appeal to those keen on 'back to nature' experiences. The 175 pitches set in the dunes are charmingly private with tall hedges, 3A electricity, and many have artificial shade. Some are alongside the beach and very secluded. The low key restaurant and bar have a fair choice of food and drinks at reasonable prices. Do not expect too much by way of entertainment here but you will get peace by the bucketful.

Facilities

Three blocks have basic but clean services, but only the central block has hot showers (tokens) and it is some distance from some pitches. Baby facilities in restaurant toilets. Motorcaravan services. Supermarket. Bar. Restaurant. Beach bar (high season). Takeaway food. Live musical entertainment in peak season. Direct access to beach. Basic play area. Tennis. Bicycle hire. WiFi in bar area (charged). Mobile homes and chalets for rent. Dogs are accepted. Off site: Riding 10 km. Capalbio 12 km. Lago di Burano Nature Reserve 4 km. Saturnia hot springs and thermal spa 30 km. Walking and cycle trails.

Open: 1 April - 22 September.

Directions

Head south from Livorno and Pisa on the SS1 (Via Aurelia). Shortly after passing the Lago di Burano, ignore sign to Capalbio to the left, but take the next road to the right (signed Chiarone Scalo). Site is well signed from here. GPS: 42.381027, 11.446606

Charges guide

Per unit incl. 2 persons and electricity	€ 24.00 - € 44.00
extra person	€ 8.00 - € 14.00

Capoliveri
Camping Lacona Pineta
Località Lacona, Capoliveri, I-57031 Isola d'Elba (Tuscany) T: 056 596 4322.
E: info@campinglaconapineta.com alanrogers.com/IT66860

Camping Lacona Pineta is a neat and very tidy site with an excellent large, heated swimming pool complex (2012). The 179 well shaded pitches (150 for touring units with 6A electricity) are well kept. The soft sand beach is just 50 m. away, so it is easy to stay cool here. The site has a great combined restaurant/pizzeria/snack bar and a pleasant bar with entertainment in high season. This would make a good base for exploring the natural beauty of this sub-tropical paradise or for a beach holiday relaxing by the turquoise bay. Cars are parked separately in designated areas. Dogs are accepted.

Facilities

Basic sanitary facilities have mainly Turkish style toilets and free hot water. Laundry with iron and ironing board. Well stocked shop. Bar, pizzeria and excellent restaurant. Large, heated swimming pool. Play area. Entertainment and activities for adults and children in high season. Diving school. Bicycle hire. Only charcoal barbecues provided by site are allowed. Infirmary. WiFi over site (charged).

Open: 1 April - 30 October.

Directions

From the port at Portoferraio follow the site signs. GPS: 42.75978, 10.3133

Charges guide

Per unit incl. 2 persons and electricity	€ 20.40 - € 58.80
extra person	€ 6.80 - € 14.90
child (3-10 yrs)	€ 4.20 - € 9.00
dog	free

For latest campsite news, availability and prices visit

alanrogers.com

Casale Marittimo
Camping Valle Gaia

Via Cecinese 87, I-56040 Casale Marittimo (Tuscany) T: 058 668 1236. E: info@vallegaia.it
alanrogers.com/IT66320

Valle Gaia is a delightful family site with a friendly, laid back atmosphere, which is in marked contrast to some of the busy sites on the coast. Just 9 km. from the sandy beaches at Cecina, this pretty site has two enticing pool complexes with a great 'lagoon' pool, both with children's pools and generous sunbathing terraces. The 196 pitches are of a reasonable size (80-120 sq.m), well shaded by pine or cypress trees and surrounded by oleanders. All have 6A electrical connections, 58 are fully serviced and sited on an elevated terrace with an excellent sanitary block. The bar and restaurant are both popular, the latter located in a converted farmhouse and specialising in reasonably priced local cuisine.

Facilities

Three toilet blocks of modern construction are maintained to a high standard with mainly British style toilets and provision for disabled visitors. Some washbasins in cubicles. Excellent facilities for children and baby bath. Washing machines. Bar. Restaurant. Pizzeria. Shop stocks a good range of provisions including local produce. Swimming pools. Tennis. Games room. Bicycle hire. Satellite TV. Internet access and WiFi. Daily entertainment. Only gas or electric barbecues are permitted.

Open: 1 week before Easter - 6 October.

Directions

From A12 take Rosignano Marittimo exit, follow SS1 signs towards Roma then take Cecina Centro exit and follow signs to Casale Marittimo. Site is clearly signed from here. GPS: 43.29999, 10.61664

Charges guide

Per unit incl. 2 persons and electricity	€ 16.40 - € 33.30
extra person	€ 4.45 - € 9.00
No credit cards.	

Casciano di Murlo
Camping le Soline

Via delle Soline 51, I-53016 Casciano di Murlo (Tuscany) T: 057 781 7410. E: camping@lesoline.it
alanrogers.com/IT66650

Le Soline is a country hillside site with wonderful views of the Tuscan hills from its steep slopes. Just 20 km. south of Siena and 1 km. from the village of Casciano, it has 80 neat pitches for large units and 60 for tents on seven terraces, all with electricity. Many trees including olive provide shade for the pitches, and most have views. There is a full entertainment programme in high season and some free guided tours of the area (includes a dip in the lake). The kind and attentive Broggini family spare no efforts in making your stay a pleasant memory and are extremely hard working to this end.

Facilities

A good quality, heated sanitary block is on the third terrace, providing mixed British and Turkish style WCs and showers on payment. Facilities for disabled campers. Motorcaravan services. Gas supplies. Laundry. Freezer. Restaurant. Pizzeria. Well stocked shop (15/3-15/10). Swimming pools (Easter-15/10). Whirlpool. Playground. Excursions (June-Aug). Donkey and pony rides for children. Barbecue area (not allowed on pitches). Free WiFi. Mobile homes and bungalows to rent.

Open: All year.

Directions

From Siena, turn off SS223 (Siena-Grosseto) left to Fontazzi (20 km) and keep right for Casciano, following signs. Alternatively, from Via Cassia SS2 turn at Lucignano d'Arbia for Murlo. GPS: 43.1552, 11.3323

Charges guide

Per unit incl. 2 persons and electricity	€ 25.00 - € 26.50
extra person	€ 8.00

Castagneto Carducci
Camping le Pianacce

Via Bolgherese, I-57022 Castagneto Carducci (Tuscany) T: 056 576 3667. E: info@campinglepianacce.it
alanrogers.com/IT66350

In a quiet situation in the Tuscan hills, six kilometres from the sea at Donoratico, this high quality site has an attractive medium sized pool, overlooked by a restaurant/bar terrace that also has commanding views over the area. The site is on steeply rising ground and has 101 shaded pitches for touring units, all with 3/6A electricity in tiered rows on fairly narrow terraces. Access to most is not easy because the limited space between the small dividing hedges and the high bank of the next terrace restricts manoeuvring so installation is sometimes made by the site's tractor.

Facilities

Three toilet blocks have British style WCs, washbasins with hot water and free hot showers. Baby room. Washing machines. Gas supplies. Motorcaravan services. Shop. Restaurant/bar/takeaway. Swimming pools with water games. Archery. Tennis. Minigolf. Bicycle hire. Playground. Entertainment in season. Barbecues on a communal area only. WiFi. Free bus to beach. Animals are not accepted.

Open: One week before Easter - 30 September.

Directions

Site is south of Livorno. Turn off main S1 just north of Donoratico in hamlet of Il Bambolo to Castagneto Carducci. After 3 km. turn left at signs to Bolgheri and site. GPS: 43.16589, 10.6149

Charges guide

Per person	€ 5.50 - € 11.00
child (0-10 yrs)	€ 4.00 - € 8.00
pitch incl. electricity	€ 9.00 - € 25.00

FREE Alan Rogers Travel Card
Extra benefits and savings - see page 10

Castiglione della Pescaia
Camping Maremma Sans Souci
I-58043 Castiglione della Pescaia (Tuscany) T: 056 493 3765. E: info@maremmasanssouci.it
alanrogers.com/IT66600

This delightful seaside site is owned and run by the Perduca family and sits in natural woodland on the coast road between Follonica and Grosseto. The minimum amount of undergrowth has been cleared to provide 370 individually marked and hedged, flat pitches for camping enthusiasts. This offers individual settings with considerable privacy. There are 6A electrical connections for all caravan and motorcaravan pitches and 40 have a satellite TV point. Some are small and cars may not remain with tents or caravans but must go to a shaded and secure car park near the entrance. There is a wide road for motorcaravans but other roads are mostly narrow and bordered by trees (this is a protected area, so they cannot fell them).

Facilities	Directions
Five small, very clean, older style toilet blocks are well situated around the site. Free showers, plus extras such as hairdryers, soap dispensers etc. Three blocks have private cabins each with WC, basin and shower. Separate facilities for disabled campers. Motorcaravan services. Laundry. Shop. Excellent restaurant. Bar with snacks. Bicycle hire. ATM. WiFi (charged). Torches required in some areas. Dogs are not accepted 16/6-31/8. Off site: Excursions organised to Elba and Rome.	Site is 2.5 km. northwest of Castiglione on road to Follonica on the S322. GPS: 42.77343, 10.84392

Open: 1 April - 31 October.

Charges guide

Per unit incl. 2 persons	
and electricity	€ 24.00 - € 43.00
extra person	€ 7.00 - € 13.00
child (3-5 yrs)	free - € 7.00

Camping Cheques accepted.

Castiglione della Pescaia
Camping Village Baia Azzurra
Le Rocchette, I-58043 Castiglione della Pescaia (Tuscany) T: 0039 0564 941092. E: info@baiaazzurra.it
alanrogers.com/IT66690

Encircled by hills, Baia Azzurra is a cool green site with lots of trees. There are 260 pitches with 170 average sized, grassy pitches for touring units. These are flat, shaded by tall trees and some have artificial shade. All have 3A electricity, and eight also have water and drainage. The focal point of the site is the new lagoon-shaped pool, restaurant and entertainment complex. The new pool has a pretty bridge feature, lots of loungers and also within the fenced complex is an entertainment area with a playground and small café. Once sited, cars are parked away from pitches.

Facilities	Directions
Three refurbished sanitary blocks offer a slightly confusing range of unisex facilities with British style toilets, plus units for disabled visitors in one block. Hot showers but otherwise the water is cold. Washing machines. New market/bazaar, bar and restaurant/pizzeria (all season). Swimming pools. Large play area. Bicycle hire. Evening entertainment and animation. Miniclub (high season). WiFi (charged). ATM. Off site: Beach 150 m. Riding 10 km.	From SS1 Livorno-Roma road take Grosseto exit on SS322. Follow SS322 north from Castiglione della Pescaia and turn left for Rocchette. Site is 3 km. on the right. GPS: 42.7778, 10.79392

Open: 28 March - 20 October.

Charges 2013

Per person	€ 7.50 - € 16.00
pitch	€ 10.00 - € 25.00

Camping Cheques accepted.

Castiglione della Pescaia
Camping Village Rocchette
SP62 delle Rocchette, I-58043 Castiglione della Pescaia (Tuscany) T: 056 494 1123.
E: booking@rocchette.com **alanrogers.com/IT66760**

Camping Village Rocchette can be found at the heart of the Maremma woods, 6 km. to the north of Castiglione della Pescaia. The well maintained site extends over 70,000 sq.m. of pinewood with a path leading to the sandy beach, just 300 m. away. Pitches are well shaded and of varying sizes, many with electrical connections. The site also offers 75 well equipped brick bungalows for rent. Good on-site amenities include a large swimming pool with spa baths and two pools for children, as well as a tennis court and sports field. This is a popular site in high season, when bookings are for a minimum of 15 days.

Facilities	Directions
Sanitary facilities include private cubicles and facilities for disabled visitors. Laundry facilities. Supermarket and other shops. Bar. Restaurant. Swimming pool with spa baths. Two children's pools. Tennis. Sports field. Play area. Bicycle hire. WiFi (charged). Entertainment and activity programme (2/6-31/8). Direct access to beach 300 m. Bungalows for rent. Off site: Shops and restaurants in Castiglione 6 km. Fishing and beach 300 m. Riding 10 km.	Approaching from the north, take the Follonica Nord exit from the E80/S1 superstrada and head south to Castiglione on the S322. Before Castiglione, turn right towards Roccamare and Rocchette. Site is well signed from here. GPS: 42.77926, 10.801234

Open: 23 March - 18 October.

Charges 2013

Per unit incl. 2 persons	
and electricity	€ 23.00 - € 44.00

Camping Cheques accepted.

Limite Sull'Arno
Camping Village San Giusto

Via Castra, 71, I-50050 Capraia e Limite (Tuscany) T: 055 871 2304. E: info@campingsangiusto.it
alanrogers.com/IT66075

Camping San Giusto is a friendly, family run site in an unspoilt, typically Tuscan setting within the Montalbano National Park. There are 100 terraced touring pitches, the lower ones with 6A electricity and well shaded. Some of these pitches have superb views over the Tuscan countryside, while almost all of the upper pitches enjoy spectacular views. Amenities include a restaurant specialising in wonderful Tuscan food cooked by the father of the family owners and a pleasant, small, well stocked shop which also sells delicious home-made cakes. San Giusto will suit those looking for the peace and quiet of a traditional campsite with reasonable rates in a natural setting. At busy times vehicles are parked in a large car park at the front of the site. This site is a good base for exploring Tuscany, especially by using the site's shuttle bus to the local station which has regular rail services to destinations throughout Tuscany. The beautiful small town of Vinci, best known as Leonardo's birthplace is 20 minutes away. Florence, the cradle of the Renaissance, is 30 minutes. A little further afield, Pisa and Volterra are also highly recommended. The Montalbano National Park has a great wealth of walking and mountain biking tracks, and the site's owners will be pleased to recommend routes.

Facilities

Four sanitary blocks provide a variety of services. Most toilets are Turkish style. The small upper block is new (2012). Washing machines. Bar and snack bar. Excellent restaurant. Shop. Swimming and paddling pools. Playground. Games room. WiFi (free). Communal barbecue area. Shuttle bus service. Mobile homes and chalets for rent. Off site: ATM 5 km. Bicycle hire 10 km. Walking and cycling. Florence, Siena, Vinci and Volterra.

Open: 15 March - 5 November.

Directions

From A1 Milan - Rome autostrada take Firenze exit, then the Firenze, Pisa, Livorno road towards Empoli and Pisa. Leave at Montelupo and head towards Limite sull'Arno and on to Castra. Site is signed on the left after Castra. GPS: 43.783251, 10.988329

Charges guide

Per unit incl. 2 persons and electricity	€ 22.50 - € 38.00
extra person	€ 7.00 - € 9.00

Via Castra 71 - 50050
Capraia e Limite (FI)
www.campingsangiusto.it
info@campingsangiusto.it
Tel. 055 8712304
Fax 0558711856
Cell. 3939091852 - 3939439646
GPS: 43° 46' 58.00" N
10° 59' 18.26" E

We offer our guests the following: bar, restaurant, mini-market, playgorund for children, sport camp, common kitchen and the newness of the year: two swimmingpools in the open. Bus to the railwaystation from where you can take the train to reach all important cities of Italy.

How to reach us:

> Leave the road at Florence Scandicci - freeway FI-PI-LI direction Pisa - leave the road at Montelupo Fiorentino and from there follow the indications for Capraia and Limite.
> Leave the road A11 Pisa airport- freeway FI-PI-LI direction Florence - leave the road at Empoli center and form there follow the indications for Capraia and Limite.

Marina di Bibbona
Camping Free Time

Via dei Cipressi, I-57020 Marina di Bibbona (Tuscany) T: 058 660 0934. E: info@freetimecamping.it
alanrogers.com/IT66330

Camping Free Time is 700 m. from the beach and 500 m. from the little resort of Marina di Bibbona. The site is attractively landscaped with numerous flowers, and trees provide welcome shade to most of the level grass pitches (80 sq.m) which have 10A electricity. Of the 111 pitches, 44 have their own thatched private facilities with toilet and shower, outside kitchen and patio. The bar and waiter service restaurant/pizzeria complex overlooks a lagoon style pool and paddling pool and offers a reasonably priced and varied menu. There is also a superb thatched open-air gym and sauna by the very large fishing lakes that are linked to the site.

Facilities

Modern toilet blocks are well maintained. Facilities for disabled visitors. Some pitches have private sanitary facilities (extra charge). Motorcaravan service point. Fishing. Play area. Lively entertainment programme in peak season. Sauna. Gym. Internet access and WiFi. Tourist information. Off site: Beach 700 m. Cecina 10 km.

Open: 24 April - 20 October.

Directions

Site is south of Livorno. From Livorno-Civitavecchia road (autostrada) take La California exit and follow signs to Marina di Bibbona. Site is well signed. GPS: 43.25235, 10.5309

Charges 2013

Per unit incl. 2 persons and electricity	€ 26.50 - € 53.00

Marina di Bibbona
Camping Il Gineprino
Via dei Platani 56a, I-57020 Marina di Bibbona (Tuscany) T: 058 660 0550. E: info@ilgineprino.it
alanrogers.com/IT66370

This is a pleasant part of Tuscany with many interesting places within visiting distance. Il Gineprino, a small, family run site is on the edge of Bibbona but not directly on the coast. Of the 194 pitches, 70 are for touring and are located across the beach access road. The friendly owner, Roberto, was an architect and designed the main part of the site where the facilities can be found. There is an unusually shaped pool and a small but pleasant restaurant with terrace, serving reasonable food.

Facilities

Two modern sanitary blocks have British and Turkish style WCs, washbasins and showers. Laundry. Facilities for disabled visitors. Motorcaravan services. Shop, restaurant with terrace. Swimming pool with paddling pool and aquagym. TV room. Bicycle hire. Some entertainment in high season. Excursions. Only small pets are accepted – contact owner. WiFi is planned. Off site: Bus 100 m. Beach and fishing 500 m. Riding 10 km.

Open: 1 April - 30 September.

Directions

Site is south of Livorno. Leave the SS1 coast road between La California and Marina di Bibbona. Follow signs to Marina di Bibbona where there are site signs. GPS: 43.236377, 10.535352

Charges guide

Per unit incl. 2 persons and electricity	€ 20.00 - € 34.00
extra person	€ 6.50 - € 11.50
No credit cards.	

Marina di Campo
Camping Ville degli Ulivi
Via della Foce 89, Marina di Campo, I-57034 Isola d'Elba (Tuscany) T: 056 597 6098. E: info@villedegliulivi.it
alanrogers.com/IT66680

Camping Ville degli Ulivi is an impressive site with many quality activities for families and a great atmosphere. In a pleasant setting amongst pines and olives, it has access through a rear gate to a pretty sandy bay with a safe beach and all manner of watersports. Of the 285 pitches, about 50 are available for touring units. There is a very large contingent of tour operators and some bungalow and apartment accommodation. The good quality touring pitches are of a reasonable size, flat and most have natural shade. All have 6A electricity. Cars are not allowed to stay on the site. There is some aircraft noise from a local airport. Watch for the extras.

Facilities

Toilet facilities are good with hot showers, baby rooms and facilities for disabled visitors. Laundry. Bar/restaurant. Pizzeria. Takeaway. Shop. Swimming pool. Play area. Bicycle and scooter hire. Diving centre. Multisports pitch. Amusement arcade. Entertainment (May-Sept). Aquagym, Miniclub. Excursions. Internet access. WiFi over part of site (charged). No charcoal barbecues. Off site: Local markets. Watersports on the beach. Village 1 km.

Open: 20 April - 20 October.

Directions

From Portoferraio ferry port follow signs for Procchio, then Marina di Campo. Before Marina di Campo village, turn left towards La Foce-Lacona. In 800 m. turn right to site. GPS: 42.7519, 10.24502

Charges guide

Per unit incl. 2 persons and electricity	€ 24.00 - € 52.00
extra person	€ 6.50 - € 15.00

Marina di Grosseto
Camping le Marze
Strada Provinciale 158, km. 30,200, I-58046 Marina di Grosseto (Tuscany) T: 056 435 501.
E: lemarze@boschettoholiday.it **alanrogers.com/IT66620**

This natural site within open woodland is 4 km. north of Marina di Grosseto and has 224 generously sized pitches for touring units. Some are separated by hedges, all have 3A electricity and many enjoy natural shade from mature pine trees. On sand and with easy access, there is a background noise of cicadas (crickets) from the lofty pines and squirrels entertain high above. A private beach is accessed via a walk across the main road and then through the pine woods. Bicycles are an asset and you could also enjoy a cycle ride to the town along a beach track. The beach is worth the long walk as it is the strongest feature here, being soft sand which shelves slowly.

Facilities

The four toilet blocks are of a good standard, with Turkish and some British style WCs. Limited facilities for disabled campers in two blocks, with baby facilities and private bathrooms for rent. Motorcaravan service point. Market and bazaar. Bar, restaurant, pizzeria and takeaway (15/5-15/9). Swimming pool (15/6-15/9). Aquarobics. Play areas. Entertainment in season, excursions and activities. Barbecue areas. Bicycle hire. WiFi (charged). Torches recommended. Cars parked away from pitches.

Open: 30 March - 3 October.

Directions

Site is on the road between Castiglione delle Pescaia and Marina di Grosseto, known as the SS322 or SP158 in places. Site is well signed 3 km. from Marina di Grosseto. GPS: 42.74523, 10.94805

Charges guide

Per unit incl. 2 persons and electricity	€ 20.15 - € 45.85
extra person	€ 4.80 - € 13.40
Camping Cheques accepted.	

For latest campsite news, availability and prices visit
alanrogers.com

Montecatini Terme

Camping Belsito

Via delle Vigne, localitá Vico, I-51016 Montecatini Terme (Tuscany) T: 057 267 373. E: info@campingbelsito.it
alanrogers.com/IT66010

The owners of this site wish it to be for families and thus the emphasis is on peace and tranquillity. Whilst the towns below are blisteringly hot, the cool breezes here do make it as the name says, Belsito – a beautiful place. There are now 200 pitches of varying size, all with electricity (6-8A) and some with shade. It is very much a touring site with no permanent occupants and only six bungalows for hire. There are 64 pitches with a private sanitary unit for hire on the pitch. The views are excellent from most pitches, and from an amazing new swimming pool on the upper terrace.

Facilities

Two sanitary blocks (one new) plus 64 private units for hire. Hot water is provided throughout. Facilities for disabled visitors. Washing machines. Good shop, bar/restaurant, snack bar with takeaway (all April-Sept). New swimming pool. Play area. Book exchange. Communal freezer and barbecue area. Satellite TV. WiFi throughout (charged). Off site: Bus 100 m. from gate to railway station. Collodi – Pinnocchio's town!

Open: 1 April - 30 September.

Directions

From A11 Firenze-Mare autostrada take exit for Montecatini Terme. Follow brown signs for site and take Montecatini Alto road (do not use sat nav as you may end up in a very narrow village street). Site is on the left in 3 km. GPS: 43.90480, 10.78783

Charges guide

Per unit incl. 2 persons and electricity	€ 22.50 - € 36.00
extra person	€ 6.00 - € 9.00

Montopoli

Camping Toscana Village

Via Fornoli 9, I-56020 Montopoli (Tuscany) T: 057 144 9032. E: info@toscanavillage.com
alanrogers.com/IT66610

This area was once a forest surrounding the attractive medieval Tuscan village of Montopoli. Toscana Village has been thoughtfully carved out of the hillside under mature pines and it is ideal for a sightseeing holiday in this central area. The 150 level pitches (some large) are on shaded terraces and are carefully maintained. Some pitches have full drainage facilities and water, most have 6A electricity. The amenities are centrally located at the top of the hill in a pleasant modern building. English is spoken by the helpful reception staff who also organise a programme of visits and events.

Facilities

Two modern toilet blocks have excellent facilities including British style toilets, hot water at all the stylish sinks, private cabins and two large en-suite cubicles which may be suitable for disabled campers. Washing machines and dryer. Motorcaravan services. Shop. Bread to order. Gas. Restaurant (limited menu, evenings only). Takeaway. Swimming pool. Play area. Organised activities. Torches useful. Off site: Montopoli village 1 km. Fishing 6 km. Golf and riding 7 km.

Open: All year.

Directions

From A12 (Genova-Florence) take Pisa Centro exit. Take F1,P1,L1 and then Montopoli exit. Follow signs to Montopoli village. Look for cemetery on right. Opposite is Via Masoria leading to Via Fornoli and site. Note: follow brown signs to site; ignore sat nav. GPS: 43.67611, 10.75277

Charges guide

Per unit incl. 2 persons and electricity	€ 25.50 - € 33.50

Camping Cheques accepted.

Pisa

Camping Torre Pendente

Viale delle Cascine 86, I-56122 Pisa (Tuscany) T: 050 561 704. E: info@campingtorrependente.com
alanrogers.com/IT66080

Torre Pendente is a most friendly site, well run by the Signorini family who speak good English and make everyone feel welcome. It is amazingly close to the famous leaning tower of Pisa and obviously its position means it is busy throughout the main season. It is a medium sized site, on level, grassy ground with some shade from trees and lots of artificial shade. There are 220 touring pitches, all with electricity. All site facilities are near the entrance including a most pleasant restaurant, swimming pool complex with pool bar and a large terrace.

Facilities

Three new toilet blocks are very clean and smart with British style toilets and good facilities for disabled campers. Private cabins for hire. Hot water at sinks. Washing machines. Motorcaravan services. Well stocked supermarket. Pleasant restaurant, bar and takeaway. Swimming pool with pool bar, paddling pool and spa. Playground. Boules. Entertainment in high season. WiFi. Accommodation. Off site: Bicycle hire. Bus 100 m.

Open: 1 April - 15 October.

Directions

From A12, exit at Pisa Nord and follow for 5 km. to Pisa. Do not take first sign to town centre. Site is well signed at a later left turn (Viale delle Cascine). GPS: 43.7252, 10.3819

Charges guide

Per person	€ 8.00 - € 9.50
child (3-10 yrs)	€ 4.50 - € 6.00
pitch	€ 10.00 - € 15.00

No credit cards.

Portoferraio
Camping Rosselba le Palme

Localitá Ottone 3, Portoferraio, I-57037 Isola d'Elba (Tuscany) T: 056 593 3101. E: info@rosselbalepalme.it
alanrogers.com/IT66880

Rosselba le Palme is a fabulous, large resort style campsite with a tropical feel, set beneath a towering medieval castle set on the cliff top. Of the 280 steeply terraced pitches, 150 are available for touring, all with electricity (1.5-3A). The large pool complex has slides, jacuzzi and a great new (2012) children's pool feature. There is also a terraced poolside bar and entertainment area here. The range of sporting facilities is diverse and children can enjoy the kids' club with its young explorers course. There is a superb restaurant specialising in fish dishes, with a terrace leading into the botanical gardens.

Facilities

Eight modern, attractive and clean toilet blocks are spread over the site, but the steep terrain may be difficult for those with mobility problems. Laundry with washing machines and ironing facilities. Supermarket. Restaurant, pizzeria, pool bar and café/bar. Large pool complex with swimming courses and aquarobics. Tennis with coaching. Volleyball. Archery. Five-a-side football. Basketball. Trampolines. Bicycle track. Bicycle and motorcycle rental. Secure car park. Botanical gardens. WiFi (charged).

Open: 21 April - 5 October.

Directions

From ferry at Portoferraio follow signs for Porto Azzurro to begin. Then turn left towards Bagnaia and follow campsite signs, on the right, just after a fork to the left. GPS: 42.80146, 10.36488

Charges guide

Per unit incl. 2 persons and electricity	€ 13.20 - € 50.40
extra person	€ 4.80 - € 15.00
child (3-8 yrs)	free - € 11.20

Portoferraio
Camping Scaglieri

Localitá Scaglieri, Portoferraio, I-57037 Isola d'Elba (Tuscany) T: 056 596 9940. E: info@campingscaglieri.it
alanrogers.com/IT66850

Camping Scaglieri is a small coastal site on a steep slope with a steep entrance and relatively high prices. A small pool is directly alongside reception at the top of the site, as is the restaurant and bar, all enjoying great views. The 55 touring pitches are of varying sizes, all on terraces with 3A electricity and views over the bay, but the slopes are interesting! Some pitches have shade from attractive trees. The campsite is part of a group with two hotels and the facilities there may be used by camping guests. Due to the steep slopes this site is not recommended for disabled or infirm campers, and there is a maximum van length of 7.5 m. This is a small neat site which may appeal to young campers.

Facilities

One central toilet block is kept very clean with good fittings. WCs are mostly British style. Baby room. Washing machines. Motorcaravan service point. Fridge hire. Bar, restaurant and takeaway. Gelateria and small shop. Swimming pool. Play areas. Entertainment programme in season. No barbecues allowed on pitches (communal area). Car hire. Torches very useful. Internet access. WiFi over site (charged). Off site: Golf and beach 200 m.

Open: 20 April - 21 October.

Directions

Site is west of Portoferraio on the coast. From Portoferraio ferry take the Procchio road. After 5 km. and on a hilltop turn right towards Biodola and Scaglieri. Site entrance is on the right after 2 km. GPS: 42.80349, 10.27072

Charges guide

Per unit incl. 2 persons and electricity	€ 30.00 - € 61.00
extra person	€ 7.50 - € 15.50

Punta Ala
Baia Verde International Camping

Via delle Collacchie, I-58040 Punta Ala (Tuscany) T: 056 492 2298. E: info@baiaverde.com
alanrogers.com/IT66740

Baia Verde is a large, mature, sprawling family site with direct access to a sandy private beach. The informally sited, level pitches are totally shaded by mature pines and vary considerably in size. The site boasts a good range of amenities, notably a very open shopping and restaurant complex. This is a lively site in peak season with an extensive entertainment programme including a beach gym, various sports tournaments and evening discos. There is plenty to do on the beach – pedaloes and canoes are available for hire, along with loungers and parasols – and there's plenty to see in the area.

Facilities

Nine mature but clean sanitary blocks provide a mixture of British and Turkish style toilets. Hairdresser. Laundry. Motorcaravan service point. Shopping centre. Bazaar. Bar/restaurant. Pizzeria with terraces. Takeaway. Picnic area. Beach bar. Play area. Games room. Bicycle hire. Boat and canoe hire. Evening entertainment (high season). Dogs are not accepted 20/6-31/8. WiFi (charged).

Open: 24 April - 13 October.

Directions

From the north, take E80 to Rosignano and join Via Aurelia (SS1) leaving at Follonica Sud exit. Follow signs to Punta Ala and site is well signed from here. GPS: 42.83446, 10.77988

Charges guide

Per unit incl. 2 persons and electricity	€ 21.00 - € 48.50
No credit cards.	

Punta Ala
PuntAla Camping Resort

Localitá Punta Ala, Castiglione della Pescala, I-58043 Punta Ala (Tuscany) T: 056 492 2294.
E: info@campingpuntala.it **alanrogers.com/IT66730**

This very large site was established some 35 years ago but almost all of the infrastructure has been rebuilt recently (2012) and is superb. The touring unit/tent pitches are shaded, secluded and vary tremendously in size. They are on flat sand (with 3/6A electricity, 67 also have water and drainage) There is something for everyone here, with a very busy entertainment programme in high season. The beach is safe and of soft sand, with easy access for disabled campers. A lively, green and friendly site which will suit families.

Facilities

Eight blocks are modern, and the ninth requires updating. Facilities are clean with private cabins to hire. Excellent units for disabled campers. Washing machines and dryer. Motorcaravan services. Bars, restaurants and takeaway. Shop. Bazaar. Entertainment. Play areas. Free WiFi over site. Bicycle hire. Tennis. Beach with watersports. ATM. Communal barbecue areas – no barbecues allowed on pitches. Excursions. Dogs are not accepted. Torches essential. Off site: Bus service 800 m. from the gate. Golf and riding 3 km. Town 6 km.

Open: Easter - 15 October.

Directions

From E80/S1/Aurelia superstrada take Follonica Nord exit onto S322 for Punta Ala and Castiglione della Pescaia. Watch for district of Pian d'Alma on maps. Site is now signed to the right along a narrow road. GPS: 42.84143, 10.7796

Charges guide

Per unit incl. 2 persons and electricity	€ 31.50 - € 67.60
extra person	€ 1.70 - € 4.00
child (2-17 yrs)	€ 1.10 - € 4.00

San Baronto di Lamporecchio
Camping Barco Reale

Via Nardini 11, I-51035 San Baronto di Lamporecchio (Tuscany) T: 057 388 332. E: info@barcoreale.com
alanrogers.com/IT66000

Just forty minutes from Florence and an hour from Pisa, this site is beautifully situated high in the Tuscan hills close to the fascinating town of Pistoia. Part of an old walled estate, there are impressive views of the surrounding countryside. It is a quiet site of 15 hectares and the 250 terraced pitches enjoy shade from mature pines and oaks. Some pitches are huge with great views and others are very private. Most are for touring units, although some have difficult access (the site provides tractor assistance). All 187 touring pitches have electricity and 40 are fully serviced. A member of Leading Campings group.

Facilities

Three modern sanitary blocks are well positioned and kept very clean. Good facilities for disabled visitors (dedicated pitches nearby). Baby room. Laundry facilities. Fridge hire. Motorcaravan services. Dog shower. Shop. Restaurant. Bar. Supervised swimming pools (10.00-18.00, caps required). Ice cream shop. Playgrounds. Bowls. Bicycle hire. Internet point. WiFi over part of site. Disco. Entertainment. Cooking lessons for Tuscan style food. Excursions. Charcoal barbecues not permitted. Off site: Village and shops 1 km. Markets. Fishing 8 km. Golf 15 km.

Open: 31 March - 28 September.

Directions

From Pistoia take Vinci-Empoli-Lamporecchio signs to San Baronto. From Empoli signs to Vinci and San Baronto. Final approach involves a sharp bend and a steep slope. GPS: 43.84190, 10.91130

Charges 2013

Per unit incl. 2 persons and electricity	€ 25.10 - € 42.00
extra person	€ 7.30 - € 12.50
child (3-11 yrs)	€ 4.00 - € 7.70
dog	€ 2.00 - € 3.50

Discounts for longer stays in low season.

San Gimignano
Camping Boschetto di Piemma
Localitá Santa Lucia 38/C, I-53037 San Gimignano (Tuscany) T: 057 790 7134. E: info@boschettodipiemma.it
alanrogers.com/IT66270

The medieval Manhattan of San Gimignano is one of Tuscany's most popular sites and this new campsite lies just 2 km. from the town. There are 100 small pitches here, all with 6A electricity and some with shade from mature trees. The site is in woodland surrounded by olive groves and vineyards and has been developed with much care for the environment, using rain water for irrigation and with many solar panels. Located with a sports centre, the site has use of many of the sporting amenities (tennis carries an extra charge). The swimming pool alongside the site is shared with the public, but site security is good.

Facilities

Excellent sanitary block includes facilities for disabled visitors. Cool room with fridge and freezer for campers. Shop (specialising in local produce), restaurant/pizzeria and bar (all 1/4-30/10). Heated outdoor swimming pool (1/6-15/9, small charge). Tennis (charged, lessons available). Sports centre. Playground. Entertainment and activity programme in high season. WiFi (charged). Dogs accepted with lead and muzzle. Apartments for rent. Off site: San Gimignano 2 km. Bus service to town. Cycle and walking trails. Bicycle hire 2 km. Riding 10 km.

Open: 15 March - 31 October.

Directions

From the Florence-Siena superstrada take exit for Poggibonsi Nord and follow signs to San Gimignano. At first roundabout follow signs to Volterra, then take first road to the left, signed Santa Lucia. Site is well signed close to the sports area.
GPS: 43.4533, 11.0536

Charges guide

Per unit incl. 2 persons and electricity	€ 21.00 - € 34.00
extra person	€ 6.70 - € 11.00

San Piero a Sieve
Camping Mugello Verde
Via Massorondinaio 39, I-50037 San Piero a Sieve (Tuscany) T: 055 848 511.
E: mugelloverde@florencecamping.com **alanrogers.com/IT66050**

Mugello Verde is a country hillside site with 200 good sized pitches for motorcaravans and caravans, and smaller pitches for tents. All have 6A electricity. Some are on flat ground, others are on steep terraces where mature trees provide shade. The big attraction here is the site's proximity to the international Mugello racing track, just 5 km. away. It is used by Ferrari for practice runs and is also an international car and motorcycling track. The site has a pleasant, open feel and the accommodation for hire does not impinge on the touring area.

Facilities

Two toilet blocks are well positioned and the facilities are clean with mixed British and Turkish style WCs. Hot water throughout. Facilities for disabled visitors. Laundry facilities. Shop. Restaurant/bar and pizzeria (all season). Swimming pool (1/6-18/9; no paddling pool). Play area. Tennis. WiFi (charged). Off site: Mugello racing track 5 km. Riding, golf, bicycle hire and fishing all within 5 km.

Open: Easter - 31 October.

Directions

From A1 autostrada take Barberino del Mugello exit and follow SS65 towards San Piero a Sieve and before town, turn left and just past Tamoil garage turn right to site. GPS: 43.96148, 11.31030

Charges guide

Per unit incl. 2 persons and electricity	€ 19.00 - € 32.00
extra person	€ 7.50 - € 9.50

San Vincenzo
Camping Park Albatros
Pineta di Torre Nuova, I-57027 San Vincenzo (Tuscany) T: 056 570 1018. E: parkalbatros@ecvacanze.it
alanrogers.com/IT66380

Camping Albatros is situated on the historic Costa Degli Etruschi where natural parks abound. There is a theme of circles throughout the site in the form of round buildings and the placing of mobile homes in curves. Of the 1000 pitches, the 300 for touring are in a separate area on flat ground. All have water, drainage, 10A electricity and shade. The pools at this ultra modern site are outstanding and the facilities are superb. A great site for family holidays.

Facilities

Two superb toilet blocks and brilliant room for children. All WCs are British style and the showers are really good, as are facilities for disabled visitors. Washing machines. Huge air-conditioned supermarket. Bazaar. Lagoon complex with five amazing pools (one covered and heated). Central area includes two bars, two restaurants and pizzeria with large terrace. Takeaway. Daily entertainment programme in season. Disco. Miniclub (4-12 yrs). Play areas. Diving organised. Bicycle hire. No barbecues allowed. Internet points and WiFi. Train around site in high season.

Open: 16 April - 25 October.

Directions

Site is northwest of Grosseto and south of Livorno on the coast. From the SS1 take San Vincenzo exit. Site is well signed in San Vincenzo and is 6 km. south of village along the beach road.
GPS: 43.04972, 10.55861

Charges guide

Per unit incl. 2 persons and electricity	€ 26.50 - € 50.70
extra person	€ 7.50 - € 14.90
child (2-12 yrs)	free - € 11.90

For latest campsite news, availability and prices visit
alanrogers.com

Sarteano
Parco delle Piscine

Via del Bagno Santo 29, I-53047 Sarteano (Tuscany) T: 057 826 971. E: info@parcodellepiscine.it
alanrogers.com/IT66450

Sarteano is an ancient spa town, and this large, smart site utilises that spa in its very open environs. This site is well run with an excellent infrastructure, if a little expensive. There is a friendly welcome from the English speaking staff. The 500 individual, flat pitches, (389 for touring) are all 100-150 sq.m. in size with high neat hedges giving real privacy. Electricity (6A) is available. The three unique swimming pools fed by the natural thermo-mineral springs are a novel feature here. These springs have been known since antiquity as Del Bagno Santo (Holy Bath), which flows at a constant temperature of 24 degrees.

Facilities

Two heated toilet blocks are of high quality with mainly British style WCs, many cubicles also with bidet. Gas supplies. Motorcaravan services. Restaurant/pizzeria with bar. Takeaway. Coffee bar. Swimming pools (one all season). Excellent play area for children. TV room and mini-cinema with 100 seats and very large screen. Tennis. Exchange facilities. Free cookery lessons and art classes in high season. Free guided cultural tours. Internet. Free WiFi over site. Dogs are not accepted.

Open: 1 April - 30 September.

Directions

From autostrada A1 take Chiusi/Chianciano exit, from where Sarteano is well signed (6 km). In Sarteano follow camping/piscine signs to site (entrance sign reads Piscine di Sarteano). GPS: 42.9885, 11.8639

Charges guide

| Per unit incl. 2 persons and electricity | € 36.00 - € 61.00 |
| extra person | € 10.00 - € 16.20 |

No credit cards.

Scarlino
Camping Butteri

I-58020 Scarlino (Tuscany) T: 056 695 9958. E: camping@rivadeibutteri.info
alanrogers.com/IT66780

This is a sister site of Camping Baia dei Gabbiani (IT66770) and is closer to Follonica. The site is just 100 m. from the public beach and 15 minutes walk from the town centre. The 150 marked pitches are located beneath low trees and most have 3A electricity connections. The site has a good range of leisure amenities including a restaurant, bar and supermarket. A varied activity and entertainment programme is organised in peak season, including activities for children. This is a suitable site for a reasonable overnight stay whilst travelling in the low season.

Facilities

Sanitary facilities include hot showers (payment by token) and provision for visitors with disabilities. Laundry facilities. Motorcaravan services. Shop and newsagent, restaurant, bar and takeaway (all open as site). Playground. Mountain bike hire. Entertainment and activity programme in high season. Miniclub. Security wristbands used. Dogs not accepted 6/8-19/8. Chalets for rent. Off site: Nearest beach 100 m. Follonica 3 km. Siena, Florence and Pisa are all within 2 hours drive.

Open: 24 April - 12 September.

Directions

From Livorno take southbound Via Aurelia (S1). Leave at Follonica Nord exit. Head initially towards Follonica and then towards Grosseto. Site is signed to left just as you leave Follonica. GPS: 42.9111, 10.7736

Charges guide

| Per unit incl. 2 persons and electricity | € 28.10 - € 42.40 |

No credit cards.

Scarlino
Camping Village Il Fontino

Localitá Il Fontino, Maremma Toscana, I-58020 Scarlino (Tuscany) T: 056 637 029. E: info@fontino.it
alanrogers.com/IT66720

The name means Little Fountain as springs provide all the drinking water here. The Maurizio family have worked hard to provide a most pleasant site for campers. There are 60 terraced pitches for touring units on a sloping site, all with 3/6A electricity and shade from mature olives. Once settled on the pitch cars are parked separately. The 25 m. pool with its separate paddling pool is the site's strength – it is stunning, safe and free. As you swim you can enjoy the views over the town of Follonica below you, whilst in turn the village of Scarlino sits hundreds of metres above on the cliff top.

Facilities

Two dated sanitary blocks provide hot showers (timer). Mostly Turkish style toilets, cold water at washbasins. Single facility for disabled visitors. Washing machines and dryer. Bar/restaurant and takeaway. Shop. Swimming and paddling pools. Entertainment programme and miniclub (high season). Play area. Bicycle hire. WiFi over part of site (charged). Free bus in high season to beach (watersports).

Open: 24 April - 30 September.

Directions

From E80/S1 autostrada take Scarlino exit. Head for the hills and Scarlino. On approach to town look for site signs to site (towards Grosseto). Site is 1.4 km. on the left. GPS: 42.91101, 10.84347

Charges guide

| Per unit incl. 2 persons and electricity | € 22.50 - € 36.00 |

No credit cards.

FREE Alan Rogers Travel Card
Extra benefits and savings - see page 10

Siena
Camping Colleverde

Strada Scacciapensieri 47, I-53100 Siena (Tuscany) T: 057 733 2545. E: info@sienacamping.com
alanrogers.com/IT66245

Camping Colleverde enjoys a panoramic setting overlooking the beautiful Tuscan city of Siena and the surrounding Chianti hills. The proprietor Andrea Sassolini and his family are on hand to ensure you have an enjoyable stay. Open for a long season, this is a great base for visiting Siena and the Chianti region. A bus stop is just 100 m. away and the railway station is 1.5 km. There are 221 pitches arranged on terraces, many with hardstanding and 97 with 10A electricity. On-site facilities include a swimming pool, a pizzeria/restaurant, bar and a shop, all newly built in 2009. There are 25 mobile homes, which can be reserved for short stays.

Facilities

Three new top quality sanitary facilities include those for disabled visitors. Laundry. Motorcaravan services. Shop, bar, restaurant/pizzeria (all March-Oct). Swimming and paddling pools (June-Sept). Play area. WiFi over site (charged). Mobile homes for rent. Bicycle hire. Bus tours to major attractions arranged. Off site: Railway station 1.5 km. City centre 2 km. Bicycle hire 3 km. Riding 10 km. Chianti countryside. Cycle and walking tracks.

Open: 1 March - 31 December.

Directions

Site is north of the city. Approaching from the north, leave RA3 superstrada (Florence-Siena) at Siena Nord exit. Turn right and follow signs for Hospital (Ospedale) and Camping. Site is 1 km. from the hospital, well signed and is the only campsite here. GPS: 43.33771, 11.33048

Charges 2013

Per unit incl. 2 persons and electricity	€ 32.00 - € 36.00
extra person	€ 9.50 - € 11.00
child (3-11 yrs)	€ 5.00 - € 6.00

Sovicille
Camping la Montagnola

Strada della Montagnola, I-53018 Sovicille (Tuscany) T: 057 731 4473. E: montagnolacamping@libero.it
alanrogers.com/IT66250

An agreeable, reasonably priced alternative to sites closer to the centre of Siena, la Montagnola is set in secluded woodland to the north of the village of Sovicille. The owners have worked hard to provide a good basic standard of amenities. The 52 pitches are 60-80 sq.m. in size and some offer privacy. Clearly marked and with shade, all are suitable for caravans and motorcaravans, all having electricity connections (some need long leads). However, there are just three water points on the site. There is a large wooded area and an overflow field for tents with no electricity and another field has a play area for children. A friendly bar/shop area offers snacks and many provisions including wines.

Facilities

A single toilet block provides free hot showers and mainly British style toilets – not luxurious, but adequate and clean. Small, well stocked shop and bar. Play area. Torches definitely required in tent areas. WiFi throughout (charged). Off site: Small supermarket in Sovicille 2 km. Large supermarket in San Rocco a Pilli and Rosia 6 km. Two restaurants in the village. Bus service to Siena. Golf 10 km.

Open: Easter - 30 September.

Directions

From north on Firenze-Siena motorway take exit for Siena Ouest. Turn left on SS73 and at Malignano turn right towards Sovicille. Turn left just before mini roundabout. Site is 2 km. on the right. From south (Grosseto) take SS223 turn at crossroads to Rosia from where site is signed. GPS: 43.2811, 11.2199

Charges guide

Per unit incl. 2 persons and electricity	€ 25.00
extra person	€ 8.00
child (2-10 yrs)	€ 4.00

For latest campsite news, availability and prices visit
alanrogers.com

Tirrenia

Camping Saint Michael

Via della Bigattiera 24, I-56218 Pisa (Tuscany) T: 050 330 41. E: info@campingstmichael.com

alanrogers.com/IT66085

Camping St Michael is a small, family owned site and is quietly situated close to the Migliarino National Park and around 600 m. from a private sandy beach. Beneath the site's pine trees there are 150 level pitches, 40 of which are occupied by seasonal units, all with 4A electrical connections. Around the perimeter there are 30 mobile homes for rent. This site is mainly used by Italian holiday makers and there is plenty to do here in high season with much activity focused on the beach. There is also a children's club catering for different ages. Tirrenia is 2 km. distant and has all the amenities of a typical Italian resort. The Massaciuccoli National Park is very close and well worth a visit.

Facilities

The modest facilities are centrally placed and include sanitary facilities with British style WCs, open washbasins with cold water, controllable showers (charged). Facilities for children and disabled visitors. Laundry facilities. Small shop for basics. Bar. Restaurant, pizzeria and takeaway meals. Play area. Multisports court. Children's club. Bicycle hire by arrangement. WiFi (charged). Dogs are not accepted. Off site: Swimming pool, tennis, riding, fishing and golf. Private beach 600 m. Tirrenia 2 km. Cycle and walking trails.

Open: 1 June - 10 September.

Directions

Tirrenia is 12 km. north of Livorno. From the south, take SS224 to Tirrenia and continue towards Marina di Pisa. Site is 2 km. further north and is well signed. GPS: 43.64694, 10.295

Charges guide

Per person	€ 6.50 - € 8.00
child (3-10 yrs)	€ 5.00 - € 6.50
pitch incl. electricity	€ 10.00 - € 14.00

Torre del Lago

Camping Europa

Viale dei Tigli, I-55049 Torre del Lago Puccini (Tuscany) T: 058 435 0707. E: info@europacamp.it

alanrogers.com/IT66060

Europa is a large, flat, rectangular site with roads on all four sides of the site. There are 400 pitches in 17 rows, with the 200 touring pitches occupying six rows at the far end of the site. To reach these, you need to pass rows of very close together, well established permanent pitches and bungalows available for rent. The site's facilities including a bar, shop and air-conditioned restaurant, are in rows five and six. The touring pitches are flat, very sandy and close together (55-70 sq.m). Some have shade from small trees or artificial cover and 6A electricity is available to most. The site has been owned by the Morescalchi family since 1967 and they are very keen that you have an enjoyable stay. The pool (free) and its separate paddling pool are near the site entrance and a jacuzzi is built into one end. The beach is a brisk 20 minute walk through a forest 1 km. away; a bicycle would be useful. However, there is a site minibus service to the beach and once there the sand is soft and the beach shelves gently into the water. Europa is conveniently situated for visiting many of the interesting places around, such as Lucca, Pisa, Florence and the wealth of Puccini related historical items.

Facilities

Two sanitary blocks provide hot and cold showers (€ 0.50 token from reception). Toilets are mixed Turkish and British style. Facilities for disabled visitors. Laundry facilities. Cleaning goes on non-stop here. Motorcaravan service point outside gate. Bar/restaurant (air conditioned), takeaway, small shop (all open all season). Good swimming pool (1/5-23/9, caps required). Large play area. Entertainment. Miniclub. Bicycle hire. Satellite TV. Internet access. Dogs are not accepted (3/8-23/8). Torches useful. Off site: Beach 1 km. Fishing. Riding 2 km. Golf 17 km.

Open: 28 March - 13 October.

Directions

From A11-12 to Pisa Nord take Marina di Torre del Lago exit following the sign 'mare' towards the sea for Marina di Torre Lago Puccini. Follow clear signs for site. GPS: 43.83083, 10.27055

Charges guide

Per unit incl. 2 persons and electricity	€ 18.00 - € 41.00
extra person	€ 4.50 - € 9.50
child (2-11 yrs)	€ 2.50 - € 4.50

FREE Alan Rogers Travel Card
Extra benefits and savings - see page 10

Torre del Lago
Camping Italia

Viale del Tigli 52, I-55048 Torre del Lago (Tuscany) T: 058 435 9828. E: info@campingitalia.net
alanrogers.com/IT66260

This is a large site with a traditional Italian style that in 2009 benefited from the addition of a range of new facilities. There are 100 pitches for touring units which are set apart from 340 used by permanent units. The touring pitches are arranged informally with a degree of shade from mature trees and all pitches have 6A electricity. There is some road noise to one side. The site has been owned by the Forti family since 1969 who have recently completed the construction of a modern restaurant and bar, a well stocked small supermarket and new toilet facilities.

Facilities

One clean unisex toilet block is on the touring side, with toilets in the new amenity block. All WCs are British style, showers are pushbutton (on payment). Facilities for disabled visitors. Baby bath. Washing machines. Well stocked supermarket. Bar, restaurant with varied menu and pizzeria/takeaway. Swimming pool (1/6-31/8). Play area. TV in bar. Entertainment programme. Bicycle hire. Bungalows to rent. Site minibus to beach. WiFi (charged). Dogs are not accepted in high season. Torches useful.

Open: 21 April - 23 September.

Directions

Torre del Lago is on the west coast 15 km. north of Pisa. From A8 northbound leave at Viareggio exit, when heading south use Pisa North exit. Then take the S1 heading for Pisa. Continue towards the village of Torre del Lago where site is well signed. GPS: 43.81666, 10.26666

Charges guide

Per unit incl. 2 persons and electricity	€ 18.50 - € 30.50

Troghi
Camping Il Poggetto

Via Il Poggetto 143, SP Aretina no. 1, I-50067 Troghi (Tuscany) T: 055 830 7323.
E: info@campingilpoggetto.com **alanrogers.com/IT66110**

This superb site has a lot to offer. It benefits from a wonderful panorama of the Colli Fiorentini hills with acres of the Zecchi family vineyards to the east adding to its appeal and is just 15 km. from Florence. The charming and hard working owners Marcello and Daniella have a wine producing background and you can purchase their fine wines at the site's shop. Their aim is to provide an enjoyable and peaceful atmosphere for families. All 106 touring pitches are of a good size, kept neat and tidy and have 6A electricity. On arrival you are given a joining pack and escorted to view available pitches then assisted in taking up your chosen pitch.

Facilities

Two spotless sanitary blocks offer British style WCs. Three private sanitary units for hire. Five very well equipped units for disabled visitors. Separate facilities for children and baby room. Laundry facilities. Motorcaravan services. Gas supplies. Shop. Bar. Restaurant. Swimming pools and jacuzzi (1/5-30/9). Fitness room. Bicycle and scooter hire. Playground and entertainment for children. Excursions and trekking. Wine and oil tastings. WiFi over site (charged).

Open: 25 March - 15 October.

Directions

Exit A1 at Incisa southeast of Florence and turn right on the SS69. After 4 km. turn left following signs for Pian dell Isola. At next crossing turn right towards Firenze. Follow site signs: village streets are steep and narrow, ignore sat nav. GPS: 43.701415, 11.405262

Charges guide

Per unit incl. 2 persons and electricity	€ 29.50 - € 39.50

Vada
Camping Baia del Marinaio

Via Cavalleggeri 177, I-57018 Vada (Tuscany) T: 058 677 0164. E: info@baiadelmarinaio.it
alanrogers.com/IT66280

This well run, family owned site provides an inclusive holiday experience where all of your requirements are catered for without needing to set foot outside the campsite. The resident owner has overseen the development of the site to a high standard and first class leisure facilities are provided close to the magnificent pool complex. The site is split into sections with the 200 touring pitches positioned away from sections of 200 bungalows (50 of them are available to rent). Most of the fairly small pitches (60-70 sq.m) have good shade and 6A electricity is provided. The restaurant, bar and a well stocked shop are open all season.

Facilities

Six toilet blocks, fitted out to a good standard, provide British style WCs, hot showers and washbasins. Laundry with washing machines. Good facilities for disabled visitors. Shop. Bar and restaurant serving traditional dishes. Large swimming pool complex with 30 m. water slide. Multisports court. Tennis courts. Bicycle hire. WiFi (charged). Bungalows for rent.

Open: 25 April - 12 October.

Directions

From the S1/E80 take Cecina exit and follow road towards Vada. Site is well signed and is on the left side of the road towards Marina di Cecina. GPS: 43.33512, 10.461114

Charges guide

Per unit incl. 2 persons and electricity	€ 22.00 - € 40.00
extra person	€ 6.00 - € 11.00

For latest campsite news, availability and prices visit

alanrogers.com

Vada

Camping Molino a Fuoco

Via Cavalleggeri 32, I-57018 Vada (Tuscany) T: 058 677 0150. E: info@campingmolinoafuoco.com
alanrogers.com/IT66420

This is a relatively small and quiet site with an attractively light and open feel. The 123 touring pitches are light and airy, with some natural shade. Motorcaravans are placed in pairs on very large 170 sq.m. shaded plots. Cars are parked away from the pitches in designated areas. Pleasant permanent pitches do not encroach on the touring units. This family owned site is part of the 'Tuscan For You' group and the Storace family will make you feel very welcome (they speak excellent English). The site is pristine and everything is spotlessly clean and smart. This is a great site for families that enjoy quality combined with peaceful surroundings.

Facilities

Three very clean toilet blocks provide British style WCs and good hot showers. Excellent facilities for disabled visitors. Baby bath and block for children. Washing machines. Bar, excellent restaurant and pizzeria, all with terraces. New swimming pool complex (mid May-end Sept). Good play area. Bicycle hire. Watersports. Fishing. Entertainment programme in season. Miniclub. Weekend entertainment. Communal barbecue area. ATM. WiFi (charged). Torches very useful. Bungalows to rent.
Open: 20 April - 19 October.

Directions

Site is south of Livorno and Vada. From the SS1 take Cecina exit and the site is well signed from here towards Marina di Cecina. GPS: 43.33196, 10.45966

Charges 2013

Per unit incl. 2 persons and electricity	€ 22.00 - € 38.00
extra person	€ 5.50 - € 9.00
dog (not accepted 29/6-25/8)	€ 2.00

Vada

Camping Tripesce

Via Cavalleggeri 88, I-57016 Vada (Tuscany) T: 058 678 8017. E: info@campingtripesce.it
alanrogers.com/IT66290

Neat and tidy, this family owned and run site has the great advantage of direct beach access through electronically controlled gates with CCTV. The beach is of fine sand and shelves gently – super for children, with watersports and a lifeguard in season. This great beach makes up for the lack of a pool on the site and the fairly small size of the 230 pitches. All have 4A electricity and 60 are serviced with water and drainage. Some shade is provided by trees and by artificial shading. The site is contained within a rectangle and bungalows for rent are discreetly placed near reception.

Facilities

Three clean, fresh toilet blocks provide hot and cold showers (water is solar heated and free). British and Turkish style toilets. Facility for disabled visitors. Washing machines. Motorcaravan service points. Bar/restaurant and takeaway. Shop. Excellent beach. Aquarobics and aerobics (high season). Play area (supervision required). Miniclub (high season). WiFi throughout (free). Fishing. Bicycle hire. Dogs are not accepted 23/5-4/9. Charcoal barbecues are not permitted. Off site: Bus service 300 m.
Open: 30 March - 16 October.

Directions

From S1 autostrada (free) between Livorno and Grosetto head south and take Vada exit. Site is well signed along with many others as you approach the town. GPS: 43.34301, 10.45825

Charges guide

Per unit incl. 2 persons and electricity	€ 20.00 - € 32.00
extra person	€ 5.00 - € 8.00
No credit cards.	

Vignale Riotorto

Camping Pappasole

Carbonifera 14, I-57025 Vignale Riotorto (Tuscany) T: 056 520 420. E: info@pappasole.it
alanrogers.com/IT66400

This lively site offers an amazing array of services and activities and is located 200 metres from its own sandy beach facing the island of Elba. It is a large site on flat, fairly open ground offering 477 pitches, of which 427 are for touring units. The pitches are 90-100 sq.m. with electricity and water (cars must be parked separately for most pitches). They are separated by bushes with shade from mature trees and artificial shade in other areas. The four excellent swimming pools are a strong feature, complete with cascades and hydro-massage sections, in an open garden setting (the children's pool is huge).

Facilities

Four modern sanitary blocks have free hot water for washbasins and showers and British style WCs. Laundry facilities. Motorcaravan services. Supermarket. Good deli. Wet fish shop (high season). Hairdresser. Restaurant. Snacks. Bar. Swimming pools (18/5-13/10). Play area. Tennis. Bowls. Football. Watersports. Minigolf. Bicycle hire. Fishing. Medical services. WiFi over site (charged).
Open: 5 April - 20 October.

Directions

From SS1 motorway take Follonica Nord exit onto SS322 and follow signs toward Piombino, not Follonica. After 1 km. turn east (Torre Mozza). Site is 1.5 km. on this road (north). GPS: 42.94893, 10.6863

Charges 2013

Per unit incl. 2 persons and electricity	€ 24.00 - € 62.50
extra person	€ 5.00 - € 15.00

FREE Alan Rogers Travel Card
Extra benefits and savings - see page 10

Digital iPad editions

FREE Alan Rogers bookstore app
- digital editions of all 2013 guides

alanrogers.com/digital

Known as the 'green heart of Italy', Umbria is a beautiful region of rolling hills, woods, streams and valleys that gives way to high mountain wilderness. It is well known for the beauty and profusion of its medieval hilltowns.

UMBRIA HAS TWO PROVINCES: PERUGIA AND TERNI

Umbria's main attraction is the Vale of Spoleto and the hill towns of Spoleto and Assisi. The birthplace of Saint Francis, Assisi attracts vast numbers of art lovers and pilgrims throughout the year who visit his burial place, the Basilica di San Francesco, built in 1228, two years after his death. With a scenic woodland setting, Spoleto was once an important Roman colony. The town has the remains of a Roman amphitheatre, reputedly where ten thousand Christian martyrs were slaughtered, and a variety of Romanesque churches. It also boasts an impressive 14th-century aqueduct. Near Perugia, the regional capital, is Lake Trasimeno, the fourth largest lake in Italy. It has plenty of opportunities for fishing, swimming and watersports. The lakeside town of Castiglione del Lago is a good place to relax and unwind on the small sandy beaches; from here, boats make regular trips to the Isola Maggiore, one of the lake's three islands. Further north is Gubbio, the most thoroughly medieval of all the Umbrian towns. A charming place full of twisting streets with soft pink stone houses and terracotta tiled rooftops, its beauty is enhanced by the forest-clad Apennine mountains looming up behind.

Places of interest

Deruta: town renowned for its ceramics.

Monte Cucco Regional Park: offers organised trails and outdoor activities.

Monti Sibillini: national park with good walking trails.

Norcia: mountain town, birthplace of St Benedict.

Orvieto: boasts one of the greatest Gothic churches in Italy.

Spello: renowned for frescoes in the 12/13th-century church of Santa Maria Maggiore, Roman ruins.

Todi: striking hilltown, 13th-century church and palaces.

Cuisine of the region

Simple pastas and roast meats are popular, especially pork and *la porchetta* (whole suckling pig stuffed with rosemary or sage, roasted on a spit). Truffles can be found in abundance, particularly in Noria, which also produces some of the country's best hams, sausages and salamis. The rivers yield fish such as eel, pike, trout and crayfish. Locally grown vegetables include lentils, beans, celery and cardoons. Good quality olive oil is readily available. Orvieto is a popular Umbrian white wine.

Agnello alla cacciatora: lamb with a sauce of anchovies, garlic and rosemary.

Crescionda: rich traditional cake prepared with almond biscuits, lemon rind and bitter chocolate.

Fichi: candied figs with almonds and cocoa.

Tartufo nero: black truffles.

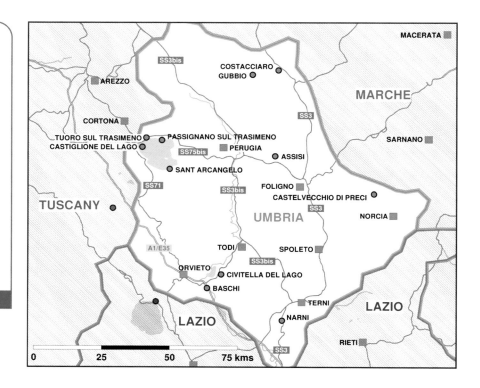

Assisi

Camping Village Assisi

San Giovanni in Campiglione 110, I-06081 Assisi (Umbria) T: 075 813 710. E: info@campingassisi.it
alanrogers.com/IT66550

Camping Village Assisi is an excellent site situated on the west side of Assisi and provides a good base to visit both Saint Francis' city and nearby Perugia and Lake Trasimeno. The 100 flat pitches, with 6A electricity, vary in size and some are specifically for motorcaravans. It can be very hot in this part of Italy, and a welcome relief is the site's pleasant, large pool. The excellent restaurant serves reasonably priced meals, ranging from pizzas to local Umbrian dishes. A large terrace can be completely enclosed. A regular shuttle bus is available to the city which is lit up in the evenings to provide a beautiful backdrop from some areas in the site.

Facilities

The neat and clean toilet block is central and provides free hot showers, mainly Turkish style WCs (only four British style in each block) and facilities for disabled visitors. Washing machine. Gas supplies. Motorcaravan services. Campers' kitchen. Restaurant/pizzeria with self-service section. Bar with snacks. Shop. Swimming pool, jacuzzi and circular paddling pool (1/6-5/9, charged, caps mandatory). Bicycle hire. Tennis. Five-a-side. Volleyball. No charcoal barbecues on pitches. Communal barbecue. WiFi throughout (charged). Off site: Riding 2 km. Fishing 3 km. Excursions to Assisi centre. Bus service to city four times daily from the site.

Open: 1 April - 31 October.

Directions

From the SS75 take the exit for Ospedalicchio Sud and follow the SS147 towards Assisi for 5 km. The site is well signed on the right. GPS: 43.07510, 12.5744

Charges guide

Per unit incl. 2 persons and electricity	€ 24.00 - € 40.00
extra person	€ 8.00 - € 10.00
child (3-9 yrs)	€ 4.00 - € 5.00
dog	free

For latest campsite news, availability and prices visit
alanrogers.com

Sant Arcangelo

Camping Villaggio Italgest

Via Martiri di Cefalonia, I-06063 Sant Arcangelo-Magione (Umbria) T: 075 848 238. E: camping@italgest.com
alanrogers.com/IT66520

Villaggio Italgest is a mature but pleasant site with 208 touring pitches (with 6A electricity) on level grass and plenty of shade. Cars are parked away from the pitches and the site offers a wide variety of activities with tours organised daily. The pools and restaurant are dated, but enjoyable. Directly on the shore on the south side of Lake Trasimeno, Sant Arcangelo is ideally placed for exploring Umbria and Tuscany. The area around the lake is fairly flat but has views of the distant hills and can become very hot during summer. There is some entertainment for children and adults in high season, Italian style.

Facilities

The one large and two smaller sanitary blocks have mainly British style WCs and free hot water in the washbasins and showers. Children's toilets. Baby room. Facilities for disabled visitors. Motorcaravan services. Washing machines and dryers. Well equipped campers' kitchen. Bar, restaurant, pizzeria and takeaway (all season). Shop. Recently enlarged swimming pool with flume and slides. Paddling pool. Spa. Tennis. Play area. TV (satellite) and games rooms. Disco. Films. Watersports, motorboat hire and lake swimming. Fishing. Charcoal barbecues not permitted, communal available. Picnic area by pond. Mountain bike and scooter hire. Internet and WiFi (charged). Wide range of activities, entertainment and excursions. Off site: Bus outside gate. Golf, parachuting, riding, canoeing and sailing nearby.

Open: 1 April - 30 September.

Directions

Site is on the southern shore of Lake Trasimeno. Take Magione exit from the Perugia spur of the Florence-Rome autostrada, proceed southwest round the lake to San Arcangelo where site is signed. GPS: 43.0881, 12.1561

Charges guide

Per unit incl. 2 persons	
and electricity	€ 20.00 - € 31.50
extra person	€ 6.00 - € 8.50
child (3-9 yrs)	€ 4.00 - € 6.50
dog	€ 2.00 - € 2.50

Camping Cheques accepted.

Tuoro sul Trasimeno

Camping Village Punta Navaccia

Via Navaccia 4, I-06069 Tuoro sul Trasimeno (Umbria) T: 075 826 357. E: info@puntanavaccia.it
alanrogers.com/IT66490

Situated on the north side of Lake Trasimeno close to two of the lake's islands. It is run by the three ebullient Migliorati sisters and is a large site with 400 flat, shaded touring pitches with 6A electricity, mostly near the lakeside. The campsite is ajacent to a soft sand beach, and has a dock with facilities for mooring and launching your boat. The hub of the site is bustling with a full animation programme for children and adults. A huge amphitheatre stages entertainment, and is located close to all the other services. This is a great and very Italian site, where families will have fun at reasonable prices.

Facilities

Three sanitary blocks with varied facilities are in the areas of seasonal campers. Washing machine and dryer. Motorcaravan services. Heated swimming and paddling pools (1/5-30/9). Shop and bar (1/4-30/9). Restaurant and takeaway (1/4-30/9). Play area. Tennis. Huge covered amphitheatre. Cinema screen. Miniclub. Entertainment is organised in high season (in Italian, English, German and Dutch). Boat launching. Daily boat trip around island (free). Fitness room. Fishing. Bicycle hire. WiFi (charged). Off site: Sandy beach, windsurfing, sailing and canoeing 200 m. Excursions and tours. Boat trips.

Open: 15 March - 31 October.

Directions

Going south on the A1 (Florence/Firenze-Rome), take exit for Val di Chiana to Perugia near Bettole. After 15 km. take Tuoro sul Trasimeno exit. Site is well signed. GPS: 43.19191, 12.07665

Charges guide

Per unit incl. 2 persons	
and electricity	€ 19.00 - € 28.50
extra person	€ 6.00 - € 8.50
child (2-9 yrs)	€ 4.00 - € 6.50
dog	free

FREE Alan Rogers Travel Card
Extra benefits and savings - see page 10

Lying between the Adriatic Sea and the Apennine mountains, Marche boasts a pretty mixture of woods and remote hills, medieval towns and seaside resorts, sandy beaches and sleepy coves, plus the snow-capped peaks of the Monti Sibillini.

THERE ARE FOUR PROVINCES IN MARCHE: ANCONA, ASCOLI PICENO, MACERATA AND PESARO E URBINO

Marche is not as well known or publicised as other regions, but despite that it has plenty to offer. The medieval town of Urbino with its spectacular Renaissance palace is one of the highlights, as is Ascoli Piceno, which also boasts a medieval heritage, various churches and an enchanting town square. The dramatic fortress at San Leo is considered to be one of the best, while nearby San Marino is Europe's oldest republic. A tiny area with no customs regulations, its borders are just seven miles apart at its widest point. The republic has its own mint and army and produces its own postage stamps. South of Ancona, the regional capital, and overlooked by the dramatic white cliffs of Monte Cónero, is the Cónero Riviera, an impressive stretch of coast with small beaches, coves and picturesque little resorts, including Portonovo, Sirolo and Numana. Along the coast is Loreto, one of Italy's most popular pilgrimage destinations, and more beaches can be found at San Benedetto del Tronto. Further inland, near the Verdicchio wine-producing hilltop villages around Jesi, is the Grotte di Frasassi, one of Europe's largest accessible cave networks. And the mountainous region of Monti Sibillini in the south offers good walking trails and stunning views.

Places of interest

Ancona: regional capital and Adriatic's largest port.

Fano: beach resort with old centre and historic monuments.

Jesi: medieval town walls, Renaissance and Baroque palaces.

Macerata: university town surrounded by lovely countryside, famous for its annual outdoor opera and ballet festival.

Numana: seaside resort on Cónero peninsula, boat trips to the offshore islets of Due Sorelle.

Sarnano: spa town.

Urbania: palace with art gallery and museum.

Ússita: winter sports resort.

Cuisine of the region

The food is a mix of seafood along the coastline and country cooking inland, involving locally grown produce – tomatoes, fennel and mushrooms. Typical seafood dishes include *zuppa di pesce* (fish soup with saffron) and *brodetto* (fish broths). Rabbit and lamb are popular plus *porchetta* (roast suckling pig). The region is best known for its Verdicchio wine although it does produce a variety of others.

Coniglio in porchetta: rabbit cooked with fennel.

Cicercchiata: balls of pasta fried and covered in honey.

Olive ascolane: olives stuffed with meat and herbs, served with *crema fritta*, little squares of fried cream.

Vincisgrassi: baked pasta dish with ham and truffles.

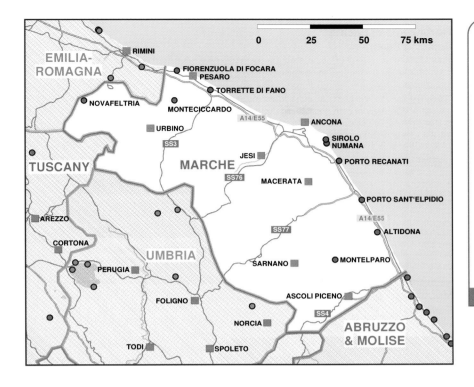

Altidona

Centro Vacanze Riva Verde

Via Aprutina 75, I-63017 Altidona (Marche) T: 073 493 2012. E: info@rivaverde.it

alanrogers.com/IT65240

An extremely well run site, Riva Verde offers everything a camper could require. The site stretches 1.5 km. beside the Adriatic with an escalator to bring clients back up the steep slope from the beach. A shuttle bus runs along the coast from the site entrance. There are 450 small pitches, with 420 for touring (electricity 6-10A), shaded by mature trees and with views over the Adriatic. Private toilet and bathroom facilities are available at a supplement. A large aqua park provides slides, swimming pools and children's pools, all surrounded by a sunbathing area. All the pitches are terraced above the road, motorway and railway and some noise must be expected at all times. Entrance to the site is via a tunnel, and the access road is steep. This is a lively site with plenty of on-site activities catering for all the family.

Facilities

Eight well equipped and maintained toilet blocks with all necessary facilities including for those with disabilities. Bar, restaurant, takeaway, pizzeria. Shops. Swimming pool complex. Solarium. Disco. Games/TV room. Tennis. Minigolf. Dogs and other animals are not accepted. Off site: Fishing 1 km. Bicycle hire 2 km. Pedaso 2 km. Sailing, boat launching 5 km. Porto San Giorgio 6 km. Riding 10 km. Golf 12 km.

Open: 25 May - 14 September.

Directions

Heading south on A14, leave at junction for Fermo and Porto San Giorgio, and join southbound SS16. The entrance to site is 5 km. south of San Giorgio on right – look for the flags. Sat nav co-ordinates are for site entrance, not reception.
GPS: 43.119521, 13.831884

Charges guide

Per unit incl. 2 persons and electricity	€ 30.00 - € 58.00
Per person	€ 7.00 - € 12.00
child (2-6 yrs)	€ 5.00 - € 7.00

Pitches available with washbasin or bathroom.
Long stay low season offers.

FREE Alan Rogers Travel Card
Extra benefits and savings - see page 10

Fiorenzuola di Focara
Camping Panorama

Strand Panoramica, I-61121 Fiorenzuola di Focara Pesaro (Marche) T: 072 120 8145.
E: info@campingpanorama.it **alanrogers.com/IT65070**

Camping Panorama is a peaceful site located on a scenic coastal drive within a small national park (Parco del San Bartolo) and quite close to the delightful town of Pesaro. The site lies 100 metres above the sea and a pleasant path nearby leads to the beach below. There are 120 touring pitches ranging in size from 50-100 sq.m, all have 6A electrical connections and are well shaded. Leisure amenities include a magnificent swimming pool (with smaller children's pool) and a sports court. This is largely an undeveloped area and has many opportunities for walking and mountain biking.

Facilities

Four toilet blocks. Washing machines. Motorcaravan service point. Swimming pool and children's pool. Bar, pizzeria and shop (all season). TV room. Games room. Play area. Sports court. Tourist information. No gas or electric barbecues. WiFi over part of site. Off site: Nearest village is Fiorenzuola di Focara, perched over the sea with bars, shops and restaurants 2 km. Fishing 3 km. Bicycle hire 6 km. Pesaro 6 km. Golf 8 km. Riding 10 km. Urbino 35 km. San Marino 42 km. Mountain biking and walking.

Open: 15 April - 30 September.

Directions

From A14 (Bologna-Taranto) take Cattolica exit and join SS16 southbound towards Siligata. Join coast road (Strad Panoramico) towards Fionenzuola. Site is beyond this town and Fiorenzuola di Focara but before Pesaro. GPS: 43.941683, 12.84585

Charges guide

Per unit incl. 2 persons and electricity	€ 26.00 - € 36.00

No credit cards.

Monteciccardo
Camping Podere Sei Poorte

Via Petricci 14, I-61020 Monteciccardo (Marche) T: 072 191 0286. E: info@podereseipoorte.it
alanrogers.com/IT65080

Podere Sei Poorte is owned and run by Hans and Sietske Poorte, who in just a few years have transformed a derelict farm into a stress-free haven of rustic charm and tranquillity. On arrival you will be welcomed with a smile and a drink. The restaurant offers good, Italian-style food in a convivial setting. The site is laid out on two terraces so everyone has good views. The 130 spacious, grassy pitches (100 for touring units with 6A electricity) are almost flat, and some have shade. A little uphill walking and some steps are required to reach reception, the restaurant and the pool, which may be inaccessible to disabled visitors.

Facilities

One main toilet block near reception, and nine smaller ones around the site are modern and tiled with free hot water. Facilities for disabled visitors. Motorcaravan service point. Shop. Bar and restaurant. Swimming pool with stunning views (8x16 m; all season). Play area. Off site: Beach 25 minutes by car. Medieval town of Fano.

Open: 28 April - 29 October.

Directions

From St Angelo in Lizzola (inland from Pesaro and A14) follow SP26 to Mombaroccio. At Villa Ugolini look for P-6-P campsite sign and turn into Via Petricci and site is 1.4 km. on the right. GPS: 43.8009, 12.82113

Charges guide

Per unit incl. 2 persons and electricity	€ 23.00 - € 37.50

Montelparo
Agricamp Picobello

Ctra Cortaglie 24, I-63853 Montelparo (Marche) T: 073 478 9012. E: info@agricamppicobello.com
alanrogers.com/IT65260

Situated only 28 km. inland from the Adriatic coast at Pedaso, this very small site caters for campers who like to go back to basics. Catering only for tents, the site offers up to 15 pitches, some with shade. There is a hammock house in the central area where campers can rig their hammocks in a shady and peaceful spot. Rob and his partner, Erna, are keen outdoor people and are very enthusiastic about keeping the spirit of true camping aflame. Rob will be your guide for hiking tours to the Sibillini mountains and also organises rock climbing. A relaxing campsite for the purist camper away from the hectic atmosphere of some of the coastal sites.

Facilities

The central toilet block is well maintained and very clean. Small bar. Small kitchen and social area for preparing light meals with fridge and freezer space. Bicycle hire. Undercover playroom and a new climbing wall. Free WiFi over site. No barbecues. Dogs are not accepted. Off site: Lively little village with supermarket, shops, bars and café 3.5 km. Riding 5 km. Fishing 15 km.

Open: 1 April - 15 October.

Directions

From Pedaso on SS16 turn southwest onto SP238 towards Comunanza. Just after Oretezzano, turn right following brown signs (PicoBello, not Agriturismo). GPS: 43.02703, 13.55552

Charges guide

Per person	€ 6.00 - € 7.00
pitch	€ 8.00 - € 9.50

Electricity by arrangement (3A).

For latest campsite news, availability and prices visit
alanrogers.com

Novafeltria
Camping Perticara

Via Serra Masini 10/d, Perticara, I-61015 Novafeltria (Marche) T: 054 192 7602.
E: info@campingperticara.com **alanrogers.com/IT66170**

High in the Marche hills, not far from San Marino, Ravenna and Rimini, is Camping Perticara, a purpose built camping site with glorious views across a valley to the mountains and the nearby traditional village of Perticara. Each of its 80 generous pitches have water and drainage, all arranged on terraces to take advantage of the fabulous scenery. Good sized trees have been planted to provide shade in the future. The shop, bar and restaurant are attractively presented, with a terrace overlooking the swimming pool which shares the incredible vistas.

Facilities

Two immaculate modern units provide really excellent facilities with all the extras. Facilities are all in large luxury cabins with shower, toilet and basin. Units for disabled visitors are of the same standard. Washing machine and dryers. Gas. Small shop. Restaurant (limited menu but good value). Snack bar. Swimming and paddling pools. Play areas and field for games. Entertainment (miniclub) in high season. Suggested walking/hiking trails are free from reception. Dogs are not accepted. WiFi over site (charged). Off site: Fishing 10 km. Golf 25 km.

Open: 15 May - 20 September.

Directions

After Bologna on A1 take A14 (Ancona) and exit for Rimini Nord. After 200 m. turn right (San Leo), over several roundabouts (San Leo, Montefeltro). At traffic lights turn right to Novafeltria (32 km). At Novafeltria, 400 m. after lights, turn right towards Perticara. Climb for 7 km. and at top turn left towards Santa Agata Feltria. After 400 m. turn right to site and descend with care. GPS: 43.89609, 12.24293

Charges guide

Per unit incl. 2 persons	
and electricity	€ 22.00 - € 36.00
extra person	€ 5.50 - € 9.50
child (4-12 yrs)	€ 3.50 - € 7.50

Numana
Numana Blu Camping Village

Via Costaverde 37, I-60026 Numana (Marche) T: 071 739 0993. E: info@numanablu.it
alanrogers.com/IT66190

Numana Blu lies on the Cónero Riviera, south of Ancona, just 300 metres from the sea, and close to the town of Marcelli. Beneath the site's 12,000 trees there are 330 shady pitches, most offering electrical connections. Separate areas have a range of rentable accommodation, including chalets and bungalows. There is plenty to do here but the site retains a relaxed atmosphere. In peak season there are several children's clubs catering for different ages. The site also boasts an impressive array of leisure amenities including an excellent swimming pool, a restaurant/pizzeria and a small supermarket.

Facilities

Supermarket, bar, restaurant/pizzeria and takeaway meals (all 28/5-10/9). Swimming pool with a children's section (28/5-10/9). Playground. Bicycle hire. Basketball/volleyball court. Football pitch. Two tennis courts. Games rooms. Children's clubs. Entertainment programme in high season. WiFi over site (charged). Off site: Beach 300 m. Riding 1 km. Golf 6 km. Cónero Riviera, Monte Cónero (at 572 m. the highest peak in the area) and Ancona. Cycle and walking trails.

Open: 24 April - 30 September.

Directions

Take the Loreto Porto Recanati exit from the A14 autostrada and follow signs to Numana. Site is south of Numana, 1.5 km. from the small town of Marcelli. GPS: 43.47641, 13.63381

Charges guide

Per unit incl. 2 persons	
and electricity	€ 24.50 - € 54.00
extra person	€ 4.90 - € 12.40
child (under 6 yrs)	€ 3.20 - € 7.90
dog	€ 2.00

Porto Recanati
Camping Bellamare

Lungomare Scarfiotti 13, I-62017 Porto Recanati (Marche) T: 071 976 628. E: info@bellamare.it

alanrogers.com/IT65180

Situated on the Cónero Riviera, just south of the River Musone, this site is ideal for campers who enjoy a well ordered and efficiently run site. The grounds are maintained to a meticulous standard. Unlike most sites along the Lungomare Adriatico, it does not suffer from either train or motorway noise. There are 355 flat, grassy pitches which are separated by maturing trees offering some shade. Touring pitches are of average size, centrally located and easily accessed. Most beach holiday activities are provided on site or within easy walking distance.

Facilities

Large, very clean central toilet block with two smaller blocks having mainly Turkish style toilets. Free cold showers, hot showers need electronic key supplied on registration. Shop, bar, restaurant, takeaway. Swimming and paddling pools (1/6-1/9). TV/games room. Play areas. Football. Bicycle hire. Organised family activities (high season). WiFi (charged). Dogs are not accepted. Overnight stay facility. Off site: Go-karts adjacent. Fishing and sailing 2 km. Riding 3 km. Golf 5 km.

Open: 24 April - 30 September.

Directions

From A14 take exit for Porto Recanati. Follow the beach road (Recanati-Porto Recanati) towards Numana. Site is well signed in both directions. GPS: 43.47095, 13.6412

Charges guide

Per unit incl. 2 persons and electricity	€ 19.00 - € 48.00
extra person	€ 4.50 - € 14.00
child (under 4 yrs)	free

Porto Sant'Elpidio
Villaggio Turistico Le Mimose

Via Faleria 15, I-63821 Porto Sant'Elpidio (Marche) T: 073 490 0604. E: info@villaggiolemimose.it

alanrogers.com/IT65200

Le Mimose is a quiet site away from the town centre, bordering the extensive and well kept single beach. There are 65 grassy or sandy pitches, all for touring, with electricity (6A). The touring pitches, scattered among the holiday apartments, are surrounded by hedges and mature trees giving good shade. Space may be a little tight in high season. The short walk to the beach is very pleasant – as is a stroll along the promenade. The site, with its bar and restaurant, are now open all year.

Facilities

Two central toilet blocks with all necessary facilities, including those for campers with disabilities. Shop (1/6-30/9). Bar and restaurant. Takeaway (1/1-30/9). Swimming and paddling pools (1/6-12/9). Wellness centre. Two children's playgrounds. Sports facilities. Bicycle hire. Beach adjacent. ATM in reception. WiFi over site. Off site: Tennis adjacent. Boat launching 1 km. Fishing 3 km. Golf 10 km. Riding 15 km.

Open: All year.

Directions

From SS16 Adriatico in Porto Sant Elpidio follow well marked signs to site. Access through town difficult for large outfits (4 m. height, 3 m. width restrictions) and care is needed passing through the gate. GPS: 43.23768, 13.77365

Charges guide

Per person	€ 4.50 - € 9.00
pitch	€ 6.50 - € 22.00
electricity	€ 2.50

Sirolo
Camping & Club Internazionale

Via San Michele 10, I-60020 Sirolo (Marche) T: 071 933 0884. E: info@campinginternazionale.com

alanrogers.com/IT65150

This is a high quality site with a particularly attractive, cliffside location within the Parco del Cónero. The 230 pitches (110 for touring units, most with 10A electricity) are on terraces shelving down towards two bays. Most pitches have fine sea views and all have shade. The terrain and access are steep, and the pitches small (25-50 sq.m), so large caravans and motorcaravans may find this site unsuitable. It may also prove challenging for those who find hills a problem. However, the site is efficiently run and well maintained with a good range of leisure amenities. The restaurant and bar are very popular, thanks no doubt to their magnificent views and good local cuisine.

Facilities

Two large toilet blocks cater well for this busy site, with adequate hot water to sinks and showers. Facilities for disabled visitors. Small shop with delicatessen. Bar and restaurant/pizzeria, takeaway (all season). Outdoor swimming pool (25/5-10/9). Play area. Children's club (high season). Entertainment programme in high season. WiFi over part of site (charged). Chalets and mobile homes for rent. Dogs are not accepted. Off site: Beach adjacent. Cónero Riviera. Ancona. Urbino. Riding.

Open: 10 May - 23 September.

Directions

From A14 autostrada take Loreto Porto Recanati exit and follow signs to Numana and Sirolo. Follow brown signs, taking care in Sirolo itself where manoeuvring can be tight. GPS: 43.523706, 13.620472

Charges guide

Per unit incl. 2 persons and electricity	€ 24.00 - € 54.00
extra person	€ 5.00 - € 11.00
child (1-6 yrs)	free - € 7.00

For latest campsite news, availability and prices visit

alanrogers.com

Torrette di Fano

Camping Stella Maris

Via A Cappellini 5, I-61032 Torrette di Fano (Marche) T: 072 188 4231. E: stellamaris@camping.it

alanrogers.com/IT66180

This clean, modern Adriatic coast site is, without doubt, the best in the area. The owner, Francesco Mantoni, is friendly, enthusiastic and proud of his site. There are 161 pitches, 100 for tourers, all with electricity (6A), water and drainage. In an informal setting, touring pitches, permanent sites and cabins are blended together with pleasing results. For swimming and relaxing there is the choice of a clean, long, soft sand beach or an excellent pool complex with loungers, umbrellas, jacuzzi and paddling pool. Alongside the pool is a most attractive restaurant with table service, a varied menu and good selection of wine. A site for holidays and touring, where a high standard of service is provided in all areas.

Facilities

Clean, modern sanitary blocks are nicely decorated with separate male and female areas and include hairdryers. Facilities for babies and disabled campers. Laundry facilities. Motorcaravan services. Well stocked shop. Restaurant/bar. Snacks. Large swimming pool. Games room. TV room. Hard court with arena style seating used for organised games. Children's activities day and evening in season. Entertainment. Beach. Free WiFi over site. Dogs or other animals are not accepted.

Open: 21 April - 30 September.

Directions

Site is between Fano and Falconara. From autostrada take Pesaro exit and follow signs on the SS16 for Ancona, site is 3 km. past Fano on the inner coast road. Well signed.
GPS: 43.79826, 13.09547

Charges guide

Per person	€ 7.40 - € 10.80
child (2-6 yrs)	€ 4.60 - € 7.90
pitch incl. electricity	€ 14.50 - € 18.50

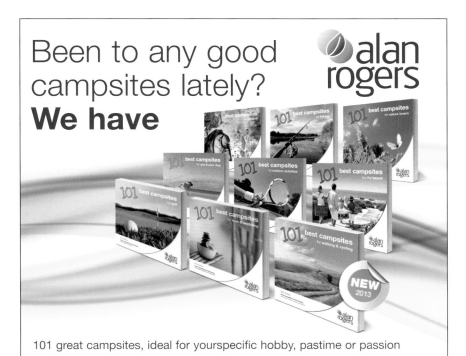

Lazio lies between the Apennines and the Tyrrhenian Sea, with the Pontine marshes in the south and wooded hills in the north. Home to the historic city of Rome it also has numerous lakes and coastal resorts which provide the perfect antidote to the heat of the city and its crowds.

LAZIO HAS FIVE PROVINCES: FROSINONE, LATINA, RIETI, ROMA AND VITERBO

Rome, the capital city of Italy, is crammed full of history, boasting a dazzling array of architectural and artistic masterpieces of the ancient world. Within Rome lies the Vatican City, the world capital of Catholicism, ruled by the Pope, Europe's only absolute monarch. It's also the world's smallest state, occupying 43 hectares within high walls watched over by guards. More historical sites can be found just outside Rome, including the ruins of Villa Adriana, just outside the hilltown of Tivoli. Once a favoured resort of the ancient Romans, the town is also home to the 16th-century Villa d'Este, renowned for its beautiful gardens. Nearby Ostia Antica boasts one of the finest Roman sites. For 600 years it was the busy, main port of Rome, and the site is well preserved. Viterbo, in the north, is a medieval town with grand palaces and churches enclosed by preserved medieval walls. For recreation, there are numerous lakes including Lakes Bolsena, Bracciano, Vico and Albano. These lakes were created by volcanic activity which also left Lazio with hot springs, most notably those around Tivoli and Fiuggi. Popular coastal resorts include Sperlonga, Anzio and Nettuno, with some of the best beaches lying between Gaeta and Sabaudia.

Places of interest

Anguillara: pretty medieval lake town on the shore of Lake Bracciano.

Bolsena: lakeside beach resort on Lake Bolsena with medieval castle.

Caprarola: medieval village 4 km. from Lake Vico, with grandiose Renaissance villa.

Fiuggi: spa town.

Rome: Colosseum, Forum, Palatine Hill, Pantheon, Trevi Fountain, the list is endless.

Sermoneta: pretty hilltown overlooking the Pontine Plains, with medieval houses, palaces and churches.

Tarquinia: archaeology museum, frescoed tombs of the necropolis.

Vatican City: St Peter's church, Sistine Chapel with famous painted ceiling by Michelangelo, museums.

Cuisine of the region

Pasta is eaten with a variety of sauces including *aglio e olio* (garlic and oil), *cacio e pepe* (percorino cheese and black pepper) and *alle vongole* (with baby clams). The well known dish *spaghetti alla carbonara* was first devised in Rome. Fish and offal are popular. Mushrooms and, in particular, artichokes (*carciofi*) are used in a variety of dishes, and rosemary, sage and garlic are used frequently for seasoning. Local wines include Frascati and Torre Ercolana, one of the few red wines produced in Lazio. Fresh drinking water is freely available in the numerous fountains scattered around Rome.

Risotto alla Romana: rice with sauce of liver, sweetbreads and Marsala.

Saltimbocca: veal with ham and sage.

Torta di Ricotta: cheesecake made with ricotta, Marsala and lemon.

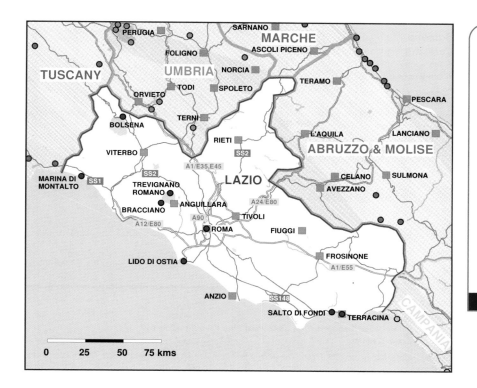

Bolsena

Lido Camping Village

Via Cassia km. 111, I-01023 Bolsena (Lazio) T: 076 179 9258. E: info@lidocampingvillage.it

alanrogers.com/IT67680

Lido Camping Village is located on the edge of Lake Bolsena, 1.5 km. south of the fascinating town of Bolsena. This landscaped site has a fine pool (with a high additional charge). There are 600 flat, sandy pitches of an average size with 3A electricity. Some have shade. Sadly all the lakeside pitches are occupied by seasonal or tour operator units. An attractive, modern restaurant, bar, pizzeria and terrace are located on the edge of the lake and have wonderful views over the black sand. Some entertainment is provided. There are a disco, entertainment area and cinema on the site and the site's sports facilities are of a high standard. Watch for the extra charges here!

Facilities

Modern facilities include showers (charged). Expect them to be under pressure in high season. Supermarket, bar, restaurant and pizzeria (all open all season). Swimming pools (mid June-Aug; high extra charges). Dance area, cinema and music area. Tennis. Windsurfing and water skiing. Lake swimming and boat launching. Playground (but dated equipment needs strict supervision). Limited entertainment in high season. WiFi over site (charged). Dogs are not accepted. Off site: Bolsena 1.5 km. Excursions. Watersports.

Open: 25 April - 30 September.

Directions

Site is by Lake Bolsena south of the town of Bolsena off the S2 (Via Cassia). It is well signed.
GPS: 42.62716, 11.99524

Charges guide

Per unit incl. 2 persons	
and electricity	€ 23.50 - € 31.00
extra person	€ 7.00 - € 9.00
child (3-10 yrs)	€ 3.00 - € 5.50

Bolsena

Camping Internazionale Il Lago

Viale Cadorna 6, I-01023 Bolsena (Lazio) T: 076 179 9191. E: anna.bruti@libero.it

alanrogers.com/IT67700

Camping Internazionale Il Lago is enchanting. A tiny and simple, rustic site with only 34 pitches, it is in a peaceful garden setting on the lake shores of Bolsena, only 500 metres from the centre of the town. The flat and grassy pitches, all for touring units, are spread around the lake. Electricity (4A) is available and there is shade from many trees, good hedging and two gravel roads. The same family has owned the campsite for over 50 years and some English is spoken. A small bar and café offers snacks, with four restaurants within 100 metres of the campsite and more in the town. If you enjoy small, uncomplicated and very friendly sites, this is perfect.

Facilities

The single well cared for sanitary block is clean and has mixed style toilets and good showers. Facilities for disabled visitors. Drinks and snack bar. Fishing. Lake swimming. Boat launching. WiFi over part of site (very small charge). Off site: Restaurants nearby. Bicycle hire 500 m. Riding 3 km. Sailing.

Open: Easter - 30 September.

Directions

Site is beside Lake Bolsena in the southeast area of the town of Bolsena. In town follow lake and camping signs and site is easy to locate.
GPS: 42.63833, 11.98472

Charges guide

Per unit incl. 2 persons and electricity	€ 18.00 - € 25.00
extra person	€ 5.00 - € 6.50
No credit cards.	

Bracciano

Camping Porticciolo

Via Porticciolo, I-00062 Bracciano (Lazio) T: 069 980 3060. E: info@porticciolo.it

alanrogers.com/IT68130

This is a small, family run site. Useful for visiting Rome, it has its own private beach on the lake and is overlooked by the impressive Bracciano Castle. The 170 pitches, some with lake views, and 120 having electricity (4-6A) are level, peaceful and shaded by very green trees. The bar/restaurant/takeaway and wood-fired pizzeria have two large terraces. Alessandro and his wife, Alessandra, have worked hard to build up this basic site since 1982. They are charming and speak excellent English.

Facilities

Three sanitary units with children's toilets and showers are showing some signs of wear and tear. Hot showers. Laundry facilities. Motorcaravan services. Gas supplies. Small shop (basics). Bar. Trattoria/pizzeria/takeaway. Tennis. Play area. Bicycle hire. Fishing. Internet point and free WiFi. Torches required in some areas. Excursions. Off site: Bus service from outside the gate runs to central Rome. Air-conditioned train service from Bracciano (1.5 km) into the city – the site runs a connecting bus (09.00 daily). Riding 2 km.

Open: 1 April - 30 September.

Directions

From Rome ring road (GRA) northwest side take Cassia exit to Bracciano S493 (not Cassia bis which is further northeast). 2 km. before Bracciano village, just after going under a bridge, follow site signs and turn along the lake away from Anguillara. Site is 1 km. on the SP1f and has a fairly steep entrance.
GPS: 42.10582, 12.18928

Charges guide

Per unit incl. 2 persons and electricity	€ 17.50 - € 31.00
extra person	€ 5.00 - € 7.00

Bracciano

Camping Roma Flash

Via Settevene Palo km. 19,800, I-00062 Bracciano (Lazio) T: 069 980 5458. E: info@romaflash.it

alanrogers.com/IT68120

This excellent site is in a superb location with magnificent views over Lake Bracciano, the source of Rome's drinking water. When we visited, although it was busy, it was still peaceful and relaxing. There are 275 flat, shaded pitches with 6A electricity (Europlug). A pleasant, covered restaurant set alongside a lake has a large terrace, as does a small indoor area. Elide and Eduardo speak excellent English and happily go out of their way to ensure guests enjoy their holiday. Many of the visitors told us that they return year after year, some staying for 8-12 weeks at a time, enjoying all that the Lazio region has to offer.

Facilities

Two large, modern toilet blocks have free hot water and fully adjustable showers. Facilities for disabled visitors and children. Laundry facilities. Gas. Bar/restaurant/pizzeria, small shop (all open as site). Swimming pool (1/6-31/8, caps compulsory). Play area. Watersports. Games room. Entertainment for children in high season. WiFi over site (charged). Excursions. Private bus daily to Roma San Pietro and return. New sports area. Off site: Riding 6 km.

Open: 1 April - 30 September.

Directions

From A1/E45 north of Roma take exit for Orte and Viterbo (SS675), Vetralla, Sutri (SS2), Trevignano Romano (SP12d) and then towards Bracciano (SP4a). GPS: 42.130113, 12.173527

Charges 2013

Per unit incl. 2 persons and electricity	€ 16.00 - € 37.00
extra person	€ 7.00 - € 9.50
Camping Cheques accepted.	

For latest campsite news, availability and prices visit

alanrogers.com

Lido di Ostia
Camping Internazionale Castelfusano

Via Litoranea 132, I-00122 Lido di Ostia (Lazio) T: 065 623 304. E: info@romacampingcastelfusano.it
alanrogers.com/IT67790

For a beach holiday this site is ideally situated with easy access across the road to a lovely long sandy beach. It is a rustically attractive site with 65 pitches interspersed on undulating ground among mature trees. Although they offer plenty of shade, there are many low hanging branches (they are protected) and, as a result, some pitches are small and inappropriate for larger units. However, tents and smaller units can tuck themselves away in interesting nooks and crannies. The soil is sandy but the access roads are mostly tarmac and gravel. Most of the pitches have 3A electricity. Reception is a pleasant wooden building near a large flat area that can accommodate larger units.

Facilities	Directions
Three toilet blocks with functional facilities including hot showers but only cold water for dishwashing and laundry. Unit for disabled visitors. Washing machine and dryer. Well stocked shop (March-Oct). Bar/restaurant (closed Jan. and Nov) with terrace. Live music (high season). Playground. Games area. Entertainment for children twice a week (July/Aug). Internet access and information in reception. Children's pool. Off site: Beach 50 m. Bicycle hire 1 km. Riding 2 km. Ostia 3 km. Rome 25 km.	Site is southwest of Rome. From GRA exit 26 or 27 (depending on direction) onto Via Cr. Colombo towards Flumicino. Continue on V. Cr. Coloumbo to end (beach). Keeping in left lane, follow road to right then immediately left and left again in 100 m. Turn right in 150 m. and site is 1.5 km. on right. GPS: 41.706075, 12.340111

Open: All year.

Charges guide

Per unit incl. 2 persons
and electricity € 21.00 - € 35.00

Marina di Montalto
California International Camping Village

SS1 Aurelia km. 105,500, I-01014 Marina di Montalto (Lazio) T: 076 680 2848.
E: info@californiacampingvillage.com **alanrogers.com/IT68160**

The first vision of California Camping on the approach is the excellent lagoon-style pool complex with its bridges and large fountain surrounded by palms. All facilities are shared with the large population of holidaymakers in rental accommodation. A smart bar, pizzeria and restaurant complex are in an octagonal building overlooking the pools. The 420 pitches for touring units (4A electricity) are large, arranged mainly in close, level, shaded rows. Cars are parked separately in high season. The long, grey sand/shingle beach is cleaned daily; it is virtually private and easily accessed.

Facilities	Directions
Nine refurbished blocks contain varying facilities including those for disabled campers. Hot water for showers but only cold at sinks. Showers are concentrated in one block (a long walk for some). Supermarket. Excellent restaurant, bar and takeaway. Large lagoon pool complex. Minigolf. Amphitheatre. Tennis. Discos. Play areas. Entertainment. Miniclub. Boat hire. Fishing. WiFi (charged). Communal barbecues. No charcoal barbecues on pitches. Dogs are not accepted. Off site: Town nearby with all amenities.	Site is 100 km. north of Rome off the SS1 between Ortobello and Civitavecchia. At Montalto di Castro take minor road to the coast and Montalto Marina. On approach to town, site is clearly signed. GPS: 42.3055, 11.62333

Open: 1 May - 15 September.

Charges guide

Per unit incl. 2 persons
and electricity € 21.00 - € 39.50
extra person € 7.00 - € 12.50

Marina di Montalto
Camping Pionier Etrusco

Via Vulsinia snc, I-01014 Marina di Montalto di Castro (Lazio) T: 076 680 2807. E: info@campingpe.it
alanrogers.com/IT68165

This family run site has 250 pitches (with 3A electricity), just under half of which are used for seasonal units. On sandy ground, all the pitches are under tall pine trees resulting in full shade. Oriented towards families, this site in a small seaside town would make a good base for touring the local Etruscan ruins or perhaps as a transit stop. The beach is about 100 m. away and is of dark volcanic sand. There is a bright new bar, restaurant and café here now, and the promenade and beach are just 100 m. away.

Facilities	Directions
Two mature, but well maintained sanitary blocks provide toilets (some Turkish style), washbasins and unisex hot showers. Motorcaravan service point. Shop. Bar. New restaurant (self-service), pizzeria and café. Bicycle hire. Dogs are not accepted 1/6-31/8. Bungalows to rent. WiFi over part of site (charged). Off site: Bars, shops, beach and all you would expect at a busy seaside resort.	Leave SS1 at exit for Marfina di Montalto di Castro and go towards the coast. At roundabout turn left, then right and at T-junction right again. Site is off to left and is clearly signed. GPS: 42.32706, 11.58155

Open: 1 April - 30 September.

Charges guide

Per unit incl. 2 persons
and electricity € 18.00 - € 40.00
extra person € 7.00 - € 12.00

FREE Alan Rogers Travel Card
Extra benefits and savings - see page 10

147

Roma

Camping Seven Hills Village

Via Cassia 1216, I-00189 Roma (Lazio) T: 063 031 0826. E: info@sevenhills.it

alanrogers.com/IT68100

Close to Rome, this site has both quiet and lively areas on steep slopes set in a delightful, lush green valley, flanked by two of the seven hills of Rome. The 250 well tended pitches for touring units are on steep terraces, mostly shaded, with 6A electricity. Two fine restaurants and the pizzeria/snack bar, with a takeaway, cater for everyone. The site runs a regular shuttle bus, and a daily bus to Rome. The pool (extra charge), also with bar snacks, is great for cooling off and relaxing after a busy day in the city. English is spoken. All cash transactions on the site are made with a card from reception. This is a bustling site and there can be many touring buses with their occupants on site during high season.

Facilities

Three soundly constructed sanitary blocks are well situated around the site, with open washbasins, and hot water in the average sized showers. Facilities for disabled campers. Well stocked shop. Bar. Two excellent restaurants with terraces. Money exchange. Swimming pool at the bottom of the site with bar/snack bar and a room where the younger element tends to congregate (separate pool charge). Disco. Excursions. Bungalows and apartments to rent. Free WiFi. Off site: Golf 4 km. Excursions to Tivoli gardens.

Open: All year (on request).

Directions

From autostrada ring road exit 3 take Via Cassia (signed SS2 Viterbo, NOT Via Cassia Bis) and look for site signs. Turn right after 1 km. and follow small road, Via Italo Piccagli, for 1 km. to site. This narrow twisting road is heavily parked on during the day. GPS: 41.993, 12.41685

Charges guide

Per unit incl. 2 persons and car	€ 24.90 - € 32.20
extra person	€ 8.00 - € 9.50
child (5-12 yrs)	€ 6.00 - € 7.50
dog	free

Roma

Camping Tiber

Via Tiberina km. 1,400, I-00188 Roma (Lazio) T: 063 361 0733. E: info@campingtiber.com

alanrogers.com/IT68090

An excellent city site with extensive facilities, which also caters for backpackers. Although a lively site, the thoughtful layout and the division of different areas with flowering shrubs makes it surprisingly peaceful. It is ideally located for visiting Rome with a free shuttle bus every 30 minutes to the station and then an easy train service to Rome (20 minutes), with trams operating late at night. The 350 touring pitches (with electricity) are mostly shaded under very tall trees and many have very pleasant views over the River Tiber. This mighty river winds around two sides of the site boundary (safely fenced) providing a cooling effect for campers. The site is extremely well run with friendly and helpful staff and especially good for campers with disabilities.

Facilities

Fully equipped, very smart sanitary facilities include hot water everywhere, private cabins, a baby room and very good facilities for disabled campers. Laundry facilities. Motorcaravan service point. Shop. Bar, restaurant, pizzeria and takeaway. Swimming pool (hat required) and bar. Play area. Internet access. Shuttle bus (on payment) to the underground station every 15 or 30 minutes according to season. Torches useful. WiFi. Off site: Local bars, restaurants and shops. Golf and riding 20 km.

Open: 25 March - 20 October.

Directions

From Florence, exit at Rome Nord Fiano on A1 and turn south onto Via Tiberina and site is signed. From other directions on Rome ring road (GRA) take exit 6 northbound on S3 Via Flaminia following signs to Tiberina. GPS: 42.0095, 12.50233

Charges guide

Per person	€ 9.50 - € 10.00
child (3-12 yrs)	€ 6.50 - € 7.00
motorcaravan	€ 10.50 - € 12.60
caravan and car	€ 12.00 - € 14.30

For latest campsite news, availability and prices visit

alanrogers.com

Roma
Camping Village Roma

Via Aurelia 831, I-00165 Roma (Lazio) T: 066 623 018. E: campingroma@ecvacanze.it
alanrogers.com/IT67800

Perched high on a hilltop on the edge of Rome, this is another venture by the Cardini/Vanucchi family, who have other quality city sites in Italy. Camping Village Roma has been brilliantly redeveloped over the past three years into possibly the best city campsite in Europe. The diverse range of facilities are designed in particular to meet the needs of young travellers and the aim here is to provide a friendly helpful service all year round. There are 150 pitches of varying sizes on level terraces. Motorcaravans are mostly placed in a separate area where 80 pitches are fully serviced. There is some shade and most have attractive views.

Facilities	Directions
Two superb toilet blocks with British style WCs and showers. Good facilities for disabled visitors and children. Baby baths. Washing machines. Motorcaravan services. New supermarket. Large restaurant/late night bar with DJ. Pizzeria with terrace and poolside bar. Swimming pool and jacuzzi. Huge TV screen. Evening entertainment/disco and regular themed parties. Play area. Internet.	Site is west of Rome. From A1 autoroute take Roma North exit towards Fuimcino airport. Take GRA and exit 1 'Aurelia' towards San Pietro-Citta del Vaticano-Centro. At 831 km. marker site is well signed. GPS: 41.8877, 12.4042

Open: All year.

Charges guide

Per person	€ 8.70 - € 11.30
pitch	€ 9.30 - € 12.80

Roma
Flaminio Village Camping Bungalow Park

Via Flaminia Nuova 821, I-00189 Roma (Lazio) T: 063 332 604. E: info@villageflaminio.com
alanrogers.com/IT68140

Camping Flaminio is an attractive campsite with many flowers, shrubs and trees giving some shade. Being 400 metres from the main road it is protected from traffic noise. Although it is quite a large site there are only 250 pitches, all with 6A electricity, which are approached by environmentally approved brick access roads. There is reasonable space allocated to touring units and the majority of pitches in the lower areas are of average size. Pitches are situated away from the main facilities so there is quite a walk between the two. There are 120 well equipped bungalows in a village-style setting on the slopes.

Facilities	Directions
The sanitary facilities are of a high quality including provision for disabled visitors and a very good baby room. Bar/pizzeria and restaurant. Shop. Swimming pool (hats required), pool bar and solarium (15/6-5/9). Bicycle hire. Internet access. Bus service. Torches useful. Pick-up service to and from Ciampino airport. WiFi. Off site: Shops, service station, bank and access to cycle route alongside river into the city. Buses and trains outside the gate. Fishing 3 km.	From ring road north of city take Flaminia exit (towards Rome centre). After 3-4 km. follow Flaminia signs, bear left where road splits to avoid tunnel and follow direction to Corso di Francia. Warning: site entrance appears suddenly on right as central barrier ends 150 m. after passing tunnel entrance. GPS: 41.95618, 12.4824

Open: All year.

Charges guide

Per unit incl. 2 persons and electricity	€ 28.00 - € 40.00

Camping Cheques accepted.

Roma
I Pini Camping

Via delle Sassete 28, Fiano Romano, I-00065 Roma (Lazio) T: 076 545 3349. E: ipini@ecvacanze.it
alanrogers.com/IT68110

I Pini was built just a few years ago by a family of experienced campers, many of whom remain involved in the operation of this site to make your stay enjoyable. The 117 pitches, with 6-10A electricity, are set on shaded grassy terraces with views of the nearby hills. Access is easy for all units via tarmac roads and everything is here, including a well stocked and reasonable supermarket. The beautifully designed restaurant, with a very large terrace, is typical of the thought that has gone into making I Pini a place where you can relax.

Facilities	Directions
The single sanitary block is spotless and hot water is free. Children's shower. Two well equipped units for disabled visitors. Washing machines and dryers. Motorcaravan services. Bar. Restaurant with large terrace. Snack bar and pizza oven. Pleasant market. Bazaar. Swimming pools (with lifeguard). Tennis. Play area. Entertainment (1/6-30/8). WiFi in bar. Torches handy. Buses to Rom.	From Rome ring road (GRA) take A1 exit to Fiano Romano. As you enter the town turn right along via Belvedere opposite an IP petrol station and follow camping signs. GPS: 42.1558, 12.5732

Open: 20 April - 29 September.

Charges guide

Per unit incl. 2 persons and electricity	€ 26.50 - € 38.00
extra person	€ 9.00 - € 12.00

FREE Alan Rogers Travel Card
Extra benefits and savings - see page 10

Salto di Fondi

Camping Village Bungalow Park Settebello

Via Flacca km. 3,6, I-04020 Salto di Fondi (Lazio) T: 077 159 9132. E: settebello@settebellocamping.com

alanrogers.com/IT68190

The SS213 hugs this beautiful coast line for many miles, running between small towns and villages and alongside the pine forests that are directly behind the beach. Camping Settebello, a large, attractive and well managed site, is in a rural area but unfortunately the site straddles this busy road and inevitably there is a great deal of traffic noise. The touring pitches are all on the beach side of the site in a wooded area and all are limited to 3A electricity supply. The ground rises before the beach and this is where many of the bungalows for rent have been built. With a total of 500 pitches about 260 are available for touring units. There is direct access to the beach, which also has a fine restaurant overlooking the sea.

Facilities	Directions
Five toilet blocks include showers, WCs (Turkish and some British style) and washbasins. Facilities for disabled visitors. Motorcaravan service point. Well stocked shop, fruit and vegetable shop, bar and restaurant/takeaway (1/6-31/8). Swimming pool and children's pool (at extra cost 51/5-31/9). Skating. Tennis. Minigolf. Entertainment and children's club. Disco. Amphitheatre and cinema. WiFi. Dogs (or cats) only accepted by advance request. Bungalows and mobile homes to rent. Bicycle hire.	The Via Flacca is a comparatively short stretch of the SS213 between Sperlonga and Terracina. The site straddles this road at km. 3.6 which is close to Terracina. Turn towards the beach to find reception. GPS: 41.29028, 13.33111

Charges guide

Per unit incl. 2 persons	€ 25.00 - € 60.00
extra person	€ 8.00 - € 16.00
Camping Cheques accepted.	

Open: 1 April - 30 September.

Terracina

Camping Romantico

Via Flacca km. 0,45, I-04019 Terracina (Lazio) T: 077 372 7620. E: romantico@camping.it

alanrogers.com/IT68180

This is a pleasant small site of only 70 pitches, but most are taken over by seasonal units, with only approximately 27 pitches available for touring units. These are set randomly among the seasonal units and consequently there is a feeling of being part of a typical Italian holiday experience. Although it is near the busy SS213, it is far enough away for traffic noise not to be a problem, and the only noise we did hear was from the occasional small boat going down the river and this was hardly noticeable. The small pitches of about 40 sq.m. are all marked by tidy hedges and are shaded under pine trees. The site enjoys a semi-rural location alongside a private beach which campers may use.

Facilities	Directions
One main toilet block includes showers, WCs (Turkish and British style) and washbasins. Facilities for disabled visitors. Motorcaravan service point. Washing machine. Small shop. Bar and restaurant/pizzeria. Children's club and entertainment in high season. Five bungalows and mobile homes to rent. Off site: Terracina 3 km. Sandy beach with sunbeds and shades.	Site is 3 km. south of Terracina on Via Flacca, the small coast road, and down the road by the river just before estuary. Coming through Terracina tunnel take first exit and turn back towards town. GPS: 41.298383, 13.28155

Charges guide

Per unit incl. 2 persons and electricity	€ 28.00 - € 40.00

Open: 1 April - 30 September.

Trevignano Romano

Camping Internazionale Lago di Bracciano

Via del Pianoro 4, I-00069 Trevignano Romano (Lazio) T: 069 985 032. E: camping.village@gmail.com

alanrogers.com/IT67850

Lago di Bracciano, just 45 km. north of Rome, is of a size that provides excellent opportunities for watersports and is inevitably very popular with windsurfers. With some pitches alongside a little beach, the site provides 110 pitches of which about 50 are for touring units. Our pitch had a full view of the lake and the gentle breeze made the temperature at the end of June quite bearable. Some shade is provided by large trees. A bar and restaurant near the entrance are behind the site's small swimming pool and play area. The local bus has a regular service to Rome.

Facilities	Directions
The single toilet block is well equipped. Facilities for disabled visitors. Washing machine. Motorcaravan service point. Small shop. Bar and restaurant/pizzeria. Small swimming pool (15/5-15/9). Play area. Barbecue area (not allowed on pitches). WiFi and Internet access. Mobile homes and bungalows to rent. Off site: Lago di Bracciano.	From Rome GRA take exit 5 on SS2 (Cassia). Turn left at Trevignano exit (km. 35) and follow SP4a to lake where site is on left. Access road and gate are max. 2.6 m. wide. GPS: 42.144717, 12.26865

Charges guide

Per unit incl. 2 persons and electricity	€ 23.00 - € 28.00
per person	€ 6.00 - € 7.00

Open: 1 April - 30 September.

For latest campsite news, availability and prices visit

alanrogers.com

Until 1963, Abruzzo and Molise were combined in one region known as Abruzzi. With some of the wildest terrain in Italy, Abruzzo is bordered by the Apennine mountain range with vast tracts of forest, while Molise has a gentler countryside with high plains, soft peaks and valleys.

THE REGIONS ARE DIVIDED INTO THE FOLLOWING PROVINCES: ABRUZZO: CHIETI, L'AQUILA, PESCARA AND TERAMO, MOLISE: CAMPOBASSO AND ISERNIA

A popular attraction in Abruzzo is the medieval hilltown of Scanno. Surrounded by high peaks looming above, the town hosts a range of activities in the summer including riding, boating and a classical music festival. Close by is Italy's third largest national park. With mountains, rivers, lakes and forests it is an important wildlife refuge, home to bears, wolves and the golden eagle. It also offers good walking, with an extensive network of paths, plus riding, skiing and canoeing. Around Scanno are the historic mountain towns of L'Aquila and Sulmona, and the village of Cocullo, where the bizarre Festival of Snakes takes place in May; a statue of a local saint is draped with live snakes and paraded through the streets. Along the Abruzzo coast is Pescara, the main resort, which has a 16 km. long beach. Ferries to Croatia and the Dalmatian islands depart from here. Nearby are the small hill towns of Atri, Penne, and Loreto Apruntino, one of the region's most important market towns. In Molise, the city of Isernia is where traces of a million-year-old village were unearthed in 1979, the most ancient signs of human life ever found in Europe. And the quiet resort and fishing port of Térmoli, from where Italian and Central European time is set, is a good place to relax.

Places of interest

Alba Adriatica: most northern of Abruzzo's coastal resorts.

Atri: 13th-century cathedral, archaeology and ethnography museums.

Celano: pretty village with turreted castle.

Lanciano: historic town.

Larino: medieval town centre, cathedral, amphitheatre.

Pineto: coastal resort.

Saepinum: ruined Roman town.

Téramo: remains of Roman amphitheatre, theatre and baths.

Cuisine of the region

As sheep farming dominates the regions, lamb is popular: *abbacchio* (roasted baby lamb), and *castratro* (castrated lamb) is used to make *intingolo di castrato*, a casserole prepared with tomatoes, wine, onion and celery. Chilli is another favourite ingredient, known locally as *pepdinie* (*peperoncino* elsewhere in Italy). Abruzzo is famous for *maccheroni all chitarra*, pasta made by pressing sheets over a wooden frame, and other local pastas include *stengozze* and *maltagliati*, usually served with a lamb sauce.

Ceci e Castagne: chickpeas and chestnuts.

Coniglio all zafferano: rabbit with saffron.

Linguine d'Ovidio: pasta with pancetta and truffles.

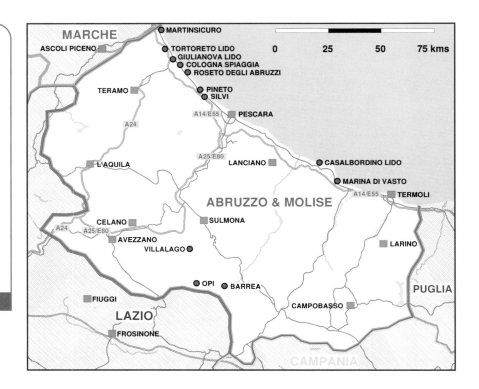

Barrea

Camping la Genziana

SS83 Ctra Tre Croci, Parco Naz. d'Abruzzo, I-67030 Barrea (Abruzzo) T: 086 488 101. E: info@pasetta.it

alanrogers.com/IT68080

This is the place to get away from it all – situated in the middle of Italy, high in the peaceful Abruzzo mountains with magnificent views over the Barrea lakes. The 105 touring pitches (4A electricity) are set on a hillside amongst wild flowers and grasses. The ebullient owner Tomasso Pesetta d'Amico and his family make everyone welcome to this peaceful, natural site. Pasetta is an expert in Alpine walking and a great raconteur. Ask him about 'calling wolves' – he really does and has appeared on BBC World in this role! The site has limited facilities, but swimming, riding and fishing are all possible nearby.

Facilities

Single clean, modern sanitary block with hot water throughout (honesty payment in high season). Mainly British style toilets. Laundry facilities. Motorcaravan services. Bar, coffee bar and small shop. WiFi (free). Torches are essential. Off site: Village of Barrea and ATM 500 m. Lake beach 3 km. Canoeing, fishing and sailing all within 3 km. Bicycle hire 3 km. Riding 7 km. Trekking and walking information.

Open: April - October.

Directions

From A25 take route 83 from Celano and site is signed 4 km. before Barrea. Alternatively route 17 from Pratola/Sulmona through Castel di Sangro. then right to route 83 and site is 1 km. before Barrea. GPS: 41.74267, 13.98867

Charges guide

Per unit incl. 2 persons and electricity	€ 27.50 - € 31.50
extra person	€ 8.20
child (under 9 yrs)	€ 4.00
dog	€ 3.00

No credit cards.

Casalbordino Lido
Centro Vacanze Poker
Ctra Termini 27 Lungomare sud, I-66021 Casalbordino Lido (Abruzzo) T: 087 391 8321.
E: info@centrovacanzepoker.it **alanrogers.com/IT67960**

This is an extraordinary campsite. The 15 luxury pitches (6A electricity) are set among attractive palms at one end of the hotel grounds (some rail noise). They are an integral part of a five-star hotel which has beautifully landscaped gardens, cleverly complementing a plush restaurant/bar complex. The adjacent beach is a mixture of sand and small rocks, but fabulous swimming and paddling pools and a jacuzzi compensate. Popular and a little pricey, Vacanze Poker is a great family site.

Facilities

15 medium pitches each with a private bathroom nearby (key entry). Swimming pools and jacuzzi. Restaurant and bar. Ambitious entertainment programme. Dogs allowed. WiFi over part of site (charged). Off site: Beach adjacent (lifeguard, loungers and toilet facilities). Amenities at Casalbordino Lido. Watersports.

Open: 1 June - 15 September.

Directions

Leave the A14 at Torino di Sangro and join the SS16 south. In Casalbordino Lido go under the railway, continue south along the seafront road. The hotel complex is well signed. GPS: 42.19094, 14.64433

Charges guide

Per unit incl. 2 persons	
and electricity	€ 49.00 - € 89.00
extra person	€ 12.00 - € 22.00

Cologna Spiaggia
Stork Camping Village
Via del Mare 11, I-64020 Cologna Spiaggia (Abruzzo) T: 085 893 7076. E: info@storkcampingvillage.com
alanrogers.com/IT67860

This is a relaxed site set back from the SS16 Adriatica in a 21-acre park with a selection of pitches for larger caravans and motorcaravans, mainly around the perimeter. The 457 touring pitches (all with 6-16A electricity) are well laid out between mature trees that offer good shade, but many can be difficult to access. Some pitches are available adjacent to the beach, for a small supplement. There is direct access to a sandy beach with a range of amenities on offer, including a beach bar and beach volleyball. A lively entertainment programme is organised in peak season, including a children's club and aquagym.

Facilities

Two central toilet blocks provide a mixture of British and Turkish style WCs. Hot water for showers and basins is restricted to certain times. Shop. Bazaar. Bar. Restaurant/pizzeria. Beach bar. Swimming pool. Children's pool (swimming lessons available). Play area. Tennis. Beach volleyball. TV room. Entertainment and children's activities (July/Aug). WiFi over site (charged). Chalets for rent. Gas barbecues only. Off site: Fishing and bicycle hire 1 km. Rafting and canoe trips. Excursions.

Open: 15 May - 15 September.

Directions

From A14 motorway (Bologna-Taranto) take the Teramo-Giulianova exit and join SS80 towards Giulianova, and then continue towards Cologna Spiaggia. Site signed. GPS: 42.72119, 13.98901

Charges guide

Per person	€ 4.50 - € 11.50
pitch incl. electricity	€ 7.00 - € 17.50
Camping Cheques accepted.	

Giulianova Lido
Don Antonio Camping Residence
Via Padova s/n, I-64021 Giulianova Lido (Abruzzo) T: 085 800 8928. E: info@campingdonantonio.it
alanrogers.com/IT68020

Set alongside the beautiful Adriatic coast with its sandy beaches, this site has 350 pitches, all with 6A electricity, 200 with water and waste water. There is an excellent reception building and swimming pool, but other facilities, although very clean, are rather basic. The site does, however, benefit from the facilities of its larger, adjacent sister site, Camping Holiday (IT68010), with its pool, restaurant, games and supermarket. Many of the campers also pop next door to join in the organised entertainment. Parts of this generally quiet site may be subject to some noise during the evening and music in the daytime from the other campsites in the immediate area.

Facilities

Four traditional units provide a mixture of British and Turkish sanitary facilities. The new units for disabled campers are of a high standard. Swimming pool with slides and whirlpool (June-Sept). Washing machine. Snack bar. Beach bar. Bicycle hire. Torches useful. Dogs are not accepted 8/7-20/8. Off site: All resort facilities in town. Beach fishing. Golf 35 km.

Open: 14 May - 11 September.

Directions

Leave autostrada E14 north of Pescara and take SS80 to Giulianova Lido. Follow numerous site signs. Take care to find bridge under railway with a 3.6 m. clearance (north of town). All other bridges have 'car only' clearance, so do not use sat nav. Site is 400 m. on left after bridge. GPS: 42.777322, 13.951178

Charges guide

Per unit incl. 2 persons	
and electricity	€ 19.00 - € 49.00
extra person	€ 5.00 - € 12.00

Marina di Vasto

Camping Villaggio Il Pioppeto

SS16 Sud km. 521, I-66055 Marina di Vasto (Abruzzo) T: 087 380 1466. E: infocampeggio@ilpioppeto.it

alanrogers.com/IT67970

Il Pioppeto lies to the south of Pescara and is a clean and friendly family site. It is well maintained and tidy, with 110 level pitches with 5A electricity and plenty of shade. The local food offered in the small, unassuming restaurant is superb and reasonably priced (cash only). Diners can eat inside or enjoy the atmosphere on the terrace, although there is some road noise. The delightful beach just outside the site is long and very wide, so there is no difficulty in escaping from the maddening crowd.

Facilities

The four toilet blocks of differing sizes are of a good standard, although some washbasins have only cold water. Excellent new motorcaravan services. Supermarket. Bar and snack bar. Restaurant. Play area. Games room. Entertainment and children's club in peak season. Adjacent beach. Tourist information. Chalets for rent. Bicycle hire. WiFi over part of site. Off site: Riding centre (owned by site) 700 m. Disco. Tennis. Roller skating rink.

Open: 15 May - 15 September.

Directions

From the A14 motorway (Bologna-Taranto) take Vasto exit and join SS16 towards Vasto from where site is well signed. GPS: 42.088, 14.73667

Charges guide

Per unit incl. 2 persons	
and electricity	€ 19.60 - € 44.30
extra person	€ 4.90 - € 9.60
child (2-8 yrs)	€ 3.70 - € 7.20

Credit cards accepted during high season.

Martinsicuro

Camping Riva Nuova

Via dei Pioppi 6, I-64014 Martinsicuro (Abruzzo) T: 086 179 7515. E: emanuele.dionisi@rivanuova.it

alanrogers.com/IT67980

Situated at the south end of the small town of Martinsicuro on the Adriatic coast, this excellent site offers a first class camping experience with a great ambience. Set in pleasant, neat, landscaped gardens and obviously well planned, there are 334 pitches for touring units varying in size from 60 to 120 sq.m. There are 140 pitches with water, drainage and electricity and a further 23 with a private bathroom on the pitch. Across a beach road is a long beach of soft sand and a promenade with the usual seaside facilities. This is a great site for low or high season, especially for families with children.

Facilities

An exceptional, central sanitary block provides everything to the highest standard. Ample toilets, showers and washbasins. Children's bathroom. Facilities for disabled visitors. Private bathrooms to rent. Laundry facilities. Bar, restaurant and shop. Swimming pool (extra daily charge) and sunbathing area. Gym. Boules. Tennis. Entertainment in high season. Bicycle hire. Sailing. ATM. WiFi (charged). Dogs are not accepted. Off site: Fishing and boat launching 100 m. Martinsicuro. Tremano.

Open: 1 May - 18 September.

Directions

Leave the A14 at San Benedetto and take SS16 to Martinsicuro. Turn onto the coast road and go south of the town to the site in Via dei Pioppi (well signed). Be sure to follow the campsite signs as other access roads to the beach road are mostly dead ends. GPS: 42.8801, 13.9205

Charges guide

Per unit incl. 2 persons	
and electricity	€ 16.90 - € 45.90
extra person	€ 4.00 - € 11.50

Martinsicuro

Camping Village Duca Amedeo

Lungomare Europa, 158, I-64014 Martinsicuro (Abruzzo) T: 086 179 7376. E: info@ducaamedeo.it

alanrogers.com/IT67982

Duca Amedeo is a small site on the seafront and promenade with access to a broad, sandy beach across a busy road. There are 150 flat, closely placed pitches here, of which 50 are available to touring units. Of a reasonable size, some have shade from trees and 6A electricity is provided. This is a very Italian site with lots of loud holiday noise and music until 23.30. There is no shop, but a supermarket is 300 m. away and the bar/restaurant of the hotel next door (owned by family members) is used by campers. There are many loyal Italian families here in well established long term pitches.

Facilities

One main sanitary block with a confusion of facilities, some modern, some not. Hot water at sinks and showers. Toilets for children. Some private bathrooms for hire. Motorcaravan service area (very close to pitches). Swimming and paddling pools. Picnic area. Barbecue area. Games room. Playground. Beach games area. Sports field. Bocce. Animation in high season. Fishing. Mobile homes and chalets for rent. WiFi throughout (charged). Off site: Town of Martinsicuro.

Open: May - 15 September.

Directions

The site is on the seafront at Martinsicuro. Leave the A14 autostrada at the Martinsicuro exit, to the south of San Benedetto del Tronto. Follow signs to the town centre and then to the site. GPS: 42.88118, 13.9207

Charges guide

Per unit incl. 2 persons	
and electricity	€ 16.00 - € 44.00
extra person	€ 4.00 - € 11.00

For latest campsite news, availability and prices visit

alanrogers.com

Opi

Camping Il Vecchio Mulino

SS Marsicana 83 km. 52, I-67030 Opi (Abruzzo) T: 086 391 2232. E: ilvecchiomulino@tiscalinet.it

alanrogers.com/IT67920

Il Vecchio Mulino enjoys a fine woodland setting on the slopes of Monte Marsicano, at the heart of the Abruzzo National Park. The site is open all year and is popular for walking and cycling in the summer and is well located for the Pescasseroli and Macchiarvana ski resorts in the winter. The focal point of the site is the old mill and the attractively restored farm buildings housing the restaurant and bed and breakfast accommodation. The 70 pitches here are spacious and level and all are equipped with a wooden picnic table and electrical connection.

Facilities

Centrally located toilet block. Motorcaravan services. Small shop (local produce). Bar/restaurant. Snack bar. Sports field. Play area. Games room. Barbecue area. Tourist information. Off site: Village centre 1 km. Bus service from site entrance. Abruzzo National Park. Mountain biking and walking.

Open: All year (but check with site).

Directions

Take Pescina exit from the A24/A25 Rome-Pescara motorway and join the SS83 through Passo del Diavolo to Pescasseroli from where site is well signed (1 km. from Opi). GPS: 41.780017, 13.867767

Charges guide

Per unit incl. 2 persons	
and electricity	€ 21.00 - € 26.50
extra person	€ 6.00 - € 9.50

Pineto

International Camping

Ctra Torre Cerrano, I-64025 Pineto (Abruzzo) T: 085 930 639. E: into@internationalcamping.it

alanrogers.com/IT68060

This small, very Italian, family run site, just north of Pescara and south of Pineto, is situated between the coastal railway line and a sandy beach. Inevitably there is some railway noise but it is not too intrusive. Access to the site is via a 4 m. high bridge followed by a sharp right-hand turn, then through gates to reception about 300 m. ahead. The 100 small pitches for touring units (cars parked away from pitches), all have 3A electricity, but access to many of them is difficult due to an abundance of trees and hedges. There are ten mobile homes to rent. It is quieter than the larger sites that are usually found on this coast.

Facilities

One sanitary block provides ample toilets (British and Turkish style) washbasins and hot showers (token). Children's bathrooms and baby changing room. Good facilities for disabled visitors. Shop (1/5-15/9). Bar, restaurant and takeaway (all season). Beach. WiFi and Internet point. Entertainment (high season). Excursions organised. Mobile homes and bungalows to rent. Dogs are not accepted 1/6-30/9. Off site: Pineto. Riding and bicycle hire 3 km. Golf 15 km.

Open: 1 May - 23 September.

Directions

On the SS16 at 431.2 km. marker just past the Cerrano tower, turn towards the beach and under the railway (4 m. bridge). Then turn immediately right to site. GPS: 42.58140, 14.09290

Charges guide

Per unit incl. 2 persons	
and electricity	€ 22.00 - € 51.00
extra person	€ 5.50 - € 13.00
No credit cards.	

Roseto degli Abruzzi

Camping Village Eurcamping

Lungomare Trieste Sud, I-64026 Roseto degli Abruzzi (Abruzzo) T: 085 899 3179. E: eurcamping@camping.it

alanrogers.com/IT68040

Eurcamping is about 2 km. south of the small town of Rosette degli Abruzzi, at the end of the coastal road which runs parallel to the SS16. This is a relatively quiet site, situated beside the sea, but with no direct access to it. There are 265 well defined pitches, many under green screens, and all with 3/6A electricity. Accessing the site is not difficult, but you have to pass under the coastal railway line so must use the bridge with 4 m. headroom. There is some road noise but little from the railway.

Facilities

Three sanitary blocks with free hot showers. Facilities for disabled visitors. Motorcaravan services. Laundry. Bar. Restaurant. Takeaway. Pizzeria. Shop. Swimming pools (hats must be worn) with solarium terrace. Play area and sports ground. Tennis. Bowling. WiFi (charged). Bicycle hire. Entertainment in high season. Clubs for children and teenagers. Pets are allowed only on assigned pitches. Bungalows to rent. Off site: Beach. Canoe and pedalo hire.

Open: 1 May - 31 October.

Directions

From north or south on A14 motorway, take exit Roseto degli Abruzzi exit. Turn onto SS150 to Roseto degli Abruzzi. Pass under 4 m. bridge below railway at south end of town, and right onto coast road. From Rome and L'Aquila on A24 motorway take Villa Vomano-Teramo exit onto SS150 (Roseto degli Abruzzi). GPS: 42.6577, 14.0353

Charges guide

Per unit incl. 2 persons	
and electricity	€ 18.00 - € 42.50
Camping Cheques accepted.	

FREE Alan Rogers Travel Card
Extra benefits and savings - see page 10

Silvi

Camping Europe Garden

Ctra Vallescura n. 10, I-64028 Silvi (Abruzzo) T: 085 930 137. E: info@europegarden.it

alanrogers.com/IT68000

This site is 13 kilometres northwest of Pescara, and lies just back from the coast about 2 km. up a very steep hill from where it has pleasant views over the sea. The site predominantly consists of bungalows and chalets for hire, with around 40 spaces at the top of the site available for smaller touring units and tents. These are mainly on level terraces, but access to some may be difficult. All have 6A electricity. If installation of caravans is a problem a tractor is available to help. Cars remain with units on some of the pitches or in nearby parking spaces for the remainder. Most pitches are shaded.

Facilities	Directions
The toilet block provides a mixture of British and Turkish style WCs. Hot showers. Washing machines. Shop, bar, restaurant, takeaway (all season). Swimming pool (May-Sept. 300 sq.m; caps compulsory), small paddling pool and jacuzzi. Tennis. Playground. Entertainment programme. Free weekly excursions (15/6-8/9). Free shuttle bus service (18/5-7/9) to site's own private beach. WiFi. No dogs. Barbecues are not allowed on pitches. **Open:** 18 May - 14 September.	Turn inland off SS16 coast road at km. 433 for Silvi Alta and follow site signs. From autostrada A14 take Pineto exit from north or Pescara Nord exit from the south. GPS: 42.56738, 14.09247

Charges guide

Per unit incl. 2 persons and electricity	€ 23.50 - € 42.50
extra person	€ 5.00 - € 11.00

Tortoreto Lido

Camping Village del Salinello

Lungomare Sud, I-64018 Tortoreto Lido (Abruzzo) T: 086 772 31. E: info@salinello.com

alanrogers.com/IT67990

This large, attractive site with 250 seasonal pitches, and a further 250 small pitches for camping under trees lies at the southern extremity of Tortoreto Lido. It also provides over 300 chalets and bungalows to rent. With an adjacent sandy beach alongside the turquoise Adriatic, the site has an excellent location and is close to both the SS16 and the A14 autostrada. Access to the coast road and Lungomare involves passing under the railway, and care must be taken to use the new underpass since many of the bridges have less than 2 m. headroom.

Facilities	Directions
Two large, well maintained sanitary blocks have a mixture of British and Turkish toilets, showers in cubicles and open plan washbasins. Facilities for disabled visitors. Private bathrooms to rent. Swimming complex (charged). Bars. Restaurants. Commercial centre and open-air cinema/theatre. Full programme of entertainment (1/6-31/8). Tennis and 5-a-side pitches (on payment). ATM. WiFi (charged). No dogs. Off site: Tortoreto Lido. **Open:** 15 May - 15 September.	From A14 join SS16 via either Valvibrata or Teramo exit and head for Tortoreto. In the town turn left into Viale Napoli, the last turning before the site (site sign on main road). Turn south on Lungomare to site. Do not use sat nav for final approach and beware low bridges to coast road. GPS: 42.784129, 13.952664

Charges guide

Per unit incl. 2 persons and electricity	€ 18.50 - € 37.00

Villalago

Camping I Lupi

Riviera di Villalago, Lago di Scanno, I-67030 Villalago (Abruzzo) T: 086 474 0625. E: campingilupi@libero.it

alanrogers.com/IT67930

I Lupi is a traditional, friendly and very peaceful site in a beautiful location within the Abruzzo National Park on the banks of the Lago di Scanno. The 170 medium sized pitches (6A electricity) are informal, with little shade, but many have fine views of the lake and mountain scenery. There is an attractive bar/restaurant (opening may be limited to high season). Although amenities on site are sometimes limited, campers have access to the facilities of the nearby Albergo Acquevive Hotel, which is linked to the site. Campers seeking a no frills, back-to-nature site will enjoy I Lupi.

Facilities	Directions
Two well appointed toilet blocks have good facilities with hot water throughout. Motorcaravan services. Communal freezer. Small shop. Bar, snack bar. Bread and milk to order. Supermarket. Play area. Children's club in peak season. Tourist information. Shuttle bus (high season). Games room. Sports field. Direct access to lake. Accommodation for rent. Torches essential. Off site: Riding 20 m. Lake beach 200 m. Sailing and fishing 300 m. Boat launching 400 m. Bicycle hire 1 km. **Open:** 1 June - 1 September, also Easter and Christmas.	From the A25 motorway (Rome-Pescara) take the Cocullo exit and join the SP60 towards Anversa Degli Abruzzi. At this town, join the SR479 towards Scanno and you will reach the Lago di Scanno and site (well signed) shortly after passing Villalago. GPS: 41.92009, 13.859081

Charges guide

Per unit incl. 2 persons and electricity	€ 24.90 - € 26.90
extra person	€ 6.40

For latest campsite news, availability and prices visit

alanrogers.com

Campania boasts one of the finest coastlines in Italy, incorporating the dramatic Amalfi coast, the beautiful Bay of Naples, and the enchanting islands of Capri, Ischia and Prócida. It is also home to some of the best preserved ancient sites, most notably Pompeii, plus the historic city of Naples.

THE REGION HAS FIVE PROVINCES: AVELLINO, BENEVENTO, CASERTA, NAPOLI AND SALERNO

Filled with palaces, churches and convents, the regional capital of Naples also boasts an archaeology museum housing artefacts excavated from the nearby Roman sites of Pompeii and Herculaneum. Situated on the Bay of Naples, these sites were buried after Mount Vesuvius erupted in 79 AD, leaving them frozen in time. Although still active (the only one on mainland Europe) it is possible to scale up the volcano. Not far from Pompeii is the popular holiday destination of Sorrento and off the coast of the bay are the islands of Ischia, Capri and Prócida. The largest is Ischia, which along with Capri, attracts vast numbers of tourists; Prócida is the smallest and least visited. All three can be explored on day trips from the mainland. Further south is the Amalfi coast, a spectacular stretch of coastline littered with superb beaches and resorts, including Positano, Amalfi and Ravello. The busy port of Salerno is near to the ancient Greek site of Paestum, with temples dating back to the 6th century BC, and the area known as the Cilento, a mountainous region with a quiet coastline. It has a number of seaside resorts including Agropoli, Acciaroli and Palinuro plus the inland villages of Castelcivita and Pertosa, both of which have cave systems open to the public.

Places of interest

Benevento: once an important Roman settlement, monuments include the Arch of Trajan and the Roman theatre.

Campi Flegri: area known as the Fiery Fields, with volcanic craters and hot springs.

Caserta: opulent royal palace with gardens open to the public.

Ravello: offers best view of the Amalfi coast.

Salerno: medieval old quarter, 11th-century cathedral, annual fair in May.

San Marco: picturesque fishing village.

Santa Maria Capua Vetere: ruined Roman amphitheatre with a series of tunnels beneath it.

Cuisine of the region

Naples is the home of pizza, pasta and tomato sauce. Aubergines and courgettes are frequently used in pasta sauces. Seafood is widely available along the coast including fresh squid, octopus, clams and mussels. Cilento produces strawberries, artichokes and mozzarella cheese. Made with buffalo milk, mozzarella is usually accompanied by tomatoes.

Calzone: stuffed fried pizza with ham and cheese.

Marinara: pizza topped with tomato, garlic and basil, no cheese.

Sfogliatella: flaky pastry case stuffed with ricotta and candied peel.

Zuppa di cozze: mussels with a hot pepper sauce.

Zuppa Inglese: dessert made with sponge fingers, peaches, custard, brandy and egg whites.

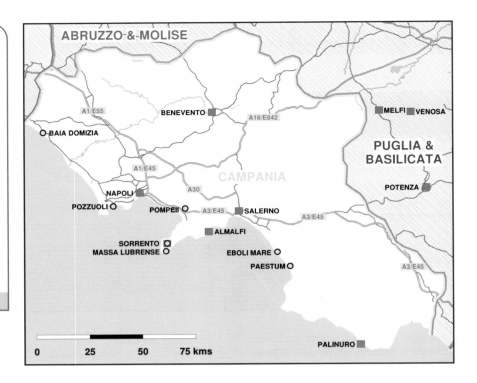

Baia Domizia

Baia Domizia Villaggio Camping

Via Pietre Bianche, I-81030 Baia Domizia (Campania) T: 082 393 0164. E: info@baiadomizia.it

alanrogers.com/IT68200

This large, beautifully maintained seaside site is about 70 kilometres northwest of Naples, and is within a pine forest, cleverly left in its natural state. Although it does not feel like it, there are 750 touring pitches in clearings, either of grass and sand or on hardstanding, all with electricity, 80 now also with water and waste water. Finding a pitch may take time as there are so many good ones to choose from, but staff will help in season. Most pitches are well shaded, however there are some in the sun for cooler periods. The central complex is superb with well designed buildings providing for all needs (the site is some distance from the town). Member of Leading Campings group.

Facilities

Seven new toilet blocks have hot water in washbasins (many cabins) and showers. Good access and facilities for disabled campers. Washing machines, spin dryers. Motorcaravan services. Gas supplies. Supermarket and general shop. Large bar. Restaurants, pizzeria and takeaway. Ice cream parlour. Swimming pool complex. Playground. Tennis. Windsurfing hire and school. Disco. Excursions. Torches required in some areas. WiFi (charged). Dogs are not accepted. Off site: Bicycle hire 100 m. Fishing and riding 3 km.

Open: 18 April - 15 September.

Directions

The turn to Baia Domizia leads off the Formia-Naples road 23 km. from Formia. From Rome-Naples autostrada, take Cassino exit to Formia. Site is to the north of Baia Domizia and well signed. Site is off the coastal road that runs parallel to the SS7. GPS: 41.207222, 13.791389

Charges 2013

Per unit incl. 2 persons	
and electricity	€ 25.50 - € 48.50
extra person	€ 6.50 - € 12.00
child (1-11 yrs)	€ 4.60 - € 9.50

For latest campsite news, availability and prices visit
alanrogers.com

Eboli Mare
Camping Village Paestum

Litoranea Localitá Foce Sele, I-84025 Eboli Mare (Campania) T: 082 869 1003. E: info@campingpaestum.it
alanrogers.com/IT68410

This large, family owned site is set some way back from the beach near to Paestum and the important ancient Greek temples of ancient Poseidon, built by the Greeks in the sixth century BC and taken by the Romans and renamed in 273 BC. Fast becoming a popular tourist resort, the town of Paestum is some way south of the site which enjoys a quiet, rural environment. With 540 level and well defined pitches, it has 200 allocated for international touring units and these are sited in a special area maintained for non-Italian guests on the basis that they prefer more peace and quiet.

Facilities

Five toilet blocks are well finished and provide 75% Turkish and 25% British style WCs. Hot showers and washbasins. Facilities for disabled visitors. Motorcaravan service point. Washing machines. Small shop. Bar and restaurant. Swimming pool and children's pool (swimming caps compulsory). Tennis. Entertainment and children's club. Disco. Shuttle bus to beach. WiFi (charged). Bungalows to rent. No pets. Off site: Beach 500 m.

Open: 1 May - 30 September.

Directions

Site is north of Paestum Capaccio on the coast road (SP175). From Paestum go north along main coast road. At T-junction turn left and past military zone to site 3 km. on right. From the A3 near Salerno follow signs initially for Pontecagnano, then keep south on coast road (SP175). GPS: 40.491167, 14.944583

Charges guide

Per unit incl. 2 persons and electricity	€ 22.00 - € 36.00

Massa Lubrense
Camping Nettuno

Via A Vespucci 39, Marina del Cantone, I-80061 Massa Lubrense (Campania) T: 081 808 1051.
E: info@villaggionettuno.it **alanrogers.com/IT68380**

Camping Nettuno is owned and run by the friendly Mauro family, who speak excellent English. Nestled in the bay of Marina del Cantone, it is situated in the protected area of Punta Campanella. As a result the approach roads are difficult and narrow. This tiny campsite of only 42 pitches (with 4A electricity available) is spread over three levels above the pebbly beach. Up several steps and across the road are the amenities, reception, shop, and dive centre and restaurant. Pitches are informally arranged and most with shade. They are small and close together but there is plenty of assistance to find the best place.

Facilities

The single central sanitary block includes facilities for disabled campers (and access via a ramp to the beach). Washing machine. Basic motorcaravan service point. Gas supplies. Small shop. Delightful restaurant with sea views. Bar (lively at night). Dive centre. Excursions. TV in bar area. Small play area. Free tennis arranged at court next door. Fishing. Off site: Small beach (pebbles) 5 m. from bottom of site. Excellent restaurant 100 m. Amalfi Coast, Capri, nature parks, walking etc.

Open: 20 March - 2 November.

Directions

From A3 motorway (Naples-Salerno), take Castellamare di Stabia exit onto S145. Pass Castellamare, follow signs to Meta di Sorrento via tunnel and turn off towards Positano in Meta. After 5 km. turn to Sant'Agata dei due Golfi (6.5 km) then on to Nerano and finally Marina del Cantone. Continue 100 m. then turn round to negotiate steep, narrow entrance. GPS: 40.58389, 14.35194

Charges guide

Per unit incl. 2 persons and electricity	€ 23.00 - € 36.50

Camping Cheques accepted.

Paestum
Camping Villaggio Athena

Via Ponte di Ferro, I-84063 Paestum (Campania) T: 082 885 1105. E: vathena@tiscalinet.it
alanrogers.com/IT68530

This is a rather basic site, but has the benefit of direct access to the beach. Most of the 120 touring pitches are undefined, but are set amongst mature trees that give some good shade. Part of the site is in woodland. The access is easy and the staff are friendly, but little English is spoken. There are 11 bungalows available for rent. Limited entertainment is staged in July and August. The management, the Prearo brothers, aim for a happy environment and visit most days to keep an eye on things.

Facilities

Toilet facilities in two blocks are basic and have mixed British and Turkish style WCs, washbasins and cold showers. Hot showers are available in the small block adjacent to the beach. Toilets for disabled campers. Small shop (all season). Watersports. WiFi. Dogs are not permitted. Off site: Restaurant/pizzeria close to site entrance. Tennis 1 km. Hourly bus service.

Open: 1 March - 30 October.

Directions

Take SS18 through Paestum and, at southern end of town before the antiquities, turn right as signed and follow to sea. Left at crossroads and a little further turn right. Site signed, but some are obscured by vegetation. GPS: 40.42061, 14.99608

Charges guide

Per person	€ 5.00 - € 9.00
pitch incl. electricity	€ 8.50 - € 15.00

FREE Alan Rogers Travel Card
Extra benefits and savings - see page 10

Pompeii

Camping Zeus

Via Villa dei Misteri, I-80045 Pompeii (Campania) T: 081 861 5320. E: info@campingzeus.it
alanrogers.com/IT68300

The naming of this site is obvious once you discover it is just 50 metres from the entrance to the fantastic ruins at Pompeii (closer than the car park). It is a reasonably priced, city-type site perfect for visiting the famous Roman archaeological sites here. The site's 100 pitches, all for touring units, are on flat grass under mature trees that give shade. All have access to 10A electricity. Larger units use the tarmac parking area. This site provides a safe central location and is of a high standard for the area, albeit with none of the holidaying trimmings.

Facilities	Directions
The single sanitary block is basic but clean and modernised, with British and Turkish style WCs. Showers have hot water with cold water in washbasins. No facilities for disabled campers. Washing machines. Shop. Gas supplies. Bar/restaurant at site entrance with daily menu at lunch times (evenings only in high season). WiFi (charged). Accommodation to rent. Off site: Pompeii, Sorrento, Herculaneum, Amalfi coast. **Open:** All year.	Leave Napoli-Salerno autostrada at the Pompeii Ovest exit. Turn left towards the ruins and go under the autostrada. A further 100 m. turn left towards Pompeii and the site. Site is straight ahead past the railway station. GPS: 40.74958, 14.4724

Charges guide

Per unit incl. 2 persons and electricity	€ 17.00 - € 25.00
extra person	€ 5.00 - € 6.00

Pozzuoli

Camping Il Vulcano Solfatara

Via Solfetara no. 163, I-80078 Pozzuoli (Campania) T: 081 526 7413. E: info@solfatara.it
alanrogers.com/IT68250

This is truly a unique site situated within the crater of an active volcano. Solfatara is one of the many volcanoes that surround Naples, Vesuvius being the most widely known. Here you can camp in a pleasant wooded area with basic but modern facilities, yet be just a couple of minutes from the other side of the crater with its steaming fumaroles. There are no designated pitches, but there are 100 electricity connections (4A), and you are free to pitch where you like. This is a site for tents and small units only, definitely not for any larger units, the problem being the access arch to the site.

Facilities	Directions
The single sanitary block provides toilets (British and Turkish style), hot showers and washbasins. No facilities for disabled visitors. Washing machine. Motorcaravan service point. Bar and small shop. Natural sauna and small swimming pool. WiFi (charged). Small volcano museum. Off site: The Solfatara Natural Park and the living, breathing volcano! **Open:** All year.	Take the Naples tangenziale from the autostrada and exit at exit N11 (Agnano). Follow signs (Pozzuoli) and turn right at traffic lights at top of hill. Site is 3.5 km. along this road on the right. Local traffic can be a problem. GPS: 40.82858, 14.13583

Charges guide

Per person	€ 8.00 - € 9.90
pitch	€ 4.50 - € 14.50

Sorrento

Village Camping Santa Fortunata

Via Capo, 39, I-80067 Sorrento (Campania) T: 081 807 3574. E: info@santafortunata.eu
alanrogers.com/IT68340

Village Camping Santa Fortunata is situated on the hillside just outside Sorrento among olive and lemon groves. There is plenty of shade but low hanging branches make some of the pitches unsuitable for larger units. There is a steep tarmac approach to some but the stunning views over the bay more than compensate. Pitches are of average size with several spaces for larger units and there is a feeling of spaciousness as many are separated by trees and shrubs intersected with wooden constructed walkways. Two small beaches can be reached via long steep inclines.

Facilities	Directions
Five older style refurbished sanitary blocks with adjustable hot showers. Hot water for dishwashing but not laundry sinks. Washing machine. Good restaurant/bar. Small well provisioned shop. Swimming pool. WiFi. Off site: Beach 300 m. Boat launch and bicycle hire 1 km. Riding 3 km. Bus to Sorrento. Boat trips to Capri. Amalfi, Naples, Pompeii and Positano are all within easy reach. **Open:** 1 April - 25 October.	From the A3 (Naples-Salerno) follow signs to Pensisola Sorrentina. Exit at Castellammare di Stabia and on through Sorrento. Then take SS145 towards Massa Lubrense, running along Via Capo. Site is 1.5 km. past Sorrento (the best time to travel this busy coastline is 13.00-15.00 during siesta). GPS: 40.62753, 14.35736

Charges guide

Per unit incl. 2 persons and electricity	€ 20.00 - € 45.00

For latest campsite news, availability and prices visit
alanrogers.com

Puglia is the long strip of land that forms the heel of the Italian 'boot', with the Gargano Peninsula as its spur. A popular destination, holidaymakers are attracted to its sandy beaches and clean seas. Lying next to it is Basilicata, a remote and wild region that has remained largely unspoilt.

PUGLIA HAS FIVE PROVINCES: BARI, BRINDISI, FOGGIA, LECCE AND TARANTO

BASILICATA HAS TWO: MATERA AND POTENZA

Made into a national park in 1991, the Gargano peninsula in Puglia boasts a diverse landscape of beaches, lagoons, forests and mountains. Up in the hills is the town of Monte Sant'Angelo. Home to one of the earliest Christian shrines in Europe, it attracts pilgrimages from all over the country. Further inland is the Forest of Shadows, an area covering 11,000 hectares with a variety of wildlife, ideal for walking. The seaside towns of Vieste, Rodi Garganico, Péshici and Manfredonia are popular with tourists, as are the Trémiti Islands – including San Nicola, San Domino and Capraia – off the Gargano coast. Heading south is Trani, one of the most important medieval ports with an ornate cathedral, and Bari. Ferries to Greece depart from Bari, as well as from Bríndisi. At the southern tip of Puglia is Lecce, renowned for its Baroque architecture, and the Salentine peninsula. Good beaches can be found along the western coast of the peninsula around Gallipoli. To the west Basilicata is mostly upland country, scattered with ruins. The brooding town of Melfi has a formidable Norman castle, while nearby Venosa was once the largest Roman colony. The town has an archaeology park with remains of Roman baths and an amphitheatre.

Places of interest

Alberobello: home to white-washed circular buildings with conical roofs known as *trulli*, there are *trulli* restaurants, shops plus a cathedral.

Galatina: important wine-producing town, famous for its *tarantella* dance performed on the feast day of Saints Peter and Paul in June.

Lucera: ruins of Roman amphitheatre, 13th-century castle with fortified walls and towers.

Matera: town perched on edge of a ravine.

Mattinata: popular, small resort in Gargano.

Metaponto: Roman ruins, museums.

Vieste: holiday capital of Puglia with excellent beaches.

Cuisine of the region

Puglia is the main source of Italy's fish. It also produces some of the country's best olives and is famous for its almonds, tomatoes, figs, melons and grapes. Lamb is commonly eaten, often roasted with rosemary and thyme, and as there is little poultry, beef or pork in the region, horsemeat is popular, particularly in the Salento area. Peppers and *zenzero* (ginger) are widely used in dishes throughout Basilicata. Local cheeses include *ricotta*, *mozzarella*, *scamorza*, *burrata* (soft and creamy, made with cow's milk), and *caprini* (small fresh goat's cheese preserved in olive oil).

Braciole di cavallo: horsemeat steaks cooked in a rich tomato sauce.

Latte di mandorla: almond milk.

Panzarotti alla barese: pasta stuffed with meat sauce, egg and cheese, deep fried in olive oil.

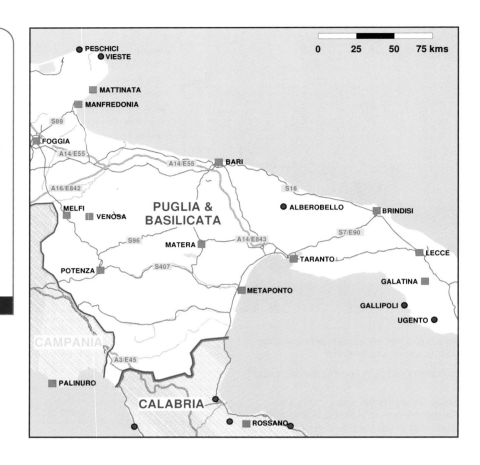

Alberobello

Camping Dei Trulli

Via Castellana, SP113 Monopoli-Alberobello km. 17, I-70011 Alberobello (Puglia) T: 080 432 3699.

E: info@campingdeitrulli.it **alanrogers.com/IT68700**

The UNESCO listed site at Alberobello is just 17 km. inland from the coast and offers the chance to see the unusual trulli properties. It is a dry, almost arid, landscape which is covered with olive groves, orchards, vineyards and the trulli (strange circular buildings with conical roofs and domed within, built from local limestone without mortar). Camping Dei Trulli is a short stay site offering visitors a chance to explore the area. It has 120 small pitches all with 6A electricity. Bungalows and caravans are available to rent. The grottos of Castellana are not far away.

Facilities

The toilet block includes facilities for disabled visitors although it also holds the washing machine and is used for emptying chemical toilets. Small shop. Bar. Restaurant (Aug. only). Swimming pool and children's pool (1/6-15/9). Pool table and electronic games. Indoor disco during the winter months. WiFi over site. Off site: Alberobello (trulli properties). Grottos of Castellana.

Open: 1 April - 30 September.

Directions

From E55 coast road south of Bari take Alberobello exit (SP113) and bear left then right. Site is 17 km. along this road. At crossroads go straight ahead (Alberobello) and the site is on the left 1.5 km. before the town. GPS: 40.801283, 17.251217

Charges guide

Per person	€ 6.00 - € 8.00
child (3-8 yrs)	€ 4.00 - € 5.00
pitch	€ 5.00 - € 7.00
electricity	€ 2.50

Gallipoli
Camping Baia di Gallipoli
Litoranea per Santa Maria di Leuca, I-73014 Gallipoli (Puglia) T: 083 327 3210. E: info@baiadigallipoli.com
alanrogers.com/IT68660

The western shoreline of Puglia offers beaches of excellent quality, interspersed with small villages and some holiday complexes. The Baia di Gallipoli campsite is in a quiet rural area to the southwest of the town on a minor coast road. It offers 600 pitches, all with electricity, under pine and eucalyptus trees. Cars are parked in a separate area and access for vehicles is strictly controlled which gives the site a quiet, peaceful ambience. Although it is about 1 km. from the beach it has solved that problem in partnership with others by providing regular shuttle buses to the beach car park. The sites jointly fund a bar and restaurant on the beach with toilets and showers. This is a good, quiet site in low season and also great for family holidays in July and August when excursions and entertainment are always on offer.

Facilities

Five toilet blocks include facilities for disabled visitors, both on the site and at the beach. Motorcaravan service point. Washing machines. Shop. Bar and restaurant (1/4-31/10). Swimming pool (1/6-30/9). Tennis. Shuttle bus to beach (1 km). Off site: Gallipoli.

Open: 1 April - 30 September.

Directions

The SS101 motorway south of Bari heads first to Lecce, then turns southwest towards Gallipoli. Join the SS274 towards Santa Maria di Leuca and exit at Lido Pizzo. Follow the coast road (SP215) towards Gallipoli and site is on the right 4 km. before Gallipoli. GPS: 39.998317, 18.0265

Charges guide

Per unit incl. 2 persons	
and electricity	€ 23.50 - € 48.00
extra person	€ 8.50 - € 13.50
child (3-8 yrs)	free - € 8.00
dog	€ 1.50 - € 3.00

Camping Cheques accepted.

Gallipoli
Centro Vacanze La Masseria
I-73014 Gallipoli (Puglia) T: 083 320 2296. E: info@lamasseria.net
alanrogers.com/IT68655

Located near the Torre Sabea and within an ancient farm, this site provides 300 pitches under pinewood. During the low seasons most pitches are unmarked in two large areas, but in high season the lines of marked pitches at the end of the site with their high net screens come into use. Gallipoli is just a short ride away and the site operates a shuttle bus in high season. The old town has much to offer and the fish market and restaurants near the port entrance are well worth a visit. The beach is just across the coastal road at the side of the site. However, a new swimming complex is likely to be very tempting to campsite guests. The site restaurant and bar are complimented by another restaurant near the site entrance (this appeared to be quite upmarket).

Facilities

Five sanitary blocks and 36 private bathrooms (to rent) provide ample toilets, showers and washbasins. Bar, restaurant and shop. Washing machines. Motorcaravan service point. Large swimming pool complex. Shuttle bus to Gallipoli in high season. Wine and oil tasting on site. Off site: Gallipoli.

Open: All year.

Directions

From the SS101 (Lecce-Gallipoli) leave at km. 30 towards the Porto. Site is close by and is well signed. Reception is beyond the restaurant and pools. GPS: 40.07417, 18.00889

Charges guide

Per unit incl. up to 3 persons	€ 21.00 - € 38.00
extra person	€ 6.00 - € 10.00

FREE Alan Rogers Travel Card
Extra benefits and savings - see page 10

Peschici

Centro Turistico San Nicola

Localitá San Nicola, I-71010 Peschici (Puglia) T: 088 496 4024. E: sannicola@sannicola.it

alanrogers.com/IT68450

This large site occupies a hillside position, sloping down to a cove with a 500 metre beach of fine sand – a special feature is an attractive grotto at the eastern end. Hard access roads lead to 800 terraced, sand/grass pitches (5A electricity), some with real shade. Some pitches are on the beach fringes (no extra charge) and there is a separate area for campers with animals. The infrastructure was beginning to look a little tired when we visited. Cars have to be parked away from the pitches in high season. The site is popular with German campers (tannoy announcements and most notices in German only) although English is spoken. If you are looking for a site with fine sand on the beach and the chance to explore the Gargano National Park, then San Nicola may be for you.

Facilities

Four toilet blocks of variable standards with British and Turkish style toilets, some with hot water in the washbasins and hot showers. One in the beach area had queues for showers when we visited (late June). Laundry facilities. Supermarket. Beach bar and snacks. Large bar/restaurant with terraces and pizzeria. Games room. Multisports area. Tennis. Watersports. Playground. Organised activities and entertainment for children (July/Aug). ATM. Dogs are not accepted in high season. Off site: Peschici town 1 km. Riding 6 km. Coach and boat excursions. Gargano National Park.

Open: 1 April - 15 October.

Directions

Leave autostrada A14 at exit for Poggio Imperiale, and SS693 towards Peschici and Vieste. It is a winding coast road to Peschici. Follow signs to San Nicola and follow campsite signs. Take care as there are two campsites very close to each other with virtually the same name. You want the second on the approach. The site is 1.5 hours drive from the motorway. GPS: 41.94291, 16.03493

Charges guide

Per unit incl. 2 persons and 6A electricity	€ 23.80 - € 49.40
extra person	€ 6.80 - € 13.40
child (3-11 yrs)	€ 3.90 - € 8.20

Min. 1 week stay in high season.

Ugento

Camping Riva di Ugento

Litoranea Gallipoli, Santa Maria di Leuca, I-73059 Ugento (Puglia) T: 083 393 3600. E: info@rivadiugento.it

alanrogers.com/IT68650

There are some campsites where you can be comfortable, have all the amenities at hand and still feel you are connecting with nature. Under the pine and eucalyptus trees of the Bay of Taranto foreshore is Camping Riva di Ugento. Its 850 pitches are nestled in and around the sand dunes and the foreshore area. They have space and trees around them and the sizes differ as the environment dictates the shape of most. The sea is only a short walk from most pitches and some are at the water's edge. The site buildings resemble huge wooden umbrellas and are in sympathy with the environment. The area is sandy but well shaded, and the sea breezes scented with pine give the site a cool, fresh feel.

Facilities

Twenty toilet blocks all with WCs, showers and washbasins. New bathrooms. Bar. Restaurant and takeaway. Swimming and paddling pools (10/6-15/9). Tennis. Bicycle hire. Watersports incl. windsurfing school. Cinema. TV in bar. WiFi. Entertainment for children. Dogs are not accepted. A new play area for children has been added. Beach volleyball. WiFi. Off site: Fishing. Riding 500 m. Boat launching 4 km. Golf 40 km.

Open: 15 May - 30 September.

Directions

From Bari take the Brindisi road to Lecce, then SS101 to Gallipoli, then the SR274 towards Santa Maria di Leuca. Continue to Felline exit, and continue towards Torre San Giovanni, following the signs for Riva di Ugento. Site is well signed, turn right at traffic lights on SS19. GPS: 39.87475, 18.141117

Charges guide

Per unit incl. 2 persons, 1 child and electricity	€ 21.00 - € 45.00
extra person (over 2 yrs)	€ 5.00 - € 12.00

Camping Cheques accepted.

For latest campsite news, availability and prices visit

alanrogers.com

Vieste
Camping le Diomedee

CP289, I-71019 Vieste (Puglia) T: 088 470 6472. E: info@lediomedee.com
alanrogers.com/IT68460

Diomedee is situated at the far end of the Gargano peninsula, close to the Foresta Umbra, and is part of a chain. The site has 170 level touring pitches (6A), Some shade is obtained from mature trees and screens, and there are some flat, beachside pitches. The pleasant beach is of soft sand or you can jump into the swimming pool. The beach-front restaurant/pizzeria offers a value tourist menu and is great for a sunset meal in the cooling summer breezes. English is spoken at reception but most signs are in Italian and German. A very popular site for wind- and kite-surfing and there is a professional school here. This is a very pleasant beachside holiday location popular with German campers.

Facilities

The large, modernised toilet block has hot water throughout, showers, British style WCs and washbasins. Facilities for disabled visitors. Washing machines. Motorcaravan service point. Shop and fruit stall. Bar. Restaurant/pizzeria/takeaway. Large swimming pool with loud music. Windsurfing school. Tennis. Beach volleyball. Children's entertainment (high season). Free WiFi in pool area. Charcoal barbecues are not permitted. Dogs are not permitted on the beach. Off site: Vieste and the Gargano park area. Excursions.

Open: 1 May - 22 September.

Directions

Site is 5 km. from Vieste on the winding P52 coast road towards Peschici. Allow extra time for the coast road. GPS: 41.91195, 16.124083

Charges guide

Per unit incl. 2 persons and electricity	€ 20.50 - € 53.50
extra person	€ 6.00 - € 15.50
child (3-12 yrs)	free - € 9.00
dog	free

Vieste
Punta Lunga Camping Village

CP339, localitá Defensola, I-71019 Vieste (Puglia) T: 088 470 6031. E: puntalunga@puntalunga.com
alanrogers.com/IT68480

Punta Lunga is located in the spectacularly beautiful Gargano region, a huge National Park, and nestles in an attractive bay. The 150 medium sized, terraced, sandy pitches (3.5-6A) are flat, mostly set on steep slopes, and some have shade. Camping along the shore is less formal and in some cases less shaded, but some pitches have spectacular views. There is a choice of restaurants. The upper one is finer dining, while the lower one is an informal beach restaurant. The site is well suited for energetic windsurfer types, but not for infirm or disabled visitors. This is a delightful place to relax by the sea and to explore the dramatic wilderness of the Gargano peninsula with its coves, cliffs and coastal towns.

Facilities

Two toilet blocks, some distance from pitches, have a mixture of unisex showers and dedicated toilets, mostly Turkish. The facilities are clean and fresh. Access difficult for infirm and disabled campers. Laundry facilities. Hairdresser. Small shop. Gas. Excellent restaurant with pleasant views. Beach bar with snacks. Gym. Children's clubs (high season). Small play area. Bicycle hire. Windsurfing school. Excursions. WiFi (charged). Dogs are not accepted. Off site: Restaurants, bars and shops. Boat launching 3 km. Riding 10 km.

Open: 15 May - 25 September.

Directions

From north take A14 exit for Poggio Imperiale, then to Vico Gargano and Vieste. From south take A14 exit Foggia, then towards Manfredonia, Mattinata and Vieste. GPS: 41.89798, 16.15047

Charges guide

Per unit incl. 2 persons and electricity	€ 17.00 - € 47.00
extra person	€ 5.00 - € 14.00
child (3-12 yrs)	free - € 8.00

FREE Alan Rogers Travel Card
Extra benefits and savings - see page 10

The toe of the Italian 'boot', Calabria, like its neighbouring region, is a sparsely populated region with unspoilt countryside. The coastline boasts fine, sandy beaches, while the interior features the rugged Aspromonte and Sila mountains, which dominate the landscape.

THERE ARE FIVE PROVINCES IN CALABRIA: CATANZARO, COSENZA, CROTONE, REGGIO DI CALABRIA AND VIBO VALENTIA

One of the main towns in the region is Cosenza, which is completely enclosed by mountains – the Sila to the east, the Catena Costiera to the west, separating it from the sea. The Sila massif is divided into three parts: the Sila Greca, Sila Grande and the Sila Piccola. Lying in the Sila Greca are the villages of Santa Sofia, San Sosmo and Vaccarizzo, which come alive during annual festivals held throughout the year. There are ski slopes in the Sila Granda plus numerous lakes, ideal for fishing. Camigliatello is one of the best known resorts here offering winter sports, riding and hiking. Lastly, Sila Piccola is the region's most densely forested section, which has been designated National Park status. South of Cosenza along the Tyrrhenian coast is the picturesque town of Tropea, whose old town clings to the cliffside, offering superb views of the sea and beaches. There are more sandy beaches nearby at Capo Vaticano, while across on the Ionian coast is the popular resort of Rossano Scalo. Just inland from here is the attractive hilltown of Rossano while further south are the vineyards of Cirò. To the north of Rossano is Sibari, home to the world's largest archaeological site, covering 1,000 hectares; excavations have revealed evidence of ancient Greek and Roman civilisations.

Places of interest

Aspromonte: scenic mountainous region in the southernmost tip of Italy's boot.

Capo Colanna: Greek ruins, nearby beaches.

Gerace: impressive cathedral, ruined castle.

Locri: Greek ruins.

Pizzo: picturesque town with small castle and beaches.

Reggio di Calabria: national museum.

Soverato: popular resort with good beaches.

Stilo: home to the 10th-century, five-domed Cattolica.

Cuisine of the region

Food is largely influenced by Greek cuisine – aubergines, swordfish and sweets made with figs, almonds and honey. Many biscuits and cakes are made in honour of a religious festival or saint's day; they can be deep fried in oil, soaked in honey or encrusted with almonds. Pasta is popular as are pork and cheeses such as *mozzarella* and *pecorino*. Locally produced wines include the Greco di Bianco, a sweet white wine, and those from Cirò.

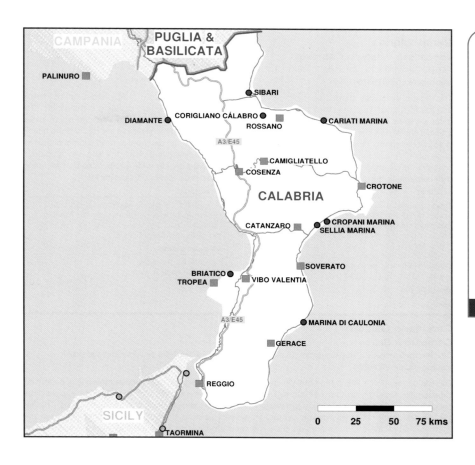

Briatico
Villaggio Camping Dolomiti sul Mare

SS522 per Tropea km. 16,5, I-89817 Briatico (Calabria) T: 096 339 1355. E: info@dolomitisulmare.com
alanrogers.com/IT68900

Set high above the Gulf of Eufemia, 300 m. from the beach, Dolomiti is a large sprawling site where the focus is on bungalows. The pitches are informally laid out in a large, somewhat dusty olive grove where the ground slopes to the sea (chocks useful). Campers share the pool, bar, restaurant and entertainment with the other residents, but the high standards of the main complex make a stay worthwhile. It is popular with Italians and the village area within the resort is growing fast resulting in a little chaos at times, especially at reception and the restaurant. Unsuitable for disabled visitors (rough terrain). This is an excellent stopover point when in the area and compares favourably with other local sites.

Facilities
One unit with mixed British and Turkish style toilets and hot showers provides adequate, clean facilities. Washing machines. Motorcaravan service point. Shop. Bar and terrace. Self-service restaurant and snack bar. Swimming pool and spa. Play area. Amphitheatre with entertainment and miniclub. Dogs are accepted but contact site first. Torches useful. Off site: Riding and beach 500 m.

Open: 14 May - 16 September.

Directions
Take E45 Cosenza-Reggio road and leave at Serre exit. Head for Vibo Valentia, then take the coast road and Briatico. The site is well signed on the SS522 at the 165 km. marker. GPS: 38.7191, 16.0589

Charges guide

Per person	€ 6.00 - € 14.00
pitch	€ 7.00 - € 18.00
dog	€ 3.00 - € 6.00

Cariati Marina

Vascellero Villaggio Camping

I-87063 Cariati Marina (Calabria) T: 098 391 127. E: villaggio@vascellero.it

alanrogers.com/IT68750

The superb, irregularly shaped pool with its bar and gelateria are the hub of Vascellero. Signora Franca and her family aim to please their guests, whether it is for summer holidays or skiing in the winter. The camping area just inside the gate is modest, but there are 100 pitches of gravel and sand under artificial shade and giant poplars. The pool area is a delightful place to while away the day and the beach is equally tempting. However these facilities are not normally used by campers and an additional charge is payable. A sophisticated beach bar serves food on terraces overlooking the sea. An ambitious programme for children runs during the day, and evening entertainment for adults is held in an arena with a spacious building set aside for games, movies and special events on satellite TV.

Facilities

The single toilet block, kept clean at all times, provides mixed Turkish and British style toilets. Washing machines. Motorcaravan services. Pizzeria. Good swimming pool with pool bar (charged). Two good play areas. Hairdresser. Tennis. Bicycle hire. Miniclub, entertainment and aerobics. Beach 250 m. Beach restaurant. Watersports. Excursions. Dogs are not accepted in Aug. Off site: Riding 500 m. Sailing. Fishing. Boat launching 3.5 km.

Open: All year.

Directions

Take SS106 Taranto-Reggio road. At km. 299.2 marker in village of Cariati turn towards beach at campsite signs. Site is well signed over the railway line. GPS: 39.4856, 16.9976

Charges guide

Per unit incl. 2 persons	€ 15.00 - € 40.00
electricity (meter in winter)	€ 1.50
dog	€ 1.50 - € 5.00

Corigliano Cálabro

Camping Il Salice

Ctra Ricota Grande, I-87060 Corigliano Cálabro (Calabria) T: 098 385 1169. E: info@salicevacanze.it

alanrogers.com/IT68580

The site's reception is inside the hotel which forms part of this holiday complex and this site is becoming increasingly popular with tour operators. The advantage is there are many choices here – to visit the hairdresser, have a massage, enjoy the warm Ionian sea or have a relaxing drink by the pool. The flat pitches are under tall pines and eucalyptus, many with views of the beach, some right alongside the sand. It is a real treat to stay here and enjoy the excellent facilities and we think it well worth the drive. In the distance the mountains of Pollino National Park can be seen. Nearby are the famous sites of Archaic Sybaris, the capital of Magna Greece and many other attractions.

Facilities

One large heated and two small unheated toilet blocks provide high quality facilities including excellent units for disabled campers. Laundry. Restaurant, pizzeria, takeaway and bar. Shop. Hairdresser. Massage. Very large outdoor pool (fairly hefty family charge in high season € 36-62). Solarium. Tennis. Bicycle hire. Electronic games. Internet access. Amphitheatre and entertainment. Pedaloes. Windsurfing. Off site: Excursions to historic sites of Sybaris 3 km. and Park National of Calabria. Fishing. Boat launching 4 km. Golf 20 km.

Open: All year.

Directions

From A3 Salerno-Reggio Calabria autostrada take Sibari exit, then SS106 road towards Crotone. Before km. 19 marker look for campsite sign and turn for Centro Vacanze Il Salice towards beach. Site well signed through small housing estate. GPS: 39.6814, 16.52165

Charges guide

Per person	€ 2.50 - € 13.00
child (3-6 yrs)	free - € 9.00
pitch incl. electricity (3-6A)	€ 6.00 - € 22.00

For latest campsite news, availability and prices visit

alanrogers.com

Cropani Marina
Camping Casa Vacanze Lungomare

Viale Venezia 40, I-88050 Cropani Marina (Calabria) T: 096 196 1167. E: info@campinglungomare.com
alanrogers.com/IT68830

The Ionian coast of Calabria is a mixture of industrial areas (there is off-shore oil and gas), rural areas and large and small holiday resorts. Cropani Marina is definitely at the smaller end of the holiday spectrum and it is some considerable way south on a road that gets progressively slower as you travel. The site has 120 pitches in total but has mobile homes, static caravans and tent only areas. This means that there are perhaps only 40 pitches for touring caravans and motorcaravans, all with 6A electricity. The sandy beach is just across a small access road.

Facilities	Directions
Two toilet blocks include showers (tokens required), WCs (Turkish and British style). Facilities for disabled visitors (Portacabin style). Washing machine. Motorcaravan service point. Bar and restaurant/pizzeria. All weather tennis court/football pitch. Accommodation to rent. Off site: Sandy beach and local bars and restaurants.	Site is on the main coast road (SS106) south of Crotone on the way to Catanzaro. Just south of the resort of Botricello you come to Cropani Marina. Site is well signed at the junction towards the beach and is 500 m. on the right. GPS: 38.908917, 16.80945
Open: 1 April - 30 September.	**Charges guide**

Per person	€ 5.00 - € 9.80
pitch	€ 4.80 - € 9.50
electricity	€ 2.50

Diamante
Villaggio Turistico Mare Blu

Cirella di Diamante, I-87020 Diamante (Calabria) T: 098 586 097. E: mareblu.villaggio@libero.it
alanrogers.com/IT68950

Mare Blu is a large site with lots of watersports activities and an open feel to the site, and is aimed at Italian families spending their holidays by the sea. This is a good site for a short stay to get a taste of the Italian way of camping, or a transit site whilst passing as it is one of the best in the area with many amenities. The 100 touring pitches are flat with some grass, 40 have electricity (3A) and most enjoy shade from trees. There is beach access under the railway line and the fine sand provides a safe area for children. Here you will find the many watersports and a beach bar.

Facilities	Directions
Two units provide mixed British and Turkish style toilets. Facilities are in separate blocks – showers from toilets. Unit for disabled visitors. Laundry facilities. Motorcaravan service point. Shop. Restaurant. Bar and terrace with views. Snack bar. Play area. Minigolf. Tennis. Animation on the beach. Boat, mountain bike and bicycle hire. Evening animation. Disco. Miniclub. Beach (300 m). Canoes. Windsurfing. Communal barbecue. Off site: Riding 2 km.	From E45 Salerno-Cosenza road take Cosenza Nord and SS107 to Paola. Then SS585 coast road north to Diamante. Site is well signed before reaching the village of Cirella. GPS: 39.7035, 15.814
	Charges guide
Open: 1 May - 30 September.	

Per person	€ 10.00 - € 21.00
child (3-10 yrs)	€ 7.00 - € 15.00

Marina di Caulonia
Camping Calypso

Via Nazionale, I-89040 Marina di Caulonia (Calabria) T: 096 482 028. E: info@calypso.st
alanrogers.com/IT68860

This site is at the southern end of the SS106 Taranto-Reggio road and it would take some hours to get there by this route. However, the road from Rosarno to Siderno (SS582) has been improved, with numerous tunnels, and the 36 kilometres across the toe of Italy can now be covered in as many minutes. Camping Calypso is a simple site providing 96 pitches for touring use with some shade offered by the olive and eucalyptus trees. The beach adjacent to the site is rocky but just 50 metres away, there is a long sandy beach.

Facilities	Directions
The toilet block includes showers (charged), Turkish and British style WCs and open style washbasins. Washing machines. Motorcaravan service point. Bar and restaurant (high season only). Off site: Sandy beach 50 m. Supermarket 800 m.	From the north, approach via the A3 and leave at the Rosarno exit. Then turn left on SS582 towards Siderno and from there turn north along the SS106. The site is at 123.2 km. Turn sharp right down towards a railway bridge. The access road is poor, steep and bumpy. GPS: 38.354117, 16.484917
Open: 1 April - 1 October.	**Charges guide**

Per unit incl. 2 persons and electricity	€ 18.50 - € 35.00
No credit cards.	

FREE Alan Rogers Travel Card
Extra benefits and savings - see page 10

Sellia Marina

Camping Costa Blu

Localitá Finocchiaro, I-88050 Sellia Marina (Calabria) T: 044 960 232. E: info@costabluresidence.it

alanrogers.com/IT68850

This tiny campsite of just 50 clean flat pitches has remarkable features for its size plus an attractive Italian ambience. This is a great site if you think small is beautiful and is a cut above the other sites in this area and the prices in low season are very favourable. The generously sized pitches (with electricity) are shaded by pines and eucalyptus. The clean beach is just 30 m. through a secure gate and it is excellent for relaxing and enjoying the tranquil atmosphere, to soak up the sun or swim in the cool Ionian sea. The pool has a slide and separate paddling pool and close by there is a small amphitheatre for children and adult entertainment, which again is unusual in a site this size.

Facilities

One block of sanitary facilities has mixed Turkish and British style toilets and unisex coin operated showers (20c). Washing machine. Motorcaravan service point. Pleasant small pool complex with a slide. Paddling pool. Play area. Beach volleyball. Small amphitheatre. Animation and miniclub. Off site: Watersports. Fishing. Restaurants, bars and shops.

Open: 1 June - 18 September.

Directions

Take SS106 Crotone-Reggio road. At km. 199.7 marker in village of Sellia Marina take a turn towards beach indicated by campsite signs. Site well signed over railway line. At tall eucalyptus trees, turn left then left again and right where indicated. Narrow turn into site. GPS: 38.8929, 16.7634

Charges guide

Per unit incl. 2 persons and electricity	€ 12.00 - € 36.00
extra person (over 3 yrs)	€ 3.00 - € 9.00
dog	€ 1.00 - € 4.00

Sibari

Camping Pineta di Sibari

Ctra da Fuscolaro, I-87011 Sibari (Calabria) T: 098 174 135. E: info@pinetadisibari.it

alanrogers.com/IT68600

Calabria was immortalised in the drawings of Edward Lear who, travelling on a donkey in 1847, was transfixed by the landscape. Camping Pineta di Sibari is on the Ionian Sea coast and provides 500 touring pitches, all with electricity (3-6A), under pine and eucalyptus trees. Most are of average size and many have sea views. The large sandy beach stretches for miles in both directions and the backdrop is the mountains of the Pollino National Park. This is a rural area and is away from the industrial areas found further south along this coast. Karin Rudolph runs a happy site where peace and quiet are prime features. This is a good site for a long stay in low season or for family holidays in the summer months, but expect to find the site very busy then as it is very popular with German and Italian campers.

Facilities

Five toilet blocks include showers, WCs (Turkish and British style) and open style washbasins. Facilities for disabled visitors. Motorcaravan service point. Bazaar and shop (1/6-10/09). Bar, restaurant and takeaway (all 15/5-16/9). Bicycle hire. Tennis. Sandy beach with sun beds and shades (to rent). Mobile homes to rent. WiFi. Off site: Ancient Sibari. Pollino National Park. Golf and riding 4 km.

Open: 1 May - 19 September.

Directions

Take SS106 south towards Reggio Calabria. South of Trebisacce take Villapiana Scalo exit (third Villapiana exit). Turn right along coast road (SS106R), then left at sign for site and over level crossing. To avoid narrow tunnel (2.8 m. headroom), after level crossing turn right and go straight on as road bears left. Site is 700 m. GPS: 39.781, 16.41932

Charges guide

Per unit incl. 2 persons and electricity	€ 19.90 - € 41.00
extra person	€ 5.00 - € 9.50
child (3-6 yrs)	free - € 4.90
dog	€ 3.00 - € 4.90

For latest campsite news, availability and prices visit

alanrogers.com

The largest island in the Mediterranean, Sicily has seen a range of settlers come and go, from the early Greeks and Romans to the Arabs and Normans, French and Spanish. With its beach resorts, volcanic islands, ancient sites and varied cuisine, Sicily is also home to Mount Etna.

SICILY COMPRISES THE FOLLOWING PROVINCES: AGRIGENTO, CALTANISSETTA, CATANIA, ENNA, MESSINA, PALERMO, RAGUSA, SIRACUSA AND TRAPANI

The capital of Sicily is the bustling city of Palermo. With its medieval streets and markets, it has the island's greatest concentration of sights, and architecture that boasts a range of styles from Arabic to Norman, Baroque and Art Nouveau. Boats depart from here to the tiny volcanic island of Ústica, renowned for its marine life and popular with divers. Along with Milazzo and Messina, the capital also provides connections to the Aeolian Islands, of which Lípari is the most popular. Outside the capital is Monte Pellegrino, which offers superb views of the city, plus the seaside resort of Mondello. Europe's highest volcano, Mount Etna is situated in the east. Still active, its lower reaches are accessible on foot or by public transport. The closest town to the summit is Randazzo, built entirely of lava, as is Catania, situated further down the Ionian coast. Engulfed by lava in 1669 followed by an earthquake in 1693, Catania has been rebuilt on a grand scale. The coastline also bears traces of ancient Greek cities, most notably at Megara Hyblaea and Siracusa. More Greek ruins can be found near Agrigento, on the south-west coast, while around to the west is Marsala, famous for its fortified wine, and the harbour town of Trápani, a jumping off point for the Egadi Islands.

Places of interest

Acireale: spa centre, hosts one of Sicily's best festivals in February.

Agrigento: nearby archaeological area known as the Valley of the Temples.

Enna: Sicily's highest town.

Erice: medieval town, cathedral.

Marsala: home of the famous wine, in production since the 18th century.

Segesta: ancient temple, nearby ruins of an ancient theatre where summer concerts are held.

Taormina: lively resort with sandy beaches, ancient Greek theatre and 13th-century cathedral.

Vulcano: Aeolian Island, with hot mud baths and fine black beaches.

Cuisine of the region

Given its location, Sicily has attracted an endless list of invaders which has impacted on its food, resulting in one of Italy's most varied cuisines. Fish is abundant, including anchovies, sardines, tuna and swordfish, often teamed with pasta, as in *spaghetti con le sarde.* Sicily is famous for its sweets, in particular *cannoli,* fried pastries stuffed with sweet ricotta. Made from sheep's milk, ricotta is used in a variety of desserts, with *pecorino* and *provolone* cheeses also widely available. Wines include Marsala, Corvo and Regaleali.

Maccheroni con le sarde: sardines cooked with fennel, raisins, pine nuts, breadcrumbs and saffron.

Pesce spada: swordfish steak, grilled or pan-fried with lemon and oregano.

Sicilin cassata: ice-cream made with ricotta, nuts, candied fruit and chocolate in a sponge cake.

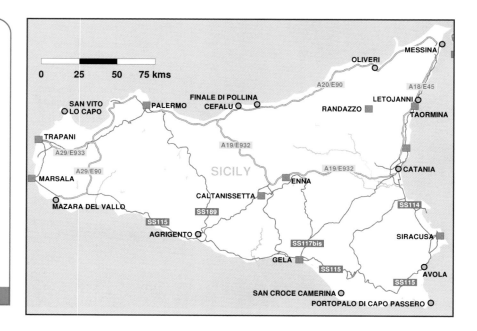

Agrigento

Camping Internazionale Nettuno

Via Lacco Ameno N3, Santa Leone, I-92100 Agrigento (Sicily) T: 092 241 6268

alanrogers.com/IT69180

Internazionale Nettuno is a small site with about 50 pitches for touring units. It would be a good place to get an early start to see the amazing ruins before the heat of the day. Alternatively, it would make a quiet place to stay after touring the ruins as it is alongside a beautiful sandy beach. The pitches are on shady level terraces, some with their own beach access. There is a bar and a small shop. The sanitary facilities were clean when we visited (unisex, as half were closed in early season), but required some maintenance as did the motorcaravan service area. With improvements to the sanitary facilities this would be a good site, when seen it was just acceptable.

Facilities	Directions
One large central sanitary block (unisex in low season) provides adjustable hot showers and small cabins. Motorcaravan service area. Bar. Restaurant and pizzeria. Off site: Valley of the Temples 4 km. Bar, restaurants and excellent white sandy beach nearby.	Site is by the beach at San Leone, 5 km. south of Agrigento on the south coast of Sicily. From S115 road follow signs to San Leone from where site is well signed some 2 km. east of the town. Access is a steep climb just after road leaves the coast.
Open: All year.	GPS: 37.24306, 13.61556

Charges guide

Per person	€ 6.00 - € 7.00
caravan and car	€ 11.00 - € 13.00
motorcaravan	€ 9.00 - € 10.00
tent	€ 5.00 - € 12.00

For latest campsite news, availability and prices visit
alanrogers.com

Agrigento
Camping Valle dei Templi

Viale Emporium, I-92100 Agrigento (Sicily) T: 092 241 1115. E: info@campingvalledeitempli.com

alanrogers.com/IT69175

This site shares its name with Sicily's premier attraction, the UNESCO World Heritage listed complex of temples and old city walls of the ancient town of Akragas, although these are about 2.5 km. to the north. Built as a beacon for homecoming sailors, the five Doric temples built on a ridge are an impressive sight even at a distance. This site is therefore a good base from which to explore these ruins, together with the numerous coach loads of tourists. With 195 unmarked pitches, about half are suitable for caravans and campers. The majority have access to 6A electricity.

Facilities	Directions
The single sanitary block in the centre of the site provides good WCs, showers and washbasins. Facilities for disabled visitors. Motorcaravan service point. Washing machine. Shop, bar, restaurant and takeaway service (all year). Swimming pool. Children's playground. Off site: Fishing 1 km. Riding 2 km. Valle dei Templi and Agrigento.	From the main SS115 road or the SS640, follow signs to San Leone, just east of Agrigento. Site is on left just as you enter the town, 700 m. before the coast. GPS: 37.26935, 13.5835

Open: All year.

Charges guide

Per unit incl. 2 persons and electricity	€ 19.00 - € 29.50
extra person	€ 5.50 - € 7.50

Avola
Camping Sabbiadoro

Ctra da Chiusa di Carlo, I-96012 Avola (Sicily) T: 093 156 0000. E: info@campeggiosabbiadoro.com

alanrogers.com/IT69215

This is truly one of Sicily's hidden gems and the Alia family will ensure your stay is pleasant and peaceful at this delightful campsite with 100 pitches. With over 100 different species of trees and flowers around the site, it is awash with colour and has good shade. A small, sandy beach complements the site's natural charm. When we arrived, a party was in progress to celebrate the natural products of the area and a huge copper pot was being used to make ricotta cheese, which within an hour was being distributed around the site, with local bread. It was delicious!

Facilities	Directions
The site confirms that a brand new toilet block is now open with facilities for disabled visitors. Motorcaravan service point. Shop, bar (1/5-31/10). Restaurant (15/5-15/9). TV room. Sandy beach. WiFi over part of site (charged). Off site: Avola with its unusual town planning.	On the SS115 north of Avola the site is 400 m. down a narrow twisting lane. GPS: 36.93639, 15.17472

Open: All year.

Charges guide

Per person	€ 10.00
pitch	€ 10.00 - € 14.00
electricity	€ 4.00

No credit cards.

Camping Cheques accepted.

Catania
Camping Jonio

Via Villini a Mare 2, Ognina, I-95126 Catania (Sicily) T: 095 491 139. E: info@campingjonio.com

alanrogers.com/IT69230

This is a small, uncomplicated and tranquil city site with the advantage of being on top of a cliff at the water's edge. The 70 level touring pitches are on gravel with shade from some tall trees and artificial bamboo screens. There are some clean, high quality sanitary facilities (also some private facilities for hire). There is no pool, but the views of the water compensate and there are delightful rock pools in the sea just a few steps from the campsite. A new attractive restaurant offers food in the summer high season. Camping Jonio is ideal for a short stay to unwind.

Facilities	Directions
Sanitary facilities are modern and clean in two blocks, one small block for men and another for women. Laundry with roof top drying area. Motorcaravan services. Shop. Bar and restaurant. Basic old style playground (supervision recommended). Entertainment (high season). Diving school. Access to small gravel beach. Excursions. Dogs are not accepted in July/Aug. Off site: Large town of Catania, many historical sites and Mount Etna.	From A18 Catania exit follow signs to the coast road (SS114) towards Ognina. Site is off the SS114 (signed) on the northeast outskirts of town. Access to site is off the small one way system and via the site's separate car park. GPS: 37.53232, 15.12012

Open: All year.

Charges guide

Per person	€ 6.50 - € 10.00
pitch	€ 6.50 - € 13.50
car	€ 4.00 - € 6.00
electricity	€ 3.00

Camping Cheques accepted.

FREE Alan Rogers Travel Card
Extra benefits and savings - see page 10

Cefalu

Camping Costa Ponente

Ctra da Ogliastrillo, SS 113, I-90015 Cefalu (Sicily) T: 092 142 0085. E: info@hotel-kalura.com

alanrogers.com/IT69360

The pleasant Costa Ponente site, with easy access from the A20 and SS113 roads, is located between the small coastal railway line and the beach. However, its layout does much to minimise the impact of the infrequent trains. There are 150 pitches, all with 2A electricity, of which 120 are used for touring units. Arranged on terraces and with over 25% having water and drainage on the pitch, the site has a good ambiance and views. An area for tents near the swimming pools caters for large groups travelling by coach. There is access to the beach, as well as sunbathing areas near the bar and pools.

Facilities

Four sanitary blocks provide good facilities with ample toilets (British and Turkish style), washbasins and hot showers. Facilities for disabled visitors. Washing machine. Motorcaravan services. Bar (all season). Shop. Snack bar/takeaway (July/Aug). Swimming pools. Dogs are not accepted in August. WiFi. Off site: Bicycle hire 1 km. Cefalu 2 km. Riding 3 km. Golf 15 km.

Open: 1 April - 31 October.

Directions

From the A20 Cefalu exit take the SS113 towards the town. Site is at the 190.2 km. marker on the left down a slope and across a level crossing. GPS: 38.02684, 13.9828

Charges guide

| Per unit incl. 2 persons and electricity | € 23.00 - € 37.00 |
| extra person | € 6.50 - € 8.50 |

Finale di Pollina

Camping Rais Gerbi

Ctra Rais Gerbi, SS113 km. 172.9, I-90010 Finale di Pollina (Sicily) T: 092 142 6570. E: camping@raisgerbi.it

alanrogers.com/IT69350

Rais Gerbi provides very good quality camping with excellent facilities on the beautiful Tyrrhenian coast not far from Cefalu. This attractive terraced campsite is shaded by trees and the good sized pitches vary from informal areas under the trees near the sea, to gravel terraces and hardstandings. Most have stunning views, many with their own sinks and with some artificial shade to supplement the trees. From the mobile homes to the unusual white igloos, everything here is being established to a high quality. The pool and the restaurant, like so much of the site, overlook the rocky coastline and aquamarine sea.

Facilities

Excellent new sanitary blocks with British style toilets, free hot showers in generous cubicles. Small shop. Casual summer terrace and indoor (winter) restaurant. Communal barbecue. Entertainment area and pool near the sea. Tennis. WiFi over site (charged). High quality accommodation and tents for rent. Rocky beach at site. Dogs are not accepted in August. Off site: Small village of Finale 500 m. Larger historic town of Cefalu 12 km.

Open: All year.

Directions

Site is on the SS113 running along the northeast coast of the island, km. 172.9, just west of Finale (the turn into the site is at end of the bridge on the outskirts of the village). It is 12 km. east of Cefalu, 11 km. north of Pollina. GPS: 38.02278, 14.15389

Charges guide

| Per unit incl. 2 persons and electricity | € 23.50 - € 45.00 |
| extra person (over 3 yrs) | € 5.00 - € 10.00 |

Letojanni

Camping Paradise

Via Nazionale 2, SS114 km. 41, I-98037 Letojanni (Sicily) T: 094 236 306. E: campingparadise@campingparadise.it **alanrogers.com/IT69260**

Forty kilometres south of the ferry port at Messina, Camping Paradise is situated on a long narrow strip along the sea with direct beach access. Most of the pitches have views over the crystal clear waters that are a delight to bathe in on a hot day. The level, grass and gravel pitches are fairly small with paved access roads and shade from well established, mainly olive trees. This site with a mountain backdrop is very popular so you may need to book ahead in high season. There is some noise from the local train all along this coast.

Facilities

One large centrally located sanitary block has mainly Turkish style toilets, fully adjustable hot showers and facilities for disabled visitors. Small shop for essentials. Large bar/restaurant with views over the sea. Off site: Rich in history, the area has many antiquities. Good crystal clear beaches. Nearby town Letojanni is a popular seaside resort. Mount Etna within easy reach.

Open: May - October.

Directions

From the A18 motorway between Messina and Catania take Taormina exit and then turn north on the S114 towards Letojanni. The site is on this road (S114) at the 41 km. marker just north of Letojanni. There is quite a sharp bend on entering the site and a 3.1 m. bridge. GPS: 37.89717, 15.32699

Charges guide

Per person	€ 6.00 - € 10.00
pitch	€ 6.00 - € 13.00
electricity	€ 3.00 - € 4.00
car	€ 4.00 - € 5.00

Mazara del Vallo
Sporting Club Village & Camping

Ctra Bocca Arena, I-91026 Mazara del Vallo (Sicily) T: 092 394 7230. E: info@sportingclubvillage.com
alanrogers.com/IT69160

Mazara del Vallo can be found on Sicily's southwest coast. As the crow flies, Tunisia is not far, and the town has a distinct Arabic influence in its winding streets. The site is 2.5 km. from Mazara and boasts some good amenities including a large swimming pool, surrounded by tall palm trees. Pitches here are grassy and generally well shaded. This is a lively site in high season with a wide range of activities and a regular entertainment programme. The nearest beach is 350 m. away and the site is also adjacent to a nature reserve. Sporting Club's focal point, however, is its restaurant with typical Sicilian dishes.

Facilities

Good sports club with swimming pool, gymnasium, floodlit football pitches, tennis and volleyball. Restaurant, bar and large reception/function room. Off site: Beach 350 m. Mazara 2.5 km. Various excursions organised by the site, for example to the Acropolis at Selinunte (25 km) and the island of Mozia.

Open: 1 April - 5 October.

Directions

From A29 take the Mazara del Vallo exit and head towards the town. Straight over the first roundabout and after 1.5 km. right at traffic lights towards the beach. At roundabout exit left and straight ahead to site, not over the bridge. GPS: 37.63647, 12.61631

Charges guide

Per unit incl. 2 persons	
and electricity	€ 20.50 - € 41.80
extra person	€ 4.50 - € 7.90

Messina
Camping Il Peloritano

Ctra Tarantonio SS 113 dir., Rodia, I-98161 Messina (Sicily) T: 090 348 496. E: il_peloritano@yahoo.it
alanrogers.com/IT69250

Set in a 100-year-old olive grove providing shade for 50 informally arranged pitches, Camping Il Peloritano is a quiet uncomplicated site off the coast road, with excellent clean facilities. It is a 200 m. walk to the sandy beach and approximately 2 km. to the nearby village. The friendly owners, Patrizia Mowdello and Carlo Oteri, will help to arrange excursions to the Aeolian Islands, Taormina and Mount Etna, and do everything to make your stay a pleasant one.

Facilities

Single refurbished toilet block provides hot showers (by token). Good facilities for disabled visitors. Washing machine. Motorcaravan service point. Small shop and bar. Meals can be ordered in from local restaurants. Communal barbecue. WiFi over part of site. Excursions arranged. Bowls. Off site: Sandy beach 200 m. Small seaside village 2 km. Riding 2 km.

Open: 15 March - 15 October.

Directions

From Messina on the A20 motorway take Villafranca exit then follow Messina dir and Tarantonio for 2 km. From Palermo on the A20, take exit for Rometta and signs for Messina and Tarantonio for 5 km. GPS: 38.25932, 15.46782

Charges guide

Per unit incl. 2 persons	
and electricity	€ 21.00 - € 33.50
extra person	€ 5.50 - € 9.00

Messina
Nuovo Camping Dello Stretto

Via Circuito, Torre Faro, I-98614 Messina (Sicily) T: 090 322 3051. E: info@campingdellostretto.it
alanrogers.com/IT69255

This delightful campsite is just 15 minutes from the port of Messina. The restaurant alongside the two pools is one of the best we have seen in our travels. With 60 pitches for caravans and motorcaravans to the rear of the site, all with 3A electricity, this offers a peaceful resting place after the long journey south. The site's restaurant and pizzeria are set alongside the pools in a beautiful garden and are such that you will not want to walk to the other local establishments. At the time of our visit a new hot water system was under construction for the two sanitary blocks.

Facilities

Two sanitary blocks provide ample toilets, showers and washbasins. Facilities for disabled visitors (plus another in the restaurant). Motorcaravan service point. Exceptional restaurant and pizzeria. Two swimming pools with lifeguard. Miniclub (July/Aug). WiFi (charged). Off site: Messina and Taormina.

Open: 1 June - 30 September.

Directions

Site is well signed from Messina Port. At the port exit turn right at traffic lights and head north along Viale della Liberta, then Consolare Pompea (SS113). Go through Ganzirri with lake on your right. At first crossroads turn right again alongside the lake and at T-junction turn left. Site is on the left where the road forks. GPS: 38.26167, 15.63333

Charges guide

Per unit incl. 2 persons	
and electricity	€ 20.00 - € 25.00

FREE Alan Rogers Travel Card
Extra benefits and savings - see page 10

Oliveri
Camping Villaggio Marinello
Via del Sol 17, I-98060 Oliveri (Sicily) T: 094 131 3000. E: marinello@camping.it
alanrogers.com/IT69300

Camping Marinello is located alongside the sea with direct access to a lovely uncrowded sandy beach with an informal marina at one end and natural pool areas with a spot of sand at the other. The 220 gravel touring pitches here are shaded by tall trees. We enjoyed a delicious traditional meal in the excellent terraced restaurant with its lovely sea views. The Greco family have been here for over 30 years and work hard to ensure that their guests enjoy a pleasant stay. There is some noise from the coastal rail line which runs along the length of the site.

Facilities

Two sanitary blocks with free hot showers, one is not currently used and is awaiting a much needed refurbishment and heating. Washing machines. Bazaar, market and supermarket. Bar with sea views. Restaurant and terraced eating area also with views. Electronic games. Piano bar in high season. Dogs are not accepted in July/Aug. Tours arranged (including Mount Etna, Taormina, Aeolian Islands). Off site: Seaside resort-style town of Oliveri.

Open: All year.

Directions

From A20 motorway take Falcone exit and follow Oliveri. At town turn north towards beach, then west along beach and continue 1 km. to site. Turn right immediately before a small narrow bridge (2.2 m. high and 2.5 m. wide). GPS: 38.13246, 15.05452

Charges guide

Per person (over 3 yrs)	€ 4.50 - € 9.00
pitch incl. electricity	€ 13.00 - € 21.00
car	€ 3.00 - € 5.00

Portopalo di Capo Passero
Camping Residence Capo Passero
Ctra da Vigne Vecchie, I-96010 Portopalo di Capo Passero (Sicily) T: 093 184 2333. E: info@italiaabc.com
alanrogers.com/IT69210

Camping Residence Capo Passero is located on the southeast point of Sicily. There are often nice sea breezes at the campsite which has a clean and well maintained appearance, although when we visited the shade was patchy due to the Italian custom of trimming trees aggressively. The touring pitches are generally level and all have 6A electricity connections. The sandy beach, only 50 m. walk away, is inviting and there is a very good pool area with grassy areas to sunbathe. The nearby village is quite interesting for the region and has a number of restaurants and bars.

Facilities

Three older style toilet blocks, all clean when visited with washbasins but only cold showers. There are six warm showers near reception but tokens are required. Facilities for disabled visitors in one block. Attractive typical style restaurant and bar area. Excellent pool. Play area. Disco area. Boules. Tennis. Good access to sandy beach. Off site: Town with bars, restaurants and marina 1-1.5 km.

Open: Easter - 15 October.

Directions

From SS115 road follow signs to Pachino, then Portopalo di Capo Passero. Site is located west of the town on the beach and there are some signs from the village. Low bridges may cause problems on some routes. GPS: 36.6775, 15.1208

Charges guide

Per person	€ 6.50 - € 9.00
pitch	€ 4.00 - € 15.00
car	€ 3.50

San Croce Camerina
Camping Scarabeo
I-97017 San Croce Camerina (Sicily) T: 093 291 8096. E: info@scarabeocamping.it
alanrogers.com/IT69190

Camping Scarabeo is a beautiful site located in Punta Braccetto, a little fishing port in Sicily's southeast corner. It is a perfect location with exceptional facilities to match. Split into two separate sites (just 50 m. apart) with a total of 80 pitches, it is being constantly improved with care by Angela di Modica. All pitches are well shaded, some naturally and others with an artificial cane roof and have 3/6A electricity. Scarabeo lies adjacent to a sandy beach and the little village is close by. The site layout resembles a Sicilian farm courtyard and is divided into four principal areas.

Facilities

Exceptional sanitary blocks provide personal WC compartments (personal key access). Ample hot showers (free low season). Facilities for disabled visitors. Washing machine. Direct access to beach. Playground. Entertainment programme in high season. WiFi over site (charged). Mobile homes for rent. Off site: Restaurant/café 500 m. Riding 3 km. Supermarket 4 km. Golf 6 km. Cycling and walking trails.

Open: All year.

Directions

Site is 20 km. southwest of Ragusa. From Catania, take S194 towards Ragusa and, at Comiso, follow signs to San Croce Camerina, then Punta Braccetto, from where site is well signed. Use second entrance for reception. GPS: 36.81645, 14.46964

Charges guide

Per person	€ 4.00 - € 8.50
pitch	€ 4.00 - € 11.00

Camping Cheques accepted.

For latest campsite news, availability and prices visit
alanrogers.com

San Vito Lo Capo
El Bahira Camping Village

Ctra da Makari-Localitá Salinella, I-91010 San Vito Lo Capo (Sicily) T: 092 397 2577. E: info@elbahira.it
alanrogers.com/IT69140

El Bahira is a popular site in quite a remote area overlooking the Gulf of Makari toward Monte Cofano. The views are outstanding and the location is good as it is near the sea, nature reserves and ancient cities such as Segtesta and Selinunte with their awe inspiring antiquities. Partners Maurizio, Maceri, Sugameli and Michele, who speak good English, have chosen this area to develop a campsite of a high standard. The 200 fairly small pitches are on sloping gravel (chocks required), most are shady and all have electricity. There are also numerous statics which unfortunately rather spoil the look of the site. There is a separate area for tents. The excellent restaurant, pizzeria and the pool all have views of the sea and there are very good entertainment and sporting facilities. Sanitary facilities with the exception of the showers are very good. The unisex showers are by timed token (outside the cabin) and the cubicles are tiny. Book ahead for this site in July and August as sites this good are few and far between in Sicily. Mothia with its prehistoric caves with early signs of man is also nearby, as is the enchanting Erice where time appears to have stood still and you can meander the ancient streets and enjoy the Norman castle and wonderful Duomo.

Facilities

Three well placed sanitary blocks, showers are by token (€ 4 for 8 showers), these are unisex, in tiny cabins. Motorcaravan service point. Supermarket. Restaurant and pizzeria. Swimming pool. Two entertainment areas. Tennis. Sub-aqua facilities. Boat launching at rocky beach on site. Off site: Popular resort village of San Vito Lo Capo 3 km.

Open: 1 April - 4 October.

Directions

From the east follow the A19 motorway and take Castellammare del Golfo exit then follow the S187 towards Trapani. After 16 km. turn right and follow signs to San Vito Lo Capo and site is well signed off the road approaching the town.
GPS: 38.150707, 12.73191

Charges guide

Per unit incl. 2 persons	
and electricity	€ 20.40 - € 37.60
child (0-3 yrs)	€ 3.00
pitch	€ 13.50 - € 19.80
small pitch	€ 9.00 - € 15.50

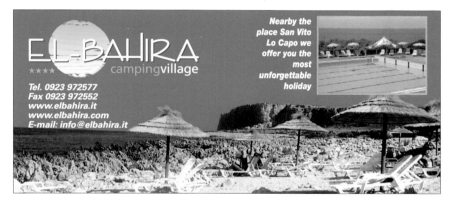

With dramatic, rolling
uplands covered
with grassland, and
a beautiful coastline
boasting isolated coves,
long sandy beaches and
hidden caves, Sardinia offers
more than just sunshine and clear
waters: littered around the island
are thousands of prehistoric
nuraghic remains.

SARDINIA HAS FOUR PROVINCES: CAGLIARI, NUORO, ORISTANO AND SASSARI

The busy port of Cágliari is the island's capital. Attractions include the city walls, archaeology museum and cathedral plus an impressive Roman amphitheatre. More ruins can be found just outside the city at Nora, while some 7,000 or so nuraghi are dotted all around the island. Unique to Sardinia, these stone-built constructions are remnants of Sardinia's only significant native culture. The most famous of them is at Su Nuraxi, the oldest and largest nuraghic complex, dating from around 1500 BC. The island's second city, Sássari, is known for its spectacular Cavalcata festival on Ascension Day; festivities include traditional singing and dancing plus a horse race. Not far from Sássari is Alghero, a major fishing port and the island's oldest resort. Surrounded by walls and defensive towers, the old town is full of narrow, cobbled streets with flamboyant churches and brightly coloured houses. Boat or car trips can also be made to Neptune's Grotto, a spectacular, deep marine cave, around the point of Capo Caccia. Sardinia's best known resort is the Costa Smeralda, one of the Mediterranean's loveliest stretches of coast, a 10 km. strip between the gulfs of Cugnana and Arzachena. Beaches can be found at Capriccioli, Rena Bianca and Liscia Ruia.

Places of interest

Bosa: small, picturesque seaside town.

Cala Gonone: bustling seaside resort and fishing port, with good beaches, isolated coves and natural caves including the famous Grotta del Bue Marino.

Carloforte: an attractive town on the island of San Pietro.

Dorgali: in the wine-growing region of Cannonau.

Maddalena Islands: popular tourist attraction, sandy and rocky beaches.

Oristano: nearby lagoon is home to one of the island's largest populations of flamingo.

Cuisine of the region

Fresh ingredients are widely used to create simple dishes: seafood, especially lobster, is grilled over open fires, as is suckling pig. Fish stews and pasta are popular. The island also produces a variety of breads. Cheeses tend to be made from ewe's milk, including *pecorino Sardo*. Nougat is a sweet Sardinian speciality and pastries are often flavoured with almonds, lemons or oranges. Vernaccia is the island's most famous wine.

Agnello arrosto: roast lamb, roasted on a spit or in casseroles with rosemary and thyme.

Bottarga: a version of caviar made with mullet eggs.

Culigiones: massive ravioli stuffed with cheese and egg.

Maloreddus: saffron flavoured pasta.

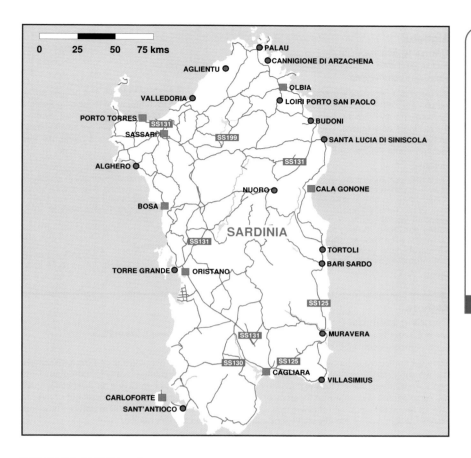

Aglientu

Camping Baia Blu la Tortuga

Pineta di Vignola Mare, I-07020 Aglientu (Sardinia) T: 079 602 200. E: info@campinglatortuga.com

alanrogers.com/IT69550

Tortuga is named after the giant turtle-like rock off the site's beautiful beach, and is a large, professionally run campsite. The 450 sizeable touring pitches (all with 3/10A electricity) are on grass and coarse-grained sand and shaded by tall pines with banks of colourful oleanders and wide boulevards providing easy access. This is a busy, bustling site with plenty to do, with its attractive bars and restaurants by the beach, which shelves rather steeply. The excellent play areas are cleverly placed to allow parents a break and the entertainment is first class. We were impressed by this quality family site. A member of Leading Campings group.

Facilities

Four excellent sanitary blocks (most with solar panels for hot water) with free hot showers, WCs, bidets and washbasins. Facilities for disabled campers. Quality private shower/washbasin cabins for rent. Laundry facilities. Motorcaravan services. Supermarket, beachside restaurant and bars, self-service restaurant, snack bar and takeaway. Gas. Bazaar. Gym. Hairdresser. Doctor's surgery. Playground. Tennis. Games and TV rooms. Windsurfing and diving schools. Internet point and WiFi area (charged). Massage centre (July/Aug). Entertainment and sports activities (mid May-Sept). Excursions. Barbecue area (not permitted on pitches). Two specially adapted mobile homes are available for family members with disabilities. Off site: Disco 50 m. Riding 18 km. Ferry to Corsica.

Open: 28 March - 14 October.

Directions

Site is on the north coast road (SP 90) between the towns of Costa Paradiso and Santa Teresa di Gallura (18 km) at Pineta di Vignola Mare and is well signed around the 47 km. marker.
GPS: 41.12436, 9.067594

Charges 2013

Per unit incl. 2 persons,	
water and electricity	€ 17.20 - € 52.80
extra person	€ 5.88 - € 14.20
child (3-9 yrs)	€ 3.80 - € 12.20
dog	€ 3.50 - € 8.00

FREE Alan Rogers Travel Card
Extra benefits and savings - see page 10

Alghero
Camping Mariposa
Via Lido 22, I-07041 Alghero (Sardinia) T: 079 950 360. E: info@lamariposa.it
alanrogers.com/IT69960

Mariposa is a sprawling beachside site with its own access to a fine sand beach. The pitches are of various sizes (50-80 sq.m); those on uneven ground are best suited for tents, while those on gravel are for caravans and motorcaravans (some alongside the sea). Some pitches have shade but all have 6A electrical connections. Cars must be parked away from the pitches. There is an entertainment programme in high season. The amenities are by the site entrance and include a pizzeria, bar and restaurant with TV. The small shop is also here.

Facilities

The brightly coloured, open plan sanitary facilities are clean, with cold water to washbasins. Hot showers (€ 0.50 token). Laundry facilities. Motorcaravan service point. Shop. Restaurant and bar. Bicycle hire. Kite surfing. Diving. Windsurfing. Stand-up paddling. Sailing. Surfing. Paragliding. (Courses available at extra charge). Communal barbecue. Dogs are not accepted in August. Off site: Site-owned restaurant in town (The Kings) offers 10% discount to campers. Neptune Caves.

Open: 1 April - 15 October.

Directions

Alghero is on the northwest coast, 35 km. southwest of Sassari. Mariposa is at the north end of the town. Follow the signs on the beach road, but watch for one-way systems which you have to navigate. GPS: 40.57885, 8.31253

Charges guide

Per unit incl. 2 persons	
and electricity	€ 23.00 - € 44.00
extra person	€ 10.00 - € 13.00
child (3-12 yrs)	€ 5.00 - € 9.00

Alghero
Camping Torre del Porticciolo
Localitá Porticciolo, Sede lagale via G Ferret 17, I-07041 Alghero (Sardinia) T: 079 919 010.
E: info@torredelporticciolo.it **alanrogers.com/IT69950**

Torre del Porticciolo is set high on a peninsula with fabulous views over the sea and old fortifications. It is a friendly, family owned site with striking traditional old buildings, attractive landscaping and large pools. A really huge site in terms of area, the camping area is under pine trees and totally shaded. There are some pitches with views, although most are tucked in under the pine trees. A walk out of the site down a very steep slope with stunning views, leads to the attractive beach and warm waters. The owner Marisa Carboni and her friendly staff speak a little English and are very helpful.

Facilities

Two clean toilet blocks have mainly Turkish style toilets and free showers. Washing machines. Motorcaravan service point. Large supermarket. Restaurant. Good supervised pool and paddling pool. Aerobics. Fitness centre. Play areas. Bicycle hire. Miniclub. Entertainment. Excursion service. Beach 100 m. down fairly steep slope. Excellent diving. Off site: Fishing. Sailing. Riding 1 km.

Open: 15 May - 10 October.

Directions

Take SS291 Sassari-Alghero road east, then the SS55 to Capo Caccia. Turn to Porticciolo town where site is well signed. GPS: 40.6423, 8.1906

Charges guide

Per unit incl. 2 persons	
and electricity	€ 19.50 - € 47.00
extra person	€ 6.00 - € 14.00
junior (3-12) or senior (over 60 yrs)	€ 4.00 - € 12.00
Camping Cheques accepted.	

Alghero
Camping Village Calik Blu
SS 127 bis, Fertilia, I-07041 Alghero (Sardinia) T: 079 930 111. E: info@campeggiocalik.it
alanrogers.com/IT69970

Camping Village Calik Blu is a large site, pleasantly placed between the sea and a huge lagoon, the beach being directly across the road from the site. Most of the 600 pitches (450 for touring units) have 6A electricity and are shaded with pine and eucalyptus trees. Some pitches are in the trees, others are on level ground in long rows, the end ones enjoying lagoon-side positions. A considerable number are fully serviced. On-site amenities are close to the entrance and include a novel white, canvas-roofed restaurant/pizzeria plus a self-service restaurant.

Facilities

Four renovated sanitary blocks provide a high standard of facilities. Units for disabled campers. Restaurant/pizzeria. Self-service restaurant. Takeaway. Supermarket. Play area. Activity and entertainment programme. Bicycle hire. Boat launching. Internet and WiFi (payment). Watersports. Sea fishing. Mobile homes and chalets to rent. Off site: Alghero town. Outdoor swimming pool, golf and riding 2 km.

Open: 1 April - 31 October.

Directions

The site is to the north of Alghero on the northwest coast of Sardinia. It is close to the 41 km. marker on the coast road (SS127) near Fertilia. The site is well signed. GPS: 40.594571, 8.29152

Charges guide

Per unit incl. 2 persons	
and electricity	€ 16.00 - € 46.00
extra person	€ 5.40 - € 11.50

For latest campsite news, availability and prices visit
alanrogers.com

Bari Sardo
Camping l'Ultima Spiaggia

Localitá Planargia, I-08042 Bari Sardo (Sardinia) T: 078 229 363. E: info@campingultimaspiaggia.it
alanrogers.com/IT69720

L'Ultima Spiaggia (the ultimate beach) is an apt name as the beach really is extremely pleasant, although coarse grained. There are four great paddling and swimming pools, and the facilities have bright, colourful décor. The 252 pitches all have 3/6A electricity, are terraced on sand and some enjoy limited sea views. The ambitious entertainment programme can be enjoyed from the terrace of the restaurant, which offers a variety of good food. Mobile homes occupy the top area of the site away from the pitches, and access to the beach (with lifeguard) and a variety of watersports is gained through a security gate.

Facilities

Two modernised toilet units include facilities for babies and disabled visitors, but are some way from the lower pitches. Laundry facilities. Motorcaravan service point. Small supermarket. Restaurant and snack bar. Play areas. Domestic animal area with donkeys. Windsurfing, diving and sailing. Aerobics. Riding. Tennis. Minigolf. Canoeing. Bicycle hire. Miniclub. Multisports area. Entertainment. WiFi (charged). Torches useful. Off site: Restaurants, bars and shops. Fishing. Boat launching. Kite surfing.

Open: 20 April - 30 September.

Directions

Site is on east coast of Sardinia, well signed from the main coast road, the SS125 in the village of Bari Sardo. GPS: 39.819003, 9.670484

Charges guide

Per unit incl. 2 persons	
and electricity	€ 25.50 - € 54.00
extra person	€ 7.00 - € 15.50
child (1-12 yrs acc. to age)	€ 4.50 - € 12.50
dog	€ 4.50 - € 6.50

Budoni
Camping Pedra & Cupa

Via Nazionale, I-08020 Budoni (Sardinia) T: 078 484 4004. E: info@pedraecupa-camping.com
alanrogers.com/IT69650

This attractive site has had much thought put into its planning and construction. Modern bungalows (for rent) screen the camping area from the coastal road. It is close to the white sands of the lovely beach and enjoys the shade of eucalyptus and pine trees along the coast. The 55 level, grassy pitches have 6A electricity and artificial shade. The bar, pool and restaurant complex offers a variety of refreshments and food, along with entertainment in high season on a stage close to the terraces. The site is divided by a river, which is safely fenced.

Facilities

Twin sanitary blocks provide toilets (mainly Turkish style), open style washbasins and hot showers (€ 0.50/3 mins). Motorcaravan service point. Shop. Restaurant. Bar. Takeaway (all 15/6-15/9). Swimming pool and terrace. Tennis. Football. Entertainment (high season). WiFi (charged). Off site: Riding. Walks and cycle routes.

Open: 1 May - 30 September.

Directions

Site is at the southern end of Budoni town and well signed. GPS: 40.700315, 9.71395

Charges guide

Per unit incl. 2 persons	
and electricity	€ 26.00 - € 50.00
extra person	€ 6.50 - € 15.00
child (2-11 yrs)	€ 3.50 - € 9.00

Cannigione di Arzachena
Isuledda Holiday Centre

Localitá Laconia, I-07021 Cannigione di Arzachena (Sardinia) T: 078 986 003. E: info@isuledda.it
alanrogers.com/IT69630

This large, high quality, natural campsite has something for everyone, with an amazing choice of activities and entertainment. Some of the 600 good sized, gravel pitches (with 4A electricity) have magnificent views over the Archena Gulf. We loved the outstanding pitches perched directly over the sea and the beaches. Other pitches enjoy shade from eucalyptus trees and are flat. Cars are parked outside the entrance. The central area buzzes with activity, although it is possible to find a quiet area to relax. It is crowded in high season (5-20 August). You are advised to book early for the best pitches.

Facilities

Six toilet blocks include British and Turkish style toilets and facilities for disabled campers. Showers. Washing machines. Motorcaravan service point (charged). Large supermarket. Restaurant, pizzeria and snack bar. Aerobics. Play areas. Boat, car, bicycle and scooter hire. Windsurfing. Sailing. Sub-aqua. Marina. Miniclub. Entertainment. Excursions. Disco and beer bar (can be noisy until late). WiFi (charged). Dogs are not accepted. Off site: Riding 10 km. Golf 15 km.

Open: 1 April - 30 October.

Directions

Site is on the Costa Smeralda in the northeast of Sardinia. From SS125 Olbia-Cannigione road, south of Arzachena, take road north towards Baia Sardinia. Then follow road north to Cannigione, go through town and further north for 2 km. where the site is well signed. GPS: 41.1302, 9.4387

Charges guide

Per unit incl. 2 persons	
and electricity	€ 20.50 - € 61.00
extra person	€ 5.00 - € 13.00
Camping Cheques accepted.	

FREE Alan Rogers Travel Card
Extra benefits and savings - see page 10

Loiri Porto San Paolo

Camping Tavolara

SS125 km. 300,300, Porto San Paolo, I-07020 Loiri Porto San Paolo (Sardinia) T: 078 940 166.
E: info@camping-tavolara.it alanrogers.com/IT69640

This smallish site has just 200 pitches (with 3/10A electricity), which are flat and well shaded, with a garden atmosphere created by flowers and hedging. South of Olbia and just 30 minutes from the ferry port and airport, it is a quiet and pleasant site. It is 500 m. from the beach (shuttle bus provided). This is a great location opposite Isola Tavolara, literally a mountain rising from the sea. It is famous for the legendary 'goats with golden teeth', a phenomenon caused by the grass they eat. The restaurant and bar with their terraces are very welcome in the cool evenings.

Facilities	Directions
Two sanitary blocks provide toilets (mainly Turkish style), washbasins and showers (torch required). Facilities for disabled campers. Motorcaravan service point. Restaurant and bar. Pizzeria. Shop (all facilities open Easter-Sept). Diving school. Archery. Bocce. Football. Tennis. Excursions and entertainment (high season). WiFi (charged). Caravans and mobile homes to rent. Off site: Tourist town of Porto San Paolo 2 km. Isola Tavolara. Costa Smeralda. Olbia.	Site is at 300 km. marker on the SS125 south of Olbia. From the port follow signs for Aeroporto and pass the airport heading towards San Teodoro. Site is on the left just past Porto San Paolo. GPS: 40.858612, 9.642753

Open: 1 April - 30 October.

Charges guide

Per unit incl. 2 persons	
and electricity	€ 26.50 - € 50.00
extra person	€ 9.00 - € 11.00

Muravera

Camping 4 Mori

Localitá Is Perdigonis, I-09043 Muravera (Sardinia) T: 0709 991 10. E: info@4mori.it
alanrogers.com/IT69730

Camping 4 Mori (the four moors) is a modern site with many good facilities which would suit families. There are 88 touring pitches with 3/6A electricity. Some have shade and all have easy access. The superb beach is close by with a great bar/snack bar, loungers and umbrellas (extra charge), and lifeguards. On site, the pleasant pools also have lifeguards. After a swim, try the bar and restaurant which are bright and friendly. The site is decked with colourful plants and bushes. English is spoken and there is always a smile. You will not need to leave 4 Mori as everything is here.

Facilities	Directions
The slightly tired condition of the six sanitary blocks is disappointing as is the need for shower tokens (€ 0.25 for 2 minutes). Good facilities for disabled campers. Bar and restaurant. Full animation programme. Sub-aqua school. Watersports. Fishing. Bicycle hire. Excursions. WiFi in the bar (charged). Off site: Riding 5 km.	Site is in the southeast section of Sardinia. Take the SS125 and site is well signed from the 58 km. marker. GPS: 39.375897, 9.59917

Open: 27 April - 13 October.

Charges guide

Per unit incl. 2 persons	€ 17.00 - € 41.50
extra person	€ 4.00 - € 12.00

Muravera

Camping Capo Ferrato

Localitá Costa Rei, I-09040 Muravera-Castiadas (Sardinia) T: 070 991 012. E: info@campingcapoferrato.it
alanrogers.com/IT69770

Situated at the southern end of the magnificent Costa Rei, this small, friendly and well managed site has 83 touring pitches, many in great positions on the fine, white sand beachfront. They all have 3/6A electricity, are on sand, shady and of generous proportions. On the fringes of Costa Rei, the site benefits from close proximity to the shops and restaurants, yet enjoys absolute tranquillity. The charming restaurant holds it own against the village competition. This site is brilliant for beach lovers and windsurfers, and offers many watersports. The beach shelves safely for children.

Facilities	Directions
Two sanitary blocks include toilets, washbasins and free hot showers. No facilities for disabled visitors. Washing machine. Baby room. Motorcaravan service point. Bar. Restaurant. Pizzeria. Well stocked shop. TV room. Bicycle hire. Tennis. Football and basketball pitch. New, comprehensive, well shaded children's play area. Entertainment (high season). WiFi (charged). Dogs are not accepted in July/Aug. Bungalows to rent. Off site: Sailing and boat launching 200 m. ATM in village. Riding 3 km. Golf 20 km. Costa Rei, Castiadas, Muravera.	Capo Ferrato is in the southeast of Sardinia and can be reached by using the SS125 and heading off to Capo Ferrato. Then take the Costa Rei signs and the site is well signed on the southern edge of the village of Costa Rei. GPS: 39.24297, 9.56941

Open: 1 April - 2 November.

Charges guide

Per unit incl. 2 persons	
and electricity	€ 20.40 - € 47.20
extra person	€ 5.60 - € 13.20
child (3-12 yrs)	€ 4.00 - € 9.90

Camping Cheques accepted.

Muravera
Tiliguerta Camping Village

SP 97 km. 6, localitá Capo Ferrato, I-09043 Muravera (Sardinia) T: 070 991 437. E: info@tiliguerta.com
alanrogers.com/IT69750

This family site situated at Capo Ferrato has changed its owners, name and direction (2011). The new owners have made many improvements, all of them in sympathy with the environment. The 186 reasonably sized pitches are on sand and have 3A electricity. Some have shade and views of the superb, fine beach and sea beyond. There are some permanent pitches used by Italian units. The traditional site buildings are centrally located and contain a good quality restaurant using only fresh ingredients. This has a charming ambience with its high arched ceilings. Shaded terraces allow comfortable viewing of the ambitious entertainment programme. Cars must be parked away from pitches. The staff are cheerful and English is spoken. Consideration is given to the environment at every turn. There are numerous activities on offer – basketball, beach volleyball, riding and watersports, and in high season yoga, tai-chi, Pilates and dancing are possible. There is a full entertainment programme. We believe Tiliguerta is becoming a good quality, environmentally friendly site.

Facilities	Directions
Three sanitary blocks. One is newly renovated with private bathrooms, and facilities for children and disabled visitors. The two older blocks have mixed Turkish/British style toilets. Washing machine. Motorcaravan service point (extra charge). Shop. Restaurant and snack bar. Play areas (due for replacement by 2012). Miniclub and entertainment in high season. Tennis. Water aerobics. Sub-aqua diving. Windsurfing school. Riding. Torches essential. Bicycle hire. WiFi over site (charged). Communal barbecue areas. Off site: Sailing 1.5 km.	Site is in southeast corner of Sardinia in the north of the Costa Rei. From coast road SS125 or the SP97 at km. 6, take the turn to Villaggio Capo Ferrato. Site is well signed from here. GPS: 39.2923, 9.5987

Open: 27 April - 27 October.

Charges guide

Per unit incl. 2 persons and electricity	€ 21.50 - € 47.54
extra person	€ 5.00 - € 15.00
child (3-9 yrs)	€ 3.50 - € 10.00
dog	€ 3.00 - € 6.00

Muravera
Camping le Dune

Localitá Piscina Rei, I-09043 Muravera (Sardinia) T: 070 991 9057. E: info@campingledune.it
alanrogers.com/IT69740

The Costa Rei in southeast Sardinia is a popular seaside resort which has not as yet been over developed. A white sandy bay and the turquoise sea make it a perfect holiday location. There are 100 pitches for touring units on sand, mostly under shade, all with 3/6A electricity, plus 100 for accommodation, but there is little overlap on site. This is a family oriented site with excellent beach access. We watched quality entertainment with approximately 300 campers having great fun.

Facilities	Directions
Three sanitary blocks provide a mixture of British and Turkish style toilets, washbasins (open style) and showers. Washing machines. Restaurant. Bar. Shop. Swimming pool. Tennis and football. Sailing and boat launching. Entertainment (high season). WiFi (charged). Off site: Costa Rei town. Diving. Riding 1 km.	Site is in southeast corner of Sardinia in the north of the Costa Rei. From SS125 go towards Villaggio Capo Ferrato and then Costa Rei. Site is well signed in the village. GPS: 39.2767, 9.5821

Open: 10 April - 30 September.

Charges guide

Per unit incl. 2 persons and electricity	€ 17.00 - € 45.00
extra person	€ 4.50 - € 10.00

FREE Alan Rogers Travel Card
Extra benefits and savings - see page 10

Muravera

Camping Torre Salinas

Torre Salinas, I-09043 Muravera (Sardinia) T: 070 999 032. E: info@camping-torre-salinas.de

alanrogers.com/IT69735

This is a small and simple site which will suit the pockets of some campers. The site is on a slope with some terraced pitches. On sand and grass, some are shaded and all have 4A electricity. Access is good on the site and it is very peaceful. All the facilities are at the entrance and a small friendly bar is faced across the main site road by a little restaurant/pizzeria which serves good food at sensible prices. English is spoken and the staff is most friendly. There is little sophistication at Torre Salinas but everything is clean and neat.

Facilities	Directions
The single central sanitary block was new in 2011 and one of the best we saw on any small site in Sardinia. Spotless throughout it supplies hot water (solar) everywhere and has excellent facilities for disabled campers and children. Bar. Pizzeria/restaurant. Bicycle hire. Off site: Beach and fishing 300 m. Boat launching and sailing 1 km. Riding 3 km.	Site is on the southeast coast of Sardinia, south of the town of Muravera. From the SS125 head for the town and the site is well signed from there off the coastal SS125 road. GPS: 39.36696, 9.596322

Open: 1 April - 31 October.

Charges guide

Per unit incl. 2 persons and electricity	€ 16.00 - € 36.50
extra person	€ 4.80 - € 11.50

Nuoro

Camping Agriturismo Costiolou

SS389, I-08100 Nuoro (Sardinia) T: 078 426 0088. E: info@agriturismocostiolou.com

alanrogers.com/IT69670

Costiolou is a wonderful 100-hectare, organic farm high in the hills above Nuoro, with fantastic views in almost every direction. This is a most unusual campsite, located on the working farm run by Giovanni di Costa, cheese maker, winemaker, farmer, gardener and host. Prepare to be amazed by the courtyard with covered terrace, cellars, traditional kitchens and other charming Sardinian features. The site has just nine pitches on a flat and level area behind the farmhouse. Eagles circle overhead and many animals can be seen, including horses, which are bred here (and are available to ride).

Facilities	Directions
Toilets and showers are provided in a restored farm building alongside the pitches, including facilities for disabled visitors. Bar. Restaurant (by arrangement). Barbecues. Rooms to rent (full or half board, B&B). Riding. Dogs are not accepted. Off site: Wild Sardinian countryside for walking and wildlife.	The site is at the 90 km. marker on the SS389 Nuoro to Bitti road. It is well signed, but there is a 9 km. long roughish track to the farm. GPS: 40.3674, 9.29658

Open: All year.

Charges guide

Per unit incl. 2 persons and electricity	€ 22.00 - € 30.00
extra person	€ 7.00 - € 10.00

Cash only.

Palau

Camping Capo d'Orso

Localitá Saline, I-07020 Palau (Sardinia) T: 078 970 2007. E: info@capodorso.it

alanrogers.com/IT69600

Capo d'Orso is a large, attractive, terraced site with views of the Maddalena Archipelago. Set into a hillside that slopes down to the sea, the 350 terraced pitches (40-80 sq.m) are of gravel, grass and sand, some with views over the sea and some others set alongside the beach (10% extra in high season). Access to the pitches is good despite the rocky terrain. Cars are parked away from the pitches in high season. The very Italian restaurant atop the amenities building serves delicious meals from a set menu and has a covered terrace giving excellent sea views. This site is great for families.

Facilities	Directions
Three toilet blocks are being renovated and will provide ample facilities, including hot showers, and mainly Turkish style WCs. Motorcaravan service point. Shop. Bazaar. Bar/restaurant. Pizzeria. Takeaway. Fresh fish twice weekly. Scuba diving, windsurfing, sailing school, boat excursions, boat hire and moorings (all main season). Tennis. Entertainment programmes. Excursions in high season. WiFi (charged). Off site: Scuba diving. Sailing. Windsurfing. Train and boat trips. Scooter hire 5 km.	Site is 5 km. from Palau, in the northeast of Sardinia. On the SS133 Porto Pozzo-Cannigione road. Well signed towards the beach. GPS: 41.16117, 9.403

Open: 15 May - 30 September.

Charges guide

Per unit incl. 2 persons and electricity	€ 21.50 - € 53.00
extra person	€ 6.00 - € 9.50
child (6-12 yrs)	€ 3.00 - € 6.50

Camping Cheques accepted.

For latest campsite news, availability and prices visit

alanrogers.com

Sant'Antioco
Camping Tonnara

Localitá Alasapone, I-09017 Sant'Antioco (Sardinia) T: 078 180 9058. E: tonnaracamping@tiscalinet.it
alanrogers.com/IT69860

A small, attractive campsite, Tonnara is on the west side of Sant'Antioco island in the southwest corner of Sardinia. Access to the island is via a causeway and Tonnara is located 12 km. away in the pretty Cala Sapone inlet with its delightful sandy beach and rocky outcrops. The 150 sandy pitches (with 6A electricity) are on slopes and terraces with small trees and some artificial shade. Some are very close to the beach and most enjoy fabulous views of the inlet. The local seafood is good and cooked to perfection in the small restaurant where you can sit out on the terrace and watch the sunsets.

Facilities

Two modern sanitary blocks have both Turkish and British style toilets, washbasins (cold water only) and hot showers. Facilities for disabled campers. Superb facilities for children. Baby bathing area. Washing machine. Motorcaravan service point. Shop. Restaurant and snack bar. Outdoor swimming pool (caps compulsory). Play area. Bicycle hire. Tennis. Bocce. Beach. Sub-aqua diving arranged. Excursions. WiFi (charged). No barbecues allowed. Off site: Sailing 1 km. Riding 3 km.

Open: 20 April - 30 October.

Directions

Site is on island of S'Antioco on southwest coast of Sardinia. Go over the causeway and immediately at the end, turn left and left again at T-junction towards Cala Sapone (site is well signed). GPS: 39.0053, 8.3873

Charges guide

Per unit incl. 2 persons and electricity	€ 22.00 - € 51.00
extra person	€ 9.00 - € 14.00

Santa Lucia di Siniscola
Selema Camping

Tiria Seliana, I-08029 Santa Lucia di Siniscola (Sardinia) T: 079 953 761. E: info@selemacamping.com
alanrogers.com/IT69660

Selema is a pretty site with a tropical feel. There is considerable shade from pine and eucalyptus, although access to many pitches is restricted by tall, bending trees. Flowers and cacti have been used to provide landscaping features and unusually there are grassy areas. There are 170 large pitches of grass and sand, well shaded with shallow terracing. The site runs along the Pineta coast with its long white sandy beaches and vibrant blue water and has a wide river flowing along the other side. Some pitches are near the beach and a few have views of the distant mountains.

Facilities

Two sanitary blocks have good facilities with a mixture of British and Turkish style toilets. Hot showers. Facilities for disabled visitors. Washing machine. Motorcaravan service point. Shop. Restaurant and snack bar. Play areas. Tennis. Bocce. Large screen TV. Electronic games. Bicycle hire. Windsurfing. Small boat launching. Excursions. Off site: Fishing. Riding 500 m. Sailing 4 km.

Open: 1 May - 15 October.

Directions

The site is on the SS125, 30 km. north of Orosei. Turn towards the coast, near the 254 km. marker to Santa Lucia. Site signed. GPS: 40.5785, 9.7730

Charges guide

Per unit incl. 2 persons and electricity	€ 21.00 - € 59.00
extra person	€ 5.50 - € 13.50

Torre Grande
Camping Village Spinnaker

Strada Provinciale, Oristano, I-09170 Torre Grande (Sardinia) T: 078 322 074. E: info@spinnakervacanze.com
alanrogers.com/IT69900

Set on the undulating foreshore under tall pines, with beach frontage to the camping area, Spinnaker Village is a smart, purpose built, modern beach site. The 143 pitches are sandy, with 43 suitable for caravans and motorcaravans, the remainder for tents. All pitches have 6A electricity and there are plenty of water taps. Tent pitches are large and clearly marked, each with a tree to provide shade. Cars must be parked in a car park outside the site. There are many neat, white buildings on site – the restaurant, a café and the swimming pool are set around a large square, where activities for families take place. Transponders are provided for showers and for use around the site in lieu of cash.

Facilities

Toilet blocks are modern and very clean with British style toilets and facilities for disabled campers. Showers are transponder operated (€ 0.50 per shower). Washing machine. Motorcaravan service point. Small shop. Restaurant and small snack bar. Swimming pool and pool bar. Play area. Bicycle hire. Small boat launching. Miniclub and entertainment in high season. Excursions. Torches essential. Off site: Riding 2 km. Golf 23 km.

Open: 1 April - 30 September.

Directions

Take SS131 Cagliari-Oristano road then minor road to Cabras and Torre Grande. Just before Torre Grande village by large water tower take angled left turn back on yourself to site. GPS: 39.903, 8.5301

Charges guide

Per unit incl. 2 persons and electricity	€ 23.00 - € 45.00
extra person	€ 8.00 - € 18.00
Camping Cheques accepted.	

FREE Alan Rogers Travel Card
Extra benefits and savings - see page 10

Tortoli

Camping Cigno Bianco

Lido di Orri, I-08048 Tortoli (Sardinia) T: 078 262 4927. E: info@cignobianco.it

alanrogers.com/IT69700

The small town of Tortoli is just 5 km. inland from the busy ferry port of Arbatax. Here the very friendly Pinna family run a quiet and restful site with good facilities and direct beach access. The 100 unmarked pitches are separated by the tall eucalyptus and pine trees, which also give considerable shade. They all have 6A electricity. The restaurant serves some quality Italian food and there is limited entertainment for children. There is direct access to a superb beach, with trees to give shade, and clean water for a cooling swim. This is a very reasonably priced site.

Facilities

Two well placed sanitary blocks provide toilets (some Turkish style), washbasins and showers (token required). Motorcaravan service point. Restaurant, bar and small shop. Tennis court and multisport pitch. Dogs are not accepted in July/Aug. Flats and mobile homes to rent. Off site: Riding centre 5 km. Watersports. Gennargentu National Park. Cala Sisine.

Open: 1 May - 30 September.

Directions

Site is just off the SS125, south of Tortoli. Look for and follow the large blue signs for Lido d'Orri towards the sea, and then the campsite signs. GPS: 39.9076, 9.6824

Charges guide

| Per unit incl. 2 persons and electricity | € 23.00 - € 35.00 |
| extra person | € 7.50 - € 12.50 |

Valledoria

Camping la Foce

Via Ampurias no. 110, I-07039 Valledoria (Sardinia) T: 079 582 109. E: info@foce.it

alanrogers.com/IT69500

English-speaking Matteo Lampati is the director of la Foce, which is a large, sprawling site in the Golfo del Asinara. A novel feature is the motorbarge to ferry campers to a secluded area of the sea coast on the other side of the river, which flows alongside the site, where they can enjoy the golden sand dunes and have a refreshing swim away from other beach-goers. The 300 sandy pitches (with 4/6A electricity) vary in size and are informally arranged under tall shady eucalyptus trees stretching along the length of the site, some close to the river. There is a full entertainment programme in high season.

Facilities

Three mature and one new toilet blocks house good facilities with British and Turkish style toilets plus excellent facilities for disabled visitors. Washing machine. Motorcaravan service point. Supermarket, bar, restaurant and snack bar. Two pools. Play areas. Tennis. Bocce. Excursions. Boat launching, sailing and windsurfing. Canoeing. Sub-aqua diving. WiFi (part site, free). Off site: Beach and fishing 200 m. Riding 2 km.

Open: 25 April - 30 September.

Directions

From Sassari take coast road east to Castelsardo and Valledoria. As you arrive at the village watch for campsite signs towards beach and site. GPS: 40.9335, 8.8174

Charges 2013

| Per unit incl. 2 persons and electricity | € 19.00 - € 43.00 |
| extra person | € 5.30 - € 9.00 |

Camping Cheques accepted.

Villasimius

Villaggio Spiaggia Del Riso

Campulongu, I-09049 Villasimius (Sardinia) T: 070 791 052. E: campriso@tiscali.it

alanrogers.com/IT69780

This spacious site looks well kept and is professionally run. It is split by a public road but there is an underpass for campers. Pitches on both sides of the site are mostly flat, with 3A electricity. The area beside the beach area has pitches for motorcaravans which are in the sun but have a low artificially shaded area alongside each pitch (it can be windy here in the afternoon). Pitches on the upper side are under mature trees for shade, while the lower ones have sea views. The well designed restaurant is fabulous with lots of local fare. A pleasant site which will be enjoyed by families.

Facilities

Four sanitary blocks provide mixed British and Turkish style toilets. Only cold water at washbasins and the showers are cramped with no divider or shelves, and require €0.50 tokens (torch required). Facilities for disabled visitors. Laundry facilities. Motorcaravan service point. Cafeteria. Restaurant and bar. Pizzeria/snack bar. Shop. Archery. 5-a-side football. Bicycle hire. Entertainment (high season). Communal barbecue area only. Internet and WiFi (charged). Off site: Golf and riding 500 m.

Open: 25 April - 30 October.

Directions

Site is in the bottom southeast corner of Sardinia, south of the village of Villasimius. From the SS125 take the road to Villasimius where the site is well signed. It is 2 km. towards the sea. GPS: 39.123202, 9.512658

Charges guide

| Per unit incl. 2 persons and electricity | € 26.00 - € 47.00 |
| extra person | € 9.00 - € 16.00 |

For latest campsite news, availability and prices visit

alanrogers.com

The world famous Postojna caves are well worth a visit. Guided tours by special cave trains take you through extensive and marvellous rock formations.

With its snow-capped Julian Alps and the picturesque Triglav National Park that includes the beautiful lakes of Bled and Bohinj, and the peaceful Soca River, it is no wonder that the northwest region of Slovenia is so popular. Stretching from the Alps down to the Adriatic coast is the picturesque Karst region, with pretty olive groves and thousands of spectacular underground caves, including the Postojna and Skocjan caves. Although small, the Adriatic coast has several bustling beach towns such as the Italianised Koper resort and the historic port of Piran, with many opportunities for watersports and sunbathing. The capital Ljubljana is centrally located; with Renaissance, Baroque and Art Nouveau architecture, you will find most points of interest are along the Ljubljana river. Heading eastwards the landscape becomes gently rolling hills, and is largely given over to vines (home of Lutomer Riesling). Savinja with its spectacular Alps is the main area for producing wine.

Population
2 million

Capital
Ljubljana

Climate
Warm summers, cold winters with snow in the Alps.

Language
Slovene, with German often spoken in the north and Italian in the west.

Telephone
The country code is 00 386.

Currency
The Euro (€).

Banks
Mon-Fri 08.30-16.30 with a lunch break 12.30-14.00, plus Saturday mornings 08.30-11.30.

Shops
Shops usually open by 08.00, sometimes 07.00. Closing times vary widely.

What Slovenia lacks in size it makes up for in exceptional beauty. Situated between Italy, Austria, Hungary and Croatia, it has a diverse landscape with stunning Alps, rivers, forests and the warm Adriatic coast.

Public Holidays

New Year 1, 2 Jan; Preseren Day 8 Feb; Easter Monday; Resistance Day 27 Apr; Labour Day 1-2 May; National Day 25 Jun; Assumption; Reformation Day 31 Oct; All Saints Day; Christmas Day; Independence Day 26 Dec.

Motoring

A small, but expanding network of motorways radiates from Ljubljana. A 'vignette' system for motorway travel is in place. The cost is around € 35 (for a six-month vignette) and they can be purchased at petrol stations and DARS offices in Slovenia and neighbouring countries near the border. Failure to display a vignette will lead to fines of up to € 300. Winter driving equipment (winter tyres or snow chains) is mandatory between 15 Nov and 15 March. By law, you must have your headlights on **at all times**, while driving in Slovenia. You are also required to carry a reflective jacket, a warning triangle and a first aid kit in the vehicle. Do not drink and drive – any trace of alcohol in your system will lead to prosecution.

Tourist Office

Slovenian Tourist Board Office
10 Little College Street
London SW1P 3SH
Tel: 0870 225 5305
E-mail: london@slovenia.info
Internet: www.slovenia.info

British Embassy

4th Floor Trg Republike 3
1000 Ljubljana
Tel: (386) (1) 200 3910

Places of interest

Adriatic Coast: Venetian Gothic architecture can be found at Piran, the best beach along the coast is at Fiesa.

Julian Alps: Mt Triglav is the country's highest peak, Bled Castle, Bled Island has a 15th-century belfry with a 'bell of wishes', Lake Bohinij.

Ljubljana: Municipal Museum, National Museum, Museum of Modern Art all along the banks of the Ljubljana River, Tivoli Park with bowling alleys, tennis courts, swimming pools and a roller-skating rink.

Skocjan Caves: filled with stalactites and stalagmites and housing 250 plant varieties and five types of bat.

Cuisine of the region

Traditionally the cuisine mainly consists of venison and fish, but there are Austrian, Italian and Hungarian influences.

Dunajski zrezek: wiener schnitzel

Golaz: goulash

Klobasa: sausage

Njoki: potato dumplings

Paprikas: chicken or beef stew

Struklji: cheese dumplings

Zavitek: strudel

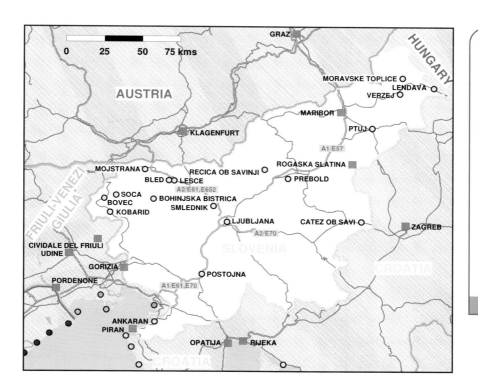

Ankaran
Camping Adria

Jadranska Cesta 25, SLO-6280 Ankaran T: 056 637 350. E: sales@adria-ankaran.si
alanrogers.com/SV4310

Camping Adria is on the south side of the Milje/Muggia peninsula, right on the shore of the Adriatic Sea and just beyond the large shipyard and oil storage depot. It has a concrete promenade with access to the sea, complemented by an Olympic size pool (June-September) with children's pool, both filled with sea water. The site has 400 pitches (250 for tourers), all with 10A electricity, set up on one side of the site close to the sea. Pitches are off tarmac access roads, running down to the sea and most are between 80 and 90 sq.m. There are six fully serviced pitches for motorcaravans with electricity, water and waste water. Pitches at the beach (used by static caravans) have beautiful views of the Adriatic and the historic ports of Koper and Izola.

Facilities

Five modern toilet blocks with British and Turkish style toilets, open style washbasins. Free hot and cold water, controllable showers. Facilities for disabled visitors. Laundry room. Fridge box hire. Supermarket. Beach shop. Newspaper kiosk. Bar/restaurant with terrace. Swimming pool (40x15 m) with large slide. Playground on gravel. Playing field. Tennis. Minigolf. Fishing. Jetty for mooring boats. Boat launching. Canoe hire. Disco and bowling club. Off site: Historic towns of Koper, Izola, Piran and Portoroz are close.

Open: 10 April - 15 October.

Directions

From Koper drive north to Ankaran. Site is immediately on the left at roundabout after entering Ankaran. Do not try to enter from Trieste/Muggia using sat nav from autobahn.
GPS: 45.57797, 13.73633

Charges guide

Per person	€ 11.00 - € 13.50
child (2-10 yrs)	€ 5.00 - € 6.50
electricity (16A)	€ 4.50
dog	€ 4.00

Bohinjska Bistrica

Camping Danica Bohinj

Triglavska 60, SLO-4264 Bohinjska Bistrica T: 045 721 702. E: info@camp-danica.si

alanrogers.com/SV4250

For those wishing to visit the famous Bohinj valley, which stretches like a fjord right into the heart of the Julian Alps, Danica Bohinj is an ideal site lying in the valley 3 km. downstream of the lake. It is spacious, stretching from the main road to the bank of the newly formed Sava river, on a flat meadow set in natural woodland. This excellent site has 165 pitches, 145 for touring units (all with 16A electricity), and forms an ideal base for the many sporting activities the area has to offer.

Facilities

Two good toilet blocks with open plan washbasins and hot showers. Facilities for disabled visitors. Laundry facilities (expensive). Motorcaravan service point. Small shop. Bar (also used by locals, open until 01.00 and can be noisy). Café. Tennis. Fishing. Badminton. Volleyball. Cross-country skiing from site. Bicycle hire. WiFi. Excursions in the Triglavski National Park. Off site: Four ski resorts. Riding 6 km. Canoeing, kayaking, rafting and numerous walking and mountain bike trails.

Open: All year.

Directions

Driving from Bled to Bohinj, in Bohinjska Bistrica stay on main road (it goes to the right). Site is 200 m. on the right-hand (north) side of the road. GPS: 46.27335, 13.94868

Charges guide

Per person	€ 7.00 - € 11.00
child (7-14 yrs)	€ 5.60 - € 9.00
electricity	€ 3.50
dog	€ 2.50

Bovec

Camping Polovnik

Ledina 8, SLO-5230 Bovec T: 053 896 007. E: kamp.polovnik@siol.net

alanrogers.com/SV4280

Camping Polovnik is a small site set in a circular field with trees in the centre, providing useful shade, and an open part to one side. There are 50 unmarked pitches (45 for tourers) all with 16A electricity, off a circular, gravel access road. To the back of the site is a separate field for groups. All pitches have good views of the surrounding mountains. This site is useful as a stopover on your way to the Postojna Caves, the Slovenian Riviera or Italy, and for touring the local area with kayaking, rafting and canoeing possible.

Facilities

One well maintained toilet block with British style toilets, open style washbasins with cold water only and preset hot showers (€ 0,50 token). Washing machine, dryer. Motorcaravan service point. Off site: Restaurant at entrance. Fishing 1 km. Bovec town.

Open: 1 April - 16 October.

Directions

Bovec is 35 km. NE of Udine (Italy). Site is south of town and well signed on the main 203 road. GPS: 46.33622, 13.55837

Charges guide

Per person	€ 7.00 - € 8.00
child (7-14 yrs)	€ 5.25 - € 6.00

Catez ob Savi

Camping Terme Catez

Topliska cesta 35, SLO-8251 Catez ob Savi T: 074 936 700. E: info@terme-catez.si

alanrogers.com/SV4415

Terme Catez is part of the modern Catez thermal spa, which includes very large and attractive indoor (31°C) and outdoor swimming complexes, both with large slides and waves. The campsite has 450 pitches, with 190 places for tourers, arranged on one large, open field, with some young trees – a real sun trap – and provides level, grass pitches which are numbered by markings on the tarmac access roads. All have 10A electricity connections. Although the site is ideally placed for an overnight stop when travelling on the E70, it is well worthwhile planning to spend some time here to take advantage of the excellent facilities that are included in the overnight camping charges.

Facilities

Two modern toilet blocks with British style toilets, washbasins in cabins, large and controllable hot showers. Child sized washbasins. Facilities for disabled visitors. Laundry facilities. Motorcaravan service point. Supermarket. Kiosks for fruit, newspapers, souvenirs and tobacco. Attractive restaurant with buffet. Bar with terrace. Large indoor and outdoor swimming complexes. Rowing boats. Jogging track. Fishing. Golf. Bicycle hire. Sauna. Solarium. Riding. Organised activities. Video games. WiFi throughout (free). Off site: Golf 7 km.

Open: All year.

Directions

Site is signed from the Ljubljana-Zagreb motorway (E70) 6 km. west of the Slovenia/Croatia border, close to Brezice. GPS: 45.89137, 15.62598

Charges guide

Per unit incl. 2 persons and electricity	€ 40.30 - € 49.50
extra person	€ 17.90 - € 22.50
child (4-11 yrs)	€ 8.95 - € 11.25
dog	€ 4.00

Bled
Camping Bled

Kidriceva 10c SI, SLO-4260 Bled T: 045 752 000. E: info@camping-bled.com

alanrogers.com/SV4200

On the western tip of Lake Bled is Camping Bled. The waterfront here has a small public beach, behind which runs a gently sloping narrow wooded valley. Pitches at the front, used mainly for overnighters, are now marked, separated by trees and enlarged, bringing the total number to 280. In areas at the back, visitors are free to pitch where they like. There is some noise from trains as they trundle out of a high tunnel overlooking the campsite on the line from Bled to Bohinj. But this is a small price to pay for the pleasure of being in a pleasant site from which the lake, its famous little island, its castle and town can be explored on foot or by boat. Unlike many other Slovenian sites, the number of statics (and semi-statics) appears to be carefully controlled with touring caravans, motorcaravans and tents predominating.

Facilities

Toilet facilities in five blocks are of a high standard (with free hot showers). Three blocks are heated. Private bathrooms for rent. Solar energy used. Washing machines and dryers. Motorcaravan services. Gas supplies. Fridge hire. Supermarket. Restaurant. Play area and children's zoo. Games hall. Trampolines. Organised activities in July/Aug including children's club, excursions and sporting activities. Mountain bike tours. Live entertainment. Fishing. Bicycle hire. Free WiFi over site. Off site: Riding 3 km. Golf 5 km. Within walking distance of waterfront and town. Restaurants nearby.

Open: 1 April - 15 October.

Directions

From the town of Bled drive along south shore of lake to its western extremity (some 2 km) to the site. GPS: 46.36155, 14.08075

Charges guide

Per unit incl. 2 persons and electricity	€ 21.50 - € 31.80
extra person	€ 8.90 - € 12.90
child (7-13 yrs)	€ 6.23 - € 9.03
dog	€ 3.00

Less 10% for stays over 6 days.

FREE Alan Rogers Travel Card
Extra benefits and savings - see page 10

Kobarid
Kamp Koren Kobarid

Ladra 1b, SLO-5222 Kobarid T: 053 891 311. E: info@kamp-koren.si

alanrogers.com/SV4270

Superbly run by its owner, Lidija Koren, this peaceful, well shaded site is located above the Soca river gorge in the countryside close to Kobarid. A small site with 90 pitches, it is deservedly very popular with those interested in outdoor sports, including hiking, mountain biking, paragliding, canoeing, canyoning, rafting and fishing. At the same time, its quiet location makes it a good site for those seeking a relaxing break. Six attractive, well equipped chalets are a recent addition. The Julian Alps, and in particular the Triglav National Park, is a wonderful and under-explored part of Slovenia that has much to offer.

Facilities

Two attractive and well maintained log-built toilet blocks. Facilities for disabled visitors. Laundry facilities. Motorcaravan services. Shop (March-Nov). Café serves light meals, snacks and drinks apparently with flexible closing hours. Play area. Bowling. Fishing. Bicycle hire. Canoe hire. Climbing walls. Communal barbecue. WiFi. Off site: Town within walking distance. Riding 5 km. Golf 20 km. Guided tours in the Soca valley and around Slovenia start from the campsite.

Open: All year.

Directions

Approaching Kobarid from Tolmin on 102, just before Kobarid turn right on 203 towards Bovec and after 100 m. take descending slip road to right and keep more or less straight on to Napoléon's bridge (about 500 m). Cross bridge and site is on left, 100 m.
GPS: 46.25075, 13.58658

Charges guide

Per unit incl. 2 persons and electricity	€ 24.00 - € 27.00
dog	€ 2.00

Kobarid
Lazar Kamp

Gregorciceva, SLO-5222 Kobarid T: 053 885 333. E: edi.lazar@siol.net

alanrogers.com/SV4265

Lazar Kamp is a fairly open site with a relaxed atmosphere, from which there are good views of the surrounding mountains. Located in the countryside 40 m. above the Soca River, popular with wild watersport fans, there are plenty of walking and mountain biking opportunities directly from the site, in this attractive region of Slovenia. The site has 50 open plan grassy pitches, all with 10A electricity, arranged in large sections divided by low openwork wooden fences. The friendly bar/restaurant (08.00-22.00) serves English breakfast, and fresh bread is available. This is a site where you really are in the countryside and have access to good well maintained facilities.

Facilities

The sanitary block is of a very good standard and includes facilities for disabled visitors. Washing machine. Fridge. Bar. Crêperie and grill with terrace area. Internet corner, WiFi. Ranch style clubroom. Excursions and lots of local sporting activities. Off site: Kozjak Waterfall. Mountain biking, walking, paragliding, touring.

Open: 1 April - 31 October.

Directions

Approaching Kobarid from Tolmin on 102 just before Kobarid turn right on 203 towards Bovec. After 100 m. take descending slip road to right, keeping straight on to Napoléon's bridge (about 500 m), then straight on down gravel road 700 m. to site (road is unsuitable for larger units).
GPS: 46.25513, 13.58626

Charges guide

Per person	€ 10.00 - € 11.00
child (7-13 yrs)	€ 6.00
electricity	€ 5.00

Lendava

Camping Terme Lendava

Tomsiceva 2a, SLO-9220 Lendava T: 025 774 400. E: info@terme-lendava.si

alanrogers.com/SV4455

Camp Terme Lendava forms part of an important thermal resort holiday complex, located at the meeting point of Slovenia, Hungary and Croatia. This is an all-year site with 430 grassy pitches, most with electrical connections and varying amounts of shade. Hotel accommodation is also available. Campers have access to a large swimming pool complex as well as the resort's various thermal facilities, including bathing in water with paraffin content, considered to be an effective treatment for rheumatic disorders. There are several good restaurants within the complex. Special facilities are also available for naturist bathers. Terme Lendava is a good starting point for excursions around the Pomurje region.

Facilities	Directions
Bar. Restaurant. Swimming pool. Thermal complex. Children's pool. Play area. Tourist information. Off site: Shops and restaurants. Golf. Excursions to Hungary and Croatia.	Approaching from the west (Maribor) on A5 motorway, take the exit to Lendava and follow signs to the site. GPS: 46.55167, 16.45842
Open: All year.	**Charges guide**

Per unit incl. 2 persons and electricity	€ 28.00 - € 30.00
dog	€ 3.00

Lesce

Camping Sobec

Sobceva cesta 25, SLO-4248 Lesce T: 045 353 700. E: sobec@siol.net

alanrogers.com/SV4210

Sobec is situated in a valley between the Julian Alps and the Karavanke Mountains, in a pine grove between the Sava Dolinka river and a small lake. It is only 3 km. from Bled and 20 km. from the Karavanke Tunnel. There are 500 unmarked pitches on level, grassy fields off tarmac access roads (450 for touring units), all with 16A electricity. Shade is provided by mature pine trees and younger trees separate some pitches. Camping Sobec is surrounded by water – the Sava river borders it on three sides and on the fourth is a small, artificial lake with grassy fields for sunbathing.

Facilities	Directions
Three traditional style toilet blocks (all now refurbished) with mainly British style toilets, washbasins in cabins and controllable hot showers. Child size toilets and basins. Well equipped baby room. Facilities for disabled visitors. Laundry facilities. Motorcaravan services. Supermarket, bar/restaurant with stage for live performances. Playgrounds. Rafting, canyoning and kayaking organised. Miniclub. Tours to Bled and the Triglav National Park organised. WiFi throughout (free). Off site: Golf 2 km.	Site is off the main road from Lesce to Bled and is well signed just outside Lesce. GPS: 46.35607, 14.14992
	Charges guide

Per unit incl. 2 persons and electricity	€ 24.70 - € 30.10
extra person	€ 10.60 - € 13.30
child (7-14 yrs)	€ 7.90 - € 9.90
dog	€ 3.50

Open: 14 April - 30 September.

Ljubljana

Camping Ljubljana Resort

Dunajska Cesta 270, SLO-1000 Ljubljana T: 015 683 913. E: ljubljana.resort@gpl.si

alanrogers.com/SV4340

Located only five kilometres north of central Ljubljana on the relatively quiet bank of the River Sava, Ljubljana Resort is an ideal city campsite. This relaxed site is attached to, but effectively separated from, the sparklingly modern Laguna swimming pool complex (open 1/6-15/9). The site has 220 pitches, mostly situated between mature trees and all with electricity connections (16A). A modern toilet block is open in summer, while a smaller, heated block is open in winter. The main building and the pool complex provide several bars, restaurants and takeaways to cater for the campsite guests and day visitors.

Facilities	Directions
The modern toilet block includes facilities for disabled campers, a baby room and children's toilet and shower. Motorcaravan service point. Laundry service. Internet access. Airport transfer service. Bicycle hire. New children's play area. Entertainment for children in July/Aug. Off site: Ljubljana centre 5 km.	From either direction on the northern city ring road, take exit no. 3 for Ljubljana-Jezica north towards Crnuce for a little over 1 km. Site is signed (blue sign) on the right just before railway crossing and bridge over the river. GPS: 46.09752, 14.5187
Open: All year except 1 January - 14 March.	**Charges guide**

Per unit incl. 2 persons and electricity	€ 18.50 - € 30.50
extra person	€ 7.00 - € 13.00
child (3-12 yrs)	€ 5.25 - € 9.75

Mojstrana
Camping Kamne
Dovje 9, SLO-4281 Mojstrana T: 045 891 105. E: campingkamne@telemach.net
alanrogers.com/SV4150

For visitors proceeding down the 202 road, from Italy or the Wurzen Pass towards the prime attractions of the twin lakes of Bled and Bohinj, a delightfully informal, little site is to be found just outside the village of Mojstrana. For those arriving via the Karavanke Tunnel, the diversion along the 202 is very well worth it. Owner Franc Voga opened the site in 1988, on a small terraced orchard. He has steadily developed the facilities, adding a small pool and two tennis courts and improving all other facilities. The little reception doubles as a bar, and locals wander up for a beer and a chat while enjoying the view across the valley of the Julian Alps.

Facilities	Directions
The small excellent sanitary block is of a high quality and well maintained. New facilities for babies and disabled visitors. Reception/bar. Small swimming pool (25/6-15/9). Two tennis courts. TV room. Mountain bike hire. Franc's English is good and his daughter Anna is fluent. Two new apartments and bungalows now available to rent. Shop (25/6-10/9). WiFi throughout (free). Off site: Walking trails.	Site is well marked on north side of the 202, 4 km. from Jesenice, just to west of exit for Mojstrana. Site is 4 km. from the Karawanken tunnel. GPS: 46.46453, 13.95787

Open: All year.

Charges guide

Per unit incl. 2 persons	
and electricity	€ 16.90 - € 20.10
extra person	€ 6.20 - € 7.30
child (5-17 yrs)	€ 4.70 - € 5.20

Moravske Toplice
Camping Terme 3000
Kranjceva ulica 12, SLO-9226 Moravske Toplice T: 025 121 200. E: recepcija.camp2@terme3000.si
alanrogers.com/SV4410

Camping Terme 3000 is a large site with 430 pitches. There are 200 places for touring units (all with 16A electricity), the remaining pitches being taken by seasonal campers. On a grass and gravel surface (hard tent pegs may be needed), the level, numbered pitches are of 50-100 sq.m. There are hardstandings available in the newer area of the site. The site is part of an enormous thermal spa and fun pool complex (free entry to campers) under the same name. There are over 5,000 sq.m. of water activities – swimming, jet streams, waterfalls, water massages, four water slides (the longest is 170 m) and thermal baths. The complex also provides bars and restaurants and a large golf course. Once you have had enough of the 14 indoor and outdoor pools, you can walk or cycle through the surrounding woods and fields.

Facilities	Directions
Modern and clean toilet facilities provide British style toilets, open washbasins and controllable, free hot showers. Laundry facilities. Football field. Tennis. Water gymnastics. Daily activity programme for children. Golf. WiFi (charged).	From Maribor, go east to Murska Sobota. From there go north towards Martjanci and then east towards Moravske Toplice. Access to the site is on the right before the bridge. Then go through a park for a further 500 m. GPS: 46.67888, 16.22165

Open: All year.

Charges guide

Per unit incl. 2 persons	
and electricity	€ 36.50 - € 40.00
extra person	€ 16.00 - € 18.00
child (6-9 yrs)	€ 8.00 - € 9.00
child (10-15 yrs)	€ 11.20 - € 12.60

For latest campsite news, availability and prices visit
alanrogers.com

Postojna
Camping Pivka Jama

Veliki Otok 50, SLO-6230 Postojna T: 057 203 993. E: avtokamp.pivka.jama@siol.net
alanrogers.com/SV4330

Postojna is renowned for its extraordinary limestone caves, which form one of Slovenia's prime tourist attractions. Pivka Jama is a most convenient site for the visitor, being midway between Ljubljana and Piran and only about an hour's pleasant drive from either. The 300 pitches are not clustered together but nicely segregated under trees and in small clearings, all connected by a neat network of paths and slip roads. Some level, gravel hardstandings are provided. The facilities are both excellent and extensive and run with obvious pride by enthusiastic staff.

Facilities

Two toilet blocks with very good facilities. Washing machines. Motorcaravan service point. Campers' kitchen with hobs. Supermarket. Bar/restaurant. Swimming pool and paddling pool. Tennis. Bicycle hire. Day trips to Postojna Caves and other excursions organised. Off site: Fishing 5 km. Riding and skiing 10 km. Golf 30 km.

Open: March - October.

Directions

Site is 5 km. north of Postojna. Leave A1/E61 autobahn Postojna exit. In Postojna follow signs to Postojna Caves (Postojnska Jama) continue past caves for 4 km. where site is signed to the right. Follow road through forest 3 km. to site. GPS: 45.80533, 14.20457

Charges guide

Per person	€ 10.40 - € 11.40
child (7-14 yrs)	€ 7.90 - € 8.90
electricity	€ 3.90

Prebold
Camp Dolina Prebold

Vozlic Tomaz Dolenja vas 147, SLO-3312 Prebold T: 035 724 378. E: camp@dolina.si
alanrogers.com/SV4400

Prebold is a quiet village about 15 kilometres west of the large historic town of Celje. It is only a few kilometres from the remarkable Roman necropolis at Sempeter. Dolina is an exceptional little site where reception and bar are housed in the beautifully converted 150-year-old stable, taking 50 touring units, 25 with 10A electricity. It belongs to Tomaz and Manja Vozlic who look after the site and its guests with loving care. It has been in existence since 1960 and was one of the first private enterprises in the former Yugoslavia. Excursions are organised to the Pekel Caves and Roman remains.

Facilities

The small, heated toilet block is immaculately maintained. Washing machine and dryer. Small swimming pool (heated 30-33°C, 1/5-30/9). Children's play area with trampoline. Large wood-fired oven with doors for traditional cooking. Sauna. Bicycle hire. WiFi. Off site: Good supermarket and restaurant 200 m. Tennis and indoor pool within 1 km. Fishing 1.5 km.

Open: All year.

Directions

Leave E57 at Sempeter/Prebold exit. Head south, after 100 m, right at roundabout, over bridge. Follow site signs to the left after 150 m. Upon reaching Prebold, site is signed to the right down a small side street. GPS: 46.24392, 15.09108

Charges guide

Per unit incl. 2 persons and electricity	€ 22.00
extra person	€ 7.36
dog	€ 3.00
No credit cards.	

Prebold
Camping Park

Latkova vas 227, SLO-3312 Prebold T: 0599 25 306. E: info@campingpark.si
alanrogers.com/SV4402

Camping Park is set on a grassy field close to the E57, directly beside the Savinja river. It provides 30 pitches (all for tourers) and is attractively landscaped with flowers and young trees. Pitching is on one large field, with some shade provided by mature trees and the high hedge surrounding the site. Pitches are not separated, but when it is quiet you can take as much space as you need. There are 18 electricity connections. Tennis courts and a riding centre are just 1 km. away.

Facilities

One traditional style toilet block with modern fittings with toilets, open plan washbasins and controllable hot showers. Laundry facilities. Fridge boxes (free). Fishing. Large barbecue area. WiFi (free). Torch useful. Off site: Riding 1 km. Outdoor pool 2km. Golf 20 km.

Open: 1 April - 30 October.

Directions

Leave the E57 motorway at the Sempeter/Prebold exit. Head south. At the roundabout just south of the motorway, turn right. Site is 250 m. on left. GPS: 46.25588, 15.09917

Charges guide

Per unit incl. 2 persons and electricity	€ 19.50
extra person	€ 8.00
dog	€ 2.00

FREE Alan Rogers Travel Card
Extra benefits and savings - see page 10

Ptuj
Camping Terme Ptuj

Pot v toplice 9, SLO-2251 Ptuj T: 027 494 100. E: info@terme-ptuj.si

alanrogers.com/SV4440

Camping Terme Ptuj is close to the river, just outside the interesting town of Ptuj. It is a small site with 100 level pitches, all for tourers and all with 10A electricity. In two areas, the pitches to the left are on part grass and part gravel hardstanding and are mainly used for motorcaravans. The pitches on the right-hand side are on grass under mature trees, off a circular, gravel access road. The main attraction of this site is clearly the adjacent thermal spa and fun pool complex that also attracts many local visitors. It has several slides and fun pools, as well as a sauna, solarium and spa bath. The swimming pools and saunas are free for campsite guests. This site would also be a useful stopover en-route to Croatia and the beautiful historic towns of Ptuj and Maribor are well worth a visit.

Facilities	Directions
Modern toilet block with British style toilets, open washbasins and controllable, hot showers (free). En-suite facilities for disabled visitors with toilet and basin. Two washing machines. Football field. Torch useful. Off site: Bar/restaurant and snack bar and large thermal spa 100 m.	From Maribor go southeast towards Ptuj or exit the new (2009) A4 motorway at exit for Ptuj. Follow Golf/Therm signs, drive past spa/therm complex, camping is a further 100 m. GPS: 46.422683, 15.85495

Open: All year.

Charges guide

Per unit incl. 2 persons	
and electricity	€ 35.00 - € 39.00
extra person	€ 15.50 - € 17.50
child (6-10 yrs)	€ 7.75 - € 8.75
dog	€ 4.00

Camping Cheques accepted.

Recica ob Savinji
Camping Menina

Varpolje 105, SLO-3332 Recica ob Savinji T: 035 835 027. E: info@campingmenina.com

alanrogers.com/SV4405

Camping Menina is in the heart of the 35 km. long Upper Savinja Valley, surrounded by 2,500 m. high mountains and unspoilt nature. It is being improved every year by the young, enthusiastic owner, Jurij Kolenc and has 200 pitches, all for touring units, on grassy fields under mature trees and with access from gravel roads. All have 6-10A electricity. The Savinja river runs along one side of the site, but if its water is too cold for swimming, the site also has a lake which can be used for swimming. This site is a perfect base for walking or mountain biking in the mountains. A wealth of maps and routes are available from reception. Rafting, canyoning and kayaking, and visits to a fitness studio, sauna and massage salon are organised. The site is now open all year to offer skiing holidays.

Facilities	Directions
Two toilet blocks (one new) have modern fittings with toilets, open plan washbasins and controllable hot showers. Motorcaravan service point. Bar/restaurant with open-air terrace (evenings only) and open-air kitchen. Sauna. Playing field. Play area. Fishing. Mountain bike hire. Russian bowling. Excursions (52). Live music and gatherings around the camp fire. Indian village. Hostel. Skiing in winter. Kayaking. Mobile homes to rent. Climbing wall. Rafting. Off site: Fishing 2 km. Recica and other villages with much culture and folklore are close. Indian sauna at Coze.	From the Ljubljana/Celje autobahn A1, take exit for Sentupert and turn north towards Mozirje (14 km). At roundabout just before Mozirje, hard left staying on the 225 for 6 km. to Nizka. Then, just after circular automatic petrol station, turn left where site is signed. GPS: 46.31168, 14.90913

Open: All year.

Charges guide

Per unit incl. 2 persons	
and electricity	€ 17.80 - € 23.00
extra person	€ 7.50 - € 10.00
child (5-15 yrs)	€ 3.50 - € 6.00
dog	€ 2.50 - € 3.00

For latest campsite news, availability and prices visit

alanrogers.com

Smlednik
Camp Smlednik

Dragocajna 14a, SLO-1216 Smlednik T: 013 627 002. E: camp@dm-campsmlednik.si

alanrogers.com/SV4360

Camp Smlednik is relatively close to the capital, Ljubljana, yet within striking distance of Lake Bled, the Karawanke mountains and the Julian Alps. It provides a good touring base, set above the River Sava, and also provides a small, separate enclosure for those who enjoy naturism. Situated beside the peaceful tiny village of Dragocajni, in attractive countryside, the site provides 190 places for tourers each with electricity (6/10A). Although terraced, it is probably better described as a large plateau with tall pines and deciduous trees providing some shade. The naturist area measuring only some 30x100 m. accommodates 15 units adjacent to the river (INF card not required).

Facilities

Three fully equipped sanitary blocks are of varying standards, but with adequate and clean provision. In the main camping area a fairly new, solar-powered, two-storey block has free hot showers, the lower half for use within the naturist area. Normally heated showers in the old block are also free. Toilet for disabled visitors. Laundry facilities. Supermarket at entrance. Bar (all year) serves food (1/5-30/9). Two good quality clay tennis courts (charged). River swimming and fishing. WiFi.

Open: 1 May - 15 October.

Directions

Travelling on road no.1, both Smlednik and the site are well signed. From E61 motorway, Smlednik and site are again well signed at the Vodiice exit 11. (Watch out for sharp right turn to site on a bend just after camping 1 km. sign). GPS: 46.17425, 14.41628

Charges guide

Per person	€ 7.50 - € 8.50
child (7-14 yrs)	€ 3.50 - € 4.00
electricity (6-10A)	€ 3.00 - € 4.00

Soca
Kamp Klin

Lepena 1, SLO-5232 Soca T: 053 889 513. E: kampklin@siol.net

alanrogers.com/SV4235

With an attractive location surrounded by mountains in the Triglav National Park, Kamp Klin is next to the confluence of the Soca and Lepenca rivers, which makes it an ideal base for fishing, kayaking and rafting. The campsite has 50 pitches, all for tourers, with 7A electricity, on one large, grassy field, connected by a circular, gravel access road. It is attractively landscaped with flowers and young trees, which provide some shade. Some pitches are right on the bank of the river (unfenced) and there are beautiful views of the river and the mountains.

Facilities

One modern toilet block and a Portacabin style unit with toilets and controllable showers. Laundry with sinks. Bar/restaurant. Play field. Fishing (permit required). Torch useful. Off site: Riding 500 m. Bicycle hire 10 km.

Open: March - October.

Directions

Site is on the main Kranjska Gora-Bovec road and is well signed 3 km. east of Soca. Access is via a sharp turn from the main road and over a small bridge. GPS: 46.33007, 13.644

Charges guide

Per person	€ 11.00 - € 13.00
child (7-12 yrs)	€ 5.50 - € 6.50
electricity	€ 3.50

Verzej
Camping Terme Banovci

Banovci 1A, SLO-9241 Verzej T: 025 131 400. E: terme@terme-banovci.si

alanrogers.com/SV4445

Terme Banovci is a comfortable, quiet, countryside site with 130 textile touring pitches plus 50 FKK naturist pitches, which are located separately. The grassy pitches have ample shade, are accessed by gravel roads and all have 10A electricity. Entry to the indoor (35-38°C) and outdoor (25-27°C) pools, with a total surface area of 2,000 sq.m, is free to campers. The pools with large outdoor slide and ample space for sunbathing are all that one expects from a modern, well equipped, thermal spa. The comfortable restaurant is built in traditional style, and drinks and food are available on the terrace beside the pool.

Facilities

Two well appointed, heated sanitary blocks. Washbasins in cabins. Facilities for disabled visitors. Laundry. Motorcaravan service point. Nordic walking. Volleyball. Tennis. Morning gymnastics. Entertainment programme. Wellness centre with three Finnish saunas. Solarium. Turkish bath. Various massage programmes (at extra cost). Off site: Numerous walking and cycling paths.

Open: 1 April - 6 November.

Directions

Site is 38 km. east of Maribor. From A5 take Vucja Vas exit and go south on 230 for 5 km. to Knzevci pri Ljutomeru. Turn northeast on 439 for 1 km. and fork right to Banovci. Site is 400 m. northeast of Banovci and signed. GPS: 46.573181, 16.171494

Charges guide

Per unit incl. 2 persons and electricity	€ 27.50 - € 29.50
dog	€ 3.00

FREE Alan Rogers Travel Card
Extra benefits and savings - see page 10

With its warm seas, crystal clear waters and over one thousand islands to explore, Croatia is an ideal place to try scuba diving. Diving centres can be found at the larger resorts.

The heart-shaped peninsula of Istria, located in the north, is among the most developed tourist regions in Croatia. Here you can visit the preserved Roman amphitheatre in Pula, the beautiful town of Rovinj with its cobbled streets and wooded hills, and the resort of Umag, well known for its recreational activities, most notably tennis. Islands are studded all around the coast, making it ideal for sailing and diving enthusiasts. Istria also has the highest concentration of campsites.

Further south, in the province of Dalmatia, Split is the largest city on the Adriatic coast and home to the impressive Diolectian's Palace. From here the islands of Brac, Hvar, Vis and Korcula, renowned for their lively fishing villages and pristine beaches, are easily accessible by ferry. The old walled city of Dubrovnik is 150 km. south. At over 2 km. long and 25 m. high, with 16 towers, a walk along the city walls affords spectacular views.

Population
4.5 million

Capital
Zagreb

Climate
Predominantly warm and hot in summer with temperatures of up to 40°C.

Language
Croatian, but English and German are widely spoken.

Telephone
The country code is 00 385

Currency
Kuna

Banks
Mon-Fri 08.00-19.00

Shops
Mainly Mon-Sat 08.00-20.00, although some close on Monday and Sundays.

Croatia has thrown off old communist attitudes and blossomed into a lively and friendly place to visit. A country steeped in history, it boasts some of the finest Roman ruins in Europe and you'll find plenty of traditional coastal towns, clusters of tiny islands and medieval villages to explore.

Public Holidays

New Year's Day; Epiphany 6 Jan; Good Friday; Easter Monday; Labour Day 1 May; Parliament Day 30 May; Day of Anti-Fascist Victory 22 June; Statehood Day 25 June; Thanksgiving Day 5 Aug; Assumption 15 Aug; Independence Day 8 Oct; All Saints 1 Nov; Christmas 25, 26 Dec.

Motoring

Croatia is proceeding with a vast road improvement programme. There are still some roads which leave a lot to be desired, but things have improved dramatically. Roads along the coast can become heavily congested in summer and queues are possible at border crossings. Drive carefully especially at night – roads are usually unlit and have sharp bends. Tolls: some motorways, bridges and tunnels. Cars towing a caravan or trailer must carry two warning triangles. It is illegal to overtake military convoys.

Remember – if you travel to Croatia via Slovenian motorways, you now require a vignette *(see Slovenia introduction)*.

Tourist Office

Croatian National Tourist Office
2 The Lanchesters
162-164 Fulham Palace Road
London W6 9ER
Tel: 020 8563 7979
Fax: 0208 563 2616
Email: info@cnto.freeserve.co.uk
Internet: www.croatia.hr

British Embassy

Ivana Lucica 4, Zagreb
Tel: (385)(1) 6009 100

Places of interest

Dubrovnik: particularly appealing is the old town Stari Grad, with marble-paved squares and steep, cobbled streets.

Risnjak and Paklencia National Parks: both have excellent areas for hiking, the latter has excellent opportunities for rock climbing.

Rovinj: an active fishing port, an excellent collection of marine life can be found at the aquarium.

Split: Diocletian's Palace, Maritime Museum.

Zagreb: the capital of Croatia, with a whole host of museums.

Cuisine of the region

Brodet: mixed fish stewed with rice

Burek: a layered pie made with meat or cheese

Cesnjovka: garlic sausage

Kulen: paprika-flavoured salami

Manistra od bobica: beans and fresh maize soup

Piroska: cheese doughnut

Struki: baked cheese dumpling

Virtually every region produces its own varieties of wine.

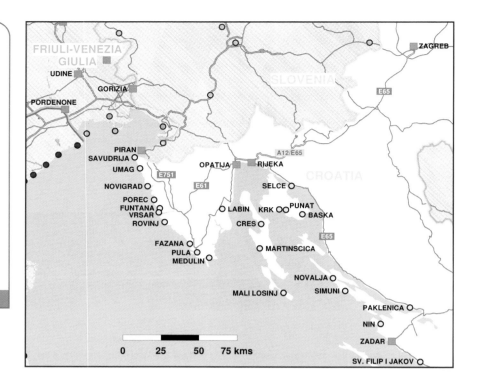

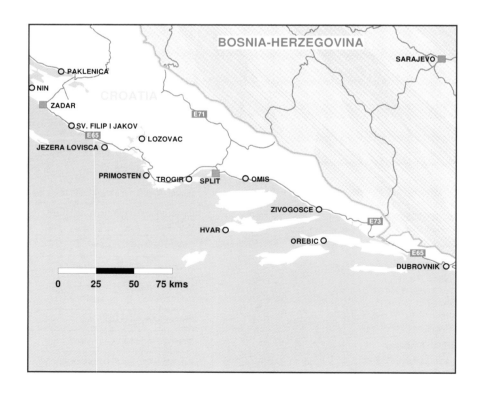

For latest campsite news, availability and prices visit
alanrogers.com

Fazana
Camping Bi-Village

Dragonja 115, HR-52212 Fazana (Istria) T: 052 300 300. E: info@bivillage.com

alanrogers.com/CR6745

Camping Bi-Village is a large holiday village in an attractive location close to the historic town of Pula and opposite the islands of the Brioni National Park. From the beach superb sunsets can be observed as the sun sinks below the sea's horizon. The site is landscaped with many flowers, shrubs and rock walls and offers over 1,000 pitches for touring units (the remainder taken by bungalows and chalets). The campsite is separated from the holiday bungalows by the main site road which runs from the entrance to the beach. Pitches are set in long rows accessed by gravel lanes, slightly sloping towards the sea, with only the bottom rows having shade from mature trees and good views over the Adriatic. Bi-Village has 800 m. of pebble beach, but also offers three attractive swimming pools.

Facilities	Directions
Four modern toilet blocks with toilets, open washbasins and controllable hot showers. Baby room. Facilities for disabled visitors. Washing machine. Shopping centre (1/5-11/10). Bars (1/5-30/9) and restaurants. Bazaar. Gelateria. Pastry shop. Three swimming pools. Play area on gravel. Playing field. Trampolines. Motorboats and pedaloes for hire. Boat launching. Games hall. Sports tournaments and entertainment organised. WiFi in some areas (charged). Dogs are not permitted on the beach.	Follow no. 2 road south from Rijeka to Pula. In Pula follow site signs. Site is close to Fazana. GPS: 44.91717, 13.81105

Directions
Follow no. 2 road south from Rijeka to Pula. In Pula follow site signs. Site is close to Fazana.
GPS: 44.91717, 13.81105

Charges guide

Per unit incl. 2 persons and electricity	€ 14.00 - € 40.00
extra person	€ 4.00 - € 10.00

Camping Cheques accepted.

Open: 30 March - 9 November.

Funtana
Naturist Camping Istra

Grgeti 35, HR-52452 Funtana (Istria) T: 052 465 010. E: camping@valamar.com

alanrogers.com/CR6726

Located in the tiny and picturesque village of Funtana, this peaceful site is part of the Camping on the Adriatic group. Istra has a fine array of facilities and, although there is no pool, it is surrounded by sparkling sea water on three sides. The formally marked pitches ring the peninsula and some are directly at the water's edge giving great views of the island off to the south (early booking is advised). There are 1,000 pitches on site with 904 for touring, most with ample shade and varying in size from about 90 sq.m. The ground is undulating and some areas have been cut into low terraces. There is 10A electricity and water points are scattered around the site. Two large, informal and central zones have sloping pitches, some with water and electricity. This is a very pleasant site with a peaceful air and eminently suitable for those who just want to relax in the sun.

Facilities
Three old and three new sanitary buildings provide toilets, washbasins, showers (hot and cold), hairdryers and some facilities for disabled campers. Laundry facilities. Small supermarket. Restaurant and bars. Play areas. Entertainment for children in high season. Organised sport. Minigolf. Tennis. Massage. WiFi near reception (free). Dogs are allowed in some areas. Charcoal barbecues are not permitted. Off site: Restaurants and shops in Funtana, a short walk from the gate. Riding 1 km.

Open: April - October.

Directions
Site is signed off Porec-Vrsar road 6 km. south of Porec in Funtana. Access for large units could be difficult off main road from Porec. If so, go past the signed turning, turn around in the night club car park a few metres further on. The problem is less when approaching from Vrsar. GPS: 45.17464, 13.59869

Charges guide

Per unit incl. 2 persons and electricity	€ 16.20 - € 30.60
incl. full services	€ 17.60 - € 39.10

Labin

Camping Marina

Sveta Marina bb, HR-52220 Labin (Istria) T: 052 879 058. E: camping@valamar.com

alanrogers.com/CR6747

Camping Marina is a very quiet site with a somewhat steep approach. Overlooked by high, tree clad hills and adjoining a small bay, there are views of the rocky coast and the island of Cres. The 293 pitches are of all types, from those in the central area on level marked areas with electricity and water, to the cliff top pitches on the outskirts of the site. The particularly clear water where there are shipwrecks and caves to explore has made Marina a haven for divers, and the campsite diving club, which has a diving school, is a past winner of Croatia's best diving club award. From the site, steps lead down to sheltered, narrow, pebble beaches and clear water, ideal places for sunbathing or snorkelling. Adjoining the site are local bars and a small, flower-decked restaurant totally in keeping with the natural surroundings. Although advertised as part of a cycle route, the roads around Marina are more suited to walking.

Facilities

The single toilet block houses British style toilets, free controllable showers and washbasins. Toilet for children and a baby room. Facilities for disabled campers. Washing machine and ironing area. Motorcaravan service point and points for washing diving/snorkelling equipment. Restaurant/bar. Church. Play area. WiFi. Dog shower and garden. Off site: Well stocked supermarket on the left at start of the entrance road to the site. Places to visit are Labin, the old town. Rabac, a popular seaside resort during the time of Tito, with hotels, restaurants, bars and a small harbour.

Open: 4 April - 4 October.

Directions

Site is 10 km. south/southeast of Labin. From E751/21 Pula-Opatija road turn off to Labin and follow signs towards Rabac. On outskirts of Labin site is signed sharp right and up a climbing cobbled road. Follow signs for Marina SV. Turn off country road for site and Marina SV is well signed to left. GPS: 45.033391, 14.157976

Charges guide

Per person	€ 4.30 - € 6.90
child (4-10 yrs)	free - € 4.00
pitch	€ 6.40 - € 9.00
dog	€ 2.60 - € 3.40

Medulin

Camp Kazela

Kapovica 350, HR-52203 Medulin (Istria) T: 052 577 277. E: ackazela@arenaturist.hr

alanrogers.com/CR6735

Camp Kazela is partly naturist and is situated close to Medulin, an attractive old fishing port. The site has 965 touring units with electricity connections (10A) and 100 pitches with electricity, water and drainage. The remaining pitches are used for chalets, seasonal guests and tour operators. The site is open with young trees and some pitches have pleasant views over the sea. Some clusters of mature trees provide a little shade, but generally this site is something of a sun trap. New to the upper part of the site is a shopping centre with supermarket, information centre and three restaurants.

Facilities

Six adequate toilet blocks have British and Turkish style toilets, open washbasins with cold water only and controllable hot showers (but they could be cleaner). Motorcaravan service point. Shopping centre with supermarket and restaurants. Two aquaparks. Sailing and diving schools. Water skiing. Parasailing. Trampolines. Entertainment team. Games hall. Disco. Live music. WiFi. Off site: Historic towns of Medulin 2 km. and Pula 10 km. Visit Venice by hydrofoil.

Open: 30 March - 4 November.

Directions

Follow the road south from Pula to Medulin. At Medulin, follow the signs for the hotels and the site is 1 km. after the hotels. GPS: 44.80540, 13.95550

Charges guide

Per unit incl. 2 persons and electricity	€ 15.60 - € 30.30
extra person	€ 4.30 - € 7.40
child (4-12 yrs)	€ 2.50 - € 4.60
dog	€ 2.60 - € 4.50

Camping Cheques accepted.

For latest campsite news, availability and prices visit

alanrogers.com

Medulin

Medulin Camping Village

Osipovica 30, HR-52203 Medulin (Istria) T: 052 572 801. E: marketing@arenaturist.hr

alanrogers.com/CR6734

Medulin is part of the Arenaturist group and it has a fabulous setting near Pula on the tip of the Istrian peninsula, enjoying great views of the offshore island and the town's twin church towers. Consisting of a peninsula about 1.5 km. long and a small island accessed by a road bridge, the site is thickly wooded with mature pine trees producing a carpet of needles. Pitches are marked and separated into three sizes. The land is undulating but there is no shortage of level areas. There are 1,040 touring pitches, all with 10/16A electricity and some mobile homes which are not intrusive.

Facilities

The sanitary blocks are kept very clean. Toilets are mostly Turkish style. Washbasins and showers are a mixture of outdoors and under cover. Most have hot water (relying on solar power). Shop, market and produce stalls. Eight restaurants or snack bars provide a large range of fare. Cocktail bar. Ice for sale. Fridge rental. Play area. Watersports. Barbecues are not permitted on pitches. Off site: Golf, fishing (with permit) and riding nearby. Restaurants and bars in Medulin village or in Pula.

Open: 27 March - 17 October.

Directions

Approaching from the north (Koper, Rovinj), on outskirts of Pula turn to follow signs for Medulin and site. Site is at far end of village and is well signed. GPS: 44.81466, 13.9316

Charges 2013

Per unit incl. 2 persons	
and electricity	€ 16.00 - € 27.10
extra person	€ 5.00 - € 7.90
child (4-11 yrs)	€ 3.00 - € 5.50

Novigrad

Camping Mareda

Mareda, HR-52466 Novigrad (Istria) T: 052 735 291. E: camping@laguna-novigrad.hr

alanrogers.com/CR6713

Backed by oak woods and acres of vineyards, Camping Mareda is located on the coast just north of the small picturesque town of Novigrad. The site is on hilly ground with 800 sloping grass and gravel pitches, most with shade from mature trees and some with views of the sea. There are 600 pitches for touring units, all with 16A electricity and 28 with electricity, water and drainage. Some are marked and numbered in two areas near the sea, the remainder are for free camping in other areas of the site where it may be difficult to find space in high season.

Facilities

Four modern toilet blocks with British and Turkish style toilets, open plan washbasins and hot showers. Child size toilets and basins. Laundry with sinks and washing machine. Motorcaravan service point. Supermarket. Coffee bar and bar with terrace. Restaurant. Play area. Tennis. Fishing. Boats, kayaks, canoes and pedaloes for hire. Games hall with video games. Entertainment. WiFi. Off site: Bicycle hire 4 km. Golf 10 km.

Open: 1 May - 30 September.

Directions

From Novigrad travel north towards Umag. After 4 km. the site is signed to the left. GPS: 45.34363, 13.54815

Charges guide

Per person	€ 4.00 - € 6.90
child (5-9 yrs)	free - € 3.80
pitch	€ 3.00 - € 11.50
electricity	€ 3.00

Porec

Autokamp Zelena Laguna

HR-52440 Porec (Istria) T: 052 410 101. E: mail@plavalaguna.hr

alanrogers.com/CR6722

Zelena Laguna (green lagoon) is a well run and long established site with 540 touring pitches, all with 10A electricity, 42 being fully serviced. Access to the pitches is by hard surfaced roads with gravel side roads. There are many mature trees providing plenty of shade and hedges separate most pitches. Part of the site is on a peninsula with terraced pitches, and the remainder are either on level or slightly sloping ground. A path circles the peninsula, below which are paved waterside sunbathing areas. Those to the right of the site are within easy reach of the cocktail bar. Further to the right is a small harbour, a restaurant and swimming pool. Part of the beach, which has Blue Flag status, is reserved for naturists.

Facilities

Six modern and well maintained sanitary blocks. The washbasins have hot water and there are free, controllable hot showers. Toilets are mostly British style. Facilities for disabled campers. Supermarket and shop. Restaurants and snack bars. Swimming pool. Tennis (tuition available). Bicycle hire. Boat hire (motor and sailing) and launching. Riding. Entertainment programme for the family. Off site: Nearest large supermarkets are in Porec 4 km.

Open: One week before Easter - 7 October.

Directions

Site entrance is 2 km. south of Porec on Vrsar-Porec coastal road. It is very well signed and part of a large multiple hotel complex. GPS: 45.19529, 13.58927

Charges guide

Per unit incl. 2 persons	
and electricity	€ 15.30 - € 30.20
extra person	€ 4.10 - € 7.80
child (4-10 yrs)	free - € 5.40

FREE Alan Rogers Travel Card
Extra benefits and savings - see page 10

Porec

Camping Lanterna

Lanterna 1, Tar-Vabriga, HR-52465 Porec (Istria) T: 052 465 010. E: camping@valamar.com

alanrogers.com/CR6716

This is a well organised site and one of the largest in Croatia with high standards and an amazing selection of activities, and is part of the Camping on the Adriatic group. Set in 80 hectares with over 3 km. of beach, there are 2,851 pitches, of which 1,887 are for touring units. All have electricity (10A) and fresh water, and 225 also have waste water drainage. Pitches are 80-120 sq.m. with some superb locations right on the sea, although these tend to be taken first so it is advisable to book ahead. Some of the better pitches are in a reserved booking area. There are wonderful coastal views from some of the well shaded terraced pitches. Facilities at Lanterna are impressive with the whole operation running smoothly for the campers. The land is sloping in parts and terraced in others. There is a pool complex, including a large pool for children, in addition to the pretty bay with its rocky beaches and buoyed safety areas. Some of the marked and numbered pitches are shaded and arranged to take advantage of the topography. Many activities and quality entertainment for all are available both on and off site – you are spoilt for choice here, including a vast choice of places to eat. Prices tend to be higher than other sites in the area but you get value for money with the supporting facilities. A member of Leading Campings group.

Facilities

The sixteen sanitary blocks are clean and good quality. Children's facilities and baby care areas, some Turkish style WCs, hot showers, with some blocks providing facilities for disabled visitors. Three supermarkets sell most everyday requirements. Fresh fish shop. Four restaurants, bars and snack bars and fast food outlets. Swimming pool and two paddling pools. Sandpit and play areas, with entertainment for all in high season. Tennis. Bicycle hire. Watersports. Boat hire. Minigolf. Riding. Internet café. Jetty and ramp for boats. WiFi (free). Mobile homes for rent (Istria Prestige). Dogs are accepted in certain areas. Off site: Hourly bus service from the reception area. Fishing. Riding 500 m. Golf 2 km. Nearest large supermarket in Novigrad 9 km.

Open: 1 April - 10 October.

Directions

The turn to Lanterna is well signed off the Novigrad to Porec road 8 km. south of Novigrad. Continue for 2 km. along the turn off road towards the coast and the campsite is on the right hand side. GPS: 45.29672, 13.59442

Charges guide

Per unit incl. 2 persons	
and electricity	€ 16.90 - € 31.00
with full services	€ 18.30 - € 32.60
extra person	€ 4.40 - € 7.90
child (4-10 yrs)	free - € 5.40

Prices for pitches by the sea are higher.

Porec

Camping Bijela Uvala

Bijela Uvala, Zelena Laguna, HR-52440 Porec (Istria) T: 052 410 551. E: mail@plavalaguna.hr

alanrogers.com/CR6724

Bijela Uvala is a large friendly campsite with an attractive waterside location and an extensive range of facilities. The direct sea access makes the site very popular in high season. The 2,000 pitches, 1,476 for touring, are compact and due to the terrain some have excellent sea views and breezes, however as usual these are the most sought after, so book early. They range from 60-120 sq.m. and all have electricity and water connections. Some are formal with hedging, some are terraced and most have good shade from established trees or wooded areas. There are also very informal areas where unmarked pitches are on generally uneven ground.

Facilities

Eight sanitary blocks are clean and well equipped with mainly British style WCs. Free hot showers. Washing machines. Facilities for disabled visitors. Motorcaravan service point. Gas. Fridge boxes. Three restaurants, three fast food cafés, two bars and a bakery. Large well equipped supermarket and a shop. Two swimming pool complexes, one with a medium size pool and the other a larger lagoon-style with fountains. Tennis. Playground. Amusements. TV room. Entertainment centre for active children. WiFi (charged). Off site: Zelena Laguna campsite facilities. Sports complex 100 m. Naturist beach 25 m.

Open: 19 March - 7 October.

Directions

The site adjoins Zelena Laguna. From the main Porec to Vrsar coast road turn off towards coast and the town of Zelena Laguna 4 km. south of Porec and follow campsite signs. GPS: 45.19149, 13.59686

Charges guide

Per unit incl. 2 persons	
and electricity	€ 15.30 - € 30.20
extra person	€ 4.10 - € 7.80
child (4-10 yrs)	free - € 5.40
dog	€ 3.20 - € 6.00

For latest campsite news, availability and prices visit

alanrogers.com

camping on the adriatic

Perfect in spring and autumn as well as summer

Camping at its best

Visit our campsites located in spectacular coastal surroundings, coloured with lush Mediterranean greenery and bordered by the clear blue waters of the Adriatic. All our campsites are fully equipped, offering a wide range of sports and fun activities intended for all age groups, and the numerous different types of accommodation units will make your choice of an ideal holiday destination easier.

Istria
Camping Lanterna***, Lanterna, Poreč
Naturist Resort Solaris***, Lanterna, Poreč
Naturist Camping Istra***, Funtana
Camping Orsera***, Vrsar
Camping Brioni, Puntižela, Pula
Camping Marina***, Sv. Marina, Labin

Island Krk
Camping Ježevac****
Camping Krk****
(ex Naturist Camping Politin)

New in 2013:
Camping Krk - for fun packed family holiday

Dubrovnik
Camping Solitudo***

New mobile homes in campsites Lanterna, Orsera, Marina, Krk and Solitudo

www.camping-adriatic.com
T +385 52 465 010 F +385 52 460 199
E camping@valamar.com
Other local telephone and skype numbers can be found on our website.

Porec
Camping Puntica
Rade Koncara 12, Funtana, HR-52449 Porec (Istria) T: 052 445 720. E: ac.puntica@plavalaguna.hr
alanrogers.com/CR6719

Puntica is a small, unassuming and old-fashioned campsite. Everything is modest here and if small is your thing, you will love it. There are 250 pitches, with 104 for tourers. Some of the flat, variably sized pitches (80-120 sq.m) are shaded amongst trees which could test larger units. The waterside pitches are lovely but many of these are occupied by permanent units. Electricity box positioning may warrant long leads in some areas (10A). The marina alongside is very active, and there are views from the terraces of the rustic restaurant and bar. There is a paved area around the tip of the site for sunbathing and ladders give access to deeper water. A member of the Plava Laguna group.

Facilities

One main sanitary block is kept clean and has reasonable facilities but is a little short on hot water for washing. British and Turkish style toilets with one locked unit for disabled campers. Washing machines and dryers operated by the 'laundry lady'. Small shop. Restaurant and bar. DIY motorcaravan services (lift the flap etc). Fishing. Basic playground. Gas barbecues permitted. Fridge box hire. Boat launching. Marina facilities. Bicycle hire. Watersports from collocated marina. Scuba diving.

Open: 23 April - 1 October.

Directions

Site is on the main road between Porec and Vrsar, near the village of Funtana, 7 km. south of Porec. Just watch for the yellow camping signs. GPS: 45.1774, 13.6033

Charges guide

Per unit incl. 2 persons	
and electricity	€ 11.00 - € 23.20
extra person	€ 3.10 - € 5.80
child (4-10 yrs)	free - € 3.40

Porec
Naturist Centre Ulika
Cervar, HR-52440 Porec (Istria) T: 052 436 325. E: reservations@plavalaguna.hr
alanrogers.com/CR6720

This naturist site is well located, occupying a small peninsula of some 15 hectares. This means that there is only a short walk to the sea from anywhere on the site. The ground is mostly gently sloping with a covering of rough grass and there are 1,000 pitches with 6A electricity connections, 420 also have water and drainage. One side of the site is shaded with mature trees but the other side is almost devoid of shade and could become very hot. There are many activities on site and an excellent swimming pool. The reception office opens 24 hours for help and information. Single men are not accepted. All in all, this is a pleasant, uncomplicated site which is well situated, well managed and peaceful.

Facilities

Six toilet blocks provide mostly British style WCs, washbasins (half with hot water) and showers (around a third with controllable hot water). Facilities for disabled visitors. Laundry. Motorcaravan services. Supermarket (seven days per week). Restaurant, pizzeria and snacks. Swimming pool. Massage. Tennis. Minigolf. Watersports. Boating and sailing – marina on site. Off site: Riding 3 km.

Open: One week before Easter - 10 October.

Directions

Site is 3 km. off the main Novigrad-Porec road, signed in village of Cervar. GPS: 45.25676, 13.58317

Charges guide

Per unit incl. 2 persons	
and electricity	€ 17.20 - € 33.30
extra person	€ 4.10 - € 7.80
child (4-10 yrs)	free - € 5.40

Pula
Camping Indije
Banjole, HR-52100 Pula (Istria) T: 052 573 066. E: acindije@arenaturist.hr
alanrogers.com/CR6739

Camping Indije is on the beautiful Adriatic coast in Banjole (Medulin), only a few kilometres from the historic centre of Pula. Medulin fronts a beautiful bay, dominated by a bell tower, with a wealth of little peninsulas and islands, all melting together with the blue sea and the green of the Mediterranean vegetation and Banjole is on one edge of it. All 416 grass and gravel pitches (50-120 sq.m) are for tourers and most are well shaded. All have 10A electricity and 16 are fully serviced. From many pitches there are wonderful open views over the sea to the islands.

Facilities

Three comfortable toilet blocks with British and Turkish style toilets, open plan washbasins and showers. Washing machine. Motorcaravan service point. Supermarket and newspaper stand. Bar and restaurant. Miniclub. Live music. Rock plateau beach. Diving centre. Boat mooring. Fishing (with permit). Boat launching. WiFi. Off site: Historic towns of Pula and Rovinj are close.

Open: 30 March - 23 September.

Directions

From Pula follow signs for Premantura and Banjole southwards. From Banjole follow site signs. GPS: 44.82382, 13.85078

Charges guide

Per unit incl. 2 persons	
and electricity	€ 16.00 - € 29.10
extra person	€ 4.50 - € 7.10
child (4-12 yrs)	€ 2.50 - € 4.40

Porec
Naturist Resort Solaris

Lanterna bb, HR-52465 Porec (Istria) T: 052 465 010. E: camping-porec@valamar.com

alanrogers.com/CR6718

This naturist site is part of the Camping on the Adriatic group and has a most pleasant atmosphere. When we visited in high season there were lots of happy people having fun. A pretty cove and lots of beach frontage with cool pitches under trees makes the site very attractive. Of the 1,448 pitches, 550 are available for touring, with 600 long stay units. There are 145 fully serviced pitches (100 sq.m) available on a 'first come, first served' basis, with an ample supply of electricity hook-ups (10-16A) and plentiful water points. As this is a naturist site, there are certain rules that must be followed. There is a small, but very pleasant swimming pool close to the sea which has a lifeguard (clothing is not allowed in the pool). Apartments and rooms are available to rent with half-board arrangements offered. For those who embrace the naturist regime or want to give it a try, this is a pleasant, quiet site with above average facilities in an Area of Outstanding Natural Beauty.

Facilities

Eleven excellent, fully equipped toilet blocks provide toilets, washbasins and showers. Some blocks have facilities for disabled visitors. Washing machines and ironing facilities. Restaurants, grills and fast food, and supermarkets. Swimming pool. Tennis. Bicycle hire. Riding. Play areas. Boat launching. Car wash. Entertainment. WiFi over site (free). Dogs are allowed in certain areas, but not on the beach. Off site: Excursions.

Open: May - October.

Directions

Site is 12 km. south of Novigrad on the Novigrad-Porec road. Turn towards the coast signed Lanterna. Continue straight on down this road and after passing the security barrier, turn left to Solaris. GPS: 45.29126, 13.5848

Charges guide

Per unit incl. 2 persons	
and electricity	€ 15.60 - € 29.40
extra person	€ 4.30 - € 7.50
child (4-10 yrs)	free - € 5.30
dog	€ 3.80 - € 5.50

Prices for pitches by the sea are higher.

Pula
Camping Brioni

Puntizela 155, HR-52100 Pula (Istria) T: 052 517 490. E: camping@valamar.com

alanrogers.com/CR6744

Situated on a small peninsula overlooking the Brioni archipelago (a National Park comprising 14 islands) and within easy reach of Pula, Camping Brioni is a quiet and useful base from which to tour in a scenically attractive and historically interesting region. The site has 420 touring pitches under ample shade, all with 10A electricity and 272 with fresh water taps. On mainly level grass and gravel, the pitches are numbered with some terracing. Part of the site is devoted to a youth hostel which shares the campsites facilities. A diving club is based on the site, the clear seawater being ideal for snorkelling. The à la carte restaurant and its terrace offer local dishes featuring seafood and pasta or, for simpler fare, try the beachside snack bar. The ten-hectare site has a long sea frontage and there are ample places to sit and enjoy the sun and the sea views.

Facilities

Three sanitary blocks, one with facilities for disabled visitors. Cleaning and maintenance needed some attention when we visited. Baby room. Laundry room. Small supermarket and kiosk selling fruit, vegetables and bread. Restaurant. Beachside snack bar. Play area. Boat rental. Internet access. Off site: Pula, Brioni National Park.

Open: All year.

Directions

Site is 7 km. northwest of Pula. Heading north on the road running alongside the harbour in Pula (Trscanska ulinka) turn left at the roundabout towards Rijeka. After 800 m. site is signed to the left (west). GPS: 44.89812, 13.80833

Charges guide

Per unit incl. 2 persons	
and electricity	€ 15.00 - € 35.00
extra person	€ 3.30 - € 6.50
child (4-10 yrs)	free - € 4.00
dog	€ 1.40 - € 2.90

FREE Alan Rogers Travel Card
Extra benefits and savings - see page 10

Pula

Camping Stoja

Stoja 37, HR-52100 Pula (Istria) T: 052 387 144. E: acstoja@arenaturist.hr

alanrogers.com/CR6742

Camping Stoja in Pula is an attractive and well maintained site on a small peninsula and therefore almost completely surrounded by the waters of the clear Adriatic. In the centre of the site is the old Fort Stoja, built in 1884 for coastal defence. Some of its buildings are now used as a toilet block and laundry and its courtyard is used by the entertainment team. The 708 touring pitches here vary greatly in size (50-120 sq.m) and are marked by round, concrete, numbered blocks, separated by young trees. About half have shade from mature trees and all are slightly sloping on grass and gravel.

Facilities

Five toilet blocks with British and Turkish style toilets, open plan washbasins with cold water only. Controllable hot showers. Child size basins. Facilities for disabled visitors. Laundry and ironing service. Fridge box hire. Motorcaravan service point. Supermarket. Bar/restaurant. Miniclub and teen club. Bicycle hire. Water skiing. Boat hire. Boat launching. Surfboard and pedalo hire. Fishing (with permit). Island excursions. WiFi. Off site: Pula (walking distance). Riding 8 km. Golf 10 km.

Open: 30 March - 4 November.

Directions

From Pula follow site signs.
GPS: 44.85972, 13.81450

Charges guide

Per unit incl. 2 persons	
and electricity	€ 19.00 - € 32.10
extra person	€ 5.00 - € 7.80
child (4-12 yrs)	€ 2.50 - € 5.00
dog	€ 3.00 - € 4.80

Rovinj

Camping Amarin

Monsena bb, HR-52210 Rovinj (Istria) T: 052 802 000. E: ac-amarin@maistra.hr

alanrogers.com/CR6730

Situated 4 km. from the centre of the lovely old port town of Rovinj, this site has much to offer. The complex is part of the Maistra group. It has 12.6 hectares of land and is adjacent to the Amarin bungalow complex. Campers can take advantage of the facilities afforded by both areas. There are 650 pitches for touring units on various types of ground, all between 70-100 sq.m. Most are separated by foliage, and 10A electricity is available. A rocky beach backed by a grassy sunbathing area is very popular, but the site has its own superb, supervised round pool with corkscrew slide plus a splash pool for children.

Facilities

Thirteen respectable toilet blocks have a mixture of British style and Turkish toilets. Half the washbasins have hot water. Some showers have hot water, the rest have cold and are outside. Some blocks have a unit for disabled visitors. Fridge box hire. Laundry service. Security boxes. Motorcaravan service point. Supermarket. Small market. Two restaurants, taverna, pizzeria and terrace grill. Swimming pool. Flume and splash pool. Watersports. Bicycle hire. Fishing (permit). Daily entertainment. Hairdresser. Massage. Barbecues are not permitted. Dogs are not allowed on beach. WiFi over part of site (charged). Off site: Hourly minibus service to Rovinj. Excursions from site including day trips to Venice. Riding 2 km.

Open: 25 April - 23 September.

Directions

Follow signs towards Rovinj and if approaching from north turn off 2 km. before town towards Amarin and Valalta. Then follow signs to Amarin and the campsite. Watch for a left turn after 3 km. where signs are difficult to see. GPS: 45.10876, 13.61988

Charges guide

Per unit incl. 2 persons	
and electricity	€ 15.50 - € 32.20
extra person	€ 4.50 - € 8.60
child (5-11 yrs)	free - € 5.30
dog	€ 4.00 - € 7.00

For stays less than 3 nights in high season add 10%.

Pula

Camping Stupice

Premantura, HR-52100 Pula (Istria) T: 052 575 101. E: marketing@arenaturist.hr

alanrogers.com/CR6737

This quiet site, which offers superb views over the sea to the nearby islands, is situated in a delightful strip of coast on the Istrian peninsula near the small village of Premantura. Most of the site is covered with undulating, dense pinewood providing ample shade with a carpet of pine needles. There are 1,000 pitches in total with 588 touring pitches in three sizes (ranging from 60-120 sq.m). They are mostly sloping and about a fifth have sea views. Access roads are bitumen or gravel. A narrow pebble beach and low rocks separate the sea from the site and provides a perfect place to relax and enjoy the view.

Facilities

The six toilet blocks, although old, were immaculately clean when we visited. Toilets are a mixture of Turkish and British style. Showers and free hot water. Washing machines. Good supermarket. Kiosk and several good small bars and grills. Minigolf. Modern playground. Activities for children and some live entertainment at the restaurant in high season. Rock and pebble beach. Marina, boat launching, jetty and scuba diving. Bicycle and beach buggy hire. Aquapark. WiFi. Off site: Bicycle hire 500 m. Premantura 1 km.

Open: 29 March - 25 October.

Directions

Site is 11 km. southeast of Pula. Follow signs to Premantura from Pula where there are site signs. GPS: 44.7978, 13.91366

Charges guide

Per unit incl. 2 persons	
and electricity	€ 15.60 - € 29.90
extra person	€ 4.30 - € 7.30
child (4-12 yrs)	€ 3.00 - € 4.60
dog	€ 2.60 - € 4.50

Camping Cheques accepted.

Rovinj

Camping Polari

Polari bb, HR-52210 Rovinj (Istria) T: 052 801 501. E: polari@maistra.hr

alanrogers.com/CR6732

This 60-hectare site has excellent facilities for both textile and naturist campers, the latter in an area of 12 hectares to the left of the main site. There is shade here from a good covering of trees. In all, the site has 1,650 pitches for touring units which are level with some shade. All have access to 10A electricity. There is something for everyone to enjoy here or you might prefer to just relax in this quiet location. An impressive swimming pool complex is child friendly with large paddling areas. The ancient town of Rovinj is well worth a visit, although parking is difficult. It is best reached via the 4.5 km. coastal cycle path or by bus from the campsite. Part of the Maistra group, a massive improvement programme has been undertaken and the result makes it a very attractive option. Enjoy a meal on the huge restaurant terrace with panoramic views of the sea.

Facilities

All the sanitary facilities have been renovated to a high standard with plenty of hot water and good showers. Washing machines and dryers. Laundry service including ironing. Motorcaravan service point. Two shops, one large and one small, one restaurant and snack bar. Tennis. Minigolf. Children's entertainment with all major European languages spoken. Bicycle hire. Watersports. Sailing school. Off site: Riding 1 km. Five buses daily to and from Rovinj 3 km. Golf 30 km.

Open: 1 April - 2 October.

Directions

From any access road to Rovinj look for red signs to AC Polari (amongst other destinations). The site is 3 km. south of Rovinj. GPS: 45.06286, 13.67489

Charges guide

Per unit incl. 2 persons	
and electricity	€ 18.00 - € 36.10
extra person (18-64 yrs)	€ 5.00 - € 9.30
child (5-17 yrs)	€ 4.00 - € 7.50
dog	€ 3.10 - € 6.50

For stays less than 3 nights in high season add 20%.

FREE Alan Rogers Travel Card
Extra benefits and savings - see page 10

Rovinj
Camping Valdaliso

Monsena bb, HR-52210 Rovinj (Istria) T: 052 802 200. E: ac-valdaliso@maistra.hr
alanrogers.com/CR6736

Camping Valdaliso has its affiliated hotel in the centre of the site. The 281 pitches are mostly flat with shade from pine trees and the site is divided into three sections all with 16A electricity. The choice of formal numbered pitches, informal camping or proximity to the sea impacts on the prices. The kilometre plus of pebble beach has crystal clear water. The entertainment programme is extremely professional and there is a lot to do at Valdaliso, which is aimed primarily at families. The variety of activities here and the bonus of the use of the hotel make this a great choice for campers. The fine Barabiga restaurant within the hotel offers superb Istrian and fish cuisine and the pool is also within the hotel. You are close to the beautiful old town of Rovinj and parts of this site enjoy views of the town. A water taxi makes exploring Rovinj very easy, compared with the impossible parking for private cars. A bus service is also provided but this involves considerable walking. Alternatively it is a 3 km. cycle ride.

Facilities

Two large, clean sanitary blocks have hot showers. The north-eastern block has facilities for disabled campers. Hotel facilities. Shop. Pizzeria. Restaurant. Tennis. Fitness centre. Bicycle hire. Games room. Children's games. Summer painting courses. Exchange. Boat rental. Watersports. Boat launching. Fishing. Diving school. Internet in both receptions. WiFi (charged). Water taxi. Bus service. Dogs are not accepted. Off site: Town 1 km.

Open: 6 April - 13 October.

Directions

Site is 7 km. north of Rovinj on local road between Rovinj and Monsena. GPS: 45.104267, 13.625183

Charges guide

Per unit incl. 2 persons and electricity	€ 15.50 - € 35.00
extra person	€ 4.50 - € 8.80
child (5-12 yrs)	free - € 5.40

Camping Valdaliso *Rovinj*

Istria

Mobil Homes! Diving center! Children's playgrounds!
ONLINE BOOKING

A green and, for the most part, forested peninsula is situated just in front of the old Rovinj's town centre and is a place of perfect peace and quiet.

tel: +385 (0)52 800 200 / fax: 800 215 / ac-valdaliso@maistra.hr

www.CampingRovinj.com

Rovinj
Naturist Camping Valalta

234

Cesta za Valaltu - Lim 7, HR-52210 Rovinj (Istria) T: 052 804 800. E: valalta@valalta.hr
alanrogers.com/CR6731

This is a most impressive site for up to 6,000 naturist campers, which has a pleasant, open feel. The passage through reception is efficient and this feeling is maintained around the well organised site. Valalta is a family oriented campsite and a friendly, family atmosphere is to be found here. All pitches are the same price and have 16A electricity, although they vary in size and surroundings. The variations include shade, views, sand, grass, sea frontage, level ground, slopes and terracing. It is not possible to reserve a particular pitch and campers do move pitches at will. The impressive pool is in lagoon-style with water features and cascades.

Facilities

Twenty high quality new or refurbished sanitary blocks, of which four are smaller units of plastic 'pod' construction. Hot showers. Facilities for disabled campers. Washing machines. Supermarket. Four restaurants (one specialising in seafood). Pizzeria. Two bars (own brewery). Large lagoon-style pool complex (15/5-15/9). Beauty salon. Fitness club. Massage. Minigolf. Tennis. Sailing. Play area. Bicycle hire. Beach volleyball. Marina with full services. Internet. Entertainment all season. Kindergarten. Medical clinic. WiFi throughout (charged). Dogs are not accepted.

Open: 1 May - 29 September.

Directions

Site is on coast 8 km. north of Rovinj. If approaching from north turn inland (follow signs to Rovinj) to drive around the Limski Kanal. Then follow signs towards Valalta 2 km. east of Rovinj. Site is at end of road and is well signed. GPS: 45.12235, 13.632083

Charges guide

Per unit incl. 2 persons and electricity	€ 18.70 - € 42.00
extra person	€ 5.10 - € 11.00
child (6-11 yrs)	€ 4.00 - € 5.50

For latest campsite news, availability and prices visit
alanrogers.com

Rovinj
Camping Vestar

Vestar bb, HR-52210 Rovinj (Istria) T: 052 803 700. E: vestar@maistra.hr

alanrogers.com/CR6733

Camping Vestar, just 5 km. from the historic harbour town of Rovinj, is one of the rare sites in Croatia with a partly sandy beach. Right behind the beach is a large area, attractively landscaped with young trees and shrubs, with grass for sunbathing. The site has 650 large pitches, of which 500 are for tourers, all with 6/10A electricity (the rest being taken by seasonal units and 60 pitches for tour operators). It is largely wooded with good shade and from the bottom row of pitches there are views of the sea. Pitching is on two separate fields, one for free camping, the other with numbered pitches. The pitches at the beach are in a half circle around the shallow bay, making it safe for children to swim. Vestar has a small marina and a jetty for mooring small boats, and excursions to the islands are arranged. There is a miniclub and live music with dancing at one of the two bar/restaurants in the evenings. The restaurants all have open-air terraces, one covered with vines to protect you from the hot sun.

Facilities

Six modern and one refurbished toilet blocks with British style toilets, open washbasins and controllable hot showers. Child size facilities. Baby rooms. Family bathroom. Facilities for disabled visitors. Laundry service. Fridge box hire. Motorcaravan services. Shop. Two bar/restaurants. Large swimming pool. Playground. Fishing. Boat and pedalo hire. Miniclub (5-11 yrs). Excursions. Internet access in reception. WiFi. Off site: Riding 2 km. Rovinj 5 km.

Open: 21 April - 1 October.

Directions

Site is on the coast 4 km. southeast of Rovinj. From Rovinj travel south towards Pula. After 4 km. turn right following campsite signs. GPS: 45.05432, 13.68568

Charges guide

Per person	€ 5.00 - € 10.00
child (5-18 yrs)	free - € 8.00
pitch incl. electricity	€ 7.00 - € 20.00
dog	€ 3.10 - € 6.50

Camping Vestar *Rovinj* — Istria Green Mediterranean.

Luxury sanitary facilities! Pitch with water supply and drain! Wi-Fi! ONLINE BOOKING

This campsite has a special charm – a warm welcome is guaranteed, in a stunning beachside setting.

tel: +385 (0)52 800 200 / fax: 800 215 / vestar@maistra.hr

www.CampingRovinj.com

Savudrija
CampingIN Pineta Umag

Istarska bb, HR-52475 Savudrija (Istria) T: 052 709 550. E: camp.pineta@istraturist.hr

alanrogers.com/CR6711

This pleasant, quiet site is set under tall pines and has direct access to the sea over fairly level rocks. It is of medium size (17 hectares) and gets its name from its setting amongst a forest of fully mature pine trees around two sides of a coastal bay. There are 460 pitches of which 160 are occupied on a long stay basis. Pitches are numbered and are 50-120 sq.m. all having access to electricity (10A). This is a site for those who prefer cooler situations as the dense pines provide abundant shade. Those who like the peaceful life will enjoy this site. Sea bathing is easy from the site and sunbathing areas are on the rocks the whole length of the site.

Facilities

Toilet blocks have been refurbished to a high standard. Hot and cold showers (plus showers for dogs). Mostly British style WCs and a few Turkish style. Excellent facilities for disabled campers. Fresh water at toilet blocks only. Motorcaravan service point. Supermarket. Six bars, three restaurants and snack bar. Tennis. Fishing (permit). Bicycle hire. Boat launching. Activities centre. Evening music. WiFi in some areas (charged). Off site: Gas is available in local garage 500 m. from the site entrance.

Open: 22 April - 25 September.

Directions

Site is 6 km. north of Umag. From Umag travel north following signs for Savudrija signs. In the village of Basanija, at the tourist office, turn left. Reception is 500 m. on the left. GPS: 45.48674, 13.49246

Charges guide

Per unit incl. 2 persons and electricity	€ 14.60 - € 27.70
extra person	€ 3.70 - € 7.00

For stays less than 3 nights in high season add 10%.

FREE Alan Rogers Travel Card
Extra benefits and savings - see page 10

Umag
CampingIN Finida Umag
Krizine 55a, HR-52470 Umag (Istria) T: 052 725 950. E: camp.finida@istraturist.hr
alanrogers.com/CR6714

Finida is a small, fairly quiet and friendly site with good sanitary facilities and with easy access from the Umag-Novigrad road. The sea runs the length of the site and offers places to swim, either from a concrete jetty or from a small beach. The site is heavily wooded affording abundant shade and from the terrace of the bar/restaurant there are views over the sea. There are 285 marked pitches (80-100 sq.m), all with 10A electricity, 103 also have water and TV connection. Finida will appeal to those who prefer the cosiness of a smaller, friendly site.

Facilities

Three new toilet blocks contain mostly British style WCs and a few Turkish style. Facilities for disabled visitors. Washing machines. Motorcaravan service point (a bit tight to drive onto). Small supermarket. Bar, snack bar and restaurant. Minigolf. Fishing (permit). Boat mooring off the beach. Pedalos. Bicycle hire. Communal barbecue areas. WiFi in some areas (charged). Off site: Five buses per day into Umag and Novigrad. Riding 3 km. Golf 10 km.

Open: 23 April - 26 September.

Directions

Site is on the right off the Umag-Novigrad road, 4 km. south of Umag. GPS: 45.39263, 13.54196

Charges guide

Per unit incl. 2 persons	
and electricity	€ 15.10 - € 31.00
extra person	€ 3.70 - € 7.60
child (5-12 yrs)	€ 2.20 - € 4.60
dog	€ 2.20 - € 3.70

Umag
CampingIN Naturist Kanegra Umag
Kanegra, HR-52470 Umag (Istria) T: 052 709 000. E: camp.kanegra@istraturist.hr
alanrogers.com/CR6710

Situated almost on the Slovenian border, this site has an open aspect with very little shade and sparkling clear waters off the rocky beach, which runs its total length. Part of the Istraturist group, the air-conditioned reception sets the tone for this very pleasant naturist site. It is located alongside the large Kanegra bungalow complex, and campers are able to share its comprehensive facilities. There are 193 level pitches here on sandy soil with sparse grass (90 are seasonal). They vary in size (60-100 sq.m), are marked and numbered and all have 16A electricity, however 156 also provide water and drainage.

Facilities

Two well equipped toilet blocks are kept very clean. Washing machine. Beach showers. No facilities for disabled visitors. Motorcaravan services. Supermarket. Two bars, three snack bars and two restaurants, all open until late. Nightly disco in the adjacent bungalow complex but reportedly not disturbing the campsite. Playground. Watersports. Use of all sporting facilities in the bungalow park. WiFi in reception (charged). Electric barbecues only. Off site: Bicycle hire and boat launching 200 m. Golf 3 km.

Open: 23 April - 25 September.

Directions

From Koper in the north just over the Italian border, follow signs to Umag, but turn north towards Kanegra 5 km. before Umag. If approaching from south, after Umag follow main coast road north towards Savudrija (do not turn off towards this town) and then Kanegra. GPS: 45.480017, 13.570717

Charges guide

Per unit incl. 2 persons	
and electricity	€ 15.10 - € 31.00

For stays less than 3 nights in high season add 10%.

Umag
CampingIN Park Umag
Karigador bb, HR-52470 Umag (Istria) T: 052 725 040. E: camp.park.umag@istraturist.hr
alanrogers.com/CR6715

This extremely large site is very well planned in that just 60% of the 127 hectares is used for the pitches, resulting in lots of open space around the pitch area. It is the largest of the Istraturist group of sites. Of the 2,090 pitches, 1,800 are for touring units, all with 10A electricity. Some pitches have shade. There are around 300 mobile homes, 70 for rent. Some noise is transmitted from the road alongside the site. The site is very popular with Dutch campers and a friendly and happy atmosphere prevails, even in the busiest times. The very long curved beach is of rock and shingle with grassy sunbathing areas.

Facilities

Ten toilet blocks include two bathrooms with deep tubs. Two blocks have children's WCs. Facilities for disabled visitors. The site has plans to update these facilities. Fresh water and waste water points only at toilet blocks. Motorcaravan service point. Shops. Supermarket. Bars, snack bars and restaurant (all open long hours). Swimming pool complex. Tennis. Fishing (permit from Umag). Minigolf. Watersports. WiFi (free in some areas).

Open: 23 April - 26 September.

Directions

Site is on the Umag-Novigrad road 6 km. south of Umag. Look for large signs.
GPS: 45.36707, 13.54716

Charges guide

Per unit incl. 2 persons	
and electricity	€ 19.00 - € 48.40
extra person	€ 4.90 - € 9.40

For stays less than 5 nights in high season add 20%.

For latest campsite news, availability and prices visit
alanrogers.com

Umag

CampingIN Stella Maris Umag

Savudrijska cesta bb, HR-52470 Umag (Istria) T: 052 710 900. E: camp.stella.maris@istraturist.hr

alanrogers.com/CR6712

This extremely large, sprawling site of 4.5 hectares is split by the Umag - Savudrija road. The camping site and reception is to the east of the road and the amazing Sol Stella Maris leisure complex, where the Croatian open tennis tournament is held (amongst other competitions), is to the west and borders the sea. Located some 2 km. from the centre of Umag, the site comprises some 575 pitches of which 60 are seasonal and 20 are for tour operators. They are arranged in rows on gently sloping ground, some are shaded. The pitches all have 10A electricity. The site's real strength is its attachment to the leisure complex, with numerous facilities available to campers.

Facilities	Directions
Three sanitary blocks of a very high standard. Hot water throughout. Excellent facilities for disabled visitors. Large supermarket. Huge range of restaurants, bars and snack bars. International tennis centre with pools and beach area. Watersports. Fishing (permit required from Umag). Entertainment programme for children. Communal barbecue areas. Excursions organised. Off site: Land train every 15 minutes into Umag and a local bus service to towns further along the coast. Riding 0.5 km. Golf 1 km.	Site is 2.5 km. north of Umag. On entering Umag look for signs on the main coast road to all campsites and follow the Stella Maris signs. GPS: 45.450417, 13.5222

Open: 23 April - 26 September.

Charges guide

Per unit incl. 2 persons	
and electricity	€ 10.10 - € 30.50
extra person	€ 2.80 - € 7.50

For stays less than 3 nights in high season add 10%.

Vrsar

Camping Porto Sole

Petalon 1, HR-52450 Vrsar (Istria) T: 052 426 500. E: petalon-portosole@maistra.hr

alanrogers.com/CR6725

Located near the pretty town of Vrsar and its charming marina, Porto Sole is a large campsite with 800 pitches and is part of the Maistra group. The pitches vary; some are in the open with semi shade and are fairly flat, others are under a heavy canopy of pines on undulating land. There is some terracing near the small number of waterfront pitches. The site could be described as almost a clover leaf shape with one area for rental accommodation and natural woods, another for sporting facilities and the other two for pitches. There is a large water frontage and two tiny bays provide delightful sheltered rocky swimming areas. In peak season the site is buzzing with activity and the hub of the site is the pool and shopping arcade area where there is also a pub and both formal and informal eating areas. The food available is varied but simple with a tiny terrace restaurant by the water.

Facilities	Directions
The five toilet blocks with mostly British style WCs are kept very clean and well maintained. Facilities for disabled visitors and children. Washing machines and dryers. Large well stocked supermarket (1/5-15/9). Small shopping centre. Pub. Pizzeria. Formal and informal restaurants. Swimming pools (1/5-29/9). Play area (alongside beach). Boules. Tennis. Minigolf. Massage. Entertainment in season. Miniclub. Scuba-diving courses. Boat launching. Off site: Vrsar 500 m. Marina and sailing 1 km. Riding 3 km.	Follow signs towards Vrsar and take turn for Koversada, then follow campsite signs. GPS: 45.142117, 13.602267

Open: 25 April - 3 October.

Charges guide

Per unit incl. 2 persons	
and electricity	€ 17.50 - € 42.50
extra person	€ 5.00 - € 8.00
child (5-12 yrs)	free - € 5.00
dog	€ 3.10 - € 6.50

Camping Porto Sole *Vrsar* — Istria — Green Mediterranean

Amazing sport centre, various entertainment programs, diving centre! NEW– winter camping available (2013/2014)! ONLINE BOOKING

A hidden oasis with clear seas and amazing underwater world. This is a true discovery for all lovers of active holidays.

tel: +385 (0)52 800 200 / fax: 800 215 / portosole@maistra.hr

www.CampingVrsar.com

FREE Alan Rogers Travel Card
Extra benefits and savings - see page 10

Vrsar

Camping Valkanela

Valkanela, HR-52450 Vrsar (Istria) T: 052 445 216. E: valkanela@maistra.hr

alanrogers.com/CR6727

Camping Valkanela is located in a beautiful green bay, right on the Adriatic Sea, between the villages of Vrsar and Funtana. It offers 1,300 pitches, all with 10A electricity. Pitches near the beach are numbered, have shade from mature trees and are slightly sloping towards the sea. Those towards the back of the site are on open fields without much shade and are not marked or numbered. Unfortunately, the number of pitches has increased dramatically over the years, many are occupied by seasonal campers and statics of every description, and these parts of the site are not very attractive. Most numbered pitches have water points close by, but the back pitches have to go to the toilet blocks for water. Access roads are gravel. For those who like activity, Valkanela has four gravel tennis courts, beach volleyball and opportunities for diving, water skiing and boat rental. There is a little marina for mooring small boats and a long rock and pebble private beach with some grass lawns for sunbathing. It is a short stroll to the surrounding villages with their bars, restaurants and shops. There may be some noise nuisance from the disco outside the entrance and during high season the site can become very crowded.

Facilities

Fifteen toilet blocks of varying styles and ages provide toilets, open washbasins and controllable hot showers. Child size toilets, basins and showers. Bathroom (free). Facilities for disabled visitors. Laundry with sinks and washing machines. Two supermarkets. Souvenir shops and newspaper kiosk. Bars and restaurants with dance floor and stage. Pâtisserie. Tennis. Minigolf. Fishing (with permit). Bicycle hire. Games room. Marina with boat launching. Boat and pedalo hire. Disco at entrance. Daily entertainment for children up to 12 yrs. Excursions.

Open: 25 April - 3 October.

Directions

Site is 2 km. north of Vrsar. Follow campsite signs from Vrsar. GPS: 45.16522, 13.60723

Charges guide

Per person	€ 4.50 - € 7.00
child (5-18 yrs)	free - € 5.30
pitch incl. electricity	€ 5.50 - € 18.50
dog	€ 2.50 - € 6.00

Camping Valkanela *Vrsar*

Istria

Seaside lots! Great offer of animation program!

ONLINE BOOKING

The deep blue sea and the vibrant colours of Mediterranean vegetation offer a real treat for those who seek to spend their summer surrounded by nature.

tel: +385 (0)52 800 200 / fax: 800 215 / valkanela@maistra.hr

www.CampingVrsar.com

Vrsar

Camping Orsera

Sv. Martin 2/1, HR-52450 Vrsar (Istria) T: 052 465 010. E: camping@valamar.com

alanrogers.com/CR6728

This is a very attractive site with a 900 m. shoreline from which there are stunning views over the sea to the islands and very often there are spectacular sunsets. This 30-hectare site with direct access to the old fishing port of Vrsar has 575 pitches of which 433 are available to touring units. Marked and numbered, the pitches vary in size with 90 sq.m. being the average. There is some terracing but the pitches to the north of the site are on level ground and offer better views. Ample shade is provided by mature pines and oak trees. All pitches have 10/16A electricity.

Facilities

The modern and well maintained sanitary blocks have mainly British style WCs. Free showers, hot and cold water to washbasins. Facilities for babies, children and disabled visitors. Motorcaravan service point. Laundry. Supermarket (1/5-15/9). Bar/restaurant and takeaway (1/5-15/9). Sports centre. Cinema. Bicycle hire. Fishing. Watersports (no jet skis). Free WiFi throughout.

Open: 1 April - 8 October.

Directions

Site is on the main Porec (7 km) to Vrsar (1 km) road, well signed. GPS: 45.15548, 13.61032

Charges guide

Per unit incl. 2 persons and electricity	Kn 122.10 - 231.70
extra person	Kn 30.00 - 57.00

Prices for pitches by the sea are higher.

For latest campsite news, availability and prices visit

alanrogers.com

Vrsar

Naturist Park Koversada

Koversada, HR-52450 Vrsar (Istria) T: 052 441 378. E: koversada-camp@maistra.hr

alanrogers.com/CR6729

According to history, the first naturist on Koversada was the famous adventurer Casanova. Today Koversada is an enclosed holiday park for naturists with bungalows, 1,700 pitches (all with electricity), a shopping centre and its own island. The main attraction of this site is the Koversada island, connected to the mainland by a small bridge. It is only suitable for tents, but has a restaurant and two toilet blocks. Between the island and the mainland is an enclosed, shallow section of water for swimming. The site is surrounded by a long beach, part sand, part paved. The pitches are of average size on grass and gravel ground and slightly sloping. Pitches on the mainland are numbered and partly terraced under mature pine and olive trees. Pitching on the island is haphazard, but there is also shade from mature trees. The bottom row of pitches on the mainland has views over the island and the sea.

Facilities	Directions
Seventeen toilet blocks provide British and Turkish style toilets, washbasins and controllable hot showers. Child size toilets and basins. Facilities for disabled visitors. Laundry service. Motorcaravan service point. Supermarket. Kiosks with newspapers and tobacco. Several bars and restaurants. Tennis. Minigolf. Surf boards, canoes and kayaks for hire. Tweety Club for children. Live music. Sports tournaments. Internet access in reception and WiFi on part of site (charged). Communal barbecue. Off site: Fishing and riding 8 km.	Site is just south of Vrsar. From Vrsar, follow site signs. GPS: 45.14288, 13.60527

Charges guide

Per unit incl. 2 persons	
and electricity (10A)	€ 18.00 - € 36.00
extra person	€ 5.00 - € 9.00
child (5-18 yrs acc to age)	free - € 6.20
dog	€ 3.10 - € 6.30

Open: 26 April - 22 September.

Naturist park Koversada *Vrsar* — Istria (Green Mediterranean)

Seaside lots! Children's club and playgrounds! Rooms and apartments! Wi-Fi! ONLINE BOOKING

A Mediterranean paradise in a superb natural setting; the gentle climate and clean seas have made this a favourite summer holiday destination for many generations of naturists.

tel: +385 (0)52 800 200 / fax:800 215 / koversada-camp@maistra.hr

www.CampingVrsar.com

Baska

Camping Zablace

E Geistlicha 38, HR-51523 Baska (Kvarner) T: 051 856 909. E: campzablace@hotelibaska.hr

alanrogers.com/CR6761

Camping Zablace is at the southern end of the beautiful island of Krk, 300 m. from the fishing village of Baska. Like most sites in Croatia it has direct access to a large, pebble beach and from the bottom row of pitches one has views over the Adriatic islands. The site has 300 pitches with 150 available for touring units. Zone 1 (nearest the beach) provides 100 individual pitches with electricity and water. The quietest zone, is further away (across a public road that splits the site in two) and has electricity and water taps. There is some shade. There are not many amenities on the site, but it is an easy five minute walk along the promenade to the centre of Baska where there are bars, restaurants and pizzerias.

Facilities	Directions
Five toilet blocks have open plan basins and controllable hot showers (key access to the toilets nearest the beach). Facilities for disabled visitors. Motorcaravan service point. Shop. Kiosks with fruit, cold drinks, tobacco, newspapers and beach wear. Off site: Giant water slide and games hall. Free swimming pool and fitness 100 m. Tennis and minigolf 200 m. Windsurfing. Diving. Marked hiking and cycling routes.	On Krk follow the D102 road south to Baska, turn right towards Baska centre and follow good signs to site. GPS: 44.96668, 14.74512

Charges guide

Per unit incl. 2 persons	
and electricity	Kn 125.00 - 215.00
extra person	Kn 30.00 - 51.00
child (7-11 yrs)	Kn 15.00 - 24.00
Camping Cheques accepted.	

Open: 1 April - 15 October.

Cres

Camping Kovacine

Melin I/20, HR-51557 Cres (Kvarner) T: 051 573 150. E: campkovacine@kovacine.com

alanrogers.com/CR6765

Camping Kovacine is located on a peninsula on the beautiful Kvarner island of Cres, just 2 km. from the town of the same name. The site has 1002 numbered, mostly level pitches, of which 952 are for tourers (300 with 12A electricity). On sloping ground, partially shaded by mature olive and pine trees, pitching is on the large, open spaces between the trees. Some places have views of the Valun lagoon. Kovacine is partly an FKK (naturist) site, which is quite common in Croatia, and has a pleasant atmosphere. Here one can enjoy local live music on a stage close to the pebble beach (Blue Flag), where there is also a restaurant and bar. The site has its own beach, part concrete, part pebbles, and a jetty for mooring boats and fishing. It is close to the historic town of Cres, the main town on the island, which offers a rich history of fishing, shipyards and authentic Kvarner-style houses. There are also several bars, restaurants and shops.

Facilities

Modern, comfortable toilet blocks (two refurbished) offer British style toilets, equipped with solar power, open plan washbasins (some cabins for ladies) and hot showers. Private family bathroom for hire. Facilities for disabled visitors plus facilities for children. Laundry sinks and washing machine. Fridge box hire. Motorcaravan service point. Car wash. Mini-marina and boat crane. Supermarket. Bar, restaurant and pizzeria. Playground. Daily children's club. Evening shows with live music. Boat launching. Fishing. Diving centre. Motorboat hire. WiFi (free). Airport transfers. Off site: Wellness and fitness centre 0.5 km. Historic town of Cres with bars, restaurants and shops 2 km.

Open: 22 March - 20 October.

Directions

From Rijeka take no. 2 road south towards Labin and take ferry to Cres at Brestova. Continue to Cres and follow site signs. GPS: 44.96188, 14.39650

Charges 2013

Per unit incl. 2 persons	
and electricity	€ 17.80 - € 36.20
extra person	€ 6.00 - € 12.20
child (3-12 yrs)	€ 2.80 - € 5.00
dog	free - € 3.00

Baska

Naturist Camping Bunculuka

Baska, HR-51523 Krk (Kvarner) T: 051 856 806. E: lolic@hotelibaska.hr

alanrogers.com/CR6760

Bunculuka is on the opposite side of the small fishing village of Baska from its sister site, Camping Zablace. It is situated in an attractive and very private, enclosed environment, bordered by trees on one side and the sea on the other. It has 400 pitches in two separate areas. The 200 plots for touring units are mainly in the open and on ground gently sloping downwards to the sea; the other area, to the rear of the site, is wooded and more hilly and is mainly used for tents. The front row of pitches has beautiful views over the sea and of the private pebble beach. Most pitches are fairly level, although the ground is a little rocky. A lounge bar/restaurant is close to the beach, but from the site entrance it is only 500 m. to the promenade in the centre of Baska where there are several bars, restaurants and pizzerias.

Facilities

Three good toilet blocks with open style washbasins and controllable hot showers, plus a small block close to the beach. Supermarket. Lounge bar/restaurant with covered and open-air terrace (Mediterranean and Thai cuisine). Small bakery and the grocery store within the restaurant. Tennis. Minigolf. Kayak rental. Deck chair and parasols rental on the beach. Safety deposit boxes for hire at reception. WiFi throughout (free). Off site: Baska with bars, restaurants and shops 500 m.

Open: 23 April - 10 October.

Directions

On Krk follow D102 road south to Baska. Do not turn into Baska centre, continue and site is on the left at the end of the D102.
GPS: 44.96923, 14.76702

Charges guide

Per unit incl. 2 persons	
and electricity	€ 16.40 - € 41.90
extra person	€ 3.50 - € 8.70
child (5-11 yrs)	€ 2.80 - € 4.90
dog	€ 3.10 - € 5.50

For latest campsite news, availability and prices visit

alanrogers.com

CAMP KOVAČINE CRES

A crystal clear sea, beautiful beaches and pine and olive trees which provide plenty of shade, make Kovacine a unique holiday destination. The campsite is situated on the Cres peninsula and is close to the village with the same name. There are 950 pitches which offer all the comfort you might wish. **Room (with breakfast), direct on the beach with sea view.**

- New, modern sanitary facilities (solar energy)
- New mobile homes for 2 and 4–6 persons
- Bar, buffet, restaurant, self service shop
- Mini-marina and boat crane
- First aid service
- Animation for children
- Sport facilities

- Diving and diving school
- Free WiFi
- Ferry costs refunded for 10 or 18 nights stay
- Special offers in low season: 7=6, 14=12 nights
- Shuttle service/Airporttransfer: Airport Rijeka – Cres and back: only € 30,–/person

Camping »Kovačine« Cres • HR-51557 Cres • Tel. 00-385/51/573-150 • Fax 00-385/51/571-086
E-Mail: campkovacine@kovacine.com • web: www.camp-kovacine.com

Krk

Camping Jezevac

HR-51500 Krk (Kvarner) T: 051 221 081. E: jezevac@valamar.com

alanrogers.com/CR6757

Camping Jezevac is an excellent and well maintained seaside site, close to the pretty town of Krk. It is a large site extending to over 11 hectares and is built on a hillside at the western side of the town. The 584 pitches, all for touring are mainly on level terraces with plenty of shade and some enjoy views of the bay below. All have 10A electricity, 120 are fully serviced. Some premium beach side pitches are available, with water and electricity, but waste water from these plots has to be taken to drainage points further up the site, which can be a problem. The toilet blocks were completely modernised and decorated to a high standard for 2010. In high season the atmosphere can be very lively and the site's 800 m. private beach is a focal point. Jezevac has benefited from extensive work in recent years. The reception area provides a warm welcome and is well equipped with information about the area. Thirty mobile homes are available for rent. A children's club is run for most of the season with a varied programme of activities. A good sports centre can be found 300 m. away. Free WiFi is available at points around the site and at reception.

Facilities

Heated toilet block with hot showers. Washing machines. Shops (1/4-15/10). Restaurants (1/5-1/10) and bars. Takeaway (1/5-30/9). Tennis. Playground. Activity and entertainment programmes and children's club (May-Sept). Fishing. Bicycle hire. Boat launching and sailing. Max. 1 dog. Off site: Sports centre 300 m. Shops, bars and restaurants in Krk.

Open: Easter - 15 October.

Directions

From the toll bridge onto Krk, follow signs to Krk town and the town centre. Take the second right turn and continue ahead for 2.2 km. At the first roundabout take the second exit. Continue for 600 m. following signs to Camp Jezevac. GPS: 45.01964, 14.57072

Charges guide

Per unit incl. 2 persons	
and electricity	€ 21.20 - € 35.60
extra person	€ 5.00 - € 6.90
child (4-10 yrs)	free - € 4.50
dog	€ 3.00 - € 4.40

Krk

Camping Krk

Politin bb, HR-51500 Krk (Kvarner) T: 051 221 351. E: camping@valamar.com

alanrogers.com/CR6758

This is an attractive site in a secluded hillside setting on the wooded peninsula of Prniba, quite close to the centre of Krk. On arrival you are assured of a good welcome from the staff, who speak good English. There are 342 clearly defined and well spaced out touring pitches, mostly on level sandy terraces, all with 10A electricity, and ranging in size from 70-110 sq.m. Of these, 130 plots are fully serviced and include 96 with satellite TV connection. There are also 55 seasonal pitches that do not impinge on the touring units. The site has an open feel to it with flowers, shrubs and grasses being allowed to develop naturally. Two sanitary blocks are clean and well decorated and provide very good toilets, hot showers and washbasins plus dishwashing facilities etc. The site has its own Blue Flag accredited private beach, and for those seeking some degree of solitude there is little need to venture out of the site. An attractive restaurant with a large outside terrace is a focal point and provides a good selection of food at reasonable prices. Snacks, drinks and takeaway foods are also available at the separate Beach Bar. BBQs are only allowed at the communal area. There is an activity programme for children during the high season. On-site amenities include a shop. Boat trips to the neighbouring islands of Rab and Cres are possible and can be arranged on site.

Facilities

Restaurant, bar and shop (all 1/5-30/9). Tennis. Playground. Children's activity programme (May-Sept). Fishing. Boat launching. Sailing. Free WiFi to most of site. New, spacious mobile homes for rent. Payphones at reception. Outdoor pool. Saunas. Off site: Fitness centre 1.5 km. Sports centre 2 km. Krk town centre. Buses from Krk serve other towns on the island.

Open: April - September.

Directions

Cross toll bridge from mainland to island of Krk, head for island's capital, Krk (28 km). On arrival head to first traffic junction and turn right. After 500 m. turn left (beyond petrol station). Continue on this road for 800 m. to site. Site is well signed. GPS: 45.02440, 14.59280

Charges guide

Per unit incl. 2 persons	
and electricity	€ 20.40 - € 37.70
extra person	€ 4.80 - € 6.90
child (4-10 yrs)	free - € 4.70
dog	€ 3.00 - € 4.50

Mali Losinj
Camping Poljana

Privlaka 19, HR-51550 Mali Losinj (Kvarner) T: 051 231 726. E: info@poljana.hr
alanrogers.com/CR6772

Autocamp Poljana lies on the narrow strip of land in the southern part of Losinj island, just north of the pleasant town of Mali Losinj. With 600 pitches, this site is bigger than it looks. The camping area has been newly laid out with some flat areas and some terraces. The pitches are marked with flowers and shrubs. There are some mature trees for shade and 600 electricity connections. Campers may be able to experience both sunset and sunrise from the same pitch! The toilet facilities are new and well maintained, while a shop and a series of bars and restaurants are available close by.

Facilities	Directions
New toilet blocks, including solar panels for hot water, are entirely up to date and adequate. Facilities for disabled visitors. Baby rooms. Motorcaravan service point. Washing machine (expensive). Daily entertainment. Bicycle hire. WiFi. Rock beach with cocktail bar. Marina. Off site: Losinj 4 km. Riding and canoeing 6 km. **Open:** 1 April - 21 October.	About 2 km. north of the town, the site occupies both sides of the road along the waterline and opposite the little marina. GPS: 44.55555, 14.44166

Charges guide

Per unit incl. 2 persons and electricity	€ 16.00 - € 45.00
extra person	€ 5.40 - € 11.50

Martinscica
Camping Slatina

Martinscica, HR-51556 Cres (Kvarner) T: 051 574 127. E: info@camp-slatina.com
alanrogers.com/CR6768

Camping Slatina lies about halfway along the island of Cres, beside the fishing port of Martinscica, on a bay of the Adriatic Sea. It has 370 pitches for tourers, many with 10A electricity, 50 new individual ones (29 fully serviced) off very steep, tarmac access roads, sloping down to the sea. The pitches are large and level on a gravel base and enjoy plenty of shade from mature laurel trees, although hardly any have views. Whilst there is plenty of privacy, the site does have an enclosed feeling. Some pitches in the lower areas have water, electricity and drainage. Like many sites in Croatia, Slatina has a private diving centre.

Facilities	Directions
Four new and two refurbished toilet blocks provide toilets, open style washbasins and controllable hot showers. Facilities for disabled visitors. Laundry facilities. Car wash. Shop. Bar, restaurant, grill restaurant, pizzeria and fish restaurant. Playground. Minigolf. Fishing. Bicycle hire. Diving centre. Boat launching. Pedalo, canoe and boat hire. Excursions to the Blue Cave. WiFi (charged). Only gas and electric barbecues permitted. Off site: Martinscica with bars, restaurants and shops 2 km. **Open:** 1 April - 10 October.	From Rijeka take no. 2 road south towards Labin and take ferry to Cres at Brestova. From Cres go south towards Martinscica and follow site signs. GPS: 44.82333, 14.34083

Charges guide

Per unit incl. 2 persons and electricity	€ 15.00 - € 22.00
extra person	€ 5.00 - € 8.00
child (7-12 yrs)	€ 3.00 - € 5.00

Punat
Camping Pila

Setaliste Ivana Bruscia 2, Punat, HR-51521 Krk (Kvarner) T: 051 854 020. E: pila@hoteli-punat.hr
alanrogers.com/CR6755

Autocamping Pila is right beside the bustling seaside resort of Punat on the biggest Croatian island of Krk, which is connected to the mainland by a toll bridge. Krk is the first island you reach as you travel south into Croatia and the Romans called it the 'Golden Island'. Autocamp Pila is just 100 m. from the Adriatic and has 400 grass or gravel pitches for tourers. Of these, 250 are numbered and many benefit from the shade of mature trees. All pitches have 10A electricity, plus 130 premium pitches have electricity, water and drainage. It can get very busy in high season and pitching can become cramped.

Facilities	Directions
Three modern toilet blocks with toilets, basins and showers. Child size showers and basins. Baby room. Facilities for disabled visitors. Kitchen with cooking rings. Motorcaravan service point. Small shop. Bar with terrace and restaurant. Snack bar. Play area with basketball. Minigolf. Aerobics and aquarobics. Video games. Daily evening programme for children in high season. WiFi throughout. Pebble beach. Gas and electric barbecues only. Off site: Supermarket 50 m. Aqua slide, pedalo and boat hire 200 m. Punat with shops, bars, restaurants. **Open:** Easter - 15 October.	On Krk follow D102 road south towards Baska and take exit for Punat. In Punat follow good site signs. GPS: 45.01663, 14.62873

Charges guide

Per unit incl. 2 persons and electricity	€ 18.00 - € 29.70
extra person	€ 4.00 - € 7.10
child (7-12 yrs)	€ 1.80 - € 4.50
dog	€ 1.90 - € 4.00

Camping Cheques accepted.

FREE Alan Rogers Travel Card
Extra benefits and savings - see page 10

Punat
Naturist Camping Konobe

Obala 94, Punat, HR-51521 Krk (Kvarner) T: 051 854 036. E: konobe@hoteli-punat.hr
alanrogers.com/CR6756

Naturist Camping Konobe is situated south of the historic fishing port of Punat on the island of Krk in a remote and quiet location. Access is down a long, tarmac road which leads to a landscaped terrain, with terraces built from natural stone. The 400 slightly sloping pitches are part open, part wooded, with some shade from mature trees and some have beautiful views over the Adriatic. Unmarked pitches for tents are on small terraces, with numbered pitches for caravans and motorcaravans of 50-80 sq.m. on sandy grass off tarmac access roads. The remote location makes this site ideal for quiet camping among the wild charm of a rocky and still green environment.

Facilities

Three modern, comfortable toilet blocks with toilets, open basins and preset showers. Child size washbasins. Facilities for disabled visitors. Campers' kitchen with connections (no rings). Gas. Supermarket. Bar/restaurant with open-air terrace. Tennis. Minigolf. Fishing. Pebble beach. Boat launching. Evening entertainment for children. Croatian language lessons. WiFi (free). Only gas and electric barbecues permitted. Off site: Punat 4 km.

Open: 1 May - 1 October.

Directions

On Krk follow D102 road to south of the island. Take exit for Punat and follow main road through town. Site is 4 km. south of Punat and well signed. GPS: 44.99107, 14.63065

Charges guide

Per unit incl. 2 persons	
and electricity	€ 18.00 - € 30.90
extra person	€ 4.00 - € 7.50
child (7-12 yrs)	€ 1.80 - € 4.60
dog	€ 1.90 - € 4.00

Camping Cheques accepted.

Selce
Autocamp Selce

Jasenova 19, HR-51266 Selce (Kvarner) T: 051 764 038. E: kamp-selce@ri.t-com.hr
alanrogers.com/CR6750

With easy access from the E65/8 road, this terraced site, which leads down to an attractive small harbour, is ideally situated not only as a stocking up point on what must be Europe's most picturesque coastal road, but also as a site to spend some time. Relax on the large paved areas at the water's edge or visit Selce with its supermarket, banks and local market which is only a few minutes walk away along the seaside promenade with its bars and restaurants. The site has 300 level touring pitches, all with electricity, mainly on terraces and many shaded by olive and fir trees.

Facilities

Seven good toilet blocks with British and Turkish style toilets, open style washbasins and controllable, hot showers (free). Facilities for disabled visitors. Laundry service. Fridge box hire. Motorcaravan service point. Shop. Bar/restaurant with covered and open-air terrace. Barbecues permitted only in communal area. Fishing. Diving centre. Off site: Boat rental and water skiing 150 m. Boat launching and jetty 500 m.

Open: 1 April - 1 November.

Directions

Site is on the coast 40 km. south-southeast of Rijeka on the E65/8. It is on the southern edge of Selce and is well signed. GPS: 45.1541, 14.725133

Charges guide

Per unit incl. 2 persons	
and electricity	€ 107.00 - € 181.00
extra person	€ 25.00 - € 44.00
child (5-14 yrs)	€ 16.00 - € 25.00
dog	€ 16.00

For latest campsite news, availability and prices visit
alanrogers.com

Sv. Filip I Jakov

Autocamp Rio

Put Primorja 66, HR-23207 Sv. Filip I Jakov (Dalmatia) T: 023 388 671. E: autocamp_rio@hotmail.com

alanrogers.com/CR6833

In a village close to Biograd, the small Autocamp Rio provides 54 pitches of which 29 are available for tourers. All have old-type (two-pin) 16A electricity connections. The basic reception, the modest toilet block and the house of the Croatian owner are situated on the street front while behind, the site ends at a small cliff directly above the sea. Below this, a little sandy beach and a pier for boats are accessible from the site and are only used by campsite guests. The partly shaded, marked pitches are laid out in two wings around a central grassy area.

Facilities

Decent but simple toilet block has showers with curtains but no facilities for babies or disabled visitors. Washing machine. No bar or restaurant. Off site: Village within walking distance. Vransko Jezero bird reserve 10 km. City of Zadar 25 km. Komati Archipelago National Park.

Open: Easter - 15 October.

Directions

Leave main coast road 8 and (F) from centre of Sv. Filip I Jakov village, look for site sign and continue in south easterly direction parallel to sea for 1 km. Rio is on right, not far from end of village. GPS: 43.95604, 15.43521

Charges guide

Per unit incl. 2 persons and electricity	€ 16.20 - € 25.20
extra person	€ 4.00 - € 6.50
child (under 12 yrs)	free - € 3.50

Trogir

Camp Seget

Hrvatskih zrtava 121, HR-21218 Trogir Seget Donji (Dalmatia) T: 021 880 394. E: kamp@kamp-seget.hr

alanrogers.com/CR6850

Camp Seget is a simple site which is pleasant and quiet and only 2 km. from the interesting old harbour town of Trogir. The site has 120 pitches set out on both sides of a tarmac access lane that runs down to the sea. There are 56 numbered pitches to the left. They are fairly level and from most there are views of the sea. Pitches to the right are undefined, slightly sloping and mostly used for tents. Of varying sizes (40-80 sq.m) the pitches are on grass and gravel (firm tent pegs may be needed). Some benefit from the shade of mature trees. All have access to 6A electricity (long leads may be necessary).

Facilities

Two modest sanitary blocks, one of which is part Portacabin, contain toilets, washbasins and controllable, hot showers (free). Facilities for disabled visitors. Campers' kitchen. Fridge box hire. Shop (1/5-15/10). Bicycle hire. Motor scooter hire. Beach. Fishing. Boat rental. Barbecues permitted only on communal area. Off site: Bus at gate for touring. Boat launching 500 m. Golf 1 km.

Open: 15 April - 15 October.

Directions

Follow no. 8 coastal road south from Zadar towards Split. At Seget Donji, 2 km. before Trogir, look for prominent site signs, finishing in a sharp right turn into the site. GPS: 43.5186, 16.224167

Charges guide

Per unit incl. 2 persons and electricity	Kn 150.00 - 200.00

Zivogosce

Kamp Dole

Zivogosce bb, HR-21331 Zivogosce (Dalmatia) T: 021 628 749. E: auto-camp-dole@st.hinet.hr

alanrogers.com/CR6870

Kamp Dole is a spacious site with a long beach frontage in southern Croatia, close to the beautiful island of Hvar. It has 500 pitches, 400 are for tourers. The beachside pitches are numbered and marked, the remainder are used informally and are mostly in the shade of mature trees. There are great views of the sea from the pebble beach which stretches 500 m. in front of the site; at each end of the beach is a small harbour, palm-lined to the northwest, and a restaurant. The pitches at the back have beautiful views of the impressive mountains. Close to reception is a welcoming bar with terrace.

Facilities

Four renovated toilet blocks offer high quality British WCs, washbasins and controllable, hot showers (free). Fridge box hire. Several kiosks and supermarket. Bar. Jet ski hire. Paragliding. Pedalo and canoe hire. Full entertainment programme in high season. Excursions to Korcula. Barbecues only in communal area. Off site: Paintball adjacent to site. Boat launching 200 m.

Open: 1 May - 30 September.

Directions

Site is 80 km. southeast of Split beside the No.8 coastal road 3 km. southeast of Zivogosce. Well signed. GPS: 43.170833, 17.196333

Charges guide

Per person	Kn 21.00 - 39.00
child (5-12 yrs)	Kn 13.50 - 22.00
pitch	Kn 82.50 - 165.00
electricity	Kn 30.00

FREE Alan Rogers Travel Card
Extra benefits and savings - see page 10

Accommodation

Over recent years many of the campsites featured in this guide have added large numbers of high quality mobile homes and chalets. Many site owners believe that some former caravanners and motorcaravanners have been enticed by the extra comfort they can now provide, and that maybe this is the ideal solution to combine the freedom of camping with all the comforts of home.

Quality is consistently high and, although the exact size and inventory may vary from site to site, if you choose any of the sites detailed here, you can be sure that you're staying in some of the best quality and best value mobile homes available.

Home comforts are provided and typically these include a fridge with freezer compartment, gas hob, proper shower – often a microwave and radio/cassette hi-fi too, but do check for details. All mobile homes and chalets come fully equipped with a good range of kitchen utensils, pots and pans, crockery, cutlery and outdoor furniture. Some even have an attractive wooden sundeck or paved terrace – a perfect spot for outdoors eating or relaxing with a book and watching the world go by.

Regardless of model, colourful soft furnishings are the norm and a generally breezy décor helps to provide a real holiday feel.

Although some sites may have a large number of different accommodation types, we have restricted our choice to one or two of the most popular accommodation units (either mobile homes or chalets) for each of the sites listed.

The mobile homes here will be of modern design, and recent innovations, for example, often include pitched roofs which substantially improve their appearance.

Design will invariably include clever use of space and fittings/furniture to provide for comfortable holidays – usually light and airy, with big windows and patio-style doors, fully equipped kitchen areas, a shower room with shower, washbasin and WC, cleverly designed bedrooms and a comfortable lounge/dining area (often incorporating a sofa bed).

In general, modern campsite chalets incorporate all the best features of mobile homes in a more traditional structure, sometimes with the advantage of an upper mezzanine floor for an additional bedroom.

Our selected campsites offer a massive range of different types of mobile home and chalet, and it would be impractical to inspect every single accommodation unit. Our selection criteria, therefore, primarily takes account of the quality standards of the campsite itself.

However, there are a couple of important ground rules:

- Featured mobile homes must be no more than 5 years old

- chalets no more than 10 years old

- All listed accommodation must, of course, fully conform with all applicable local, national and European safety legislation.

For each campsite we have given details of the type, or types, of accommodation available to rent, but these details are necessarily quite brief. Sometimes internal layouts can differ quite substantially, particularly with regard to sleeping arrangements, where these include the flexible provision for 'extra persons' on sofa beds located in the living area. These arrangements may vary from accommodation to accommodation, and if you're planning a holiday which includes more people than are catered for by the main bedrooms you should check exactly how the extra sleeping arrangements are to be provided!

Charges

An indication of the tariff for each type of accommodation featured is also included, indicating the variance between the low and high season tariffs. However, given that many campsites have a large and often complex range of pricing options, incorporating special deals and various discounts, the charges we mention should be taken to be just an indication. We strongly recommend therefore that you confirm the actual cost when making a booking.

We also strongly recommend that you check with the campsite, when booking, what (if anything) will be provided by way of bed linen, blankets, pillows etc. Again, in our experience, this can vary widely from site to site.

On every campsite a fully refundable deposit (usually between 150 and 300 euros) is payable on arrival. There may also be an optional cleaning service for which a further charge is made. Other options may include sheet hire (typically 30 euros per unit) or baby pack hire (cot and high chair).

IT64190 Camping River

▶ see report page 35

Localitá Armezzone, I-19031 Ameglia (Liguria)

AR1 – BUNGALOW – Bungalow

Sleeping: 2 bedrooms, sleeps 5: 1 double, 3 singles, sofa bed, pillows and blankets provided

Living: heating, shower, WC

Eating: fitted kitchen with fridge, freezer

Outside: table & chairs, barbecue

Pets: accepted (with supplement)

AR2 – CH 4+2 A CN 6 – Mobile Home

Sleeping: 2 bedrooms, sleeps 6: 1 double, 4 singles, sofa bed, pillows and blankets provided

Living: heating, air conditioning, shower, WC, separate WC

Eating: fitted kitchen with fridge, freezer

Outside: table & chairs, parasol, barbecue

Pets: accepted (with supplement)

Other (AR1 and AR2): cot to hire

Open: 27 March - 3 October

Weekly Charge	AR1	AR2
Low Season (from)	€ 245	€ 399
High Season (from)	€ 680	€ 1130

IT64010 Camping Villaggio dei Fiori

▶ see report page 39

Via Tiro a Volo 3, I-18038 San Remo (Liguria)

AR1 – TYPE A/B – Bungalow

Sleeping: 2 bedrooms, sleeps 4: 1 double, 2 singles, sofa bed, pillows and blankets provided

Living: heating, TV, air conditioning, shower, WC

Eating: fitted kitchen with hobs, fridge

Outside: table & chairs

Pets: not accepted

AR2 – TYPE C/D – Mobile Home

Sleeping: 2 bedrooms, sleeps 4: 1 double, 2 singles, bunk bed, pillows and blankets provided

Living: heating, TV, air conditioning, shower, WC, separate WC

Eating: fitted kitchen with hobs, microwave, fridge, freezer

Outside: table & chairs

Pets: not accepted

Other (AR1 and AR2): cot, highchair to hire

Open: All year

Weekly Charge	AR1	AR2
Low Season (from)	€ 350	€ 650
High Season (from)	€ 791	€ 1064

IT62260 Camping Punta Lago

▶ see report page 64

Via Lungo Lago 42, I-38050 Calceranica al Lago (Trentino - Alto Adige)

AR1 – VENEZIA – Mobile Home

Sleeping: 2 bedrooms, sleeps 5: 1 double, 3 singles

Living: living/kitchen area, heating, TV, air conditioning, shower, WC

Eating: fitted kitchen with hobs, microwave, fridge

Outside: table & chairs

Pets: not accepted

AR2 – CAPRI – Mobile Home

Sleeping: 3 bedrooms, sleeps 6: 10 doubles, 4 singles

Living: living/kitchen area, heating, TV, air conditioning, shower, WC

Eating: fitted kitchen with hobs, microwave, fridge

Outside: table & chairs

Pets: not accepted

Open: 25 April - 26 September		
Weekly Charge	AR1	AR2
Low Season (from)	€ 350	€ 450
High Season (from)	€ 700	€ 800

IT62290 Camping Lago di Levico

▶ see report page 68

Localitá Pleina, I-38056 Levico Terme (Trentino - Alto Adige)

AR1 – MOBILE HOME LEVICO – Mobile Home

Sleeping: 2 bedrooms, sleeps 5: 1 double, 3 singles, bunk bed, sofa bed, pillows and blankets provided

Living: heating, TV, air conditioning, shower, WC, separate WC

Eating: fitted kitchen with hobs, microwave, dishwasher, coffee maker, fridge

Outside: table & chairs, parasol

Pets: not accepted

AR2 – MOBILE HOME SUPERIOR LEVICO – Mobile Home

Sleeping: 2 bedrooms, sleeps 5: 1 double, 3 singles, bunk bed, sofa bed, pillows and blankets provided

Living: heating, TV, air conditioning, shower, WC, separate WC

Eating: fitted kitchen with hobs, microwave, dishwasher, coffee maker, fridge

Outside: table & chairs, parasol

Pets: not accepted

Other (AR1 and AR2): bed linen, highchair to hire

Open: 23 March - 14 October		
Weekly Charge	AR1	AR2
Low Season (from)	€ 350	€ 455
High Season (from)	€ 756	€ 819

IT61990 Camping Residence Corones

▶ see report page 71

Niederrasen 124, I-39030 Rasen (Trentino - Alto Adige)

AR1 – CHALET – Chalet

Sleeping: 2 bedrooms, sleeps 6: 4 singles, sofa bed, pillows and blankets provided

Living: living/kitchen area, heating, TV, shower, WC

Eating: fitted kitchen with hobs, fridge

Outside: table & chairs, parasol

Pets: not accepted

Other (AR1 and AR2): bed linen, cot to hire

Open: All year

Weekly Charge	AR1
Low Season (from)	€ 1190
High Season (from)	€ 1925

IT60080 Camping Sabbiadoro

▶ see report page 77

Via Sabbiadoro 8, I-33054 Lignano Sabbiadoro (Friuli-Venezia Giulia)

AR1 – TYPE H – Mobile Home

Sleeping: 1 bedroom, sleeps 3: 2 singles, sofa bed, pillows and blankets provided

Living: living/kitchen area, air conditioning, shower, WC

Eating: fitted kitchen with hobs, fridge

Outside: table & chairs, parasol

Pets: accepted

AR2 – TYPE F – Mobile Home

Sleeping: 2 bedrooms, sleeps 6: 1 double, 3 singles, sofa bed, pillows and blankets provided

Living: living/kitchen area, heating, air conditioning, shower, WC

Eating: fitted kitchen with hobs, fridge

Outside: table & chairs, parasol

Pets: accepted

Open: 31 March - 7 October

Weekly Charge	AR1	AR2
Low Season (from)	€ 312	€ 606
High Season (from)	€ 504	€ 938

IT60110 Camping San Francesco

Porto Santa Margherita, I-30020 Caorle (Veneto)

▶ see report page 83

AR1 – PINETA/BEACH – Mobile Home

Sleeping: 2 bedrooms, sleeps 5: 1 double, 2 singles, sofa bed, pillows and blankets provided

Living: living/kitchen area, heating, air conditioning, shower, WC

Eating: fitted kitchen with hobs, fridge, freezer

Outside: table & chairs, parasol

Pets: accepted (with supplement)

AR2 – M50 COMFORT – Chalet

Sleeping: 2 bedrooms, sleeps 6: 4 singles, sofa bed, pillows and blankets provided

Living: living/kitchen area, heating, air conditioning, shower, WC

Eating: fitted kitchen with hobs, microwave, fridge, freezer

Outside: table & chairs, parasol

Pets: accepted (with supplement)

Other (AR1 and AR2): bed linen, cot, highchair to hire

Open: 21 April - 24 September		
Weekly Charge	AR1	AR2
Low Season (from)	€ 315	€ 427
High Season (from)	€ 1099	€ 1421

IT60200 Camping Union Lido Vacanze

Via Fausta 258, I-30013 Cavallino-Treporti (Veneto)

▶ see report page 86

AR1 – CAMPING HOME ROOF – Mobile Home

Sleeping: 2 bedrooms, sleeps 7: 1 double, 2 singles, bunk bed, sofa bed, pillows and blankets provided

Living: living/kitchen area, heating, TV, air conditioning, shower, seperate WC

Eating: fitted kitchen with hobs, microwave, dishwasher, fridge, freezer

Outside: table & chairs, 2 sun loungers

Pets: not accepted

AR2 – CAMPING HOME VERANDA LARGE – Mobile home

Sleeping: 2 bedrooms, sleeps 6: 1 double, 2 singles, sofa bed, pillows and blankets provided

Living: living/kitchen area, heating, TV, air conditioning, shower, seperate WC

Eating: fitted kitchen with hobs, microwave, dishwasher, fridge, freezer

Outside: table & chairs, 2 sun loungers

Pets: not accepted

Other (AR1 and AR2): bed linen, cot, highchair to hire

Open: 21 April - 23 September		
Weekly Charge	AR1	AR2
Low Season (from)	€ 707	€ 637
High Season (from)	€ 1162	€ 917

IT60410 Camping Village Europa

▶ see report page 89

Via Fausta 332, I-30013 Cavallino-Treporti (Veneto)

AR1 – ECOLIFE – Chalet

Sleeping: 2 bedrooms, sleeps 7: 1 double, 3 singles, sofa bed, pillows and blankets provided

Living: heating, air conditioning, shower, WC

Eating: fitted kitchen with hobs, fridge, freezer

Outside: table & chairs

Pets: not accepted

AR2 – MAXI CARAVAN CHALET EUROPA – Mobile Home

Sleeping: 2 bedrooms, sleeps 6: 1 double, 2 singles, sofa bed, pillows and blankets provided

Living: heating, TV, air conditioning, shower, WC

Eating: fitted kitchen with hobs, oven, microwave, fridge

Outside: table & chairs

Pets: not accepted

Other (AR1 and AR2): cot to hire

Open: 31 March - 30 September

Weekly Charge	AR1	AR2
Contact the site for details.		

IT60400 Camping Village Garden Paradiso

▶ see report page 91

Via F. Baracca 55, I-30013 Cavallino-Treporti (Veneto)

AR1 – BORGO FIORITO – Mobile Home

Sleeping: 2 bedrooms, sleeps 6: 1 double, 2 singles, sofa bed, pillows and blankets provided

Living: heating, TV, air conditioning, shower, WC

Eating: fitted kitchen with hobs, microwave, dishwasher, fridge, freezer

Outside: table & chairs, parasol

Pets: not accepted

AR2 – CHALET GARDEN – Chalet

Sleeping: 2 bedrooms, sleeps 5: 1 double, 2 singles, bunk bed, sofa bed, pillows and blankets provided

Living: heating, TV, air conditioning, shower, WC

Eating: fitted kitchen with hobs, microwave, fridge

Outside: table & chairs, parasol, 2 sun loungers

Pets: not accepted

Other (AR1 and AR2): bed linen, cot, highchair to hire

Open: 24 April - 29 September

Weekly Charge	AR1	AR2
Low Season (from)	€ 368	€ 287
High Season (from)	€ 921	€ 686

IT60370 Camping Jesolo International

▶ see report page 94

Viale A. da Giussano, I-30016 Lido di Jesolo (Veneto)

AR1 – HOLIDAY HOME – Mobile Home

Sleeping: 2 bedrooms, sleeps 5: 2 doubles, 1 single, sofa bed, pillows and blankets provided

Living: heating, TV, air conditioning, shower, WC

Eating: fitted kitchen with hobs, oven, microwave, grill, dishwasher, coffee maker, fridge, freezer

Outside: table & chairs, parasol, barbecue

Pets: not accepted

Other (AR1 and AR2): bed linen, cot, highchair to hire

Open: 25 April - 29 September	
Weekly Charge	AR1
Low Season (from)	€ 546
High Season (from)	€ 1225

IT60560 Camping Miramare

▶ see report page 97

Via Barbarigo 103, I-30015 Sottomarina di Chioggia (Veneto)

AR1 – MAXICARAVAN – Mobile Home

Sleeping: 2 bedrooms, sleeps 5: 1 double, 2 singles, sofa bed, pillows and blankets provided

Living: living/kitchen area, heating, TV, air conditioning, shower, WC

Eating: fitted kitchen with hobs, fridge, freezer

Outside: table & chairs

Pets: not accepted

AR2 – CHALET BURSTNER – Chalet

Sleeping: 2 bedrooms, sleeps 5: 1 double, 2 singles, bunk bed, sofa bed, pillows and blankets provided

Living: living/kitchen area, heating, TV, air conditioning, shower, WC

Eating: fitted kitchen with hobs, fridge, freezer

Outside: table & chairs

Pets: not accepted

Other (AR1 and AR2): bed linen to hire

Open: 4 April - 24 September		
Weekly Charge	AR1	AR2
Low Season (from)	€ 280	€ 315
High Season (from)	€ 840	€ 875

IT69750 Tiliguerta Camping Village

▶ see report page 183

SP 97 km. 6 - Loc. Capo Ferrato, I-09043 Muravera (Sardinia)

AR1 – BUNGALOW – Bungalow

Sleeping: 2 bedrooms, sleeps 5: 2 doubles, 1 single, sofa bed, pillows and blankets provided

Living: air conditioning, shower, WC, separate WC

Eating: grill, fridge, freezer

Outside: table & chairs, barbecue

Pets: accepted (with supplement)

AR2 – TILI SUITE – Mobile Home

Sleeping: 2 bedrooms, sleeps 5: 2 doubles, 3 singles, sofa bed, pillows and blankets provided

Living: air conditioning, shower, WC, separate WC

Eating: fitted kitchen with grill, coffee maker, fridge, freezer

Outside: table & chairs, parasol, 2 sun loungers, barbecue

Pets: accepted (with supplement)

Other (AR1 and AR2): cot, highchair to hire

Open: 27 April - 12 October		
Weekly Charge	AR1	AR2
Low Season (from)	€ 280	€ 700
High Season (from)	€ 560	€ 1350

CR6731 Naturist Camping Valalta

▶ see report page 210

Cesta za Valaltu - Lim 7, HR-52210 Rovinj (Istria)

AR1 – MOBIL HOME – Mobile Home

Sleeping: 2 bedrooms, sleeps 4: 1 double, 2 singles, pillows and blankets provided

Living: TV, air conditioning, shower, WC

Eating: fitted kitchen with hobs, microwave, coffee maker, fridge, freezer

Outside: table & chairs, 2 sun loungers

Pets: not accepted

AR2 – MOBIL HOME LUX – Mobile Home

Sleeping: 2 bedrooms, sleeps 5: 1 double, 3 singles, pillows and blankets provided

Living: TV, air conditioning, shower, WC

Eating: fitted kitchen with hobs, microwave, coffee maker, fridge, freezer

Outside: table & chairs, 2 sun loungers

Pets: not accepted

Other (AR1 and AR2): bed linen, cot to hire

Open: 27 April - 29 September		
Weekly Charge	**AR1**	**AR2**
Low Season (from)	€ 441	€ 490
High Season (from)	€ 875	€ 1050

CR6765 Camping Kovacine

▶ see report page 216

Melin I/20, HR-51557 Cres (Kvarner)

AR1 – MOBILE HOME FOR 4-6 PERSONS – Mobile Home

Sleeping: 2 bedrooms, sleeps 6: 1 double, 3 singles, bunk bed, sofa bed, pillows and blankets provided

Living: heating, shower, WC

Eating: fitted kitchen with hobs, fridge, freezer

Outside: table & chairs, parasol

Pets: accepted (with supplement)

AR2 – MOBILE HOME FOR 2 PERSONS – Mobile Home

Sleeping: 1 bedroom, sleeps 2: 2 singles, pillows and blankets provided

Living: heating, air conditioning, shower, WC

Eating: fitted kitchen with hobs, fridge, freezer

Outside: table & chairs, parasol

Pets: accepted (with supplement)

Other (AR1 and AR2): bed linen to hire

Open: 22 March - 20 October		
Weekly Charge	**AR1**	**AR2**
Low Season (from)	€ 364	€ 280
High Season (from)	€ 938	€ 574

Travelling - in Europe

When taking your car (and caravan, tent or trailer tent) or motorcaravan to the continent you do need to plan in advance and to find out as much as possible about driving in the countries you plan to visit. Whilst European harmonisation has eliminated many of the differences between one country and another, it is well worth reading the short notes we provide in the introduction to each country in this guide in addition to this more general summary.

Of course, the main difference from driving in the UK is that in mainland Europe you will need to drive on the right. Without taking extra time and care, especially at busy junctions and conversely when roads are empty, it is easy to forget to drive on the right. Remember that traffic approaching from the right usually has priority unless otherwise indicated by road markings and signs. Harmonisation also means that most (but not all) common road signs are the same in all countries.

Your vehicle

Book your vehicle in for a good service well before your intended departure date. This will lessen the chance of an expensive breakdown. Make sure your brakes are working efficiently and that your tyres have plenty of tread (3 mm. is recommended, particularly if you are undertaking a long journey).

Also make sure that your caravan or trailer is roadworthy and that its tyres are in good order and correctly inflated. Plan your packing and be careful not to overload your vehicle, caravan and trailer – this is unsafe and may well invalidate your insurance cover (it must not be more fully loaded than the kerb weight of the insured vehicle).

CHECK ALL THE FOLLOWING:

- GB sticker. If you do not display a sticker, you may risk an on-the-spot fine as this identifier is compulsory in all countries. Euro-plates are an acceptable alternative within the EU (but not outside). Remember to attach another sticker (or Euro-plate) to caravans and trailers. Only GB stickers (not England, Scotland, Wales or N. Ireland) stickers are valid in the EU.

- Headlights. As you will be driving on the right you must adjust your headlights so that the dipped beam does not dazzle oncoming drivers. Converter kits are readily available for most vehicles, although if your car is fitted with high intensity headlights, you should check with your motor dealer. Check that any planned extra loading does not affect the beam height.

- Seatbelts. Rules for the fitting and wearing of seatbelts throughout Europe are similar to those in the UK, but it is worth checking before you go. Rules for carrying children in the front of vehicles vary from country to country. It is best to plan not to do this if possible.

- Door/wing mirrors. To help with driving on the right, if your vehicle is not fitted with a mirror on the left hand side, we recommend you have one fitted.

- Fuel. Leaded and Lead Replacement petrol is increasingly difficult to find in Northern Europe.

Compulsory additional equipment

The driving laws of the countries of Europe still vary in what you are required to carry in your vehicle, although the consequences of not carrying a required piece of equipment are almost always an on-the-spot fine.

To meet these requirements we suggest that you carry the following:

- FIRE EXTINGUISHER
- BASIC TOOL KIT
- FIRST AID KIT
- SPARE BULBS

- TWO WARNING TRIANGLES – two are required in some countries at all times, and are compulsory in most countries when towing.

- HIGH VISIBILITY VEST – now compulsory in France, Spain, Italy and Austria (and likely to become compulsory throughout the EU) in case you need to walk on a motorway.

- BREATHALYSERS – now compulsory in France. Only breathalysers that are NF-approved will meet the legal requirement. French law states that one breathalyser must be produced, but it is recommended you carry two in case you use or break one.

Insurance and Motoring Documents

Vehicle insurance

Contact your insurer well before you depart to check that your car insurance policy covers driving outside the UK. Most do, but many policies only provide minimum cover (so if you have an accident your insurance may only cover the cost of damage to the other person's property, with no cover for fire and theft).

To maintain the same level of cover abroad as you enjoy at home you need to tell your vehicle insurer. Some will automatically cover you abroad with no extra cost and no extra paperwork. Some will say you need a Green Card (which is neither green nor on card) but won't charge for it. Some will charge extra for the Green Card. Ideally you should contact your vehicle insurer 3-4 weeks before you set off, and confirm your conversation with them in writing.

Breakdown insurance

Arrange breakdown cover for your trip in good time so that if your vehicle breaks down or is involved in an accident it (and your caravan or trailer) can be repaired or returned to this country. This cover can usually be arranged as part of your travel insurance policy (see below).

Documents you must take with you

You may be asked to show your documents at any time so make sure that they are in order, up-to-date and easily accessible while you travel.

These are what you need to take:

- Passports (you may also need a visa in some countries if you hold either a UK passport not issued in the UK or a passport that was issued outside the EU).

- Motor Insurance Certificate, including Green Card (or Continental Cover clause)

- DVLA Vehicle Registration Document plus, if not your own vehicle, the owner's written authority to drive.

- A full valid Driving Licence (not provisional). The new photo style licence is now mandatory in most European countries.

Personal Holiday insurance

Even though you are just travelling within Europe you must take out travel insurance. Few EU countries pay the full cost of medical treatment even under reciprocal health service arrangements. The first part of a holiday insurance policy covers people. It will include the cost of doctor, ambulance and hospital treatment if needed. If needed the better companies will even pay for English language speaking doctors and nurses and will bring a sick or injured holidaymaker home by air ambulance.

Personal Holiday insurance (continued)

An important part of the insurance, often ignored, is cancellation (and curtailment) cover. Few things are as heartbreaking as having to cancel a holiday because a member of the family falls ill. Cancellation insurance can't take away the disappointment, but it makes sure you don't suffer financially as well. For this reason you should arrange your holiday insurance at least eight weeks before you set off.

Whichever insurance you choose we would advise reading very carefully the policies sold by the High Street travel trade. Whilst they may be good, they may not cover the specific needs of campers, caravanners and motorcaravanners.

Telephone 01580 214000 for a quote for our Camping Travel Insurance with cover arranged through leading leisure insurance providers.
Alternatively visit our website at: alanrogers.com/insurance

European Health Insurance Card (EHIC)

Make sure you apply for your EHIC before travelling in Europe. Eligible travellers from the UK are entitled to receive free or reduced-cost medical care in many European countries on production of an EHIC. This free card is available by completing a form in the booklet 'Health Advice for Travellers' from local Post Offices. One should be completed for each family member. Alternatively visit www.ehic.org.uk and apply on-line. Please allow time to send your application off and have the EHIC returned to you.

The EHIC is valid in all European Community countries plus Iceland, Liechtenstein, Switzerland and Norway. If you or any of your dependants are suddenly taken ill or have an accident during a visit to any of these countries, free or reduced-cost emergency treatment is available – in most cases on production of a valid EHIC.

Only state-provided emergency treatment is covered, and you will receive treatment on the same terms as nationals of the country you are visiting. Private treatment is generally not covered, and state-provided treatment may not cover all of the things that you would expect to receive free of charge from the NHS.

Remember an EHIC does not cover you for all the medical costs that you can incur or for repatriation - it is not an alternative to travel insurance. You will still need appropriate insurance to ensure you are fully covered for all eventualities.

Travelling with children

Most countries in Europe are enforcing strict guidelines when you are travelling with children who are not your own. A minor (under the age of 18) must be accompanied by a parent or legal guardian or must carry a letter of authorisation from a parent or guardian. The letter should name the adult responsible for the minor during his or her stay. Similarly, a minor travelling with just one of his/her parents, must have a letter of authority to leave their home country from the parent staying behind. Full information is available at www.fco.gov.uk

Travelling with dogs

Many British campers and caravanners prefer to take their pets with them on holiday. However, pet travel rules changed on 1 January 2012 when the UK brought its procedures into line with the European Union. From this date all pets can enter or re-enter the UK from any country in the world without quarantine provided they meet the rules of the scheme, which will be different depending on the country or territory the pet is coming from. Please refer to the following website for full details: www.defra.gov.uk/wildlife-pets/pets/travel

Low Cost Flights

An Inexpensive Way To Arrive At Your Campsite

Many campsites are conveniently served by a wide choice of low cost airlines. Cheap flights can be very easy to find and travellers increasingly find the regional airports often used to be smaller, quieter and generally a calmer, more pleasurable experience.

Low cost flights can make campsites in more distant regions a much more attractive option: quicker to reach, inexpensive flights, and simply more convenient.

Many campsites are seeing increased visitors using the low cost flights and are adapting their services to suit this clientele. An airport shuttle service is not uncommon, meaning you can take advantage of that cheap flight knowing you will be met at the other end and whisked to your campsite. No taxi queues or multiple drop-offs.

Obviously, these low cost flights are impractical when taking all your own camping gear but they do make a holiday in campsite owned accommodation much more straightforward. The low cost airline option makes mobile home holidays especially attractive: pack a suitcase and use bed linen and towels provided (which you will generally need to pre-book).

Pricing Tips

- Low cost airlines promote cheap flights but only a small percentage of seats are priced at the cheapest price. Book early for the best prices (and of course you also get a better choice of campsite or mobile home)

- Child seats are usually the same costs as adults

- Full payment is required at the time of booking

- Changes and amendments can be costly with low cost airlines

- Peak dates can be expensive compared to other carriers

Car Hire

For maximum flexibility you will probably hire a car from a car rental agency. Car hire provides convenience but also will allow you access to off-site shops, beaches and tourist sights.

Open All Year

The following sites are understood to accept caravanners and campers all year round. It is always wise to phone the site to check as the facilities available, for example, may be reduced.

ITALY
Piedmont & Valle d'Aosta
Gofree	31
Gran Bosco	32
Mombarone	32

Ligúria
Dei Fiori (Pietra Ligure)	38
Dei Fiori (San Remo)	39
Miraflores	39
Pian dei Boschi	38
Sfinge	36

Trentino-Alto Adige
Antholz	63
Cevedale	66
Olympia	72
Sexten	71

Veneto
Fusina	93

Emília-Romagna
Castagni	104
San Marino	101

Tuscany
Michelangelo	117
Soline	113
Toscana Village	121

Marche
Mimose	142

Lázio
Castelfusano	147
Flaminio	149
Roma	149

Abruzzo & Molise
Vecchio Mulino	155

Campania
Il Vulcano Solfatara	160
Zeus	160

Puglia & Basilicata
Masseria	163

Calabria
Il Salice	168
Vascellero	168

Sicily
Jonio	173
Marinello	176
Nettuno	172
Rais Gerbi	174
Sabbiadoro	173
Scarabeo	176
Valle dei Templi	173

Sardinia
Costiolou	184

SLOVENIA
Danica Bohinj	190
Dolina Prebold	195
Kamne	194
Koren	192
Menina	196
Terme 3000	194
Terme Catez	190
Terme Lendava	193
Terme Ptuj	196

CROATIA
Brioni	207
Galeb	223
Nevio	223
Simuni	224

Dogs

Many British campers and caravanners prefer to take their pets with them on holiday. However, pet travel rules changed on 1 January 2012 when the UK brought its procedures into line with the European Union. From this date all pets can enter or re-enter the UK from any country in the world without quarantine provided they meet the rules of the scheme, which will be different depending on the country or territory the pet is coming from. Please refer to the following website for full details: www.defra.gov.uk/wildlife-pets/pets/travel

For the benefit of those who want to take their dogs with them or for people who do not like dogs at the sites they visit, we list here the sites that have indicated to us that they do not accept dogs. If you are, however, planning to take your dog we do advise you to contact them first to check as there may be certain restrictions.

Never – these sites do not accept dogs at any time

ITALY							
Al Boschetto	90	Dei Fiori (San Remo)	39	Lo Stambecco	24	Rubicone	107
Alberello	106	Del Garda	58	Malibu Beach	94	Saint Michael	127
Argentario	110	Delle Piscine	125	Marelago	82	Salinello	156
Athena	159	Delle Rose	49	Mediterraneo	88	Sant'Angelo	92
Baia Domizia	158	Europe Garden	156	Paestum	159	Serenella	48
Bella Italia	56	Framura	37	Perticara	141	Stella Maris	143
Bellamare	142	Garden Paradiso	91	Pianacce	113	Tahiti	102
Ca'Pasquali	84	Gasparina	48	PicoBello	140	Tenuta Primero	75
Ca'Savio	82	Il Tridente	81	Portofelice	93	Union Lido	86
California	147	Internazionale	142	Pra' Delle Torri	84	Villa al Mare	90
Capalonga	80	Isamar	98	Punta Lunga	165	Voltoncino	111
Cevedale	66	Isuledda	181	PuntAla	123		
Cisano & San Vito	49	Italy	86	Residence	91	**CROATIA**	
Costiolou	184	Jesolo	94	Riva di Ugento	164	Valalta (Naturist)	210
Dei Fiori (C. Treporti)	85	Lido (Bibione-Pineda)	81	Riva Nuova	154	Valdaliso	210
		Lido Village	145	Riva Verde	139		

Maybe – not accepted in high season

ITALY							
Baia Verde	122	Costa Ponente	174	Mareblu	115	Rais Gerbi	174
Baita Dolomiti	70	Don Antonio	153	Maremma	114	Riccione	106
Butteri	125	Europa (Torre-Lago)	127	Marinello	176	Romantico	150
Capo Ferrato	182	International	155	Mariposa	180	San Nicola	164
Cigno Bianco	186	Italia	128	Miramare (Chioggia)	97	Silva	88
Conca d'Oro	27	Jonio	173	Molino a Fuoco	129	Tripesce	129
		Lido (Pacengo)	55	Pionier Etrusco	147	Vascellero	168

Trentino-Alto Adige
page 62

Friuli-Venezia Giulia
page 73

Lake Garda
page 46

SLOVENIA
page 187

CROATIA
page 198

Veneto
page 79

Lombardy
page 41

Piedmont &
Valle d'Aosta
page 21

Emilia-Romagna
page 99

Ligúria
page 33

Marche
page 138

Tuscany
page 109

Umbria
page 131

Abruzzo & Molise
page 151

Lazio
page 144

Campania
page 157

Puglia & Basilicata
page 161

Sardinia
page 178

Calabria
page 166

Sicily
page 171

FREE

The Alan Rogers
Travel Card

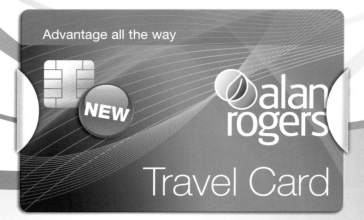

Across the Alan Rogers guides you'll find a network of thousands of quality inspected and selected campsites. We also work with numerous organisations, including ferry operators and tourist attractions, all of whom can bring you benefits and save you money.

Our brand **NEW** Travel Card binds all this together, along with exclusive extra content in our cardholders' area at **alanrogers.com/travelcard**

Advantage all the way

Carry the Alan Rogers Travel Card on your travels and save money all the way. Enjoy exclusive offers on many partner sites - as well as hotels, apartments and campsite accommodation. We've even teamed up with Camping Cheque, the low season discount scheme, so you can load your card with Cheques before you travel. So register today - hundreds of campsites already have special offers just for you.

Holiday **discounts**, **free** kids' meals, **free** cycle hire, **discounted** meals, **free** sports activities, **free** gifts on arrival, **free** wine with meals, **free** wifi, **free** tennis, **free** spa day, **free** access to local attractions.

Check out all the offers at **alanrogers.com/travelcard** and present your card on arrival.

Benefits that add up

- Offers and benefits on many Alan Rogers campsites across Europe

- Save up to 60% in low season on over 600 campsites

- Savings on rented accommodation and hotels at over 400 locations

- Free cardholders' magazine

- Exclusive cardholders' area on our website – exchange opinions with other members

- Discounted ferries

- Savings on Alan Rogers guides

- Travel insurance deals

Register today - and start saving

Step 1
Register at www.alanrogers.com/travelcard (you can now access exclusive content on the website).

Step 2
You'll receive your activated card, along with a Welcome email containing useful links and information.

Step 3
Start using your card to save money or to redeem benefits during your holiday.

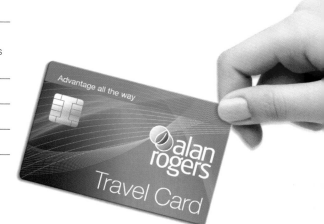

Register now at
alanrogers.com/travelcard

Start 2013
in real style...

The **ONLY SHOW** in the spring where the leading caravan and motorhome manufacturers will be displaying their **NEW 2013 SEASON MODELS**.

The Spring

CARAVAN &
CAMPING SHOW

19-24 FEB 2013 · NEC BIRMINGHAM

SUPPORTERS:

WWW.SPRINGCARAVANANDCAMPINGSHOW.CO.U

The **NATIONAL SHOW** at the NEC where you'll see the **NEW 2014 SEASON** caravan and motorhome models from all the leading manufacturers.

The **MOTORHOME &
CARAVAN SHOW**

15-20 OCT 2013 · NEC BIRMINGHAM

SUPPORTERS:

...and end it
truly inspired.

WWW.MOTORHOMEANDCARAVANSHOW.CO.U

ORGANISED BY: NCC event

Want independent campsite reviews at your fingertips?

Getting the most from off peak touring

£13.95 /night
single tariff
2 people

There are many reasons to avoid high season, if you can. Queues are shorter, there's less traffic, a calmer atmosphere and prices are cheaper. And it's usually still nice and sunny!

And when you use Camping Cheques you'll find great quality facilities that are actually open and a welcoming conviviality.

Did you know?

Camping Cheques can be used right into mid-July and from late August on many sites. Over 90 campsites in France alone accept Camping Cheques from 20th August.

Save up to 60% with Camping Cheques

Camping Cheque is a fixed price scheme allowing you to go as you please, staying on over 600 campsites across Europe, always paying the same rate and saving you up to 60% on regular pitch fees. One Cheque gives you one night for 2 people + unit on a standard pitch, with electricity. It's as simple as that.

Special offers mean you can stay extra nights free (eg 7 nights for 6 Cheques) or even a month free for a month paid! Especially popular in Spain during the winter, these longer-term offers can effectively halve the nightly rate. See Site Directory for details.

Check out our amazing Ferry Deals!

Why should I use Camping Cheques?

- It's a proven system, recognised by all 600+ participating campsites
  - so no nasty surprises.

- It's flexible, allowing you to travel between campsites, and also countries, on a whim - so no need to pre-book. (It's low season, so campsites are rarely full, though advance bookings can be made).

- Stay as long as you like, where you like - so you travel in complete freedom.

- Camping Cheques are valid 2 years - so no pressure to use them up. (If you have a couple left over after your trip, simply keep them for the following year, or use them up in the UK).

Tell me more... (but keep it brief!)

Camping Cheques was started in 1999 and has since grown in popularity each year (nearly 2 million were used last year). That should speak for itself. There are 'copycat' schemes, but none has the same range of quality campsites that save you up to 60%.

Ask for your **FREE** continental road map, which explains how Camping Cheque works

01580 214002

FREE

downloadable Site Directory
alanrogers.com/directory

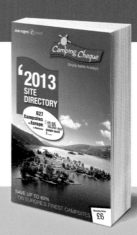

campingcheque.co.uk

Town & Village Index

Town & Village Index continued

SLOVENIA

CROATIA

Index - Campsite Number

Index by Campsite Number continued

Index by Campsite Number continued

Index by Campsite Region & Name

Index by Campsite Region & Name continued